WAR IN AMERICA TO 1775

The American Social Experience Series
GENERAL EDITOR: JAMES KIRBY MARTIN
EDITORS: PAULA S. FASS, STEVEN H. MINTZ,
CARL PRINCE, JAMES W. REED & PETER N. STEARNS

WAR IN AMERICA
TO 1775
Before Yankee Doodle

———

JOHN MORGAN DEDERER

NEW YORK UNIVERSITY PRESS

NEW YORK AND LONDON

1990

Copyright © 1990 by New York University
All rights reserved
Manufactured in the United States of America

Library of Congress Cataloging-in-Publication Data
Dederer, John Morgan.
War in America to 1775 : before Yankee Doodle / John Morgan
Dederer.
p.   cm.—(The American social experience series ; 16)
Includes bibliographical references.
ISBN 0-8147-1828-0
1. Military art and science—United States—History—18th century.
2. United States—History, Military—To 1900.   3. United States—
History—Colonial period, ca. 1600–1775.   4. United States—
History—Revolution, 1775–1783.   I. Title.   II. Series.
U43.U4D43   1990
355′.00973′09033—dc20   89-13520
CIP

New York University Press books are printed on acid-free paper,
and their binding materials are chosen for strength and durability.

Book design by Ken Venezio

To my maternal grandparents,
Oscar Joseph Mueller and Marie-Rose Schleret Mueller,
with love and respect.
Much of what I am, I owe to you.

Contents

Preface

For some, military history is anathema, the study of humankind at its worst. For others, however, it represents an investigation into an aspect of human interaction under the greatest stresses imaginable, the human condition in microcosm. The study of military history is, of course, the study of war, but battles, campaigns, and wars are only parts of the whole. Wars do not occur in a vacuum; they come about, as every good Clausewitzian knows, when conflicts between nations seemingly cannot be resolved in any other manner. But wars have also resulted from societal changes, shifts in population, economic rivalry, ideas, ambition, and a hundred other causes.

Admittedly, the decision to make war or the act of making war results from immediately irreconcilable differences, yet the underlying and root causes often can be found only by brushing away the detritus of time. Thus, if a student of military history aspires to search beyond the who, what, when, and where of war in order to comprehend the hows and whys, there must be a willingness to explore areas not normally considered as being in the military historian's purview. For as historian Charles H. Firth wrote years ago, describing his own experiences, "it was only by learning to understand the little things that it was possible to understand the important things, and to make certain of appreciating their significance."[1]

Years ago, the study of history was fundamentally the story of politics, war, and humankind, especially its heroic aspects. Then the age of specialization arrived, and history saw itself divided into various subspecialities and later microspecialities. Frequently, however, in examining an event in such increasingly minute detail, the part becomes a whole of itself. Now, the tide seems to be turning once again, and microstudies are becoming the valuable building blocks for those who wish to see things in as much of a whole as is possible. This shift does not signify a return to universal history, although the need is there, but a broader, more catholic perspective of the past. Ideas, the forces that power human development, are not being studied only for their effect on a particular event but also to find in their very origins their overall influence on a period, a culture, a people.

Tracing an idea's genealogy does not make for an easy search; there is a great deal of intermarriage and bastardization. Sometimes the most diligent inquiries result in general answers, both the bane and essence of the historian's craft. Nevertheless, even focusing on generalities, one may see how ideas beget other ideas, how these influence people, and, sometimes, how these people influence others. As military historian B. H. Liddell Hart summarized it, the "influence of thought on thought is the most influential factor in history. Yet, being intangible," and difficult to trace, "it is less perceptible than the effects of action, and has received far less attention from the writers of history." Ideas and people's ability to spawn them, he went on, are responsible for all human progress. "But, even yet, we do not fully show our recognition of this cardinal fact, either in the treatment of contemporary affairs, or in the treatment of the past."[2] When the influences of ideas upon ideas and then upon minds and thus on people are studied, Liddell Hart asserted, the philosophers and poets are recognized, but those who "produced ideas of a more concrete nature, whose thought more directly influenced the course of history, have been comparatively overlooked." We should remember and study, he advised, "the historical importance of those who have moulded the minds of men whose actions have moulded history."[3]

Thus arose the genesis of this study. Doing research for an appraisal of the development of American command and strategy during the Revolutionary War, I found myself unable to arrive at satisfactory answers to two basic questions, questions fundamental to an examination of George Washington and his key subordinates, but also elemental for any inquiry of this sort: what did Americans (as a society) think about war and its components, and where did they get their ideas on the subject? In writing military history, it has often been forgotten that armies are the products of their parent societies, and as such they must carry out the missions assigned to them by their nation's policy-makers with the tools—physical and moral—provided. To understand how a nation's military fights, its strategy, tactics, how it is supplied, who actually goes into combat, and dozens of other aspects of a national military establishment, one must first explore national attitudes toward war. Then, to understand how a nation's military actually makes war, one must examine the key influences—military and otherwise—on the thinking of its policymakers and military commanders. Yet if one wishes to understand fully what a nation thinks about war in all its aspects and which are the major influences on that nation's armed forces, there remains no other way but to delve deeply into the parent society and culture, crossing oceans and centuries as intrepidly as any fictional time-traveler. Thus, to answer these questions for the benefit of myself, my current work, and, I hope, others, I wrote what follows.

Many of the sources used in this study are from a time when the rules of grammar were highly individualistic. Although I have occasionally added a clarifying word in brackets, I have otherwise left all quoted material as I found it, eschewing the use of *sic*. In the bibliography I listed only the works cited in my notes, although these represent but a small portion of the sources I consulted. Also, I have tried to conform to the history profession's guidelines on gender-neutral language as much as possible. The final arbiters on this matter were, of course, my sources and the people and times that I have written about.

Acknowledgments

Every historian owes an unpayable debt to the work of earlier scholars, and I readily acknowledge mine. At every turn, I found the tracks of the Douglass Adairs, B. H. Liddell Harts, Michael Howards, Douglas Leachs, Forrest McDonalds, John Shys, and others who had preceded me. Their scholarship blazed the trail, making my journey so much easier. I am only sorry that I cannot thank them all.

Several institutions graciously provided funding which enabled me to research and write, unencumbered by other responsibilities. I wish to extend my sincere appreciation to the United States Army Center for Military History for a generous fellowship, and to thank former director Dr. David Trask and the current Chief of Military History, Brigadier-General William A. Stofft. The John Carter Brown Library, Brown University, provided a Visiting Scholar Fellowship, and Director Norman Fiering and his staff ensured that my time in Providence was both profitable and pleasant. Two Research Fellowships from The University of Alabama, where former university president Dr. Joab Thomas and Dean William H. Macmillan created an atmosphere conducive to academic excellence, were most beneficial. A very productive and stimulating year at Yale University was made possible by a John M. Olin Foundation Postdoctoral Fellowship in Military and Strategic History. I wish to thank Harry A. Miskimin, Chairman of Yale's Department of History, for his many courtesies and good cheer, Howard R. Lamar, Jonathan Dull, and Don Kagan for making me feel welcome, and especially Paul M. Kennedy, Dilworth Professor of History and head of the Olin program, for his many kindnesses, collegiality, and support.

My research was aided immeasurably by many archivists and librarians. I sincerely appreciated the able assistance provided by the staffs of: Duke University's Perkins Library; the Library of Congress, particularly those of the Manuscripts and Rare Books Divisions; the Amelia Gorgas Library, The University of Alabama, especially Mrs. Eloise M. Griffin of Interlibrary Loan who saved me on more than one occasion; the Pequot Library, Southport, Connecticut, where Head Librarian Stanley Crane graciously allowed me to peruse their colonial collections; and Yale University's Beinecke, Cross Campus, Divinity School, Mudd, and Sterling libraries.

Several scholars took time from their busy schedules to read all or parts of this manuscript in its several forms. Their comments, criticisms, and encouragement were all welcomed and sincerely appreciated. I wish to thank: Martin Alexander; Don Higginbotham; Robin Higham; James Michael Hill; Robert E. Johnson; Howard Jones; Douglas E. Leach; Forrest McDonald; James Kirby Martin; Pete Maslowski; Gary B. Mills; and Donald Snow. The responsibility for any errors or omissions is mine alone, but any credit is, in large measure, due to their efforts. I should add that while the following scholars did not read the manuscript, conversations with them proved illuminating and stimulating. I wish to thank: George Andreopoulos; Michael Howard; John Keegan; Michael Mallet; Peter Paret; Elihu Rose; Roger J. Spiller; and Brian Sullivan. James Muldoon not only offered encouragement but graciously sent me reprints of several of his articles. Historian and novelist Thomas Fleming buoyed my often flagging spirits, and I am most grateful to him for suggesting the title.

Two of my readers from above require special thanks. Forrest McDonald has been my mentor, editor, guidance counselor, and friend for a number of years, and for all the kindnesses he and his wife, Ellen Shapiro McDonald, have afforded my family and myself, I can only say thank you. Series editor James Kirby Martin has been a friend and a morale builder throughout the development of this work; his comments and deft editorial hand have saved me from egregious errors on more than one occasion.

Researching and writing are solitary endeavors, but I have benefited immeasurably from encouragement from senior scholars and have been sustained by many tolerant friends. My sincere appreciation and thanks go to: Martin and Rosalie Alexander; Daniel R. Campbell; Paul and Mary Lynn Clark; Cecil B. Currey; Joseph G. ("Chip") Dawson III; Jim Dingeman; Michael and Saki Dockrill; Graeme J. L. Hall; Perry Jamieson; Charles Joyner; Malcolm MacDonald; Mike McGiffert; Grady McWhiney; Robert M. Testo; Russell F. Weigley; and my associate editors and the many contributors of the *Southern Historian*, which I edited with pleasure from 1984 to 1987. In one way or another, everyone above contributed to my scholarship and mental well-being. Especial thanks are due Mrs. Sennie Granger for opening her home to me in Washington, D.C., and Gary B. and Elizabeth Shown Mills who helped a non-Southerner gain an endearing love and respect for the region.

I wish to thank Colin Jones, director, and Despina P. Gimbel, managing editor, at New York University Press for their work on this book, as well as Ann Hirst, who copyedited the manuscript with great care.

To my mother, Evelyn M. Taylor, and my late father, Douglas Morgan Dederer, I offer my love and gratitude for instilling in me an appreciation for the written word and so much more. To my daughters, Allison and Elizabeth, my love. To Melissa G. Dederer, my wife, thanks alone will never suffice; therefore, I will simply say I love you.

WAR IN AMERICA TO 1775

Introduction

Americans' conceptions of war, including the role of a military in society, played an integral part in the formation and development of the United States even before it became a nation. On 19 June 1775, the Continental Congress commissioned George Washington as "GENERAL AND COMMANDER IN CHIEF of the army of the United Colonies."[1] The situation facing the new general was unique in the annals of the eighteenth century and possibly in all of history, for here was a commander with neither army nor funds, and even the revolutionary movement he represented was unrecognized as a legitimate government. Of course, things could not have been otherwise, since scarcely a month earlier the movement had not existed. In commissioning Washington, creating an army, and assuming responsibility for sustaining this force at war, the movement in fact legitimized itself, both externally on the international stage and internally among its thirteen confused colonial members.

Looking back in 1789, Washington described the conditions he and his fellow revolutionaries had faced that June: "Not then organised as a nation, or known as a people upon the earth—we had no preparation —Money, the nerve of War, was wanting." Confronting an opponent whose resources, the Virginian noted, "were, in a manner, inexhaustible," was surely a chilling prospect even for the dauntless Washington.[2] "I am Imbarked on a wide Ocean," he wrote his brother the day after being commissioned, "boundless in its prospects & from whence,

1

perhaps, no safe harbour is to be found."[3] The nautical metaphor was apt. Great Britain, after all, had the most powerful fleet in the world, a navy that had proven itself capable of transporting, landing, and revictualing armies from Quebec to Manila, and the American colonies lay precariously perched along a narrow but lengthy band of indefensible coastline. Not a particularly large force by European standards, the British army nevertheless "had harvested laurels in every quarter of the globe" in the last war, winning victories and carving out an empire that ranged from the Ohio River to the fringes of the Pacific Basin.[4]

On paper and to eighteenth-century European thinking, Americans stood little chance of emerging from such an unequal contest with anything short of a crushing defeat. As Washington had pointed out, they were not even united as a people—they were thirteen disparate colonial entities distrustful of one another, chronically embroiled in intercolonial and regional squabbling, and beset by intracolonial factionalism. There was no national organization empowered with or capable of setting and enforcing policy, nothing that could pass as an army by even the loosest eighteenth-century definition, and no means of supporting or maintaining one even if it had existed. The colonials owned many ships, but ships and sailors alone no more constitute a navy—especially a force able to brave the awesome power of the Royal Navy—than a few men armed with muskets make an army. Gunpowder was in such short supply that every grain had to be carefully husbanded, and war matériel of all sorts was scarce or nonexistent. Yet these Americans who found themselves with little recourse other than rebellion were not foolish people given to flights of fancy, nor did they perceive themselves as martyrs, sacrificing their lives to become stirring examples to rally future generations. These colonists dreamed not of a Thermopylae but of a Marathon, not of heroic defeat but of victory.

From time immemorial, oppressed and subjugated peoples have rebelled against their masters for the amorphous but nonetheless real concept of freedom. Compared with the actual oppression that led to earlier and later uprisings, Americans could hardly be considered subjugated, and their physical oppression was minimal indeed, especially if measured against that of their contemporaries in Europe. In fact, by the winter of 1774–75, it could be argued that Americans brought many of the "oppressive" measures wrought by Great Britain upon themselves by their own civil disobedience and dissent. But this is actually illustrative of why the American rebellion-cum-revolution was unique and why it had such a great influence on and inspired subsequent revolutionary movements, for it was not merely a revolt of oppressed peoples fighting for liberty but a conflict brought about and dictated by strongly held ideas. Americans did not fight for additional lands or to increase their hegemony over the continent, although victory would ensure rights to their own property and opportunities for westward expansion. They did not fight for the superiority of their religious beliefs over others, though religion played an important role in the coming of the revolt, and increased religious toleration would result from it. Nor did Americans take up arms to redress the geopolitical balance of power, though, certainly, events which began in America reverberated throughout Europe and Europe's worldwide possessions. In fact, no matter what the ultimate result was, Americans did not rise in rebellion and initiate war for any of the reasons normal or even comprehensible to eighteenth-century European policymakers. Instead, they entered into this fray against a greatly superior foe to fight for ideals and concepts, ideas woven into the very fabric of their heritage.

This combination of long-held ideas and ideals, concepts so dear to American thinking and so much a part of the essence of these people that many risked their all for them, were theirs and theirs alone. To be sure (in a caveat inserted to forestall too many upraised eyebrows), as so many scholars have detailed, the origins of these ideas have their roots firmly implanted in the rich and ancient soils of Western political and philosophical thought.[5] The publications and writings of the colonists and of the revolutionary generation in particular fairly bulge with quotations, paraphrases, and other expressions of the ideas of Western intellectual genius. The themes and ideas developed by Bolingbroke, Trenchard, Gordon, Locke, Montesquieu, Luther, Aquinas, Calvin, and countless others and by those who influenced them, the Sallusts, Ciceros, Aristotles, and many others of the classical world, leap from the pages during the most cursory reading. As the seeds of the tiny, bitter oranges of the Old World begat luscious, sweet fruit when nurtured in the rich soil of the New, noted historian Clifford K. Shipton, so were the ideas of Western civilization and the European intellectual revolution reinvigorated in the energetic intellectual milieu of the American Enlightenment.[6] How these ancient ideas and even their seventeenth- and early eighteenth-century Europeanized interpretations were understood, how they were used, and how their often contradictory messages were juxtaposed into a whole; this, plus the very real but hard-to-define American experience and character, added up to something new, something American: a train of thought unique to the American revolutionary movement and, hence, to an American war.

A great part of this Western heritage that the early colonists transported and transformed focused on war. The Europe that they left remained incessantly embroiled in one conflict after another of varying intensity. War was an acceptable topic of discussion among seventeenth- and eighteenth-century intellectuals; it was not confined to the purview of a few generals, theorists, and enthusiasts. As war was a regular feature of society, maintaining an army in peace or war was the primary and most costly function of seventeenth- and eighteenth-century governments. In many ways war was a subject that brought dissimilar strains of intellectual energy together, and as such was considered worthy of mental rumination in Europeans salons. But it had been thus since ancient times, both for the classical Greeks and Romans and among those other influential ancients, the Hebrews of the Old Testament.

War was a chronic event with vast implications for ancient societies and played a central role in the lives of these peoples. Seventeenth- and eighteenth-century students of the classical period—and every literate person received a healthy dose of classicism—found war to be a major theme in the ancient works, whether in literature, poetry, history, or religion. War was a natural part of life to the ancients, and as with so many classical ideas, seventeenth- and eighteenth-century thought incorporated ancient attitudes about war. Not only did an intellectual bond exist, but there was a strong practical connection. As will be seen in part II of this work, eighteenth-century warfare remained closer in fact to that of the past than it would be to that of the twentieth century. Ideas developed earlier about war, warfare, the conduct of war, and the place of a military establishment continued as the basis for enlightened attempts to rationalize and minimize war's destruction. From these various strains—strains identical to those in which American political and philosophical thought or ideology originated—Americans derived their conceptions of war, warfare, and the role that a military should and would play in their society. These conceptions, already firmly held in 1775, governed American military policy during the War for Independence and would have a lasting effect on American society and the American way of war.

The first chapter of this work primarily represents an overview of what is to follow.[7] Because this study is an examination of the origins, transmission, and use of ideas, of how they are adopted and adapted to fit circumstances, how they are transmuted into new concepts, and how they influence actual practice, I thought it best to proceed as if following a schematic or lineage chart. This format benefits the author as well as the reader. Since ideas often lie dormant for centuries until, say, the political or cultural environment provides a suitable atmosphere for their reemergence (to be "rediscovered," as it were), understanding how this transmission process occurs is vital. For instance, often users of ideas are perceived as having copied directly from a single source. Upon closer examination, however, it turns out that the users were familiar with the identical original sources that had inspired the author from whom they allegedly copied. The knowledge was indisputably passed on, but perhaps the best judgment a historian can form is that the purported single source had a major influence upon the users, clarifying, summarizing, or reinforcing what they had learned from the original. And it should not be forgotten that ideas develop lives of their own. That is, the knowledge they convey can become so diffused among a society—or a whole generation or even an age—that discerning who influenced whom is impossible.[8] For all these reasons, furnishing the reader with an overview at the outset seems useful. After all, as John Trenchard and Thomas Gordon cautioned their readers years ago: "Beware, my friends, of the first Step, and know your Whole Journey before you move one Foot; when you are up to the Ears in Mire, it will be too late to look back."[9]

Chapter 1 is followed by part I (containing chapters 2 and 3) which discusses the intellectual milieu of seventeenth- and eighteenth-century America. Clearly, an introductory essay and two chapters—no matter how lengthy—cannot reproduce the massive amounts of scholarly research in this area, nor is there any reason to do so. The present work is a study of a particular aspect of the colonial and revolutionary American *mentalité*, and the objective is to remain focused on that point. Therefore, part I summarizes (and acknowledges) much of this earlier scholarship in relation to what might be described as the military culture of the colonies to the Revolution. In examining this period through a military prism, however, a fresh perspective emerges and, perhaps, new lines of inquiry are introduced.

The return of military history to the mainstream of scholarship allows for the reexamination and thus reinterpretation of ideas and events previously the sole domain of nonmilitary historians. This revitalized interest exposes new vistas for investigation. War, warfare, and military affairs in general have played a dominant (and sometimes dominating) role in all aspects of societal development. To ignore this fact belies an important part of the human condition. Part I surveys the sources Americans drew from to develop their political, philosophical, historical, and cultural ideas, the identical sources from which they derived their concepts of war (and peace). Yet these sources not only provided ideas regarding the intellectual perspective of war and society, they also furnished much of the practical knowledge Americans had about war.

In part II (chapters 4, 5, and 6) the more practical lessons on the art of war that Americans learned are addressed, although it should be noted (as it is in chapter 4) that the practical and the book-learned were inextricably intertwined. Revolutionary Americans borrowed extensively from the eighteenth-century European art of war, but then, as was the case with most colonial institutions, they sensibly adapted and refined European concepts and practices to the exigencies of the situation. This transformation occurred for several reasons, briefly summarized here as necessity, practicality, and that catchall word incorporating political and philosophical ideas, ideology. Colonial Americans, and particularly those of the revolutionary generation, learned about war in the abstract in the same way that almost every other aspiring eighteenth-century militarist from Marlborough to Napoleon did—by reading; and what Americans read was indistinguishable from what contemporary Europeans were reading. How they applied what they learned was another matter. For several reasons, Washington and his subordinates strongly urged the formation of a disciplined army based on the European model which could, if circumstances demanded it, stand up to the British in setpiece battles. A variety of shortages and stumbling blocks—not the least being time, a political culture (seen in part III) that was totally at variance with this type of army, together with long-held colonial traditions and conceptions regarding war, warfare, and the military—frustrated efforts to use all but the most fundamental aspects of conventional European doctrine and strategy.

Chapter 6 is a detailed study of the evolution of American concepts of war prior to 1775, demonstrating that Americans had already assimilated a great deal of knowledge beyond what was transported across the Atlantic. Their own experiences in the New World had much to do with how European lessons of war were understood and adapted. American colonists learned a great many valuable (and painful) lessons fighting a tough, indigenous opponent, and in the process developed firm prejudices about war and the role that the military should play in their society. Along with these practical lessons and opinions, certain myths about American martial prowess may be seen to have originated in the prerevolutionary period. Though not clearly defined, this nascent American way of war suggested that by 1775 Americans had developed a military identity of their own, as divergent in practice and theory as they themselves differed from their European cousins. Perhaps more than anything else, these conceptions (described partially in chapter 6 and in more detail in part III) would culturally, socially, politically, and philosophically preadapt Americans for the republican tenets that formed a central component of their revolutionary ideology.

Part III (chapters 7 and 8) may be summarized as the intellectual aspect of American conceptions of war. The uncontrolled degeneration of European war which began in the turmoil surrounding the Reformation and culminated in the unbridled savagery of the Thirty Years' War inaugurated a resurgence in attempts to place some controls on or limits to war's destructive power. These efforts had limited impact on actual warfare (see chapter 5), but they did help foster increased interest in thinking about war, war and society, and society and the military. Colonial Americans, of course, followed these arguments closely since they remained current with the intellectual revolution

sweeping Europe, but in general terms they were already quite familiar with them. The concepts of what constituted a just war, who was
or who was not a combatant, and a variety of other matters had
antecedents in classical Greece and Rome, in Mosaic law, and Christian theology—sources and ideas which the colonists knew quite well.
The influences of these sources (discussed in chapter 7), particularly
the biblical, had much to do with how Americans waged war and how
they perceived their opponents. To varying degrees, many colonial
settlers believed themselves to be on a mission for God, carving out a
new Zion in the wilderness or at least working under God's blessing.
Here, their concepts of fighting a war under God's ensign juxtaposed
nicely with biblical, classical, and modern perspectives on what exactly
was a just war and the very human and practical need for self-preservation. These ideas had a strong influence on the infant American
practice of war, which in turn affected how colonials thought about
war, the military, and military policy.

The relationship between colonial society and its military would
have significant implications for the development of what became the
American revolutionary ideology and on the army Washington had to
establish and constantly rebuild during the Revolution (and hence,
upon strategy and even tactics). First, and most consequential in both
short- and long-term effect, was civilian control of the military, a
zealously defended prerogative of the colonial political leadership that
actually anticipated changes in late seventeenth-century England.
Stemming equally from fears of the corruptive influences of a regular
army, Caesarism, the loss of colonial financial control to representatives of the Crown, and too much democracy, civil dominion over
military affairs formed a central tenet of colonial, then revolutionary
governance. Then, as is shown in chapter 6 and developed in chapter
7, the colonial military establishment (the militia) was actually a fairly
complex organism, fully reflective of its parent society's religious and
philosophical views, traditions, and overall antimilitarism. What was
most satisfactory to practical colonial needs, however, would prove
almost ruinous in the protracted Revolutionary War that followed.

As will be discussed in chapter 8, reliance upon a virtuous, armed
citizenry instead of a regular, professional standing army fitted well
with the radical Whig ideology of post-Cromwellian England (and the
classical citizen-soldiery of republican Greece and Rome) that became

so popular in mid-eighteenth-century America. Biblical, classical, and historical precedents, plus sensible economic and practical reasons, however, had already combined to make the concept of a standing army anathema to the colonists: thus, they were intellectually predisposed to accept the arguments made by the radical Whigs and other libertarians. Moreover, there were substantial differences between the English anti–standing army hysteria of the 1690s to the 1730s (and radical Whig theory) and English attitudes and practices in the 1760s and 1770s, differences which most Americans—separated by space and time and held in thrall to the earlier arguments—failed to perceive or ignored. Granted, being against standing armies was only one facet of both English and American republicanism, but in America after 1763, each redcoated British regular that arrived in the colonies was seen as the manifestation of English (specifically ministerial) attempts to corrupt and tyrannize Americans.[10] Rightly or wrongly, Americans perceived the British army as a threat to their lives, liberties, and properties. Opposition to standing armies (as a part of a larger antimilitarism) became a cornerstone of American revolutionary ideology, one of the primary bonds that welded Americans together. The less well-defined moderate Whig position which accepted a professional or, at least, a well-organized and well-trained military as an evil necessary for a nation's survival, had adherents among Americans such as Washington and many of his key subordinates. These officers were among the Americans who sought to balance ideology against wartime necessity and who, quite possibly, arrived at their position unaware of similar conflicts in British Whiggery. Yet such a hold did the radical Whig argument have on most revolutionaries who had loudly trumpeted its precepts that even in the face of the exigencies of wartime reality, American policymakers found it difficult—personally, ideologically, and politically—to compromise on this issue.

Following part III, a brief summarization concludes this work. It should be remarked, however, that in no way does this study presume to be definitive. Rather, it may be considered as an initial, exploratory probe into a subject which continues to have important connotations in our own times. If, in some small way, this work spurs additional examination and inquiry, then the author has accomplished his objective.

CHAPTER I

The Origins and Development of American Conceptions of War to 1775: An Overview

A nation's military mirrors its parent society; this has been true since the earliest recorded history. Whether the military represents an actual nation or national group, the values, social and cultural characteristics, fears, technologies, ideologies, and countless other aspects of a society are reflected in its armed forces. Captured in this reflection, of course, are images of national attitudes toward and conceptions of the military and of war in general. These attitudes may be observed in the emphasis a nation places on its security, how its military is organized, and in many additional ways, including how the military actually fights on the battlefield. Thus, to study a nation's military actions and policies is to lay bare the soul or character of a nation. "The quality of its courts of law and its armies," wrote Goethe, "gives the most minute insight into the essence of an empire."[1]

An old adage says that how a nation treats it young and old conveys a great deal about the country and its people, but on the world stage under the eyes of its fellow nations, a nation's armed services are a more noticeable manifestation of this national "essence" or character. Strong, confident, internally united nations do not field armed forces that are weak and in disarray. Likewise, a nation torn by internal dissent and discord projects its angst onto its armed forces. The military, therefore, is an accurate gauge of a nation's internal sociopolitical temperament, economic health, and moral well-being, a measure not unnoticed (or ignored) by fellow and rival nations.

How a nation, through its military, is perceived by other nations has considerable effect on how much influence and power it wields internationally. It is a sad but true commentary on the human condition since ancient times that the influence of a nation upon other nation-states is generally predicated upon the size and proficiency of its military arm, and, perhaps more significantly, upon its willingness to employ that arm, whether as a symbol of power or as an instrument of policy. Put another way, a nation is taken seriously only if it displays an ability to wage war and shows that it is unafraid of doing so. Accordingly, how this ability and willingness to make war are translated into action reflects not only the character or "essence" of the parent nation or movement but the will of its political leadership, for it is not armies but nations that make wars.

Thus, armed forces, no matter how rudimentary their organization, are most essential to an aspiring nation-state, for they provide the infant country with international legitimization.[2] For a revolutionary movement, fielding an armed force is especially vital. If such a revolutionary group creates a provisional government in opposition to an existing regime, the action means little unless the movement fields an active military force. Self-preservation is, after all, a fundamental goal of individuals and an aggregate of them, including governments and revolutionary movements. Whatever aspirations a political body has, it must be able and willing to defend itself, lest it be destroyed or lose its external and internal moral credibility. This means that a group or polity must be able to fight a war if it wishes to ensure its existence and win acceptance of its legitimacy. By definition, war is a legitimate act of a state; *ergo*, the ability to field and maintain an armed force constitutes a *conditio sine qua non* (a condition without which not) of sovereign statehood. To any aspiring nation-state or revolutionary movement, the ability to make war (as a means of defense or otherwise) is the legitimizing mechanism for international recognition. The inversion of this equation, however, is that the ultimate success or failure of the revolutionary movement is irrevocably bound up with that of its military, so much so that externally and even internally, a movement's military wing comes to symbolize the revolution.

But the military arm is only an instrument to carry out policy as defined and directed by national policymakers, and that policy must be compatible with the nation's (or the aspirant nation's) values and images of itself. To be sure, policymakers must ensure that the military keeps pace with the doctrinal and technological progress of rival countries. Among large, sophisticated nations, this frequently means that their militaries come to resemble one another, at least on the surface. For instance, from the late seventeenth century, European armies steadily grew more alike, a situation which eventually bordered on absurdity when Prussomania (inspired by Frederick the Great) swept drillfields and parade grounds from St. Petersburg to London.[3] For less sophisticated aspiring nations or movements, it is necessary to know how their more sophisticated opponents will fight so that they can counter them by whatever means are available. A conventionally outclassed power or movement must know how to employ ingenuity, geography, and stratagem when force is out of the question. Thus, if circumstances require a military solution, the armed forces must be ready to carry out their nation's politically defined policy. This remains as much the case today as it was in the eras of Xenophon and Clausewitz.

The implication of all this, however, is the requirement for a compact: the nation or movement, to the best of its abilities, must furnish its military with the basic, minimum requirements necessary to carry out its assigned mission with a reasonable prospect of success. A polity parsimonious toward and distrustful of its military in peacetime reduces its chances of fielding an adequate force when war comes and must share (or should bear) the burden of wartime failures. Just as a strong, efficient war machine and bulwark of patriotism cannot be expected to metamorphosize from a weak, neglected, or even hated military at the outbreak of war, a nation's armed forces must continue to receive infusions of material and moral support while carrying out its assignments. To neglect the military in the field breaks the compact, but even this failure of national will is reflective of a nation's character and values.

But the principal point is that the attitudes of a nation—and especially, but not only, its attitudes toward war—have a powerful bearing on the performance of its military when the armed forces are called upon to accomplish their mission. In sum, in composition, strategy, and every other respect, a military is representative of its nation and dependent upon what its national policy is, whether that course is set by policymakers who are absolute monarchs, cabinet ministers, or the "people."

In colonial America in 1775, there was no central authority that made policy; rather, policy evolved from a commonly held collective of ideas. These ideas included not only a loosely grouped set of inter-related political concepts that, *in toto*, have been called an ideology, but also ideas derived from every part of the colonial intellectual milieu and experience. Decisions on matters of policy were gradually assumed by the Continental Congress as a matter of necessity, but in doing so, that body did not deviate from the popular will. Instead, by its actions, Congress lent substance and definition to these collective ideas.

Among its first decisions as a national policy-making body, Congress created the skeletal organization for an army. This would be fleshed out and refined throughout the long war, but even then, Congress never strayed far from the popularly accepted understanding of what the military and its role should be. Their unswerving adherence to such a military policy should not be any surprise. For the roots of the colonials' conceptions of war, warfare, and the military were the same as those from which their resistance and rebellion and, indeed, their character as Americans had sprung. Americans' conceptions of war were so intricately bound with their revolutionary ideology and nascent national character that any deviation, even for the most critical military emergency, would have been regarded as a refutation of their heritage and principles.

What had happened in America was a spontaneous uprising of an armed populace, to which the colonial leadership as well as the British government had to respond.[4] In April 1775, British intelligence re-ported the whereabouts of several provincial leaders and a cache of gunpowder. Troops from Boston were dispatched to search out and arrest the rebels and destroy any war matériel they found. After dispersing some armed colonials at Lexington, the British burned a few buildings and skirmished with the locals. On the return march to Boston, however, hundreds, possibly thousands, of armed provincials followed the British column, sniping from behind stone walls and trees, killing and wounding scores of the regulars.[5] These farmers, laborers, and shopkeepers were not soldiers, nor were they the trained cadre of a political organization; they were simply men who believed that their families, liberty, and property were threatened, and they responded accordingly. Admittedly, some were loosely organized to cope with emergency situations, but even with those militiamen, the decision to actually take one's musket and powder horn down from the mantle and to engage in combat with British regulars was entirely personal. Within days an armed force of some twenty thousand angry men had gathered in the Boston area, effectively preventing further British incursions and confirming, by consensus and armed might, that a rebellion had begun against the Crown. Faced with circumstances beyond their control or means, local authorities in Massachusetts turned for direction to what was the only existing intercolonial body—the Continental Congress.

The Congress, which did not even convene in its second session until after the fighting had broken out, was little more than a collection of ambassadors representing thirteen confused and disjointed colonies.[6] Its members had no mandate other than to compose another petition of grievances to the Crown, and they had no specific instructions regarding war. Because of time and distance, many had only a sketchy understanding of what had taken place in Massachusetts. They returned to Philadelphia that May to find an increasingly widespread rebellion dumped in their collective lap. Events had come to a boil faster than even the most radical of them had dared to hope, and while there was spirit and ardor aplenty, little accord existed about what direction the rebellion would take. Some were clearly shocked and confused, and even prerebellion firebrands tempered their rhetoric, fully understanding the gravity of the situation. The cooler, more practical among them, however, set about organizing for war.

The delegates had at their disposal a wealth of practical experience and knowledge which could have proved something of a double-edged sword. On the one hand, the diversity of their backgrounds ensured that their knowledge was both broad and deep. Some delegates were gentlemen-politicians whose service in provincial legislatures had given them some understanding of parliamentary procedures. The many lawyers among them lent expertise in solving the constitutional and legal problems which arose. Others were merchants and planters, men of substance who understood financial matters and who were capable of decision making. Among their numbers were no professional military men, and only a few veterans of the French and Indian War who had varying measures of field experience.

On the other hand, this very diversity could render agreement or consensus—hence any action—impossible. Also, while all the representatives could offer specific expertise gained from their livelihoods—politics, practicing law, running mercantile firms and agribusinesses or some combination of these—as self-assured eighteenth-century gentlemen they believed themselves fully competent and dutybound to formulate policy in all fields. These colonial gentlemen-ambassadors required a considerable amount of tact and diplomacy, and that necessarily slowed decision making. "Our unwieldy Body moves very Slow," wrote John Adams that May. "We shall do something in Time, but [we] must have our own Way."[7] Given the circumstances, that they accomplished anything is amazing.

After all, colonial cooperation was something new, and whether it could succeed was unpredictable. The delegates were wholly representative of their colonies and of existing colonial attitudes. Some entertained suspicions of their brother delegates' motives and those of the colonies they represented. The disparity between the wealthy and those of lesser means evoked considerable uneasiness; to some, especially those without it, wealth was perceived as the antithesis of virtue. Others believed themselves more virtuous than their fellow delegates, and this sanctimoniousness played no little part in exacerbating long-standing regional distrusts. Then, too, while a general consensus prevailed that Great Britain had run roughshod over the English constitution in the 1760s and 1770s in dealing with the colonies, little overt enthusiasm existed for a complete break with the motherland. Although the concept of independence was much in the minds of the delegates, the word was rarely spoken, primarily from fears of cleaving the new-found colonial unity asunder.

From a historical perspective, the greatness of these men is apparent, but in 1775 they had not yet been deified by posterity. Certainly they had their doubts and fears; they were, after all, *de facto* leaders of a rebellion against the mother country to which they were tied culturally, socially, economically, and by blood. Granted, colonial protest against the Stamp Act in the 1760s had been widespread, and there had been a great deal of popular support for the nonimportation agreements.[8] But now the sword had been unsheathed and blood spilled. No one could predict how much support would be forthcoming from colonies that might perceive as foolish the reflexive acts of a few New England radicals. Moreover, the colonists were challenging an opponent who had crushed rebellions in Ireland and Scotland with a mailed fist, who had built and maintained an empire stretching from the Ohio Valley to the Valley of the Ganges, and who had seemingly unlimited economic and military means at its disposal.[9]

The situation was indeed grim. Congress had neither money nor means of raising any, no army, and no power, yet the colonies increasingly turned to it for leadership and direction. Looking back in 1789, one delegate neatly summarized the crisis Americans faced. Among themselves and before the world, they were thirteen British colonies, neither a nation nor even considered as separate American people. "Money, the nerve of War, was wanting," George Washington wrote. "The Sword was to be forged on the Anvil of necessity; the treasury to be created from nothing."[10] Hanging, imprisonment, confiscation of property, and exile were real possibilities. But for all their suspicions and fears, and in spite of their diverse backgrounds, these delegates reacted to the crisis with the same unflinching resolve that their fellow colonists in Massachusetts had exhibited the preceding April. They were able to do so because they (and directly and indirectly the colonies they represented) shared fundamental bonds that not only enabled them to unite with minimum acrimony but provided them with a common understanding of war, warfare, and the role that their military would play in their fight for liberty.

In his book of the same title, historian Michael Kammen described the prerevolutionary Americans as a "people of paradox," and he could not have been more correct.[11] They were at once a people of conflict and consensus, of rigidity and flexibility, of simplicity and complexity. Avowedly Christian, their God was the fierce warrior chieftain of the Old Testament Hebrews. They fled the Old World for the opportunities of the New, but for education, philosophy, heroes, and even military advice they turned back to the Old and even the Ancient. They migrated for religious freedom and brought intolerance; they bitterly opposed tyranny and made black men and women slaves.[12] They came seeking peace and considered war distasteful, but when they went to war—as they often did—they fought knowing that God was on their side, unrestrained by any rules save His. They looked wistfully at the Old World, country bumpkins fascinated by the big city's lights, and they sought and cherished products of the European intellectual and material cultures; but they also perceived the Europe of Locke, Montesquieu, and fine furniture and clothing as a sinkhole of corruption and vice, where virtuous men were rare and tyranny held sway. So, while they decried excessive pride and ambition, they conceived poverty to be a virtue, wore homespun as a badge of purity, and smugly believed themselves morally superior. Superficially, it seems that the colonists were a mass of contradictions about whom the only generalization one can make is that they were difficult to make generalizations about. But this ignores a fundamental aspect of the colonial character, one from which a common bond threaded its way through thirteen wholly different colonies—the practical nature of these people.

From the earliest settlements, they learned that they had to make do with what little they had or could create; harsh realities precluded their counting upon assistance from Europe, so they became increasingly self-sufficient, lest they do without and possibly die. Self-sufficiency eventually came to breed a sense of independence. When, after decades of virtual neglect, England sought to exercise her rights and impose her will upon her colonies, the effort would be seen as usurpation by the colonists. Self-sufficiency and self-preservation colored their ideas, their worldview, their self-perception, and their self-confidence—both as individuals and as a people—in ways that cannot be measured, except by their actions.

These colonists were eminently sensible, resourceful people who sought useful knowledge from any source. They borrowed only what they thought they needed: if it did not work, it was discarded; if it worked, it was improved and adapted for their new environment. They could not transport European institutions whole to the New World, so they borrowed extensively but selectively. For instance, from reading they actively kept abreast of changes in the European art of war, and from service alongside the British regulars against the Amerindians and on foreign expeditions they observed and learned a great deal about military affairs. No matter how they longed to build a regular, European-style army—as Washington and his lieutenants pined to do—their practical nature forbade it. Time, economics, the political culture, and a thousand other things precluded it, but so did differences in terrain and the observations Americans had made in earlier wars while fighting at the side of their English cousins (who, with few exceptions, stubbornly tried, at the cost of much blood and treasure, to impose the Old World art of war upon the New). So they adapted European lessons to what fitted their needs, unconsciously and unacknowledged, just as they liberally adopted ways and customs of the Native Americans and displaced Africans.[13] Blended with New World resources and experiences, what evolved was nothing less than a hybrid, American way—part old, part new—whose guiding principle was practicality.

The colonists' practical nature governed almost everything they did, from education to self-defense, and it helps explain why they did certain things, things that are now difficult to comprehend from a historical perspective. For instance, there were those in the postrevolutionary period who questioned the usefulness of a classical education. What need, they asked, would a land of simple farmers and mechanics have for dead languages and ancient ideas? And yet their predecessors in the revolutionary generation (some of whom were now vociferous critics) had found both a purely classical and even a classically influenced education to be of enormous worth and practicality. For it was the type of education that perhaps John Stuart Mill described best: "Education makes a man a more intelligent shoemaker, if that be his occupation, but not by teaching him how to make shoes," wrote Mill, a cobbler's grandson. "It does so by the mental exercises it gives, and the habits it impresses."[14] Settlers in the New World recognized that an ability to think clearly and logically was remarkably useful; trained to think, one could always learn particulars on the job, as it were, or by reading works specific to a task. Almost all eighteenth-century professionals in America or Europe—doctors, lawyers, military officers—learned their craft this way, as did anyone exploring means to improve his lot. Seeking to break the tobacco-debt cycle which linked him to chains running from London to Mt. Vernon, the non–classically educated but classically influenced George Washington became an agriculturist of note by immersing himself in the literature of the day, by seeking expert advice, and by careful experimentation—a methodology he carried over into war. Moreover, to be educated in colonial America, whether at school or home, or even to receive the rudiments of education given by itinerant teachers, was to acquire a healthy dosage of classicism. The medieval trivium and quadrivium, in both its classical and in its Americanized form, would furnish the revolutionary generation with a great deal of common ground, including an especial reverence for the past.

From a modern perspective, these people were doers, makers of history, but colonial Americans, particularly the revolutionary generation, were great users of history. The past was real to them, and history was their passion. It supplied them with useful knowledge, precedents, and, above all, ideas. They turned to the past to validate the present, and for a people bereft of heroes in a hero-conscious age, history gave them a long line of virtuous heroes to place in their pantheons. Colonial libraries and bookshelves were replete with histories, especially those of the great political and military writers of classical Greece and Rome. One did not have to read an ancient language, however, to enjoy the classics, as there were innumerable translations; and an even easier road to the past existed. Popular European histories of ancient times were translated into English almost as fast as they were written, and these books were eagerly read by colonists ranging from the planters of Virginia and South Carolina to the farmers and shopkeepers of New England. From reading these works average literate Americans could understand the many classical and historical allusions, names, and metaphors that permeated the political tomes, oratory, plays, self-improvement books, newspapers, and almanacs of which they were so fond. How else could the political pamphleteers have reached and influenced such a widespread audience with their classically laced polemics, and how could orators have made themselves understood to the crowd? And yet another, even more fundamental avenue to the past existed, one that was familiar to all Americans.

The Bible was a shared part of colonial Americans' cultural essence in ways that perhaps cannot be understood today. Among the delegates to Philadelphia in 1775, religious beliefs ranged from pietistic Puritanism to deism, yet in youth all had absorbed biblical knowledge and had been inculcated with a set of values that even the most deistic individual found useful. The Bible was as central to the intellectual growth and development of Western civilization and, hence, to that of the colonies, as were those other ancient tomes, the Greek and Roman classics. After all, in varying degrees, the colonists thought of themselves as God's Select, His Chosen People, or even simply that God was on their side. For the pietistic, as with their Old Testament Hebraic counterparts, if they did not transgress their covenant with God, He would stand by them in hardship and battle; among those who did not strictly adhere to covenant theology, conventional wisdom attested that God would visit them with misfortune if they broke His laws.[15] When the American Enlightenment introduced the European intellectual revolution to New World minds, the humanistic philosophies of the Old World did not supersede biblical lessons but complemented them. Even beyond religiosity, to these people the Bible dispensed values and lessons to live by. Reduced to their essence, these guidelines were identical to the beloved moral dictums of popular historians such as Rollin and Vertot, arbiters of good taste such as Addison, Steele, and L'Estrange, the extraordinarily popular and influential political writers such as Trenchard and Gordon, and, of course, in their axiomatic forms popularized in American almanacs by homegrown sages such as Benjamin Franklin. The Bible was a common source of practical knowledge for these children of the Reformation who ceaselessly tried to fix themselves, their fellow men, and their rulers in perspective.

The useful knowledge that colonists gleaned from these various sources included a considerable amount of both general and specific information about warfare. All knowledge builds upon lessons learned from the past, and the more general the knowledge, the more useful it may be over time. This occurs in all areas of human endeavor, but it is particularly noticeable in military affairs. There, distilled to their essence, lessons discovered or learned millennia ago retained their freshness and vigor through the American Revolution (and into the nuclear age). Surprise, concentration and economy of force, and many other principles of war can be easily discerned in ancient works, both historical and fictional, but even broader lessons may be seen. For instance, modern scholars have compared the Peloponnesian wars (460–404 B.C.) between the alliances led by Athens and Sparta to the cold war and the Athenian expedition to Syracuse (415–413 B.C.) with American involvement in Vietnam, using the past to illustrate and illuminate the present. Neither the wars nor the foreign interventions were the same, and the "exact analogies" do not hold true throughout. "But it is not the exact analogies that stay in a reader's mind," write Richard E. Neustadt and Ernest R. May. "It is instead the illustrations of Thucydides' proposition that human nature remains constant."[16] As much a part of ancient life as it was, it would have been more surprising if war had not been a major theme among classical Greek and Roman authors. In the Old Testament, which one scholar portrayed as an "interminable litany of battles and bloodshed,"[17] the Hebrews were constantly at war, and the Bible was a wealth of general military information to the colonists who imbibed it from youth.[18]

Admittedly, a great deal of this knowledge may be characterized as commonsensical: one does not have to be a military man to learn these lessons, but that is exactly the point. In the eighteenth century most European military officers, even the great Bonaparte, attained most of their knowledge (and, naturally, ideas) about the art of war by reading. Not only were the same books they read available to the colonists (primarily in translations) but they were very popular in America which, in spite of the intermittent Indian wars, was not a particularly martial society. But since even preclassical times, humans have been fascinated with war and the military life. Homer lamented that men become satiated "of state, Satietie of sleepe and love, satiate of ease, Of musicke, dancing, can find place, yet harsh warre still must please[,] Past all those pleasures, even past these." But as to war, "They will be cloyd with these[,] Before their warre joyes: never war gives Troy satiates!"[19] Even if colonists had no interest in military affairs and did not read what were considered even then as indispensable works on the art of war—by Saxe, Caesar, or Frederick the Great—they still absorbed a great deal of military history in their workaday reading.

But their love of history and their biblical knowledge did more than give them a general schooling in the art of war; in many ways, these not only furnished the genesis of many colonial military traditions and practices, but also predisposed them toward ready acceptance of the English radical Whig political ideas that formed such an integral part of American revolutionary ideology. The royal absolutism that filled the vacuum left in Europe by the demise of feudalism and the turmoil of the Reformation came late to England. Conflict over who should rule—between a monarch who longed to emulate his absolutist continental contemporaries and those favoring increased parliamentary power—led to civil war which resulted in more than a decade of military dictatorship. The conflict was finally resolved following the Glorious Revolution of 1688 by Parliament's gaining ascendancy, especially over the military. But beginning even before events in England came to a head, in the New World the colonists were already establishing traditions and practices that soon hardened into laws, customs, myths, and conventions that in many ways presaged those of late seventeenth-century England and continued to modern times as part of the American ethos and practice. For instance, particularly in the New England colonies, civilian control of the military was within the cautiously guarded purview of the ruling magistrates and legislators. From the Bible, the classics, European history, and their own instincts, they knew that who controlled the military controlled the state. From the classics, the fear of Caesarism and Praetorianism was all too clear. And from both a pietistic and a practical standpoint, regular armies were perceived as promoting corruption, vice, and laziness, all three being anathema especially among the relatively staid Puritans but also to their neighbors to the south. So while their English cousins fought bitterly among themselves in part to define the role of the military in their society, the colonists were already nurturing their infant conceptions of an American custom of war and thereby, unknowingly, linking themselves with bonds that would bind even the strongest colonial rifts.

From these many—but linked—sources grew the common ties that twined Americans of the revolutionary generation together and furnished them with their conceptions of war. This bond was not just among themselves: it reflected a cultural integrity that crossed both the

Atlantic and the centuries to republican Rome and Greece and to the
Hebrews before they asked God, against the advice of the prophet
Samuel, for a king.[20] Historically conscious Americans were well aware
that they had a chance to rekindle the ancient fire of liberty seemingly
snuffed out forever when Caesar uttered, "Alea iacta est" (the die is
cast), and marched at the head of his legions into Rome. To be sure,
delegates who met in Philadelphia that spring of 1775 and their fellow
colonists did not always share like interpretations of what they read. A
rich diversity of opinion existed among Americans, and many who
thought that Britain had overstepped the bounds of the constitution
with her behavior in the 1760s and 1770s were nevertheless horrified
at the thought of rebelling against the Crown. The situation demanded
a certain delicacy or diplomacy in order to promote and maintain
unity. But for those upon whose shoulders the mantle of leadership
fell, something of a cultural common ground or intellectual camaraderie prevailed that, together with long-held military traditions and practices, supplied them with a starting point for discussion and action.

The military establishment created by Congress in 1775 remained,
throughout several alterations and emergency measures, wholly representative of its parent society, the revolutionary movement, and the
ideas which governed it. Even when the dark days before Trenton saw
Washington named as virtual dictator by Congress, this was not a
deviation from the governing ideology; instead, it affirmed the ties
American revolutionaries had with republican, Cincinnatian Rome.
These generally shared conceptions of war, warfare, the military, and
the relationship between the military and civilian policymakers were
more than commonly understood ideas; they were the Revolution's
Rubicon which would not be crossed, no matter what the die read.

PART I

The Classical
Inheritance

THE impact of the classical revival on eighteenth-century Euro-Americans and their political culture has been the focus of much scholarly attention. That the writings of the ancients were regularly cited by such disparate groups as English Whigs and Tories and American and French revolutionaries is well established. Scholars disagree, however, over the extent to which classical authors actually influenced eighteenth-century thought. Some historians regard the influence as superficial: political controversialists used classical allusions in their writings simply because they lent authority to their arguments and because everyone else was doing it. Yet, evidence continues to accumulate that classical literature and ideas played an important role in forming the fashionable republican ideologies of the time and, indeed, that classicism was deeply infused throughout colonial Euro-American society as a whole.[1]

It is essential to the understanding of American conceptions of war in 1775 to comprehend how strong this classical tradition was in the American colonies. Both directly and indirectly, classicism had great influence on the development of an American revolutionary ideology, which, in turn, determined how the armed forces were to be formed and maintained and even how the war was to be fought. Then, too, from a strictly military perspective, and again both directly and indi-

25

rectly, classical influences on American conceptions and practice of war offer another, hitherto unexplored area of scholarly inquiry. And, perhaps most importantly, the colonists' sense of historical continuity —their identification with both biblical and classical times—predisposed them toward perceiving new ideas and challenges through a prism derived from ancient writings and themes. Therefore, to proceed, we must examine the depth and popularity of the classical influence in the prerevolutionary American colonies.

CHAPTER 2

Old Wine in New Skins

The vigorous intellectual fermentation of the eighteenth century arose in part from the new modes of thought associated with Bacon, Locke, and Newton; but it also flowed from the great humanistic tradition of Western civilization. The reawakening of that tradition, no less than the dawn of the Age of Reason, portended revolutionary changes, for the classical revival stimulated a rethinking of all aspects of human endeavor, from the visual arts to the art of war. The ideas and concepts of the classical Greek and Roman periods, however, were not copied and applied directly; rather, they provided a bountiful source from which inspiration, comparison, examples, and validation could be drawn. The old ideas infused eighteenth-century cultures with fresh vigor, spawning new ideas to answer old questions and to deal with conditions of the present and the future. So strong a hold did these ancient ideas obtain on several generations that what has been described as a "cult of antiquity" grew up around them. But the cult was not the exclusive domain of an intellectual elite. Technological advances—printing especially—played an important role in promulgating its ideas and disseminating them among an increasingly literate population.[1]

The British colonies in North America best illustrated this marriage of old and new. For many European intellectuals through the end of the eighteenth century, America was a living, unspoiled laboratory. There in the New World, where some believed the future of humankind lay, the ideas and ideals of Europe would be tested in a Great Experiment. Unlike the Old World with its prejudices and conflicts, America remained in a natural state, a blank canvas upon which Europe could project its own *mentalité*, seeing ideas come to life without the constraints of the past. For Europeans, America the continent and America the idea offered a liberating influence, a land of opportunity not only for the purse but for the mind and soul. Here was a chance to see if theory could be put into practice, not in the pages of a book or in a laboratory but in a real setting with real people.[2]

These real people, the European-American colonists, stayed closely attuned to what their cross-Atlantic cousins were writing and reading, and like their European counterparts they looked to and borrowed widely from the past.[3] But therein lay a crucial difference: in both the Old World and the New, history could be a beacon light, but in the Old it was a burden as well. In America all the effects were positive. By placing themselves and their actions in an ongoing stream of Western civilization from past to future, history gave Americans a vital (and exalted) sense of identity. History allowed the underlying colonial feelings of inferiority to things European, and especially things English, to be masked by a smug sense of virtuous superiority. After all, from a religious, philosophic, and historical point of view, America was the Promised Land. As Great Britain grew increasingly corrupt— in colonial eyes—Americans measured themselves morally against the mother country, and found her wanting. While railing against the sin of pride, each time Americans vitiated English society they unconsciously raised themselves in their own estimation. From their reading of history, particularly ancient history, Americans saw themselves as epitomes of virtue, as descendants of the virtuous Greek and Roman republicans.

Significantly, it should be noted, Americans of the revolutionary period by and large rejected the ancients' cyclical view of history. Language traditionally has been an accurate gauge of cultural and societal change. Heretofore, for instance, the definition of the word "revolution" was derived from the Latin *revolutio* (a rolling back or return, revolving in time). As historian I. Bernard Cohen points out, however, the impact of the eighteenth-century rage for improvements and learning in all fields, particularly science, was felt in other areas of

society, and language reflected this new thinking. A revised definition
of "revolution" emerged by the mid-eighteenth century, one that implied radical change. In fact, the third citation of Samuel Johnson's
popular *Dictionary of the English Language*, first published in 1755,
defined "revolution" as a "Change in the state of a government or
country."[4] By the American Revolution, thinking in consecutive, linear time, rather than cyclical time, was the colonial norm.

That was characteristic of these eminently practical people: they
took from the past only what they needed, refining and adapting ideas
to fit those needs. History furnished the colonists with hard facts and,
more importantly, precedents to support conclusions that they had
already worked out for themselves by experiment and through experience. The search for a usable past is a never-ending enterprise, and
few peoples have engaged in it more diligently than eighteenth-century
Americans with their passion for history. Like Diogenes, the revolutionary generation especially went about seeking the truth, recognizing
it and highlighting it when they found it, but discarding all that was
not true.[5] They valued ancient history for its still very relevant lessons:
for public affairs and personal conduct, for politics and war, the past
seemed to speak directly to the colonists, offering guidance through
ancient and timeless wisdom and example. But for all the relative
autonomy provided by three thousand miles of ocean, Americans
looked to the classical past with as much reverence as if living surrounded by vestiges of ancient Greek and Roman civilizations. For in
America, too, the cult of antiquity not only lived but thrived.[6]

To those of the age in which steam power was barely in its infancy,
the glory days of the Greek and Roman republics did not seem at all
remote. Characters in Plutarch's *Lives* and in the Bible, especially of
the Old Testament, were looked upon as familiar and entirely real
human beings. American colonists intimately knew the lives of the
ancients, their heroism and cowardice, their virtue and venality. That
was, it is true, soon to change: long-lived veterans of the American
Revolution would witness a technological transformation that, as a by-
product, all but erased the classical epoch from memory. But for the
colonists of 1775, antiquity remained easy to imagine and thus easy to
remember, for in many practical ways human progress since ancient

times could be measured in inches, if there had been any progress at all.[7]

For example, despite an eighteenth-century "rage for improvements" that increased agricultural productivity and resulted in some major engineering feats, the means of transportation and communication available to George Washington were essentially the same as those that had been available to Julius Caesar.[8] Whether one wished to travel from ancient Rome to Athens or from colonial Boston to Williamsburg, the means of getting there continued unchanged. One traveled by human power, animal power, or wind power; no alternatives existed. Moreover, communication and transportation remained virtually one and the same; the message arrived with the messenger—and not before—just as it had in Scipio Africanus's day.

Even the more advanced technologies sometimes had drawbacks compared to those of the past. The coast-hugging, human-powered triremes of ancient Mediterranean civilizations had not been particularly seaworthy, but they could weigh anchor and depart at will. Modern eighteenth-century oceangoing ships-of-the-line—the technological marvels of their day—still remained dependent upon wind and tides. Time itself had quickened but slightly by the eighteenth century, and the sunup to sundown lives of most people were certainly more akin to those of classical times than to the frenetic pace of life that was to come. And anyone who had his brains and backsides rattled and bounced trying to navigate a carriage over colonial roads could have looked back with envy to the celebrated roads of Rome.[9]

For colonists surely knew of those ancient highways and of the people who built them. When they crossed the Atlantic to America, Europeans did not leave their cultural baggage at home; their trunks contained both the Bible and classical works. And this raises a point worth emphasizing. While the Scriptures fulfilled many needs of the colonists—religious, moral, political, and practical—the close association, even empathy, that colonists felt for people of biblical times created a receptiveness for other lessons from the distant past. This is not to suggest any direct relationship between biblical study and knowledge of the classics. But if one seeks guidance, strength, and examples from one ancient tome, then one is apt to be disposed to look at others.

Evidence for such an intellectual predisposition is overwhelming. The writings of seventeenth- and eighteenth-century Americans, be they ministers, essayists, or diarists, contained an intermixture of classical themes and biblical allusions. A survey of the sources from which colonial ministers drew ideas for their sermons is most illustrative. The Bible, of course, furnished ideas for everyday and special sermons, but the writings of Thucydides, Aristotle, Plato, Cicero, Virgil, Seneca, Tacitus, Sallust, Plutarch, and Josephus frequently provided ministers with themes for their lessons. Occasionally even the words of Socrates, Demosthenes, Caesar, Horace, Juvenal, and Suetonius mixed with those from the Old and New Testaments, as preachers strove to reach their congregations using sources familiar to most.[10]

The resurgence of interest in the classics and the coming of the Age of Reason, with its intrusion of natural law into the direct line of communication between God and man, in no way lessened the importance of the Bible to colonial Americans. Although the Renaissance had kindled an intellectual fire that bathed the seventeenth and eighteenth centuries in the light of reason and rationalism, the centrality of the Bible in Western thought cannot be ignored; it stood as a keystone of Western civilization, its passages so universally known that any biblical allusion was immediately understood. In fact, while the intellectual milieu fostered by the Renaissance lasted well into the eighteenth century, the Protestant Reformation possibly had a more direct impact on focusing the political thinking of colonial Americans. As the Reformation forced individuals to rethink and reconsider their relationship with God, suggested historian Edmund Sears Morgan, they began to explore their relationships with their fellow humans, which invariably led them to a closer examination of the relationship between themselves and their rulers. For people who fled from Old World repression for the succor of New World milk and honey, the providentially dictated words of the Bible were indeed real. The colonists perceived themselves as a new Chosen People whom God would bless if they continued obedient to His laws. Even if they regressed—as they surely would, considering their gloomy view of human nature—redemption remained possible just as it had for the ancient Hebrews; God would assist them recovering their lost virtue. This theme corresponded closely—remarkably so in fact—with the highly moralistic values colonists derived from the classics and later incorporated into American republicanism.[11]

The similarity of these lessons allowed historically conscious Americans to cloak themselves in a mantle of Bible, classics, and the present. In a sense this was the heart of the American Enlightenment: a mixture of old and new ideas blended by practical Americans to fit their needs. (As John Barnard sermonized in 1734, "This Voice of Nature is the voice of God. Thus 'tis that *vox populi est vox Dei.*")[12] They recognized the value of the need for intellectual and pietistic attainment, for an understanding of reason and control of their passions, and for both science and sentiment.[13]

The use of the Exodus story was particularly representative of these people with their passion for history and precedence. The book of Exodus and the escape from Egyptian slavery under command of the "Captain General of the Hosts of Israel," Moses, was dear to the hearts and minds of all colonial and revolutionary Americans.[14] After all, the pattern of oppression, migration (forced or voluntary but filled with travail), and salvation established in Exodus "has been etched deeply" into Western "political culture." First, as scholar Michael Walzer suggested, there must be real or imagined oppression, then "hope (against all the odds of human history) for deliverance; we join in covenants and constitutions; we aim at a new and better social order." Events did not so much naturally fall into an Exodus pattern, Walzer explained, as people worked "actively to give them that shape."[15] Leaving the persecution and war of the Old World for truly only God knew what in the New, seventeenth-century Christians drew comfort from the trials of their Old Testament Hebraic antecedents.

For from the first settlements in Virginia and especially among the Puritans of New England, colonists believed that a bond existed between themselves and the Israelites of the Exodus: both groups had been providentially guided from oppression through a wilderness into a Promised Land where God would help them defeat their enemies. Faith and trust in God were their security, and He would protect them and steady their aim. The God of both the Israelites and American colonists was, after all, an active, not passive, Divinity, a God who historically came to the aid of his Chosen People.[16] "God," one Virginian wrote in 1610, "will not let us fall."[17] This providential view was a commonly held belief among all Christian settlers, although, obviously, the depth and articulation of this "covenant" or "compact" varied among different groups. Certainly, as Morgan pointed out, most "Christians agreed that the example of Israel was not to be taken too literally" for "some of the laws God prescribed for the Jews did not apply" to them, such as dietary codes. But they interpreted many Old Testament events "as prefigurations or prophecies" of events in the New Testament and, later, in colonial times.[18] For mid-eighteenth-century Americans, Exodus (and many other portions of the Bible) would present a flexible framework into which classically influenced republican ideas and ideals could easily be molded. Combining these two powerful and fundamental elements of Western civilization furnished Americans with religious and secular precedents for the exigencies of current conditions.

One passage from Exodus—of many—illustrates this point. In the Sinai, Jethro told Moses that for the sake of the people he must step down as sole leader. "This thing is too heavy for thee; thou art not able to perform it thyself alone." During their years in the wilderness, the natural increase of the Israelites was both enormous and sustained; the single charismatic chieftain who had led them out of Egypt was no longer capable of ruling so many under entirely new conditions. To provide effective and fair leadership, Jethro advised Moses to retain his overall command, but to delegate his authority among "rulers of thousands, and rulers of hundreds, rulers of fifties, and rulers of tens."[19] The message was clear: the old order was inadequate for the wilderness and certainly not suitable for the Promised Land. Therefore, a new system of government must be created in the Sinai, a system that would work equally well both in the wilderness and beyond.[20] This admonition dovetailed nicely with classical lessons and modern republican ideology for Americans ruled by a distant king and an unrepresentative Parliament. (On another level not ignored by colonials, Jethro's suggestion may be seen as sound military advice, especially to a people on the march who were subject to ambush: "Divide your forces into brigades, companies, platoons, and squads.")

Symbolic of this admixture of Old Testament and classical themes blending with modern ideology was the design agreed upon for the

Great Seal of the United States in 1776. One side was purely neoclassical, featuring a Latin inscription (*E Pluribus Unum*) with the goddesses Liberty and Justice standing armed and defiant. That the hand of providence guided this defiance may be observed in the scene from Exodus on the reverse. There, the engraver etched Pharaoh driving a chariot through the parted Red Sea while Moses, basking in the light of the Pillar of Fire, extended his hand to close the waters at God's command. Strong but realistic symbolism, indeed, for even as Congress debated its selection, a powerful British fleet was ferrying an army onto Long Island's shores, making final preparations for an assault on Washington's lines.[21]

So in many ways, the colonists drew their strength from an antiquity of mixed antecedents: part Old Testament, part classical Greek and Roman. This combination of ancient wisdom may be seen when, shortly after arriving in their new Canaan, the colonists created an educational system in the wilderness. Seeking to train an indigenous ministry and educate the next generation of leaders, the colonists turned to the educational model they knew best and laid a classical foundation.[22]

That a people in a wilderness should be even minimally interested in learning, ancient or modern, may seem surprising; but respect for the value of education was evident in America from the beginning. "Religion and learning, *Churches* and *Schools* were their first Care," one eighteenth-century minister recalled, "and for these they laid a wise and *strong* Foundation . . . to propagate a well instructed and a godly *Seed*."[23] Full participation in community life, religious and political, demanded a literate populace. After all, as the Massachusetts School Law of 1647 began, "It being one Chief Project of that old deluder Satan to keep men from the knowledge of the Scriptures," a community's spiritual and civic well-being made it essential that its members be educated.[24] The Puritans of the Massachusetts Bay colony required that all children be taught to read and write whether they wanted to or not (their education was assured, historian Samuel Eliot Morison commented, "in a community so well supplied with ministers, schoolmasters, and birch trees").[25]

Connecticut and New Hampshire followed suit, and soon, as John

Adams later remarked, "A native of America who cannot read and write is as rare an appearance, as a Jacobite or Roman Catholic, i.e. as rare as a Comet or an Earthquake."[26] Of course, "America" to Adams meant New England, and, as he admitted, there were some who believed that educating the poor promoted "idleness and vain speculation among the people," who would be better off working hard and leaving matters of importance to their betters. But "[b]e it remembred," he cautioned, ". . . liberty must at all hazards be supported," and "liberty cannot be preserved without a general knowledge among the people."[27] Therefore, "[e]very town containing sixty families, is obliged, under a penalty, to maintain constantly a school and a schoolmaster," Adams informed the Abbé de Malby, "who shall teach his scholars reading, writing, arithmetic, and the rudiments of the Latin and Greek languages."[28]

The value of education was appreciated even in colonies with diffused populations where many, if not most, children learned to read either in the classroom or at home.[29] Very early on Virginians recognized the importance of education in curbing "sloth and idleness" among young boys and girls, particularly of the poor, and from 1646,[30] the burgesses worked toward this end, albeit with mixed success, for in 1661, parents still "bewailed" the "almost general want of Schooles."[31] From colony to colony, the need for education was deemed paramount, one of the key elements, the building blocks, in the success of a community. In New England, education, along with local government, the Congregational Church, and the militia, were the four institutions, the four pillars, John Adams believed, responsible for the region's greatness.[32] (In fact, the regionally centric Adams suggested, New England's greatness could be duplicated even among the voluptuaries of Virginia if these four institutions could be adopted there.)[33] Since a fair number of the early seventeenth-century settlers—particularly among the leaders—were graduates of Cambridge and Oxford, they recognized the necessity for a school system as an "imperative matter, nearly if not as important as the institution of the churches themselves."[34]

Thus, for moral, philosophical, and political reasons, colonists were quick to establish institutions of higher learning. "After God had carried us safe to *New-England*, and wee had builded our houses, provided necessaries for our liveli-hood, rear'd convenient places for God's worship, and setled the Civill Government," one colonist wrote in 1641, explaining how Harvard College came to be established, "[o]ne of the next things we longed for, and looked after was to advance *Learning* and perpetuate it to Posterity."[35] This pattern continued with the movement westward. After girdling or chopping down trees and clearing land for some crops and loosing their hogs to forage on the natural mast, settlers turned back to the east for materials to recreate the educational system they knew best: first to England, then to Harvard, William and Mary, Yale, and Princeton.[36]

To meet entrance requirements for the colonial colleges, aspiring students received extensive preparation in a primary educational system that was uneven at best. As with any colonial institution, from the militia to local government to education, great diversity existed even within each colony as to how children were educated. Almost every colony's educational system featured formal establishments such as Boston's Latin School, pay-as-you-learn schools set up by itinerant scholars, and, for those who could afford it, private tutors; the quality of instruction from the last two modes of education was solely dependent upon the teachers, some of whom were excellent, some wastrels. In these schoolrooms, students being groomed for Harvard College or the College of William and Mary sat alongside their cousins who struggled just to master the "3 R's."

To varying degrees, however, all students received at least a modicum of classical knowledge and a surprising amount of Latin. Even those students who never construed Cicero or Sallust trained under a classical aegis, for colonial textbooks, for the most part, were translations from Latin or written by classically trained scholars. From the endless drilling and reciting, the singular rhythm and power of Latin permeated the writings of even such non–classically trained colonials as George Washington.[37] Although Washington did not read or speak Latin (or any foreign language) except for phrases in the common lexicon, his powerful, clear writing style bespeaks an education with a strong classical influence. This stemmed from his schooling in Fredericksburg under the tutelage of the Reverend James Marye, under whom the young Virginian laboriously copied the classically influenced *Rules of Civility*.[38] But among those destined for college, preparation in the classical languages was essential.

Higher education in seventeenth- and eighteenth-century colonial America—whether one studied for the ministry, law, medicine, or simply the veneer of a gentleman—was, by definition, a classical education.[39] Among the early colonists were quite a few men of education and culture who believed that a knowledge of the Greek and Roman classical authors was intrinsic to the preservation and transmission of a truly cultivated life to New England or Virginia.[40] Education was a means of raising one's status, always a prime consideration in the colonies, and this meant at least a familiarity with the classics. Admission into one of the nine colonial colleges that sprang up from 1636 to the Revolution depended, among other things, upon a student's knowledge of classical Greek and Latin. In the first years of Harvard College, for instance, students had to make "publique declamations in *Latine* and *Greeke*" once a month before an audience of "Magistrates, Ministers, and other Schollars, for the probation of their growth in Learning."[41]

These "publique declamations" were not as difficult as they might appear, for every student was already well grounded in the ancient tongues before gaining admittance. Each applicant to Harvard had to demonstrate his ability "to understand Tully, or such like classicall Latine Author *extempore*, and make and speake true Latine in Verse and Prose, *suo ni aiunt Marte* [to stand on one's own feet]," plus be able to "decline perfectly the Paradigm's of *Nounes* and *Verbs* in the Greek tongue." Only "then and not before [would the student] be capable of admission into the Colledge."[42] The Harvard laws of 1655 reaffirmed this, again stressing knowledge of "Tully."[43] In setting up these entrance requirements, Massachusetts Bay Puritans harkened back to their own undergraduate days in England; it was no coincidence, after all, that they established Harvard College in a town named Cambridge.[44]

Farther south, in New Haven, the entrance requirements at Yale were no less rigorous. The original proceedings of the Yale College trustees in 1701 explained admittance procedures. The rector of the college, neighboring ministers, and trustees gathered to examine candidates, "And finding them Duly prepared And Expert in Latin and Greek Authors both Poetick and oratorial [and] As also ready in making Good Latin," they shall be admitted.[45] Little changed by 1745, when an incoming student had to not only "bring Sufficient Testi-

mony of his Blameless and inoffensive life," but also had to be able
"Extempore to Read, Construe, and Parse Tully, Virgil, and the
Greek Testament" among other qualifications. When college masters
interviewed fifteen-year-old prodigy John Trumbull to determine
whether he was qualified to attend Yale, he had already mastered, in
Latin, Eutropius, Cornelius Nepos, Virgil, Cicero, Horace, and Juvenal. This was in addition to his reading the New Testament and the
Iliad in the original Greek.[46] As other colleges opened their doors, this
format was continued. A 1754 New York newspaper advertisement
invited applications to the newly opened King's College (now Columbia University). In order to be considered for admittance, college
president Samuel Johnson assured parents, potential students must
"have a good knowledge in the [Latin and Greek] *Grammars*, and be
able to make grammatical *Latin*, and both in construing and parsing,
to give a good Account of two or three of first select Orations of *Tully*,
and," he added, "of the first Books of *Virgil's Aeneid*."[47]

Once in college, a student's choice of classes varied little from school
to school. The earliest surviving statutes from William and Mary
(1727) describe that college's curriculum in simple terms: "As for
rudiments and grammars and classic authors of [Greek and Latin], let
them teach the same books which by law or custom are used in the
schools of England."[48] The Virginians were not alone in following the
English norm. Early Harvard students (1642) spent Wednesdays
studying Greek, while Thursday was devoted to Hebrew, Chaldee
(Aramaic), and Syriac (to enable future ministers to read the Scriptures
in their original languages).[49] At mid-eighteenth-century Yale, the
classical curriculum dominated study and was rigidly adhered to in
practice.[50] One strictly enforced requirement, for instance, stated that
"on Friday Each Undergraduate . . . Shall Declaim in the Hall in
Latin, Greek, or Hebrew and in no other language without Special
Leave from the President."[51] After the Revolution, Yale President
Ezra Stiles made what would have been considered ten years earlier a
"radical" departure from tradition: he introduced English grammar
into Yale's curriculum.[52]

Latin, and occasionally Greek, remained through the Revolution,
however, as the primary languages for all major academic papers. In
order to graduate from seventeenth-century Harvard, students had to

be able to demonstrate an ability to translate the Old and the New Testament "into the Lattin Tongue."[53] This paralleled practices at British universities and colleges, where some wealthy colonial Americans sent their children to be educated and to receive professional training in medicine and law. There, as in the colonies, major addresses and dissertations were written and delivered in one of the ancient tongues. An address given at Harvard in 1662 illustrated this point. Blending religiosity with classicism, this "Salutatory Oration" remains noteworthy only because a student delivered it in seventeenth-century rustic America. Totally written and delivered in Latin, the discourse mixed Old Testament references with selections from the classical authors most quoted in the colonies, including Cicero, Virgil, Tacitus, Xenophon, Livy, Pliny, Plato, Horace, Plutarch, and Juvenal.[54]

This medieval custom, that important orations or theses be written in Latin, turned one classically trained revolutionary away from advocacy of the classics. Dr. Benjamin Rush spent such a considerable time laboring in Edinburgh to put his doctoral thesis into passable Latin that he later sought to have all major college addresses and theses written in English. Wittily, Rush called for an end to the traditional classical education by paraphrasing Cato the Elder's "Carthage must be destroyed," writing instead, "Delenda, delenda est lingua Romana."[55] (Already during the revolutionary period—and inspired to a large measure by the spirit of change which swept the colonies—the previously stringent entrance examinations were being relaxed at most colleges.) But these anticlassical sentiments did not take hold overnight, for when Harvard awarded General George Washington an honorary LL.D. in 1776, the local newspaper printed the decree in both English and Latin.[56]

While some carped about the impracticality of a classical education —especially after the Revolution—classicism remained the standard in American colleges into the early nineteenth century. When the College of New Jersey at Princeton opened its doors in the mid-eighteenth century, little consideration was given to establishing a curriculum other than one similar to those of Harvard or Yale. As was the norm in all colonial colleges, Princeton exercised its students in the classics and, judging from the curriculum of 1764, little else. Latin,

Greek, Hebrew, some science, composition, and declamation were taught. Even the curriculum revision of 1772 on the eve of the Revolution saw few alterations. That the classical influence continued to be strong among Princeton's undergraduates may be seen in the "secret names" of the Cliosophic Society from 1770 to 1777. Upon being accepted into the society, each new member selected the name of a historical personage with whom he identified; the selections unconsciously suggest much about the psychological makeup of the student. The already martially bent Henry Lee of Virginia, for instance, selected the name "Hannibal"; the boldness the future "Light-Horse Harry" exhibited in the Revolutionary War while commanding his aptly named Legion might have had its origins in the Carthaginian's campaigns in the Second Punic War (classmate Aaron Burr's choice of the name "Cyrus" might be best left to psychohistorians!).[57]

The influence of these classically trained scholars was quite broad. Princeton graduates, to give just one example, were to be found throughout the South in the years before and after the Revolution, and there they had a great influence on developing higher education. Princeton alumnus William R. Davie of North Carolina, who served as General Nathanael Greene's quartermaster during the latter part of the war, was instrumental in establishing the University of North Carolina. He introduced a bill in the North Carolina legislature to create the university, and then brought his enormous prestige to bear to ensure its passage. Other Princetonians of the prerevolutionary classes later had cause to put their classical educations to good use, such as poets Philip Freneau and Hugh Brackenridge. And, despite his diminutive stature, another would stand out among the many classically trained delegates at the Constitutional Convention—James Madison. Many graduates returned home to become influential members of their communities, apostles, as it were, of the classical cult.[58]

It is true, as skeptics of the extent of American classicism have pointed out, that college graduates were but a very small portion of the colonial population, no matter how influential they became. Nevertheless, following matriculation and return to their communities, graduates were not isolated among barbarians. If the American cult of antiquity had depended solely upon college graduates, it would have passed away fairly quickly (and quietly) from the colonial scene. But this was not the case. For classicism had both depth and breadth in colonial American society, a society that by the eighteenth century was enjoying its own version of the Enlightenment. This period saw not the displacement of the Bible but the addition to the colonial intellectual milieu of reason and rationalism, what has been called the deification of Nature and the denaturing of God.[59] Prosperity and relative peace among coastal population centers begat a rage for knowledge. Classicism was a manifestation of this thirst for additional learning and understanding, as may be discerned by examining colonial bookshelves from those of the planters of South Carolina and Virginia to those of the Puritans of New England.[60]

Ownership of a book, to be sure, was not indicative of whether it was read, or, if read, assimilated. But a person's possessions, heroes, and books go a long way in establishing one's identity. How people act and dress, the books they own, with whom they associate, all say a great deal about who they think they are or who they would like to be. "Ancient wisdom," historian Douglass Adair wrote, "has it that as a man 'thinketh in his heart, so is he.' " The fascination of Julius Caesar with the life and campaigns of Alexander the Great and Napoleon Bonaparte's especial interest in both the Macedonian and the Roman spoke volumes about their own personalities and aspirations. "[T]he characters," Adair continued, "real or fictional, with whom any man identifies and whom he emulates are of crucial importance in crystallizing his own personality."[61] Respect for and knowledge of classical antecedents and an estimation of their own role in history led Continental officers, in the immediate aftermath of the Revolutionary War, to establish a fraternal organization, the Society of the Cincinnati. And, adds Adair, who was one of the truly innovative minds in American historical scholarship, an individual, "in choosing his heroes and in defining his villains," opens up his soul, his inner self. A person "reveals his own evaluation of himself, displays his own estimate of his potentialities, and exhibits his secret desires and hopes" of the "role he himself wishes to act on the stage of life."[62]

The classically based literature of his times certainly affected George Washington. So struck was the non–classically educated Washington with certain characters in Joseph Addison's play *Cato* that, in part, his

own singular character and actions reflected his unabashed emulation
of those not so fictional classical heroes.[63] To modern Americans for
whom Cato is known only as the Green Hornet's sidekick, the impact
that this play, based on the life and death of a first century B.C.
Roman, had on the imagination of the revolutionary generation and
what the name "Cato" came to represent are difficult to comprehend.
To use "Cato" as a pseudonym or to quote from the play meant that
one stood foursquare for virtue and liberty and against tyranny. For
instance, in an anti–Stamp Act demonstration, Bostonians paraded
effigies of the devil and a local tax man, before burning them. Around
the devil's neck was a placard bearing Cato's famous words:

> When vice prevails, and impious men bear sway,
> The post of honour is a private station.[64]

His good friends, the Fairfaxes, introduced young Washington to the
play, and while the Virginian came to recognize the play's moral and
ideological messages,[65] it no doubt first appealed to his strong romantic
strain. For Washington, as is well known, longed to play "Juba" to
Mrs. Sally Cary Fairfax's "Marcia."[66]

Washington was certainly not the only revolutionary leader infatu-
ated with the romance inherent in Addison's words; New Englanders
also knew the play intimately. "But, if I were of opinion that it was
best for a general Rule that the fair [sex] should be excused from the
arduous Cares of War and State," John Adams wrote to James Warren
in September 1775, "I should certainly think that Marcia [Mercy Otis
Warren] and Portia [Abigail Adams] ought to be Exceptions, because,"
he continued, "I have ever ascribed to those Ladies, a Share and no
small one neither, in the Conduct of our American Affairs."[67] Thus,
in a time when books were not wolfed down but savored, often read
and reread aloud, pondered over and discussed with friends and families, and when plays were performed *en famille* for entertainment and
pleasure, their impact on individuals was far more pronounced than in
modern times.

For historians, seeking this inner person, this product of literature,
culture, environment, and so on, is vitally important. An individual's
writings are an obvious starting point, but a historical detective must
be aware of even nonbarking dogs. Hence, Adair wrote (paraphrasing
Carl Becker), a personal library can provide invaluable clues, for books

"frequently [are] as revealing as personal correspondence and potentially more honest than a diary aimed deliberately at posterity."[68] This caveat was particularly true for historically conscious colonials.

The bookshelves of colonial Americans reflected a genuine love affair with classical antiquity. Booklists compiled from wills and other sources in both northern and southern colonies reveal a full range of classical Greek and Roman literature, from poetry to history. Most major Greek and Roman poets were frequently listed, Homer, Ovid, and Virgil being the most popular. Historians of ancient times— Herodotus, Thucydides, Tacitus, Plutarch, and many others—were represented in numerous collections, and authors who focused upon the classical republican periods were of especial interest. In their classical reading, Americans generally favored the practical (and valuable) lessons of the moralists and historians who promoted moral and political wisdom, those ancient authors whose works, it should be added, were replete with sage advice, admonitions similar to those in the Bible, and, of course, military history. Colonials read voraciously in the classics for knowledge, intellectual exercise, and the truth, but they also enjoyed a good story with heroes with whom they could identify, and many of these ancient heroes earned their fame and glory on the battlefield.[69]

It would be ludicrous, of course, to suggest that Americans regularly conversed in Latin or Greek. Nevertheless, colonial knowledge of these ancient tongues was fairly diffused among the populace, given that anyone with any education had acquired some language skills. In fact, Latin might be described as the *lingua franca* of the eighteenth century.[70] Officers in Rochambeau's army, for instance, were hard pressed to make themselves understood by non–French-speaking Americans, yet they were always able to find some colonial conversant enough in Latin to assist them.[71] But giving directions cannot be likened to a good reading knowledge, so colonial Euro-Americans read Aesop and Caesar just as their descendants would; that is, translated into English. For in neoclassical enlightened America of the eighteenth century, knowledge of ancient history and military practices (one and the same in most works) was widely diffused among a very large literate population, and from these common sources would come many of the conceptions about war held by Americans in 1775.

CHAPTER 3

The Diffusion of Knowledge

The interest in antiquity reached its American zenith during the second half of the eighteenth century. Following the Revolution and the creation of the United States, new-born nationalism, republican fears of elitism, and a demand for a more utilitarian educational system began the gradual erosion of classicism in America. There would be an occasional resurgence, particularly in the area of material culture, but the decline continued even into modern times. The anticlassicism of the postrevolutionary period reflected a vibrant, dynamic new society believing itself no longer wedded to the past, seeking to forge ahead on its own. This democratically inspired hubris frowned on elitist tendencies and promoted utilitarianism as the best means of bettering the individual and, hence, the nation. It might be argued that the underlying reasons for studying the writings of the ancients and for a classical education have been misunderstood. Until the postrevolutionary period, practical Americans found that a classical education was most utilitarian indeed.[1]

The traditional, classical education promoted reason, logic, and mental exercise. As the respected and popular early eighteenth-century French educator and historian Charles Rollin wrote, the first aim of education was to make people "learned, skilful, eloquent, and capable of adapting [themselves] to any career."[2] Discussing eighteenth-century education in general and Samuel Johnson's in particular, one modern historian reminds us that a classically based education, which developed in the days of the great Renaissance humanists and lasted—in modified form—into recent times, was responsible, in a large measure, for "a long, brilliant culture, off the accumulated capital of which . . . we have since been living." And he added, in words the authors of the American Declaration of Independence and Constitution would have appreciated, "if empirical results rather than mere theory are the real test of educational systems, the [classical system] has something to be said for it."[3]

A classically based or classically influenced education, with its emphasis upon knowledge of the people and lessons of history and upon how to apply abstract knowledge to practical problems, linked colonists who needed all the cohesion they could muster. Without a common bond to build upon and unify them, disciples of American republican ideology would have been likely to fracture into dozens of splinter groups; instead of a Revolution, there might have been a series of uncoordinated local insurgencies, easily repressed by powerful British forces. This crying need for unity manifested itself when the revolutionaries detailed their reasons for rebelling in a document written as much for themselves as for the world at large. The strength of this document, the Declaration of Independence, "was precisely that it said what everyone was thinking," wrote Carl Becker. "Nothing could have been more futile than an attempt to justify a revolution on principles which no one had ever heard of before."[4] For disparate colonists, knowledge of the past provided a common bond, a common reservoir of learning from which they drew inspiration (no small thing), lessons on everything from morals to child rearing to politics to military strategy, a direct linkage to ancient times, and an instant pantheon of heroes. The past offered sage advice for current dilemmas and promised hope for the future.

Therefore, from a modern perspective, comprehending the universality of ancient historical and classical knowledge among eighteenth-century Americans is difficult. The depth and breadth of that knowledge does not mean that the United States was a nation of classical scholars, although the image of a straw-chewing rustic clad in homespun topped by a tricornered hat chattering away in Latin with a coonskin-capped, buckskin-wearing passerby, elicits amusement. But if one were literate, as a great percentage of colonial Americans were, then one had at least a rudimentary knowledge of ancient history, a knowledge which, however superficial, surely surpassed that of average modern Americans about their own history.

In most of what they read, colonials were likely to receive a dose of ancient history. The late seventeenth and the early eighteenth centuries also saw a spate in the publication of interpretive ancient histories. These histories were replete with moralistic lessons that buttressed biblical admonitions. Self-improvement books, based largely on homilies and axioms gleaned from ancient writings, were very popular, and rarely did a newspaper or almanac fail to have at least a few classical quotations sprinkled about its pages. The classically influenced European essayists most popular in America filled their works with lessons from the past, and those in America who borrowed this style did likewise, for their audience expected no less. The eighteenth century proved to be the high tide of the neoclassical period in America, and, as will be shown in this chapter and more particularly in the next, that had much to do with shaping prerevolutionary American concepts about war, warfare, and the military.

A well-known anecdote somewhat facetiously described the depth of classicism in America. In 1787 Thomas Jefferson read that an English workman had invented a new wheel, "reviving a Greek idea" from a passage in Homer. Jefferson, his heart filled with national pride and his tongue firmly planted in his cheek, wrote his friend J. Hector St. John Crevecoeur that the idea actually came from a New Jersey farmer who drew upon Homer for inspiration. How could this be? Well, Jefferson wrote, "because ours are the only farmers who can read Homer."[5]

Jefferson's hyperbolic vision of a neoclassical bucolic America, with educated yeoman farmers lounging under their "vine and fig" reading Homer or Virgil, actually had some validity.[6] In all probability the Greek and Roman classics were never read so widely as in eighteenth-century America, and were read by a greater proportion of the population than at any time since antiquity. (Or listened to, for reading aloud, whether from broadsides, newspapers, or books, was a favored form of entertainment and passing information.) Critics, however,

retort that this knowledge mirrored little more than superficial learning: in modeling themselves after their English literary betters, colonial
pensmen were all too quick to pad their arguments with classical
analogy or citation.[7] And, as Voltaire said about Newton's writings
with their difficult mathematical equations: "Very few people read
Newton, because it is necessary to be learned to understand him. But,"
he added, "everyone talks about him."[8] Obviously this occurred; after
all, in the height of the classical revival, Americans would be expected
to write in the style of the times. Truly, as the learned Samuel Johnson
(a true classicist) noted with acerbity, in the eighteenth century, "classical quotation is the parole of literate men all over the world." Perhaps
Johnson's asperity stemmed from increased classical usage by nonclas-
sicist writers; he loved the words of the ancients as much as he loathed
"cant" and "modishness" in writing. In liberally dotting his own works
with these *mots d'ordre*, as he always did, he found himself in a quan-
dary.[9] One of Johnson's youthful contemporaries, Henry Fielding,
saw it another way, that eighteenth-century writers "are to the Antients what the Poor are to the Rich." The great classical authors,
Fielding wrote, were a repository to be hungrily searched over and
used. "The Antients may be considered as a rich Common, where
every Person who hath the smallest Tenement in *Parnassus* hath a free
Right to fatten his Muse."[10]

In America, the depth, breadth, and interest in antiquity precluded
mere classical name-dropping for the most part. As just one example,
John Dickinson, classical scholar and the most widely read prerevolutionary colonial essayist, wrote for a general readership, whom he
sought to enlighten, not confuse. His works were replete with classical
(and biblical) allusions and quotations in Latin. All but four colonial
newspapers republished his Farmer's Letters,[11] and many of his quotes
show up again and again as the Revolution drew near. The general
public evidently understood his scholarly references to the "*Cleons and
Clodius*'" or to how futile it was to "pursue Juno." This being so, they
surely understood his advice to stand together during the 1765 Stamp
Act crisis: "*Concordia res parvae crescunt*" ("Small things grow great by
concord").[12]

Despite this fascination with the classics and antiquity as a whole,
few Americans were fully comfortable in either of the ancient tongues.

As noted, a small number were classically trained college graduates; nonetheless, after graduation, unless they studiously worked at it, their language skills deteriorated rapidly. As with any foreign language, proficiency corresponds to regular usage: verbal and reading skills quickly atrophy if not used. That was why, for Americans, the most commonly read editions of the classics were those in translation.

That translations were favored over the original works, however, actually added to, rather than subtracted from, the widespread knowledge and influence of the classics. Translations made ancient writings available to every literate American; in all probability their impact upon the diffusion of classical knowledge proved far greater than that of the originals. A wealthy planter such as William Byrd II of Westover might look through his 3,600-volume library and read a little Hebrew, Greek, and Latin each morning just to keep in practice and sharpen his mind, but he was unusual. For ordinary Americans, translations propped open windows to the past, since practical Americans were more interested in the message than the medium. As one eighteenth-century wit wrote:

> Hang *Homer* and Virgil; their meaning to seek,
> A Man must have pok'd in the *Latin* and *Greek;*
> Those who Love their own *Tongue*, We have Reason to Hope,
> Have read them Translated by *Dryden* and *Pope*.[13]

Even Jefferson and John Adams, neither of whom was prone to taking shortcuts in scholarship, showed little compunction about reading and using (and criticizing) translations of their favorite classical works.[14] In fact, as historian H. Trevor Colbourn points out, Jefferson's use of classical works in translation may be readily discerned, as the "many uncut pages of his personal copies of Latin and Greek classics bear witness."[15]

Few translations being published locally, colonists relied upon books imported from Great Britain and the Continent. In New England, contrary to myth, the Puritans actually read well and widely. From the early seventeenth century on, most Yankee communities featured at least one bookshop or were regularly serviced by traveling booksellers who flourished in New England. For the most part, Southerners ordered books—as was the case with most everything—from Britain by mail or through their factors.[16] These disparate (and often desperate) readers learned about specific titles or authors by word of mouth, newspaper and magazine advertisements, and assorted booklists periodically sent out by British publishing houses. For the modern student, learning what classical works—in translation or in the original language—were available to the colonists is easier, however, for a published bibliography from the period provides an excellent starting point.[17]

That indispensable study is the relatively unknown work of Lewis William Brüggemann.[18] Published in 1797 with a supplement four years later, *A View of the English Editions, Translations and Illustrations of the Ancient Greek and Latin Authors* provides valuable insights into seventeenth- and eighteenth-century reading as the rich panoply of the neoclassical age unfolds for exploration. Americans oftentimes read the same editions as the British writers on liberty, morality, and republican government whom they idolized, such as Locke, Hobbes, Harrington, Sidney, Addison, Trenchard, and Gordon. Paralleling the rise of interest in classicism, Brüggemann's chronological bibliography graphically highlighted increases in popular literacy and, reflecting a growing economy, in disposable income; books, after all, were still something of a luxury, often the single luxury austere republicans allowed themselves. As the late eighteenth-century English bookseller Thomas Rede advised, in America, "Whatever is useful, sells," adding that Americans "have no ready money to spare for anything but what they *want*."[19] Because of cost, reprints or new editions depended upon an author's popularity, thus one means of gauging the influence of a particular writer was the number of editions an author's work went through, in part or in whole. One multivolume work continuously in print was the *Parallel Lives* of the Greek biographer and historian Plutarch (A.D. 50–120, and more correctly, Plutarchus), probably the most widely read classical author in the colonies.[20]

Plutarch's ancient words had great appeal to the colonists. He seemed to speak directly to them, especially those of the revolutionary generation, for his writings had a contemporaneous flavor. He was a man of reasoned intellect, a moralist with no particular religious perspective, an educated man of refined manners and morals who was greatly interested in comparing and improving government through the use of history. In short, Plutarch, as Martha Walling Howard noted in her fine study, was someone "with whom the eighteenth century could identify," or, as classicist Michael Grant added, for people of this period, he was most "congenial" to their thinking.[21] Plutarch wrote about the great Greeks and Romans, the statesmen, the generals, the orators, and philosophers with whom the neoclassicists were fascinated. In the eighteenth century (likened to a "hero factory" by one modern author), Plutarch, the "patron saint of hero worship," provided real heroes worthy of emulation, especially for hero-starved colonials.[22] To Plutarch, "great men [were] as a race apart," and his heroes were generally men of virtue who recognized that the first duty of a citizen was to the commonweal.[23] For Americans, the Greek and Roman republics featured in Plutarch represented the halcyon days of humankind, emblematic of all that was good and virtuous, "a lost world which forever disappeared when Caesar crossed the Rubicon."[24] But reading Plutarch raised hopes that the lost fires of republicanism could be rekindled.[25]

In Brüggemann, over forty Plutarchian entries prior to 1774 are cataloged, including several abridgements and reprints of well-known translations, all of which testify to their popularity.[26] The late sixteenth-century translation of the *Parallel Lives* by Sir Thomas North— used by Shakespeare for his classically thematic plays *Coriolanus, Julius Caesar,* and *Antony and Cleopatra*—remained standard into the nineteenth century[27] (Washington's aide-de-camp Alexander Hamilton filled his military paybook with marginal quotes from the 1758 edition).[28] Other popular, often reprinted authors included Virgil, with over thirty-five pages of entries; Marcus Tullius Cicero, with thirty-three; Horace, with thirty-one; and Tacitus and Sallust, with eight pages each.[29]

Julius Caesar, unpopular in republican circles and not taught in American schools until 1800, nevertheless had many editions of his *Commentaries* and *History of the Civil War* published through 1774 in both Latin and English.[30] In the eighteenth century, elementary Latin students did not begin their studies trying to understand why Gaul was divided into three parts; instead, they usually started with Cicero, then moved on to Sallust. Sallust, in particular, one eighteenth-century American wrote, was "more easily understood, and therefore in more hands. He is a School-Book: Boys learne him together with the *Latin* tongue."[31] Colonists read Caesar primarily for his military exploits and expertise, although Sallust's *War with Cataline* and *War with Jugurtha* also discoursed on general military history.

The influence of Plutarch (and others) on colonial Americans reached far beyond those who read his *Lives* and other works either in the original or in translation, for much of the colonists' knowledge of antiquity came from popular histories that synthesized the original sources. Indeed, popular synthetic histories diffused knowledge of antiquity to far more colonials than did the classics themselves, for as J. Franklin Jameson later reasoned, "histories that are read do more good than histories that are not read."[32] Colonial library holdings indicated that these shortcuts to the classics were universally popular, for while they imparted learning, addressed contemporary political and moral problems, and linked the present to the past, they also told rousing good tales.[33] For many revolutionary-era Americans, knowledge and understanding of republican Greece and Rome and of classical heroes and times were derived almost exclusively from historians such as the Frenchmen Charles Rollin and René Aubert, Abbé de Vertot.[34] Their histories were popular among common folk and intellectuals alike. Classically trained Americans held Rollin's works in high esteem, recommending them to friends and family. While her rotund husband, John, was off to Philadelphia in 1774 attending Congress, Abigail Adams embraced Rollin's massive volumes. "I have taken a very great fondness for reading Rollin's ancient History since you left me," she wrote him.[35] Adams and even the pedantic Dr. Rush noted with pleasure the interest their families took in Rollin and other ancient historians.[36]

Rollin's multivolume histories were reprinted many times in Britain and later in America and enjoyed widespread popularity well into the nineteenth century.[37] They made ancient worlds accessible and interesting to the common men and women, yet maintained standards acceptable even to scholars ("Rollin was highly admired," commented classicist Meyer Reinhold, by such different notables as Voltaire, Montesquieu, Chateaubriand, Frederick the Great, and Napoleon).[38] Rollin focused on politics and war, on great men and their effect on events, but he tastefully wrapped his often exciting narratives in a religious and moral code that satisfied even the most fastidious colonial demands. For Rollin was a teacher, and he not only offered a narrative but interpreted the past through his stern moral eye. Colonists could learn from his discourses on moral values of the ancients, many paralleling biblical themes.[39] It is highly probable that the histories of Rollin and others were instrumental in making classical terminology such an integral part of the colonial idiom.

On one level, Rollin appealed to readers simply interested in a good story. After all, as Horace noted: "Omne tulit punctum qui miscuit utile dulci" (the [author] who combines the useful with the pleasurable is most successful).[40] From the classical sources he liberally savaged for material, Rollin filled his pages with the exploits of great men and the clash of battle. As readers of the classics had done for centuries, everyday colonists now cheered on the vastly outnumbered Athenians at Marathon and admired the Spartans' selfless sacrifice at Thermopylae, all related in a stirring narrative with considerable military details and analysis.[41] Histories of this period, it should be noted, dealt almost exclusively with political and military matters, with campaigns and battles, with "How Kings and Kingdomes have florished and fallen," as Sir Walter Raleigh wrote in his very popular history.[42] To modern eyes, many of these popular histories might be considered as military histories couched in a political framework, but the writers, as good historians, were only being true to their sources—the classics.

As with the classical historians and other contemporary popular historians, Rollin cast his narrative in a Plutarchian mold, focusing on the men who made history. This filled a void for Americans; in an age when heroes were much in demand and, since they had none of their own, colonists adopted classical heroes and sought to emulate them. After all, ambitious men had few opportunities to make their mark in colonial society other than in politics or the military.[43] To be sure, ambition per se was decried, but these extremely historically conscious people could see from reading Rollin or the classics that posterity would hail as heroes epitomes of virtue who worked "selflessly" for the common good. And a vivid illustration of this widespread diffusion of classical lore can be found in none other than Parson Weems, who, in his biography of Washington, expected *children* to understand the following passage: "Washington was as pious as Numa, just as Aristides, temperate as Epictetus, patriotic as Regulas. In giving public trusts," Weems wrote, "impartial as Severus; in victory, as modest as Scipio— prudent as Fabius, rapid as Marcellus, undaunted as Hannibal, as Cincinnatus disinterested, to liberty as firm as Cato, and respectful of the laws as Socrates."[44]

For others seeking usable history, Rollin and his fellow popular historians furnished facts to support any interpretation that political circumstances demanded. Yet, in a real sense, this repeated the past when Roman writers sought validation from the writings of the Greeks, and it continued unaltered, even in modern times, where classical quotation and example have generally been replaced in political commentary and writing by the Founders' words. One sees similar use (or misuse) of their writings; the words of Thomas Jefferson, for instance, often shore up arguments from both ends of the modern political spectrum on the same issue.[45] This differed little from eighteenth-century use and abuse of the classics themselves; there, too, political opponents often employed the same quotations to buttress diametrically opposed viewpoints. Rollin's popularity, however, had even stronger roots.

In large part, Rollin's intractable sense of morality dictated his interpretation of the past. As a Jansenist (Jansenism has been described as "Calvinized Catholicism"),[46] Rollin perceived vice and corruption as sapping human will, especially those of rulers such as Alexander the Great and, by implication, the kings in Rollin's own age (criticizing monarchial foibles of long ago was a tacitly understood method of expressing dissatisfaction with the current regimes). Although studies of the Alexandrian art of war were widely read, the once-popular Macedonian was in disfavor by the eighteenth century. Moral republicans looked askance at him as a deviant and voluptuary, and he was held up in Hogarthian England as an example of what excessive alcoholic consumption could do to someone.[47] Thus, by artfully harmonizing a religiophilosophical view very close to that held by many Americans with a fairly substantial summarization of the most current (early eighteenth-century) political theory, Rollin struck a familiar chord for colonists of similar persuasion.

The rigidity of seventeenth-century colonial moral values had been tempered somewhat by changes in time, the Enlightenment, and their own intellectual maturity. God no longer dominated colonial thinking so thoroughly, although the providential perspective remained very influential. Now, however, God's law was explained through a natural interpretation. Morality became inextricably intertwined with secular politics (which, as will be seen, had a significant impact on American conceptions of war). Certainly, distance breeds fear and awe, and closeness contempt, so, in part to overcome this sense of inferiority, the colonists made themselves into paragons of virtue. They truly believed that they were morally superior to those across the Atlantic, yet they lacked confidence in their ability to resist temptation, living ever fearful of contamination from Old World vice and unmanliness and of threats from an increasingly corrupt ministerial government.[48]

Thus, with some care and a great deal of selectivity, colonists turned to contemporary British writers, wary lest they be corrupted rather than enlightened. Those writers whose works the colonists accepted, however, were embraced wholeheartedly; in fact, concepts and ideas propagated by these writers generally enjoyed a new and longer life in the colonies than they had among their original British audiences where they were now passé in substance and style. In particular Americans favored the new form of periodic self-improvement essay as anonymously written and popularized in the 1720s by Joseph Addison and Richard Steele in first, the *Tatler*, and then the even more widely read *Spectator*.[49] From the early eighteenth century through the Revolution, Addison and Steele (and others including Swift and Defoe) were arbiters of morality and good taste for colonial Americans, along with having a strong stylistic influence on writers from Samuel Johnson to Alexander Hamilton.[50] "When I was at an age which will soon be yours," seventy-year-old James Madison wrote his eleven-year-old grand-nephew upon giving him a copy of the *Spectator*, "a book fell into my hands which I read, with particular advantage. . . . Addison was of the first rank among fine writers of the age, and has given a definition of what he showed himself to be an example."[51] A writer in the early eighteenth-century English newspaper *Common-Sense*, one of many publications imitating Addison's and Steele's originals, summarized this praise. "In a word, whenever I take up the

Spectator, I am ready every minute to break out into the same exclamation," the author wrote, "that a poet of Gascogny uttered upon reading over a beautiful ode of Horace. 'D—n these ancients (says he), they have stolen all my fine thoughts.' "[52] Colonial newspapers reprinted whole numbers of the *Spectator*.[53] Bound copies of their essays—originals and many reprints—could be found on most colonial bookshelves, and Addison and Steele were easily two of the most influential writers of their day.[54]

Like Rollin, Addison and Steele were read for several reasons: superb literary craftsmanship; advice on morals, manners, and civility; and standards that were not set by court dandies but were based on common sense and Christian morality. Colonists read the often-parodied day-to-day doings of London society with horrid fascination: on the one hand, these accounts confirmed their own moral superiority and their belief that England was a corrupt, money-grubbing society sating itself on vice, while on the other they eagerly looked for ways and means to buttress themselves morally (but correctly) against contamination.[55] As a corollary, the long-lived popularity of the *Spectator* in America very likely had a significant impact on colonial perceptions of the Old Country, especially on the revolutionary generation. The early Georgian England Addison and Steele had written about in the 1720s no longer existed, but, over time, the colonial *mentalité* subsumed their parodies into truths. Nonetheless, in a century where the terms "manners and life" were "charged with meaning and value," Addison and Steele continued as guides to an exemplary life.[56]

Although Addison and Steele were classically trained and mixed Latin aphorisms throughout their work, other self-improvement books of the time had even stronger classical roots. For instance, Sir Roger L'Estrange's popular *Seneca's Morals* had widespread appeal. Colonial Americans knew that the darker side of people lay close to the surface and that temptation stood ready to lure them into sin. Therefore, among the ancients to whom they looked for guidance were those who stood unyieldingly against venality, exhibiting both public and personal virtue and courage—the Stoics. L'Estrange's oft-reprinted work carried this message in those pithy axioms in which colonists found comfort, including—as was the case with most of these works—adages related to military affairs.[57] The Stoics elicited particular admi-

ration, for they not only espoused a philosophy but lived (and, as with
Cato, died) it. In Addison's play, when Portius tries to forestall his
father's suicide, Cato, sword in hand, scolds his son:

> Wouldst thou betray me? Wouldst thou give me up
> A slave, a captive, into Caesar's hands?
> Retire, and learn obedience to a father.[58]

Some condemned Cato's suicide, but most saw the taking of his own
life, rather allowing himself to fall into Caesar's hands, as the height of
moral resoluteness and honor.[59] Finding that "there can be no shame
in Virtuous Emulation," colonists eagerly looked to the past for moral
sustenance, and in the stoicism of Seneca and Cato they uncovered
ways of new modeling their lives.[60] Thus it was that even non–
classically trained colonials such as George Washington were introduced to, accepted, and lived by philosophical tenets laid down over
two thousand years before. How strong an influence it had on them
depended, of course, upon their own temperaments.

To Washington, stoicism provided a framework within which he
constructed his life for, in the fullest sense, George Washington was a
self-made man. As a fatherless teenager saddled with a "termagant"
mother, he sought out his betters, from whom he learned the ways of
a gentleman. His great friends, the Fairfaxes, introduced him to *Seneca's Morals* and, as already seen, to Addison's very popular play, *Cato*,
the eighteenth century's introduction to Stoicism (and republicanism).
That both exerted a powerful influence on the callow youth is attested
by the many quotations, paraphrased passages, and allusions to both
works which can be found in his revolutionary and presidential writings. But these pale before examples of how Washington actually lived
his life. As a youthful surveyor in Virginia's hostile backcountry,
George learned firsthand the necessity of self-discipline, for, as Samuel
Eliot Morison wrote, "if you make the wrong decision in woods in-
fested with savages, you will probably have no opportunity to make
another."[61] And anyone who has read anything of Washington's life
will recognize the impact that both the fictional and historical Cato had
on the development of his character. For Washington the Stoic, "preferred to be," as Sallust wrote of the real Cato, "rather than to seem,
virtuous; hence the less he sought fame, the more it pursued him."[62]

Washington's frontier experience and the Stoic ideal as exemplified by Cato, with its emphasis on duty, honor, virtue, benevolence, and gentlemanly behavior (an eighteenth-century officer's ideal, in other words), merged nicely in the mind of a class-conscious young man who had laboriously copied out a set of "Rules of Civility" as a Fredericksburg schoolboy.[63]

To be sure, not everyone who read L'Estrange or saw Cato performed reacted as Washington did; but it should be noted that this urge toward moral self-improvement with its strong emphasis on classical example permeated colonial society. Plutarch, Seneca, and Cato were hailed for their moral views, but so, too, was Aesop's Fables, "a work of moral doctrine" held "suitable for the discipline of youth."[64] As Samuel Croxhall noted in a preface to his Fables of Aesop and Others, they demonstrated, "by a Kind of Example, every Virtue which claims our best Regards, and every Vice which we are most concerned to avoid."[65] The young John Adams, among others, recommended studying "Seneca, Cicero, and all other good moral writers."[66] To colonial readers, Cicero ("Tully") might have been addressing them personally over the centuries: "But as for us, let us follow nature and shun everything that is offensive to our eyes or to our ears." In De Officiis, Cicero, who no doubt influenced Addison and Steele, twinned virtue and good manners. "So, in standing or walking, in sitting or reclining, in our expression, our eyes, or the movements of our hands, let us preserve what we have called 'propriety.' "[67] This advice would be reinforced by popular political writers who, like Cicero and others, recognized that public and personal virtue were reflected in good manners, in everyday civility. "Good Breeding is the Art of shewing Men, by external signs, the internal Regard which we have for them." Poor manners "or Rudeness . . . is immoral; it is using others as you would not be used."[68] Public and political virtue were one and the same with personal virtue, so that the Stoics of ancient times were revered. In his "Silas Dogood" letters, a youthful Benjamin Franklin paid homage to both Addison and Steele (in style and sense) as well as to the moralistic views of Terence and Seneca, and later to Cato when he published James Logan's translation of Cato's Moral Distich's.[69]

The appeal of these moralists was quite broad for several reasons. The maturation of the seaboard colonial society by the eighteenth century, the American Enlightenment, the Great Awakening, and neoclassicism all combined in a rage for self-improvement. Life was still hard, but it had eased enough for colonists to begin refining their society and themselves. Many of these classical lessons were translated and reduced into maxims for parents to plague children with at every opportunity. Almanacs abounded with these axiomatic sayings that are often solely credited to Benjamin Franklin, but which, in fact, originated from Roman epigrams. On another level, these maxims blended comfortably with or even imitated similar biblical adages. But for colonists who felt themselves materially inferior to their Old Country betters, these moralistic writers turned ridiculed colonial traits into colonial virtues. Few would have argued with Hesiod's epigram: "No work is a disgrace, but idleness is a disgrace."[70] Simplicity and frugality were extolled as virtues by ancient writers and their popular interpreters such as Rollin and the Abbé de Vertot. The discipline, both domestic and military, that made republican Rome so great, Vertot wrote, "had its Rise from the Poverty of the first *Romans:* They afterward made a Virtue of what was the mere Effect of Necessity," he noted, "and Men of Courage looked upon this equal Poverty of all the Citizens as the Means to preserve their Liberty from all Usurpation."[71] Roman liberty had been ensured "by Poverty and Temperance; Love of their Country, Valour, and all the other Virtues both Civil and Military, were found always to attend it."[72]

Luxury and vice were perceived as harbingers of internal decay, as well as a decline in the warrior ethos. "What an Omen of approaching Slavery?" Vertot asked rhetorically, "None could be greater, than to see Valour less regarded in a State than luxury."[73] The abbé decried the effeminacy of Rome's young men, their affectations of voice, dress, and curried hair, certainly a slap in the face of the lisping young coxcombs and macaronis of eighteenth-century France and England. As Vertot noted, these youths were hardly adequate for defending Rome's (and France's and England's) liberties. At the battle of Pharsala during the Roman Civil Wars, he wrote, Caesar had his tough veterans thrust their javelins and swords at the faces of their young opponents; fearful of being scarred for life, Pompey's dandies turned and fled.[74] The overt fondness for luxury and ambition, "sins" so prevalent in England, would be punished by God's vengeance. These sins were also perceived by readers of *Cato's Letters* as being part of an overall ministerial conspiracy. These ministers would laugh at virtue, "disgrace Men of Virtue, and ridicule Virtue itself," all the while promoting "Luxury, Idelness, and Expence, and a general Depravation of Manners."[75] The fall of the Roman republic was a mainstay of the highly moralistic libertarian writers, blending the moral with the historical to form a strong political message. Homiletically employed in speeches, sermons, newspapers, pamphlets, and almanacs, their writing became part of the colonial vernacular, diffusing—both directly and indirectly—classical knowledge and influence.[76]

Through these mediums of print, classical knowledge infiltrated all strata of colonial society. Benjamin Franklin (for whom they were "The Sacred Classics")[77] did as much as anyone to promulgate the classical gospel. In various publications, Franklin, Isaiah Thomas, and other printers brought classical knowledge into most colonial households. Newspapers were chockful of classical terms, names, ideas, allusions, and metaphors. Almanacs, found in every colonial home, were repositories and transmitters of classical mythology. If they had specifically tried to educate Americans to ancient ideas (and they did not), they could not have done more.[78]

By the 1760s, when the colonial pamphlet wars began heating up, classical terminology and knowledge were as common and used as freely as rum punch. How else could colonials understand their own almanacs: "Ceres now halting her Winters drouze, *Wakes* Vulcan up to mend his Chains and Ploughs."[79] Few of John Dickinson's readers needed parenthetical explanations for his classical quotations, nor did Samuel Adams have to explain himself when he harangued Sons of Liberty with his admixture of classical and biblical allusions. How else could one explain an "uneducated youth" (Benjamin West) who painted "in Lancaster, Pennsylvania, at the age of fourteen, *The Death of Socrates*,"[80] or the plethora of slaves in the North and South with classical names.[81] And when, in the immediate postrevolutionary period, settlers in upstate New York created new communities in the Finger Lakes region, the town names reflected the heroic symbolism of the age: Ithaca, Cato, Lysander, Euclid, Hannibal, Seneca Hill, Syracuse, Rome, and Fabius, to name but a few.[82] "[C]lassicism blew through the American air," wrote Washington biographer James Thomas Flexner, "more constant than the scents of spring or the snows of winter. You did not have to sit in a library to be a classicist."[83]

Sweeping across colonial society, ancient terms and ideas were an accepted and unquestioned part of the colonial milieu; they were also a common thread. For in a land of thirteen separate and disparate colonies, with diverse religious, social, cultural, and economic backgrounds and requirements, with variances in governments and practices, and even language differences, commonalities were few. Yet, when Patrick Henry paraphrased a line from Addison's *Cato* and cried, "Give me Liberty or give me Death," his words reverberated along the Atlantic coast, and few who heard his stirring words failed to recognize or appreciate their origins. As Cato says to young Juba:

> . . . remember
> The hand of fate is over us, and heaven
> Exacts severity from all our thoughts:
> It is not now a time to talk of aught
> But chains or conquest, liberty or death.[84]

The last words attributed to Connecticut schoolmaster and intelligence operative, Nathan Hale, as he stood upon an English scaffold facing death, were also born in Addison's prose. In the play, Cato's son, Marcus, has just been slain battling Caesar's troops. The young man's body is brought before Cato.

> Welcome, my son! here lay him down, my friends,
> Full in my sight, that I may view at leisure
> The bloody corpse, and count those glorious wounds.
> —How beautiful is death, when earned by virtue!
> Who would not be that youth? what pity is it
> That we can die but once to serve our country![85]

No small wonder that Hale's Catoian regret that "he only had one life to give for his country" earned him quick entrance into the new nation's pantheon of heroes. Thus, the classically inspired British and Continental republican authors—from whom colonists drew many ideas—found a knowledgeable audience quite familiar with their sources, themes, and arguments. *Cato's Letters* (hailed by some as the primary source for American republicanism) was immensely popular in the colonies. Certainly, content had much to do with this, but to a public enthralled by Addison's play, by Plutarch, and by popular histories, any work bearing the name of this virtuous Roman benefited from name recognition.[86]

The use of classical names came to symbolize where one stood on particular political questions; thus, a pamphlet signed with the pseudonym "Cato," "Junius," or "Brutus," or even one using English radical John Wilkes's name told would-be readers that the author espoused radical republican ideology. This helps, it should be noted, explain why, by the 1760s and 1770s, many British were less than enthusiastic about promoting the study of classical literature, a literature that in large part favored republics over monarchies. Critics, as noted, find the use of such names mere windowdressing. But for receptive Americans, this combination of neoclassicism and republican radicalism proved to be a heady, potent brew, its effect often lasting far beyond what its makers intended. For instance, a well-known Anglo-American actor born in the late eighteenth century was given "the most patriotic of Roman names, *Junius Brutus* Booth," which he passed to his eldest son. "But one of his younger sons, who is remembered for an action in which he cried, '*Sic semper tyrannis*,' bore a name which would have seemed to [eighteenth-century Britons and Americans by] no means irrelevant—*John Wilkes* Booth."[87]

American colonists avidly used ancient history for the exigencies of their current circumstances. For them the past was a veritable groaning board filled to overflowing with useful ideas and practical knowledge. They used ancient history uncritically, however, seeing only the political wisdom, high morality, and virtuous simplicity, and somehow forgetting that the winds of time had buffed the reality and ugliness of truth into a highly polished fiction. They were groping toward an ideal of their own making, and these practical people, long accustomed by necessity to self-sufficiency and selective borrowing, unhesitantly employed any available intellectual resources that could serve their needs. They framed their institutions in great part with materials furnished by their British heritage, but they ransacked the great storehouse of Western civilization for precedents and ideas to complete their New World model home.[88]

They had little choice. Practicality is merely institutionalized improvisation, and Americans made a virtue of what was otherwise a sign of want. In almost everything, they borrowed from biblical, classical, and European precedents, but they then adapted and refined what they learned, unknowingly Americanizing it in the process.

Perhaps the best example of this process was the colonial Americans' conceptualization of war. For Americans, war "was one of those institutions, like private property and family, which were so deeply imbedded in the structure of society that," as one historian wrote, "they were generally accepted as a matter of course."[89] The classical histories of Thucydides, Herodotus, Polybius, and the others, and the popular ancient histories of Rollin, Vertot, Raleigh, and many more were, in modern parlance, histories of politics and war. For seventeenth- and eighteenth-century readers, however, they were the histories of people. Academic subspecialties, differentiating between social history and military or political history, did not exist. History, to colonial Americans, meant what is now called universal history, the cumulative record of humankind's recorded past. War was very much a part of this history, and while much can be said about the moral and social lessons of, say, Herodotus and Rollin, central to their work was a study of people at war. (Not only may Rollin's works be described as thinly disguised military history, but he had a substantial section detailing "The Art Military.")[90]

In almost all the books Americans devoured with such gusto, from the Bible to the classics to popular histories, war was a dominant theme in both ancient and modern societies; the colonists' own experiences in the wilderness and recent European history, especially British, made this evident. Of their adopted classical heroes, their favorites were either military men or solons who, by their oratorical skills, urged defense of national liberty and personal virtue against enemies foreign and internal. The popular fascination with such classical military heroes and with military history in general, which continued well into the nineteenth century, disturbed some pre–Civil War Americans who called for dropping Latin and Greek studies from grammar school and college curricula. Unlike the anticlassicists in the immediate post–Revolutionary War period who perceived a classical or classically influenced education as elitist or nonutilitarian, however, these self-styled reformers railed against the classics and popular histories because of their military content. Schoolchildren, Charles Sumner of Massachusetts noted with some disgust, are "fed like Achilles, not on honey and milk only, but on bears' marrow and lions' hearts." Young Americans, he added, draw "the nutrient of [their] soul[s] from a literature whose beautiful fields are moistened by human blood."[91] Members of antebellum antiwar societies such as Sumner and the Grimké sisters of South Carolina stridently called for eliminating study of the classics since they were "steeped in martial sentiment" and were making popular heroes out of military men.[92] But in the seventeenth and eighteenth centuries, the ancients were regarded differently by colonial Americans. Their heroes were people of virtue, honor, courage, and morality who, by their historical actions in peace and at war, taught the colonists that eternal vigilance against vice and evil was the price that people had paid for liberty in the past and must continue to pay in the future.

But from these lessons of the past, Americans' ideas about war took two separate and not entirely compatible courses, courses that would have an enormous impact on the Revolutionary War effort. For some, the past simply furnished practical military knowledge. This was obvious to anyone who read seventeenth- and eighteenth-century tomes on the art of war, and many did, as will be seen in part II. Others, however, while realizing the necessity of a military arm in time of war, noted the historical tendency of a nation's military to subvert liberty and virtue or to act as an engine pushing unscrupulous men into power, points that will be discussed in part III. These views, coming from fundamentally identical sources and conflicting as they did, dominated American conceptions of war by 1775.

PART II

Influences on American
Warfare before 1775

ALL warfare is a continuum. The lessons of war, from the earliest known conflict to the most modern, remain in a vast repository of military knowledge we call history. From there, they can be recalled, dusted off, and employed whenever the need arises. Modified, refined, and adapted to fit the conditions of time, place, and technology, these old lessons often appear under new guises bearing different terminology; nevertheless, reduced to their essence, the principle and sometimes the practice are the same.

The value and importance of the past for the present may be observed even when a technological advance appears to make all older practices of war obsolete. From the perspective of historical periodization, with its emphasis on major events along the time-space line, the development of a major technical advance portends the end of one age and ushers in the beginning of another. Looking backward historically, however, the actual time between the introduction of a technical innovation and its general deployment—usage widespread enough to play an important role—is often blurred. A particular technological advance might have immediate and major implications for a very specific area of war; but its overall impact on warfare (and society) as a whole often remains fairly limited until supporting technologies, doctrine, and training can be adapted or created to utilize its potential fully. This new technology also must be fully accepted by its actual end users—the officers and troops in the field. For an institution as conservative and tradition-bound as the military, change generally takes place grudgingly over considerable time, so that in reality, new technologies are slowly incorporated alongside older, established practices. In sum, doctrine and practice lag behind technology.

So even as heralded technological achievements and even new doctrinal changes are introduced, a great deal of practical value remains in the old forms of war. For some students of war, only the "new" lessons are valid; those of the past are outdated, providing little more than antiquarian and historical interest. Lessons from older, even ancient, military conflicts and personages, however, do retain a considerable amount of valuable and still usable, practical knowledge, and in many cases, "new" does not necessarily mean better. It is perhaps not surprising to note that among those who searched out and studied the dusty tomes of past wars (and who increased their overall learning, for knowledge is, indeed, power) are numbered the few who earned stars, batons, fame, and the sobriquet "Great Captains of War" for their "innovative" techniques and strategies. To these Great Captains, for whom—unlike most of their contemporaries—intensive study of their profession, an ability to recall these lessons, and the will to employ them, are mutually shared traits, much was to be learned from the past.

Colonial Americans certainly believed in and understood the value of history, and their conceptions of war were shaped, in great part, by their perceptions of the past. Americans developed their views on war and gained practical knowledge in the art of war just as everyone in the eighteenth century did: by reading and from experience. From the same sources that they drew upon for educational systems, moral guidance, and political ideology colonists learned about war and warfare. From their colonial military experience, especially serving alongside the British, they imbibed much practical knowledge, and because English military doctrine was influenced by current European thinking, colonists frequently saw the lessons of their reading applied in actual war. Perceptions of events learned are shaded by personal and societal views, and American conceptions of war, like their impression of the virtuous ancient republicans, incorporated myth along with reality. Born of the same sources, these concepts paradoxically followed two intertwined yet often conflicting paths of influence: the practical, which will be discussed in the following three chapters, and the intellectual, to be discussed later.

CHAPTER 4

Learning about Warfare

The Age of Reason introduced a certain formality into European and, to a lesser extent, American societies. Among the cultured or those with aspirations to culture, the Addisonian essay with its polished phraseology and moralism became de rigueur for writers and readers. Certain niceties in personal and public behavior were expected, especially among those who considered themselves ladies and gentlemen. Neoclassicism was the primary influence on art, architecture, and literature, and the well-rounded man, the *homo universale* of the Renaissance, again became the ideal in the mid-eighteenth century. For instance, to be considered a gentleman, a young man had to be proficient in all aspects of cultured life, from dancing and writing poetry to fencing and horsemanship, while young ladies learned how to be perfect mates and mothers. Among the genteel, formal gardens with intricate mazes, the stately minuet, formal manners, and powdered wigs were outward manifestations of the influence that reason had on Western culture.[1]

Formalization also held sway in professional training. Americans seeking the best professional training journeyed across the Atlantic to London's Inns of Court for the law or to Edinburgh for advanced medical degrees. There, colonials such as Joseph Reed and Benjamin Rush of Pennsylvania and Arthur Lee of Virginia received the finest professional education that the eighteenth century had to offer. But for the most part, lawyers, doctors, and military officers continued to learn about their professions as their ancient predecessors had—by "reading" alongside veteran practitioners. For lawyers and doctors, this form of refined apprenticeship was part tutorial, part practicum: one studied alongside a mentor, reading all his books, assisting him in his practice, and working under his tutelage.

With the education of military officers the practice was similar but a bit different and less formal, and it varied somewhat among nations. European officers were generally the younger sons of nobles (or at least of the gentlemanly class), and as such were considered to be "born to command." For many, parents or patrons purchased commissions in good regiments, a system with both pluses and minuses. Usually in their early teens and without the benefit of a college education, these youths were thrust into positions where they had to assimilate their roles quickly and learn their duties on the job. Their apprenticeship, such as it was, consisted of practical experience, some advice by veteran officers (and more than likely guidance from noncommissioned officers), and whatever reading they wished to do. Absent a formal structure for basic officer training and no command and staff schools or war colleges for advanced study, a great disparity existed in European officer education of the period. Many officers had little inclination or time for theoretical and historical study, preferring instead to live the life of an eighteenth-century gentleman-officer to the fullest, riding to the hounds, drinking hard and long, whoring, and gambling. The rigors of the hunt with its stress on fine horsemanship proved ideal for physically toughening and conditioning young gentlemen of the blade,[2] but more than a few officers concentrated solely on gentlemanly sport, disdaining any reading other than a deck of cards. As research has shown, however, a fairly sizable minority of officers—many promoted by merit, not birth or purchase—were students of war who combined physical with cerebral training, enhancing their professional knowledge and skills. Given the lack of any structured study of war and formal texts, however, these professional officers could only read histories and military treatises, literature which was available from booksellers to every literate person on both sides of the Atlantic, including the Saxes, Washingtons, and even Napoleons.

Throughout the eighteenth century, war remained an art, not a science, although portents of change may be discerned. Certainly, in an enlightened age when efforts were made to apply scientific principles to all aspects of human endeavor, science did make inroads into the study of war. The reduction of massive geometric bastions through sieges evolved into a highly specialized science, and by the eighteenth century several nations had established engineering and artillery schools where these special fields were scientifically taught and studied.[3] Graduates of these schools were technical experts whom their hard-drinking, fox-hunting contemporaries held in low esteem; for a gentleman, knowledge should appear to be gained effortlessly (if at all), and vocational training, not to mention working with one's hands—as engineers and artillerymen had to do—was scorned. But though the period emphasized both formalized education and warfare, surprisingly few military schools existed. Seen against the great number of military tracts published in the late seventeenth and the eighteenth century, professional officer education remained very much an individual's purview.[4] Of course, self-education has its benefits, as eighteenth-century philosopher Immanuel Kant pointed out: "What one learns the most fixedly and remembers the best is what one learns more or less by oneself."[5] For the typical, nonspecialized eighteenth-century officer, knowledge of the art of war was gained as it had been from the time of Alexander—from practical experience serving in camp and in the field, and, for those who made the effort, from reading history and books on war.

To one extent or another, all eighteenth-century commanders learned about war this way, and Napoleon is the best example of all. Bonaparte, it is true, did attend artillery school and benefit from the increasing late eighteenth-century French trend toward officer professionalization. But, for lessons on strategy and the art of command, he acted upon the advice of older officers and his own nature, and studied long and hard after hours.[6] He read voluminously, almost fanatically, sacrificing sustenance for a few more *livres* to buy additional books. This pale, thin Corsican youth devoured histories and military works, books read with almost equal ardor by fledgling American officers of a generation earlier. Also like the Americans, he followed the Plutarchian model, studying the Great Captains of history, reading deeply and broadly but also critically, analyzing both their successes and failures to refine the essence of their military prowess. When he began his meteoric rise to greatness, just as others from Philip of Macedon to Nathanael Greene had before him, he drew upon lessons gained from his study of history for many strategical and tactical ideas. Napoleon was not particularly innovative, but he developed and perfected lessons from the past, taking them beyond limits imagined by their innovators (or his opponents). A great part of Bonaparte's genius was his encyclopedic recall, his ability to draw these lessons, to analyze them, then to apply what he needed to the situation facing him, wrote historian David Chandler, for "[f]rom first to last, he was the perfecter and applier rather than the creator."[7] Napoleon summarized his views on military education thusly: "Tactics, evolutions [drill], the duties of an Engineer or an Artillery officer may be learnt in treatises," he wrote, "but the science of grand tactics [i.e., strategy] is only to be acquired by experience and by studying the campaigns of all the great Captains."[8]

Oddly enough, the most noted interpreter of Napoleonic warfare thought less about the value of studying the past than did his subject. Carl von Clausewitz, the early nineteenth-century officer and theoretician with the greatest impact on the study of war, had contradictory feelings about the importance of history. "The further one goes [from the War of the Austrian Succession (1740–48)], the less useful military history becomes, growing poorer and barer at the same time. The history of antiquity," he wrote, "is without doubt the most useless and barest of all."[9] (Later in his work, however, Clausewitz cited many valuable general lessons that may be gleaned from studying the Punic Wars.) In his disdain for the past, Clausewitz was more than likely influenced by a contemporary, the philosopher Georg Hegel, who wrote that, "Amid the pressure of world events, neither a general principle nor the remembrance of similar circumstances is of any help," adding that "something like pale recollection has no power against the vitality and freedom of the present."[10] With this Hegelian tenet and Clausewitz's subsequent dictums, the Americans of 1775 and Napoleon, some twenty years later, would have disagreed; to them, the past truly spoke to the present, and they listened.

Washington and his lieutenants for the most part were amateur officers, not professionals, and while their war anticipated the French Revolutionary and Napoleonic Wars in many aspects, it was generally different in nature. These American officers did not share Napoleon's military genius, but they were closer to the great Bonaparte in how they learned about war than they were, say, to a typical port-swilling, fox-chasing British officer of the time. The Americans were reasonably well-educated civilians who read military history for profit and pleasure: they enjoyed the literature because they were interested in the topic, and the onset of war sharpened their enthusiasm for more general and practical knowledge of military affairs. Colonials who would have field commands and those who entered Congress had equal access to and read the same works which later gave Napoleon his basic knowledge of the art of war. This literature supplied revolutionary-generation Americans with a fundamental understanding of the principles of war but also uplifted them with valuable illustrations of people challenging and triumphing over superior adversaries.

The Corsican's advice to "read and re-read" and to learn from history, however, as is the case with many lessons of the past, has often been misinterpreted. Neither he nor any other great commander ever suggested that an officer study the particular tactics employed by Alexander at Arbela (or Guagamela) or Hannibal at Lake Trasimene and Cannae in order to repeat them mechanically on some modern battlefield; time, space, terrain, technology, and a hundred other things rendered a rigid application of the past to present at least unwise and probably disasterous. To do so, as one latter-day student of warfare noted in a Procrustean metaphor, would be "akin to cutting the feet to fit the bed."[11] Nor did any intelligent commander suggest that lessons discerned from studying the campaigns of the past and reduced axiomatically to a few principles were all that history offered to modern students of war. "An absolute doctrine is impossible," General J. F. C. Fuller flatly stated.[12] Principles studied with little depth or analysis led to rigid, dogmatic thinking. "Military doctrine must be a growing science, ceaselessly developing and improving," writes Chandler, "for once it degenerates into mere dogma . . . disaster invariably looms ahead."[13] History is filled with cases of obdurate generals whose inflexibility of thought and action sacrificed thousands rather than chance modifying or breaking with existing military canons. "[O]nce a doctrine and its articles become a dogma," Fuller cautioned twentieth-century officers (to little avail), "woe to the army which lies enthralled under its spell."[14] At first, being amateurs, Washington and his lieutenants often too closely adhered to the European military doctrine of the day. Their inherent practicality, native intelligence, and experience garnered in the early campaigns of the war soon altered their thinking; these historically conscious Americans quickly learned that, as inflexibility of thought and action were the antithesis of warfare as practiced by the Great Captains of history, the precepts of European warfare had to be adapted to New World conditions.

In reality, the advice to study history was much broader and therefore more valuable, something the ancients recognized. "[I]f you essay to grow great through war," Virtue told Heracles, ". . . you must learn the arts of war from those who know them."[15] Studying their campaigns—both victorious and unsuccessful—yielded insights from the thinking, character, and actions of the Great Captains. For eighteenth-century officers of most nations save the French and Prussians, wartime provided the only opportunity to train with and maneuver large numbers of troops, and wargaming was unknown. But in studying the campaigns of the Great Captains, an officer could "see many battles fought in a short time, many towns attacked and defended, and be present as often as he pleases in the greatest feats of war," noted the Chevalier de la Valiere, whose work was widely read in the colonies. Books also allowed students of war to learn their craft "in private," finding answers to questions which they would not ask other men, "for fear of being thought ignorant."[16] Readers learned that though the Great Captains were generally sound, even brilliant, battlefield tacticians, they won acclaim by their conduct not of battles but in campaigns and wars, or, in other words, by their strategy and generalship. Great commanders perceived war in geopolitical terms, thinking and planning ahead, beyond the immediate battle or even campaign. Cognizant of limitations inherent in the warfare of their particular times and closely attuned to the realities of internal politics and economics, they employed all available resources to maximize the potential of their forces; this aspect alone raised them above their contemporaries. They clearly defined objectives, but if the winds of war shifted, they moved swiftly and decisively, pouncing upon any opportunity circumstances presented to reach their goal. For it continued equally true in ancient or modern times that the "hallmark of real strategy is that it determines what is the object and maintains it unswervingly," as Liddell Hart wrote, *adjusting both the means to the end and the end to the means.*"[17] In late 1776, during the nearly disastrous withdrawal from New York and retreat across the Jerseys, George Washington arrived at a similar conclusion.

Along with this broad, strategic view of war, history provided many general and specific observations about command. Distilling from the classics, popular histories, and other works, writers on military affairs compiled in general terms what constituted the ideal commander. From reading the biographies of the Great Captains, the Marquis de Brezé wrote in 1779, "you will see from the deeds of those great warriors that they were endowed with an active temperament, an invincible courage and an extraordinary toughness of mind." To de Brezé, "good breeding, humanity, moderation, graciousness, generosity, sobriety and so on" were important virtues, but the former were what made a general "rise above other men and command their admiration."[18] Elizabethan Thomas Styward stressed a commander's personal habits, writing in 1581 that "The General principallie ought to be a man that liveth in the fears of God, . . . [who] ought to be temperate, continent, and not excessive in eating or drinking." From his study of history, Styward recognized that a commander's character influenced his subordinate's actions, for they often modeled their behavior and thinking on his. In interacting with his lieutenants, the commander should be "Patient in travaile" and "of witte prompt." Good health was equally important. A commander "ought to be painful [have endurance], for that principallie it doth appertaine to a Generall that he in the time of turmoiles of the war, maie bee the last that is wearie."[19] But as de Brezé suggested, a general should be more than morally and physically fit, something even the Ancients were aware. He "must be resourceful, active, careful, hardy and quick-witted; he must be both gentle and brutal, at once straightforward and designing, capable of both caution and surprise," and many other things, advised Socrates.[20]

This advice was echoed from the past to the present. "A perfect general," commented Frederick the Great, "like Plato's Republic, is a figment of the imagination." Nevertheless, "Old Fritz" thought it "necessary to consider all the different talents that are needed by an accomplished general."[21] He must be "an assemblage of 'contradictory virtues'": at once honest and deceptive, brutal at one moment, magnanimous the next, and equally quick to praise and punish when necessary. A general's "principal task" was making "large projects and major arrangements," Frederick lectured, but he must also ensure that his orders were being carried out.[22] Great commanders had to be brave men with strong, virtuous characters, leaders who not only planned and directed campaigns but who remained unruffled under fire or any conditions. Few eighteenth-century army commanders actively participated on the battlefield as Alexander the Great or Gustavus Adolphus had, actually leading cavalry charges, but personal bravery and understated courage remained requisites for any gentleman-officer, especially a general. Over several campaigns, Frederick the Great had several horses shot out from under him, but merely remounted and resumed directing his troops. Young George Washington shrugged off losing two mounts and having his coat riddled with ball during Braddock's defeat, and while his generalship received a fair amount of criticism during the Revolution, his courage and Catoian resolve were never called into question. (On the other hand, British Lieutenant General George Sackville's behavior at the battle of Minden [1759]—ascribed to cowardice by some—led to his being cashiered from the army. Later, as the politically astute but strategically bereft Lord George Germain, he directed George III's war in America, and he was still sneeringly referred to as "Minden" in the letters of his officers.) For not only were planning and giving the correct orders important, from the general's personal behavior his troops "generally learn to despise or fear danger."[23]

Students of war learned that a commander must always be on duty. Seemingly simple gestures by a leader, for instance, carried with them great weight. Remembering a low-ranking subordinate's name or recognizing a veteran's face in the ranks and exchanging a few words were motivational techniques employed by commanders from the time of Cyrus the Great.[24] Cyrus, as interpreted by Xenophon, thought it strange that "while every mechanic knows the names of the tools of his trade and the physician knows the names of all the instruments he uses, the general should be so foolish as not to know the names of the officers under him."[25] Bonaparte's phenomenal memory served him well in this regard; singling out a veteran of an earlier campaign for a word, both humanized the Emperor and boosted morale. In the relatively small eighteenth-century armies, where rumors swept through camps faster than dysentery, a general's visage was carefully scrutinized by soldiers and subordinates seeking auguries in every frown or smile. Julius Caesar infected his troops with his "vigorous and cheerful countenance"—his *hilaritas*—buoying legionary spirits.[26] With his usual perspicuity and eye for detail, Shakespeare had his Henry V maintain an even demeanor before battle, strengthening his troops' resolve.

> . . . Upon his royal face there is no note
> How dread an army hath enrounded him;
> Nor doth he dedicate one jot of colour
> Unto the weary and all-watched night;
> But freshly looks, and over-bears attaint
> With cheerful semblance and sweet majesty
> That every wretch, pining and pale before,
> Beholding him, plucks comfort from his looks.[27]

It was generally held that a leader "ought therefore in no wise [ways] to seem disanimated, or doubtful," as the Earl of Orrery wrote in 1677, "but always chearful and confident."[28] Considering that the lives of thousands of men, his reputation and honor, and even his nation's freedom depended upon his actions, a wise general assumed a stoic role. Frederick, trained from childhood in the classics, military affairs, and leadership, sternly harangued his generals on the value of "dissimulation," "the art of hiding his thoughts." A commander, the Prussian monarch advised, "should be constantly on the stage . . . for the whole army speculates on his looks, his gestures, and on his mood." Even histrionics had to be carefully choreographed, and several years later, theater aficionado George Washington—who "devoured accounts of Frederick's campaigns"—took this advice to heart.[29] With very few exceptions, Washington kept his passions in check behind a stoic mask, his naturally volcanic temper allowed to erupt only when crises demanded it.

Students of their profession, the Great Captains, too, sought inspiration, guidance, and leadership techniques from history—as Alexander carried Homer and Scipio Africanus carried Xenophon's works, Frederick brought Plutarch on his campaigns.[30] The younger Scipio and Caesar, Matthew Suttcliffe noted in 1593, both spent "much time in reading of ancient deeds of Armes."[31] The past did not provide blueprints for the present: its lessons were universal, applicable to war in any age. For instance, seeking the root of the Roman army's greatness, Machiavelli, Maurice, and others discerned that discipline was vital; without disciplined soldiers, there could be no brilliant generalship, no Great Captains.[32] To make men willing to die for them, commanders had to be masters of motivation, striving to obtain personal fealty from even the lowliest soldier. "[T]he art of generalship, the art of command, whether the forces be large or small," Stonewall Jackson biographer G. F. R. Henderson wrote, "is the art of dealing with human nature." All the well-conceived plans, brilliant strategy, and outstanding generalship would go for naught if troops were unmotivated. Soldiers can undergo all types of deprivation—hunger, thirst, being loaded down like pack mules, and even fear—if their morale is good. "Human nature must be the basis of every leader's calculations," Henderson noted, whether sustaining that of his men, or breaking his opponent's morale and will to fight.[33] Henderson sought to explain what Bonaparte really learned from the campaigns of Alexander, Hannibal, and Caesar. The real knowledge Napoleon gained was not "mechanical movements and stereotyped combinations," but "a complete study of human nature under the conditions that exist in war," and how men were affected by discipline, fear, hunger, a lack of confidence and overconfidence, the weight of responsibility, politics, patriotism, distrust, and much more. Napoleon learned the "immense value of the moral element in war," and how to use it to the "utmost [until it] became instinctive, and he played upon the hearts of his enemies and of his own men," Henderson concluded, "with a skill which has never been surpassed."[34]

As Bonaparte cogently detected in his study of eighteenth-century Prussian disciplinary methods, however, discipline by fear alone was counterproductive to high morale. Ardent American republicans would have concurred but for different reasons. For instance, at Thermopylae, where King Leonidas and his three hundred Spartans and the often-neglected seven hundred Thespians stood alone before the might of Persia, republican zealots would have seen citizen-soldiers, a militia, sacrificing their lives for duty, honor, and virtue. Leonidas's famous words ("Traveler, if you come to Sparta, tell them that you have seen us lying here, as the law commanded") would be perceived by eighteenth-century Americans as the ultimate subordination of the military to the popular will.[35] The perception of a student of war, on the other hand, would be more pragmatic. Winning the hearts and minds of subordinates and troops was a leader's primary and most difficult task, even in the American and French Revolutions where revolutionary zeal initially sent thousands into the ranks. Soon, even the most ardent patriot's fervor paled in the face of the dreary routine, discipline, poor food, and sickness of camp life, as Washington quickly discovered. Patriotism was important, he believed, especially in a war such as the American Revolution, but, as he tried to make the Congress understand, "a great and lasting War can never be supported on this principle alone."[36] Revolutionary fervor might have brought Americans into the army, but as history, common sense, and experience taught him, Washington knew that discipline balanced with pay, a change of clothing, and decent food served regularly kept them under arms. (Washington, his war chest chronically empty, called money "the sinew of war" [or "the nerve of war"], employing an adage of Machiavelli— borrowed from Livy—which had entered the public domain.)[37] Washington's efforts in keeping his troops revictualed, not always successful, did earn him their personal loyalty, another trait of the Great Captains. Gaining the trust and loyalty of one's lieutenants and troops required time, thus signaling thorough preparation—another key lesson—for no matter how well trained one's subordinates were, nothing could be taken for granted in war; commanders saw to the smallest details, even making personal reconnaissance. And, perhaps a gem of wisdom which surely appealed to Napoleon, when truly great commanders deviated from accepted military doctrine, they did so boldly and decisively with *celeritas* (swiftness). These broad lessons were not lost on American revolutionary generals as they matured in command.[38]

The Greek and Roman classics, popular histories, and military treatises provided eighteenth-century militarists with a common fount of knowledge from which both Europeans and Americans drank thirst-ily. Just as Napoleon had traced the famous Frederickian oblique order of attack back to Epaminondas (who instructed a young Macedonian hostage at his court, Philip, who then passed the knowledge to his son), much of the Napoleonic way of war can be seen as being derived from the past. Bonaparte acknowledged his debt to history on many occasions. Either from reading Polybius's works or the Chevalier Fo-lard's study of Polybius, Napoleon paraphrased the ancient, advising young officers to: "Read, and re-read the campaigns of Alexander, Hannibal, Caesar, Gustavus Adolphus, Turenne, Eugène, and Fred-eric. Model yourself upon them," he urged, for "[t]his is the only means of becoming a great Captain, and of acquiring the secret of war."[39] After all, this was what he had done.

The importance of experience over study as teaching devices for generals has often been overestimated. The argument that experience and training are the best teachers versus those who emphasize formal or personal education is ancient and endless. Sallust sought to arbitrate between those who argued "whether warlike achievement succeeded more by strength of body, or ability of mind." His response was Solomon-like: "For before you enter upon action, there is need for deliberation; and when you have deliberated, there is need of a speedy execution."[40] In this, he agreed with Gaius Julius Caesar, who stated that "Generals are not born, but made—by study and experience."[41] On St. Helena, Napoleon advocated study, commenting, with some exaggeration, that "I have fought sixty battles, and I have learned nothing which I did not know at the beginning."[42] On the other hand, Lord Seaton's comments on the best way to learn war ("Fighting, and a damned deal of it") make great sense for company-level and lower-ranking field grade officers, but great warriors do not necessarily make great generals.[43] Scipio Africanus understood this well, answering critics by remarking that "his mother had given birth to a general, not a warrior."[44] Great battle leaders often lacked the overall perspective that allowed them to see the big picture, the strategic sweep. William Tecumseh Sherman thought that "he could have carried off the [Vicks-burg] campaign more effectively than" his commander, Ulysses S. Grant, "but that, unlike Grant, he could not have dared to think of it in the first place."[45] Strategy is the realm of the commander, and a general must have time to read, study, and think. "A mule who has carried a pack for ten campaigns under Prince Eugène will be not better a tactician for it, and it must be confessed," Frederick tartly wrote, "that many men grow old in an otherwise respectable profession without making any greater progress than this mule."[46] Truly, as Thucydides wrote, "war . . . is a rough schoolmaster," and yet, as history has shown on many occasions, it is only well after the battle, or even after most wars, that time allows for clear, thoughtful postaction analysis.[47] In the absence of formal advanced training, reading about the Great Captains was considered more useful than experience for those destined for or seeking high command.

Of course, a Bonaparte's fanatical study and brilliant use of the past were atypical; but in learning his craft by reading history and even to the sources he used, Napoleon, the future general and emperor, was much like any budding eighteenth-century militarist who preceded him—in Europe or in America. Perhaps even more to the point, the universality of lessons gleaned from the past made them applicable to any conflict, especially because—at their essence—the actual changes in warfare through this period "were not as great as one might imagine."[48]

The evolution of the art of war from classical antiquity to the eighteenth century was a slow, deeply involved process. To those who study the history of war and warfare as a whole—not simply specializing in a particular period or war—clearly delineated points on the time-space continuum denoting shifts from one type of warfare to another are nonexistent. Wars can have a great impact and effect upon a society, but warfare—how wars are fought—mirrors the society that is waging the war, as was indicated earlier. As European society as a whole shifted ever so slowly from feudalism to autonomous nation-states with increasingly sophisticated polities, economies, and bureaucracies, warfare inevitably reflected these changes. The heavily armored mounted knight, symbol of a way of life as well as a way of war, was already losing his dominance when he was effectively unseated by longbowmen and pikemen. The increases in the ability of states to reap the harvest of taxation from their growing economies produced also an inclination to systematize the military. For inspiration and practical lessons on organization, Europeans turned to the most efficient political-military machine the world had seen to that point—Rome.[49]

Renaissance Europeans in all fields dipped heavily into ancient cisterns; this was certainly true in the art of war, where there was little else to draw from. Leaders of city- and nation-states found themselves in a dilemma: to keep their money economies expanding, their people had to work, not make war; on the other hand, survival and growth demanded a trained army. The solution was to use some of their major product—money—to hire armies of mercenaries. One result of this was that anyone could now be a soldier; the elitism of knighthood was gone forever, and armies slowly began to increase in size. It also meant that the overlord or leader was no longer dependent upon his vassals. Thus power slowly shifted from the many to the few. To those European humanists of the Renaissance who sought to recreate the "perfect world" that had existed in classical times, however, mercenary armies were unsatisfactory, actually antithetical to the view they promulgated. Harkening back to ancient times, the decline of Rome, they felt, began when Romans no longer served their country, filling the legions' ranks and files with barbarians; for the humanists, military service, liberty, and virtue were as one, equally binding to both citizen and state—lessons not lost upon their eighteenth-century readers in America. Niccolo Machiavelli's advocacy of something akin to national military service was influenced by writers of the Roman Republic and early Empire, as were his theories on the art of politics (written for the prince) and war (written for his lieutenants).[50] The "most influential" of these classical writers was a Roman who also studied the ancients of his time to refine the essence of their greatness. This was Flavius Vegetius Renatus.[51]

Until Napoleon and his various interpreters, with the possible exception of Caesar's *Commentaries*, Vegetius's *De Re Militari* (or *Epitome rei militaris*) was—directly and even more so indirectly—the most influential military text in the Western world.[52] Mentioned by the Venerable Bede, edited to fit the needs of Charlemagne's Franks, "carried everywhere in the campaigns of the Plantagenets," especially by Henry II and Richard Coeur de Lion, and one of the first books published in England in the fifteenth century, Vegetius was a valued common source for students of war into the nineteenth century.[53] "Vegetius said that a god inspired the legion," wrote Austrian Field Marshal Prince von Ligne, "[but] as for me, I find that God inspired Vegetius."[54] Admittedly, his battle formations were generally arcane products, beautiful on paper or a parade ground but totally useless in battle. But Vegetius (and Frontinius, another important Roman military writer with whom he was often paired in print) was studied and emulated primarily for the commonsense military knowledge his writings contained, applicable in any age to any war. As Bonaparte noted, "In the Art of War—as in Nature—nothing is lost, nothing is created." (Or, as Lazare Carnot, principal architect of France's revolutionary army, said, ". . . plus ça change, plus ça reste la même chose.")[55] Vegetius also had universal appeal because his work was a foundation upon which others might build and because of his original reason for writing. Vegetius was not a military man but a patriot who saw his nation (Empire) in decline, and the decay of Rome's military emblematized the moral and societal degeneration which beset his land. Turning to the past, he sought inspiration and precedence from the halcyon days of Roman virtue and martial glory as avidly as any American republican of the revolutionary generation would fourteen centuries later.[56]

As with the Clausewitzian depreciation of most military history, critics question the value of Vegetius's writings. Historian Hans Delbrück's attitude toward Vegetius and the study of the past was as puzzling and paradoxical as Clausewitz's. Writing about war in the later Middle Ages, Delbrück stated that Vegetius was no longer important except as history. Then, however, he curiously went on to say that it was "quite understandable why [De Re Militari] was so highly regarded for such a long time and continuously studied. The practical soldier has a great need to arrive at a certain basic understanding of his profession," and in Vegetius, "one still finds . . . a series of tenets basically and clearly expressed, which are very useful for military reflection and discussion."[57] Noted twentieth-century scholar Theodore Ropp describes De Re Militari as now being primarily of "antiquarian" interest, yet he, too, lauds Vegetius as being extremely influential on thinkers and writers from Machiavelli to Montesquieu.[58] Granted, the principles espoused in Vegetius are readily apparent to any student of war and can be "grasped without the need for classical authority," but therein lies their value and universal appeal.[59]

Specific advice, received either aurally or from reading, is often quickly forgotten; general advice, usually drawn from the past in one form or another, becomes imprinted on the mind because of its widespread applicability. For instance, none other than twentieth-century military theoretician Mao Zedong, the "father of modern revolutionary war," freely credited the two thousand five hundred-year-old writings of Sun Wu Tzu with inspiring many of his theories on warfare; Maoist theory, in turn, both directly and indirectly influenced dozens of later revolutionary warriors and writers around the globe. Because of Mao's approbation, the works of Sun, who wrote concurrently with Herodotus and Thucydides, have been resurrected and enthusiastically accepted by Western students of war *and* business.[60] The direct influence of Napoleon Bonaparte on military affairs, in fact, continued to be felt on European and American military thought well into World War I. And in the best example of the even greater impact of the indirect influence of the past on the present, the Napoleonic way of war remains the centerpiece of strategic theory in the nuclear age through the writings of his number one interpreter, Clausewitz. Applying Clausewitz's disparagement of the value of older military knowledge to other fields, say, economics and literature, then Adam Smith's *Wealth of Nations* (1776) and the plays of Shakespeare are no longer relevant. Perhaps when it comes to Vegetius's *De Re Militari*, it might be held as a maxim in military history (or any history) that when the obvious is unveiled, the source is usually derogated or forgotten.

Mining many sources, Vegetius refined the essence of Roman military prowess from the Republic and early Empire. His commonsense approach, clear prose, and often brilliant analysis appealed to likeminded students of war. For many it was "studied as a military Bible."[61] Machiavelli, along with subsequent writers on the art of war such as Maurice of Nassau and the Marshal de Saxe, relied so heavily on Vegetius that in many ways their works may be perceived as modernized versions of the original. Frederick's *Instructions* and strategy, especially in the Seven Years' War, reflect a strong appreciation for the military writers of the past, for in fact he studied little other military history than what was in the classics; Vegetius's advice reverberates throughout the Prussian monarch's work.[62] To be sure, a certain inevitability in repetition exists when even great minds write endlessly on the same subject, always seeking to simplify and winnow out fundamental truths.[63] Yet the timelessness of Vegetius's advice, not original in itself and drawn from even then ancient, now lost treatises, is what makes it lasting and influential. The military writers whom future American revolutionary officers read so enthusiastically borrowed directly from Vegetius (and many of the ancients) or indirectly from other writers influenced by him. Through Vegetius's various interpreters, axioms drawn from his work entered the public lexicon, sometimes slightly paraphrased and often attributed to others, such as the following favorite of Washington's: "He, therefore, who desires peace, should prepare for war." But if the lessons of *De Re Militari* could be reduced to a single concept, what Machiavelli and others rediscovered from Vegetius was the overwhelming need for disciplined organization.[64]

Advice or knowledge most readily accepted is that to which one is already predisposed; this maxim holds true in any age. What students of the ancient Romans (including Vegetius) discerned was that what brought Rome to military ascendancy was organization. One-on-one, the Romans were good fighters, but Rome did not produce the superior individual warrior as did the undisciplined, fierce Celtic or Germanic tribesmen. But great warriors more often than not fail to make good soldiers, and as history has proven time and time again, whether the wars were in Gaul, Ireland, Africa, or along the American frontier, a disciplined, efficient, organized, well-led soldiery with good morale will eventually overcome the greatest warriors. Either in campaign or in war, Roman discipline and organization repeatedly triumphed over their poorly organized enemies in spite of losing a battle or several battles early on.[65] As is the case with any army, the Roman military arm was but an extension of the Roman political and societal body: the same sophisticated administration that collected taxes, ruled, and oversaw trade across an immense area also fielded, maintained, and reinforced its armies when hardier warrior tribesmen lost heart from inaction, starvation, or attrition. For European societies growing ever more complex, the Roman model was a provident starting point.

Thus, for prerevolutionary Americans who received a strong dose of military history from their reading of the classics and popular histories, the past provided their fundamental ideas on the concepts and practice of war. The most important lessons of the military past were those with universality, those lessons that withstood the test of time and could be applied to any war at any time. Americans did not learn these "principles" of war by rote, reciting numbers one through ten in a classroom. They learned them from reading works on the art of war, ignoring what they found irrelevant and employing what they perceived as good, commonsense ideas to use in their wars in their land. As will be seen in the following two chapters, the colonials' own practical experience and practical nature showed them that they could not emulate their European contemporaries exactly; they simply did not have the wherewithal (manpower, firepower, logistics, finances), or the ability (few if any trained officers, noncommissioned officers, or men), and their inconsiderate Amerindian opponents refused to pay them the courtesy of fighting in the European fashion.

CHAPTER 5

The European Inheritance

To ascribe to any single source primary influence on colonial American military thought and practice would be a vast oversimplification. For instance, the Greek and Roman classics and the histories of ancient times—as discussed earlier—had a direct influence, but were perhaps more influential indirectly. These ancient sources furnished a common repository of knowledge from which both Americans and Europeans drew for their concepts of and about war. European military writers were particularly dependent upon them for both general and specific ideas and practices. In turn, the Europeans' interpretative blending of ancient and contemporary ideas and practical knowledge had a substantial impact on military thinking and on American concepts of war and military affairs in general. A genealogical schematic of this family of ideas would reveal a great deal of intellectual incest and cross-fertilization.

The same proposition holds true for European societies as they developed from the Middle Ages. What appears simple at any one point in time actually masks sociopolitical-economic changes that were extremely complex and vast in magnitude. Paralleling these changes—sometimes mitigating them—were transformations in the art of war. As societies and their polities increased in size and complexity, so did their armed forces, at least on the surface, reflecting their parental societies. Homer, Herodotus, Thucydides, Polybius, Tacitus, the writers of the Bible, and many of the other ancients reminded us of this. Technological advances, economic transformations, agricultural improvements, environmental shifts (weather and the presence or absence of disease), population growth, and many other things all beget general changes in society. But just as all these societal changes directly and indirectly affect war and warfare, so does warfare effect changes upon society.

In sum, it was not just a European or, even more specifically, an English heritage that the colonists brought with them across the Atlantic; rather, within their cultural and societal DNA was a piece of Western civilization. And, for better or worse, a goodly portion of this inheritance concerned itself with war. For the legacy of Plato, Cicero, and More was also that of Alexander, Caesar, and Cromwell.

From the fourteenth through the early eighteenth century, Europe underwent a metamorphosis of titanic proportions; slowly but definitely, all society was organically altered. Strong, more sophisticated economies produced greater wealth which translated, through taxes, into regular funding for a ruler. Collection of these taxes (unless it was "farmed out" to private entrepreneurs) required an ever-increasing bureaucracy which led to a centralization of power with an increased control over politics, society, and the economy. The development of this state power and organization ensured that a like military arm was not only possible but essential. As the state grew more sophisticated (in relative terms), it grew better able to control and utilize the resources of the community. This made possible the development of a professional military which, in turn, was employed in facilitating increased state control of community resources, defense against external enemies, and suppression of internal dissent. State-provided financial support became the lifeblood of the military.[1]

Power—who shall rule—was the end result, of course, but the optimum word was control. A single ruler increasingly exercised control through a relatively complex, growing administrative bureaucracy which gradually displaced the nobility in influence. Where vassals had earlier furnished the king with men and arms—thereby serving as a check on royal ambitions—now rulers established standing armies with few ties to the populace, fueled by tax monies, and loyal only to the sovereign who paid them. Therefore, as Michael Howard notes, it was this development of a sociopolitical central nervous system—not weapons technology—that began altering and streamlining existing military structures and warfare itself. In fact, improvements in weapons technologies most likely would not have occurred and certainly could not have been utilized to their fullest if a centralized state apparatus manned by professional bureaucrats and military men had not existed.[2]

Scholars long held that the advent of gunpowder immediately and forever altered warfare and, subsequently, European society. Their interpretation, however, has been shown to be something of an exaggeration, for technology, like war and the military, does not exist independently of the the cultural and economic base and norms of a society.[3] To be sure, the introduction of gunpowder to Europe in the late fourteenth and early fifteenth centuries had an unquestionable effect on the military. In particular, the catalyst was the Turkish capture of Constantinople in 1453. When rudimentary Turkish cannon breached Constantinople's defenses, the stone shot not only destroyed the last vestige of the Roman Empire and ensured that gunpowder-fired weapons would play a significant role in European warfare, but they also knocked down important psychological walls as well: security evaporated.

The major and immediate effect, however, was on society, not on warfare. Few existing fifteenth-century castle and city walls could withstand cannon fire, and Europe suddenly believed that it stood naked and vulnerable to a few men armed with a new, awesome weapon. But even as Machiavelli lamented in 1519 that "No wall exists, however thick, that artillery cannot destroy in a few days," the momentary ascendancy that the offense achieved over the defense was all but gone.[4] First, cannon were difficult and expensive to cast and stone, then early metal, shot was only effective against weak walls. Second, the advantage besiegers held over the besieged was lost as quickly as it was attained, for centralized governments rapidly marshaled their resources and built defenses. Initially, high city walls had earthen embankments built up against them upon which existing cannon had little effect; then the walls were lowered and made thicker. Bastions and gun towers were added bit by bit, along with geometric

angles to the walls to improve fields of fire. The art of fortification—
soon altered into a science—became increasingly sophisticated and
expensive, from which two corollary effects may be observed: the city
as a strongpoint centralized trade centers, making tax collection sim-
pler, and security became the sole domain of the state.[5] Governments
then started to cast their own artillery; this did not restore equilibrium,
but it did allow a new equilibrium to emerge. Following the Renaissance, historian Geoffrey Parker writes, "much of western Europe
seemed locked into a military system in which offence and defence
were almost exactly balanced."[6]

Gunpowder would have a major impact on the military and warfare, but initially it only stimulated primary reforms which resulted
more from societal than specifically military changes. Warfare, or,
more precisely, the art of war, had not lain dormant from the decline
of the Roman Empire in the fifth century to the fall of Constantinople;
it remained constantly—albeit slowly—evolving, just as the human
body does not cease growing and functioning when a person sleeps.
Awakened, as it were, by the distant boom of Turkish guns, the art of
war, as with all Renaissance arts, began "a series of gradual and modest
adjustments to the constantly changing demands" of warfare.[7] As
economies flourished, they fueled societal changes which, almost im-
perceptibly, transformed the face of war. Discipline, systemization,
and organization—these were the credos of an evolving, more advanced society that Machiavelli linked to the military, that Maurice,
Saxe, Frederick, and Napoleon mastered and built upon to earn the
appellation Great Captains, and that George Washington vainly sought
to instill among Americans.[8]

The introduction of gunpowder to European warfare, then, actually
had a less-than-instantaneous impact upon war. Except for specialized
warfare, such as sieges, gunpowder-fired weapons never dominated
the battlefield, as scholars have observed, until the middle of the
nineteenth century. The art of war through the Age of Napoleon
remained closer to its ancient roots than to the twentieth century. The
"revolution in warfare" which occurred in the seventeenth century
proved more evolutionary than revolutionary; and ushering it in was
not technological innovation but the application of societal norms to

control an aspect of human behavior run amuck. Earlier controls which began transforming armies into instruments of state policy were only as strong as each nation's administrative organizations. Such as they were, these controls were cast aside, however, in the sixteenth-and seventeenth-century wars of religion.[9]

Warfare is controlled violence, but when kings unleashed their dogs of war to fight *jihads*, they lost all semblance of order. Wars acquired lives of their own, voraciously feeding on themselves. Wars were seemingly fought for the sake of war itself, and rational controls were ignored. War no longer was the use of force by recognized authorities to achieve political ends. Instead, it degenerated into Europe-wide anarchistic violence, war for war's sake, war begetting war. This frenzy of war rose to a fever pitch in the Thirty Years' War (1618–48).[10] The excesses generated during this long conflict were of such a magnitude that what resulted was a general, loosely held consensus among nations to endeavor to rationalize warfare as society itself was being reconstructed. European society as a whole perceived that undisciplined armies and near-anarchistic warfare, war controlled by neither prince nor pope, disrupted trade, sapping the life from their burgeoning economies, and, as historian Paul M. Kennedy writes, armies could not be considered as "predictable and reliable instruments of state."[11] Thus discipline, born of an attempt to rationalize warfare, altered doctrine which then made the increased use of gunpowder weapons feasible; this, in turn, led to further modifications and refinements in existing military structures and, ultimately, to more efficient killing machines. "It was discipline and not gunpowder," scholar Max Weber concluded, "which initiated the transformation." Gunpowder, Weber added, "and all the techniques associated with it became significant only with the existence of discipline."[12]

As was discussed earlier, discipline was a primary message in Vegetius's *De Re Militari*. Only the strongest discipline bolstered Roman legionaries in battle against fearsome, shrieking Celts and Germans wielding huge swords and battle-axes, and this same discipline sustained the Romans until their enemy lost heart. "The ancients," Vegetius wrote, "taught by experience, preferred discipline to numbers."[13] Among the ancients to whom Vegetius looked for ideas and examples was Caesar, who, like Herodotus and others before him, vastly overestimated the strength of his opponents to suit personal and patriotic needs. Vegetius and students of ancient history through the nineteenth century, however, accepted Caesar's figures as true, yet this only increased and imprinted the value of the lessons. For, Vegetius wrote, "Victory in war does not depend entirely upon numbers or mere courage, [but] only skill and discipline will insure it."[14] To Vegetius, martial discipline and training distinguished a soldier from a civilian; without discipline, "there is no longer any difference between the soldier and the peasant."[15] Although discipline did not necessarily change a soldier into a warrior, a soldier's courage, Vegetius suggested, his confidence in himself, in his abilities, his unit, and his mates, could be strengthened by training and discipline, for "[f]ew men are born brave; many become so through care and force of discipline."[16] Strong but not harsh, efficient discipline and systematic training were at the heart of Roman military success, according to the Vegetian gospel, and the two aspects went hand in hand: without a methodical system of training, discipline made no sense, and without discipline, training was worthless. Late sixteenth- and seventeenth-century readers of Vegetius and his many interpreters appreciated the worth of his relatively simple, commonsense dictums; for they were preconditioned, so to speak, by similar fundamental changes in their parent societies, societies which also drew upon the past as a source of knowledge. Vegetius and other ancient writers filled a need, and, to a large measure, inspired a modernization of warfare or a reinvention of the art of war.

In important ways, the rediscovery of discipline as a means of exacting control over an army was emblematic of modern warfare in its infancy, of its dependence upon ancient sources, and of the close ties to the past which it retained. As Michael Howard points out, from a modern perspective, where disciplined armies are considered as a matter of course among industrialized nations, it is difficult to realize just what a phenomenon this was. Borrowing directly from Vegetius, Frontinius, and others, including his contemporaries, Maurice of Nassau (or Orange) rediscovered drill in the late sixteenth century as the best means of instilling discipline (and esprit de corps). From his example, foreigners in the Dutch service quickly spread his ideas throughout Europe. The Netherlands, for at least a short time, was "the schoole of war whither the most martial spirits of Europe resort to lay downe the apprenticeship of their service in armes," noted one English writer in 1616.[17] The successes of Sweden's Gustavus Adolphus in the Thirty Years' War confirmed Maurice's concepts and were perhaps even more influential in spreading the gospel of discipline (although it should be noted that the Swedish army's effectiveness dropped precipitously when Gustavus was not in personal command). Discipline meant control, and drill was the means of achieving martial discipline. What had been unwieldy, unorganized masses, were gradually shaped by constant drilling into sophisticated, disciplined organisms ready to change shape at command and increasingly capable of refined battlefield movement. With a clearly defined chain of command that ran from the lowest-ranking noncommissioned officer back to an absolutist monarch, writes historian William McNeill, over time armies became powerful, efficient, and obedient weapons, equally fearsome to external enemies and internal dissidents. By the eighteenth century, according to historian Christopher Duffy, these armies "were more stable and more responsive to manipulation than anything known since Classical times." The rediscovery of discipline, this seemingly subtle, even minor change, proved to have an enormous impact on warfare throughout the eighteenth century.[18]

The development of disciplined, well-drilled armies paralleled an increasingly multifarious society. To build such an army required the investment of a great deal of time, effort, and treasure and was often the "most expensive and pressing activity" of sixteenth- and seventeenth-century nations; states could no longer be dependent on patriotic but ill-trained, ill-disciplined, short-term militia.[19] Therefore, the gradual movement toward permanent, paid standing armies became universal throughout Europe, finalizing the divorce of king and army (rulers) from the populace (ruled). The middle class and the landed peasantry were as effectively distanced from the army as they had been when Gaius Marius professionalized the army of the Roman Republic in the second century B.C. Previously, as in the seventeenth and eighteenth centuries, the Roman army had become like a "family" to landless peasant recruits who had few ties to the Senate and to Rome but very strong bonds to their legionary commanders. (The possibility that history might be repeating itself was not lost on late seventeenth-century libertarians, particularly those in post-Cromwellian England.)

It should be noted, however, that while the Vegetian concept of discipline as interpreted by Maurice and his "disciples" prevailed throughout Europe, implementation, systems and regularity of training, and forms of enforcing this discipline (e.g., punishment) varied greatly with each nation's armed forces at differing times.[20] Also, to reiterate a point made earlier, seventeenth- and eighteenth-century disciplinary practices should not be judged by modern attitudes toward corporal punishment.[21] Life was much harsher then and cheaper, too. This was a time after all, when the penalty for poaching a rabbit was death, when severed heads—royal or peasant—festooned city gates, when whippings, brandings, and amputation of limbs were typical sentences for even minor civilian infractions. (To modern eyes, a penalty of a "1000 lashes, well laid on" might appear to be a death sentence, but this was common in the Age of Reason. Perusing histories of the French and Indian War reveals many cases where soldiers received such a punishment only to resume their duties in less than a week. On Braddock's expedition, a young wagonmaster named Morgan, struck an officer, but a miscount let him off with *only* 999 lashes. In the next war, General Daniel Morgan and his sharpshooting riflemen paid the British back many times over.)

Such military punishments as "running the gauntlet" were not especially brutal for the period; in fact, such a punishment of soldiers by soldiers may even be considered as part of martial bonding. In this ancient Roman practice reinstituted by Gustavus of Sweden, according to Delbrück,[22] the soldier to be punished ran between files of his mates (the "gauntlet") who beat him with fists or clubs. If the miscreant was, for instance, a thief who stole from his fellows, in all likelihood their blows fell heavily, and death from this punishment was not unheard of; an officer's sycophant or sergeant's lickspittle might suffer equally. On the other hand, for a soldier guilty of a relatively minor offense, the pummeling might be eased, signifying less of a punishment and more of a right of passage, a test of manhood. Constant drilling was also multipurpose; it not only instilled discipline and kept the troops busy (an idle soldier, every sergeant knows, is mischief ready to happen),[23] but endless marching taught individual soldiers to think as one unit and built esprit de corps. For, like their ancient Roman brothers, the military created an artificial community for soldiers of the seventeenth and eighteenth century, the only community and family many knew. The troops of this period, the great-grandfathers of Wellington's "scum of the earth," were universally loathed by civilian contemporaries; for instance, eighteenth-century French inns proscribed "dogs, lackeys, prostitutes or soldiers."[24] Within their martial brotherhood, however, soldiers developed a code and credo all their own: admittedly, whoring, gambling, and drinking were part of this life, but, notes McNeill, so were "pride, punctillo, and prowess."[25]

Pride in oneself, esprit d'corps, and camaraderie were important, but strict discipline and regularly performed drill were essential features in keeping armies under control and able to accomplish their missions. In the four to six years that seventeenth- and eighteenth-century authorities deemed necessary to turn a raw recruit into a valuable soldier, in some armies men literally were whipped or beaten into obedience through discipline and drill. "Since the days when Charles V lifted his hat to the gallows as the first servant of the state," stated Theodore Ropp, beatings were as much a part of army life as bad food and long marches.[26] From history, students of war observed Hannibal's successful application of severe, even brutal discipline to keep his mixed force of Carthaginians, Celts, Spaniards, and Numidians in order, and also saw that Roman centurions employed cudgels to coax legionaries into learning their drill. But those who read closely into the past perceived that stern discipline alone would not prevent men from turning on their masters; there had to be enticements to subordination, carrots along with the sticks. As Elizabethan Matthew Suttcliffe noted, "Contrariwise due pay doeth binde the souldiers to the General, as Livy declareth in the example of Annibal."[27] Hannibal may have beaten his men, but he fed them well and allowed them to plunder. Cromwellian General George Monck summarized this wisdom: "If you intend to have a well-commanded army you must pay them punctually, and then," he added, "your general can with justice punish them severely." (Cromwell himself purportedly axiomized this, saying, "Pay well, hang well.")[28] Cromwell's New Model Army soldiers, it is true, were paid at a rate lower than common agricultural workers of the time,[29] but unlike farmhands after the crops were harvested, the soldiers never wanted for food or shelter and that, in turn, actually made theirs a better lot.

The eighteenth-century Prussians became masters at combining extremely harsh discipline with a relatively efficient administrative organization that furnished troops with regular pay, "nourishing food and annual issues of clothing."[30] Once, while reviewing his troops on parade, Frederick downplayed the precision and perfection that so excited his generals. Time, money, and attention could do that, he remarked, but what "astonish[ed]" the Prussian monarch was that he and his generals could stand there "in perfect safety," reviewing sixty thousand strong, well-conditioned, well-armed men who absolutely loathed them. Conversely, he marveled, the troops "all tremble in our presence, while we have no reason whatsoever to be afraid of them. This," he added sagely, "is the miraculous effect of order, subordination and narrow supervision."[31] Even later, during the revolutionary wars, when patriotism sent men into the army, it was pay and pride, Washington intuitively knew, that held them in the ranks. As with much of what Frederick did or wrote, however, his contemporaries often failed to grasp every nuance. One French general described Frederick as "an extraordinary man, this prince who can get such good service from his troops who detest him. Three-quarters of his men would desert if they had the choice," he commented, adding that, "nevertheless they fight like devils until the chance comes."[32]

The general's words do, however, point out drawbacks in the Frederickian method of discipline. Strict discipline was needed to weld together the polyglot armies of the seventeenth and eighteenth centuries. Most armies contained large segments of nonindigenous mercenary troops; at times rival European armies had so many Scots and Irish in their opposing ranks that battles resembled faction fights.[33] The Dutch army which faced the Spanish in 1600 fielded seventeen native companies, but its strength lay in nine German, eleven Walloon, twenty Scottish, thirty-two French, and forty-three English companies.[34] At his death in 1632, only about 10 percent of Gustavus's Swedish army was native-born, and at its height, even Frederick's army was never more than 50 percent Prussian. Employing foreign troops during wartime allowed for continued economic growth, as a

French minister explained, for each hireling was worth three Frenchmen: one more soldier for the French, one less for the enemy, and one
more Frenchman to stay at home and pay taxes.[35] But the discipline
required to ensure battlefield efficiency from this combined mercenary
and native force also drove men to desert (as did the twenty-year term
of service). So common was desertion in Frederick's army, for example, that not infrequently certain operations were curtailed: reconnaissance, skirmishing, and small foraging parties were eschewed.
Nevertheless, just as drill had a "utilitarian" role on the battlefield,
extreme discipline actually was a rational attempt to solve a difficult
problem: to get men to face the carnage and horror of the battlefield,
the punishment had somehow to be worse than doing one's duty.[36] In
his order of 11 May 1763, Frederick telescoped this concept into an
axiom for all times: "Generally speaking the common soldier must fear
his officers more than the enemy."[37] The doctrine of the day, after all,
demanded instant obedience and precision maneuvers.

Following the demise of knighthood, Europeans first sought to emulate
the ancients directly, but technological advances gradually led to modifications. Swiss pikemen had resurrected the phalanx as their basic
formation in the fifteenth century;[38] bristling with long pikes, these
phalanxes (or "battles") were impenetrable to infantry and cavalry for
some time, but their protective mass soon made choice targets for
artillery and smaller guns.[39] These weapons, especially the early hand-
held weapons, were expensive and difficult to manufacture, cumbersome, and available only to a state-sponsored and paid military. Unless
they were on active military service, few Europeans had access to or
experience with firearms of any sort until the late eighteenth century.
In part, this altered the average citizen's perspective of military affairs.
Prior to these changes, most men—the middle class and landed peasants—formed local militia units which could be mobilized in an emergency. These occasional warriors prided themselves in maintaining
their proficiency with swords, bows, and pikes, and while their efficiency might be questioned, they instilled the general populace with
martial awareness and understanding and, not least of all, patriotism.
With the advent of regular, standing armies and gunpowder weapons,
the need for this type of militia was obviated. Whereas colonial Amer-

icans became the most heavily armed people on earth by the eighteenth century because of individual hunting and security needs, their European counterparts might go a lifetime without firing a shot. Thus in Europe only those with great wealth (kings) could afford the vast amounts of new weaponry and munitions or the trained specialists needed to fire them that changes in warfare demanded.[40]

Moreover, early gunpowder weapons often proved more hazardous to those using them than to opponents. Early artillery pieces were huge, basically immobile, had a rate of fire as low as one shot per day, and blew up with alarming frequency. They were of little use other than against massed, phalanx-style formations of massed infantry or in sieges. The first handguns (so to speak) were employed primarily to defend the all-important pikemen. Early infantry weapons weighed upwards of fifty pounds with their stands, and the slow-burning fuse (match) required to ignite the powder made it a less than optimum weapon for any type of maneuver warfare. Nevertheless, the increased use of these weapons on the battlefield forced tactical adjustments; after all, a phalanx based on the Macedonian model, for instance, presented an inviting target (1,024 files, each sixteen men deep in rank), even for the inaccurate weapons of the day. These modifications began thinning the massed blocks of infantry and widening the battle-field, in part to protect the cannon and musketeers. As lighter gunpowder weapons were developed and further improved in both firepower and accuracy (by the mid-1600s, musketeers outnumbered pikemen "three or four to one", and the former now protected the latter), ranks or lines had fewer and fewer ranks and command had to be delegated among leaders of these smaller groups of troops which brought about increases in tactical maneuver. But that was in the future, for battles in the years of the dynastic wars still resembled giant chess matches.[41]

By the mid-seventeenth century, however, refinements in technology and doctrine had advanced enough to allow warfare to be divided along two lines: siegecraft and maneuver. As Paul Kennedy notes, from the late fifteenth through the late seventeenth century, "most European countries witnessed a centralization of political and military power." This gradual consolidation was "accompanied by increased powers and methods of state taxation" which required a "more elaborate bureaucratic machinery than had existed" before, or at least since classical times, although, as Kennedy advises, one should not confuse seventeenth- and eighteenth-century efficiency and bureaucracy with that of modern times.[42] In sum, money now was available to create defensive systems which would allow towns and cities—the economic hearts of the powerful new political-military bodies—to be protected. The simple town walls of medieval times which had effectively deterred bandits and small groups of armored knights were slowly being superseded by gigantic works often miles in circumference. Cities became strongpoints defended by thousands of troops. These strategic bastions could no longer be bypassed by invading armies eager to reach a nation's capital; leaving ten thousand men on your line of communication was not sound military wisdom in any age.[43] Although still few in number at the time of the Thirty Years' War (which was why, Geoffrey Parker suggests, so many battles—as opposed to seiges —took place),[44] the great, geometrically shaped walls and citadels of these bastions began forever altering the landscape of Europe. So strong had these bastions become by the mid-seventeenth century (strong enough to withstand twentieth-century artillery barrages and aerial bombardment) that sieges frequently were more destructive to the besiegers than to the besieged: starvation and disease devastated assaulting armies, forcing them to give up before a city capitulated. Doctrinal wisdom that strongpoints had to be reduced hardened into dogma, so wars consisted of sieges with opposing forces seeing which side could outlast the other. The solution to this impasse reflected then-current societal fascination for science, what Henry Guerlac called the "cult of reason and order."[45]

Rather than starvation tactics or costly and generally fruitless frontal attacks, the French (with the usual help from those ancient masters of siegecraft, the Romans) developed a siegecraft that was two parts science and one part medieval tournament.[46] Louis XIV's great engineer, Sébastian Le Prestre de Vauban, borrowing from the ancients and from Maurice of Nassau, created a highly stylized format that once begun inevitably had but one ending. A grand siege conducted by Vauban was a magnificent theatrical production with the great engineer as the impresario, all designed to impress the master of Versailles, le roi soleil. Employing an army of specialists, Vauban had a series of fortified trenches (successive parallels and zigzags) dug up to the city's fortifications. After the walls were breached, protocol but especially honor demanded that the enemy launch a brief counter-stroke and then surrender (at Yorktown in 1781, this ritual would be carefully observed by men for whom honor meant more than victory). The revolutionary godfather of Napoleon's army, Lazare Carnot, caustically described this type of formal siege not as the "art of defend-ing strong places, but that of surrendering them honorably."[47] Follow-ing capitulation, cities generally were no longer sacked and citizens slaughtered; this was, after all, a rational age, and unnecessary blood-shed was to be avoided, especially considering the time, effort, and, above all, cost it took to make a soldier. As Vauban's Dutch counter-part, Baron Coehoorn, suggested, "Burn your powder and spare your blood." These scientific sieges were made possible, it should be noted, only by the organization and prodigious efforts of Louis's war minis-ters, father Michel Le Tellier and son François Michel Le Tellier, marquis de Louvois, to use the power of the state to maintain regular logistical support. Their development of fortress magazines and wagon convoys enabled Vauban to mount (and succeed in) his spectacular siege efforts.[48] This breakthrough in logistics has been hailed as a major advance in warfare, but in reality its primary impact was on siege armies and only minimally, if at all, on field armies or armies of observation.[49]

For field armies, war was circumscribed by conditions, not an absence of strategic thought. This period—from the mid-seventeenth century to the French Revolution—is known as the age of limited warfare, delineating it from the preceding dynastic and religious struggles and from the wars of nationalism that followed. The appellation "limited" remains accurate and historically useful, but only if one clearly under-stands what exactly was "limited" about war in this period. As it has been generally used, the term "limited war" translates as a war of limited objectives, but this is historical, geopolitical terminology from a more modern period and for the seventeenth and eighteenth centuries is relevant only to sieges or, possibly, in comparison with the later Revolutionary and Napoleonic Wars.[50] For instance, a corollary of the modern usage implies that limited wars are small wars, and that they result in lower numbers of killed, wounded, and captured,[51] but there were few limits in seventeenth- and eighteenth-century battle as the extraordinary casualty rates attest: at Blenheim (1704), the British lost 24 percent of their troops and the French 40 percent;[52] later, at Malplaquet (1709) Marlborough lost fully one-third of his army; and at the battle of Zorndorf (1758), Frederick the Great's army lost 38 percent of its strength while inflicting a 50 percent casualty rate on the Russians.[53] In comparison, at bloody Gettysburg in 1863, Robert E. Lee lost 30 percent of his Confederate troops to George G. Meade's loss of 21 percent of his Federal forces.[54] (To be sure, the number of overall civilian casualties was reduced compared with the bloodbaths of earlier wars, but noncombatants in a war zone still suffered greatly.) "Limited war" also suggests limits to the area of actual operations, yet the wars of the seventeenth and eighteenth centuries crisscrossed Europe and the Atlantic; in one war alone, fighting stretched from the Vistula to the Monongahela to the Ganges, which hardly qualifies as a limited war. As to "limited objectives," the supreme practitioner of war in this period, Frederick the Great, was restricted only by organic conditions, not by his monumental ambition. For this period, the sole limitations imposed upon warfare were those set by society, technology, manpower, and agriculture.

Unlimited or total war, such as that practiced by the Romans against the Carthaginians, was unimaginable simply because unlike the Romans, it was politically inexpedient and it was totally unfeasible— no European nation had the wherewithal to accomplish it. On the former point, balance of power politics never allowed one nation to gain the upper hand. Witness the British following the Seven Years' War. So total was their victory that in the 1775–83 conflicts, all Europe except Portugal was aligned against them. Regarding the latter issue, the socioeconomic foundation laid in this period later allowed for the mass armies of the Napoleonic Wars, but through the first two-thirds of the eighteenth century societal and economic development remained in its infancy, inadequate for total war though evolving. Field armies from the late seventeenth century became much larger than those of earlier wars, but they were still small by Napoleonic standards. (For instance, Gustavus had some 150,000 troops under arms, but most were dispersed guarding supply columns, fortresses, and tied down in sieges; his field army only numbered about twenty thousand men.)[55] In part this size differential stemmed from the fact that there were simply fewer people; the general European population began to experience significant growth only as the eighteenth century progressed. Without nationalistic fervor or a *levée en masse*, these professional armies, highly trained at a great cost in both time and money, attained the maximum size that manpower and logistical constraints allowed.

Logistics, how an army feeds and maintains itself in peace but especially at war, is important for an understanding of the military and society at any time but vital to a comprehension of the art of war in this period.[56] Presaging a Napoleonic adage, Frederick described an army "as a body that travels on its stomach."[57] Commanders unable to feed their troops lost control of them, and only Frederick's well-organized supply network kept his army intact, for not even Prussian discipline could have kept hungry soldiers from deserting. The root vegetables—the simple potato—that allowed Napoleonic armies to live off of the land were not yet staples of much European agriculture. Introduced from America, potatoes provided an excellent, accessible food source; nutritious, ready to be dug up when needed, and easy to cook, potatoes and other root crops allowed Bonaparte to maintain a small "tooth-to-tail" ratio, an indispensable part of his strategy.[58] Waterborne resupply and the fortress magazines (supply depots resurrected by Vauban on the Roman model) were only partial solutions, for they limited maneuver to the course of navigable rivers or to a specific, easily identifiable line of march. As Gustavus discovered in the Thirty Years' War, every time an army moved from its river or magazine supply lines, it did so at great risk. True, Marlborough boldly cut his communications (and supply line) on his advance to Blenheim; this epic march was made possible, however, by anticipating the Napoleonic strong-arm method of enforced requisitions. Writing politely to city leaders along his route of march, Marlborough "requested" that rations be readied for his troops. With a horde of hungry soldiers bearing down on their cities, wise mayors acquiesced. This form of resupply by extortion was common in Europe, and some seventeenth-century German forces even had a *Brandmeister* who threatened towns with the torch if food was not provided.[59] In revolutionary America, however, plundering and requisition by force turned local citizens against both British counterinsurgency operations and the Continentals.

The system of magazines and depots instituted by Louvois—marshaling the power of the French state to keep Vauban's siege armies in the field—revolutionized siegecraft, but the wagon convoys this system required taxed the transport system of the period. The only decent roads in Europe at this time were, for the most part, built by the Romans centuries earlier. To supply a field army even partially, much less regularly, by animal-drawn wagons at this time was impossible as the Americans discovered in their war. An army is a great, gaping maw, devouring supplies at an incredible rate even in camp, and the first commodity to run out was invariably fodder, the fuel of premechanized armies.[60] For example, in Louvois's time, an army of 60,000 men required some 40,000 horses for cavalry, artillery, baggage, and transport. Figuring the normal ration of two pounds of bread per man per day (120,000 pounds) not counting beverages and other foodstuffs,[61] and about twenty pounds of feed per horse per day (800,000 pounds), this army required an absolute minimum of *490 tons* of basic human and animal feed on a daily basis in order to remain in the field.[62] The want of a nail might lose a kingdom, but without fodder, a hundred nails would have done that famous horse little good.

Some commanders sought to overcome these difficulties through innovation. Perhaps borrowing a page from Alexander the Great and certainly anticipating Wellington, Oliver Cromwell sent his biscuit-toting soldiers into the roadless Scottish Highlands accompanied by packhorses loaded with cheese. Some armies imitated the Irish by having herds of cattle or sheep follow them on the march, but, at one pound of meat per soldier, Parker estimates that a 30,000-man army needed 1,500 sheep or 150 bullocks daily (animals were smaller then), which proved no small hindrance to maneuver, not to ignore the problems butchering and disposing offal created in camps.[63] For field armies of the late seventeenth and eighteenth centuries, logistical innovation had little effect, and movements of armies continued to be dictated in large measure by demands of "the belly."[64] If the warfare of this period appears "petty and unenterprising" to modern students of war, historian Martin Van Creveld points out, the reason had less to do with the "supposedly exaggerated dependence of armies on their magazines and convoys, but, on the contrary, the inability of even the best organized force" of the times, the French, "to do without local supply for practically all of its fodder" and most other provisions.[65] "It is not I who commands the army," Frederick wrote in disgust, "but flour and forage are our masters."[66] Forced to operate within these constraints, commanders had to utilize every scrap of ingenuity they possessed to obtain maximum efficiency from their limited manpower and resources.

What happened in this period was nothing short of a revolution in military thinking: instead of a purely tactical mind-set, generals were now forced by necessity to think and plan strategically. Herein lay the genesis not only of Napoleonic but of all modern warfare. Until this point, warfare retained something of a medieval flavor: armies marched and did battle, and the victor retained the field, garnered the laurels, and generally, the campaign—and the war—ended. Now, hampered by the organic limitations of their times, generals had to think ahead, detailing their objectives for an entire campaign (and even beyond) just as Alexander, Hannibal, and Caesar had done before them. It was not so much that the lessons of the past were rediscovered as much as that the necessity of limitations forced generals to employ extant knowledge to its maximum potential, and the works of Vegetius, Frontinius, Caesar, and others formed the core of this knowledge.

Admittedly, the very constraints that forced the Saxes and Fredericks to explore the limits of pre-Napoleonic warfare ensured that their strategic thinking would be fairly rudimentary compared with what followed, but they were breaking ground which had lain fallow since ancient times. In fact, Frederick, in R. R. Palmer's estimation, "embodied the utmost in military achievement that was possible in Europe in the conditions prevailing before the French Revolution."[67] Battle, of course, remained the ultimate decision, the decisive moment, the *dénouement* of war just as it had in the classical period, but if the study of the art of war taught anything to military men, they learned that the enemy's will could be broken without the cost of battles. Time and space became allies, and maneuver the means for opportunity. Then, and only then, with the enemy morally and physically weakened, confused, and out of supplies, was the opportune moment for a general to choose to do battle on a field of his selection. Unless an opportunity presented itself to destroy or seriously injure the enemy, why waste invaluable supplies and irreplaceable manpower when maneuver and stratagem worked equally well?

Here the lessons of the Great Captains of the past seemed to speak directly to the Turennes, Saxes, and Fredericks. Caesar stressed flexibility, mobility, mystifying and misleading the enemy to spare his own men, and imposing his will on his enemies by making them fight only when and where he wished to give battle. Caesar never strayed from his objective, although he adapted his operational strategy and battlefield tactics to conditions. "Every plan, therefore, is to be considered, every expedient tried and every method taken before matters are brought to this last extremity [battle]," Vegetius wrote. "Good officers decline general engagements where the danger is common [to both armies], and prefer the employment of stratagem and finesse to destroy the enemy as much as possible in detail and [to] intimidate them" without exposing their own armies to destruction.[68] (Or, as Sun Tzu had written some eight hundred years before, "To subdue the enemy without fighting is the acme of skill.")[69]

One ancient method of achieving this end was popularized by Frederick: the strategy of starvation. Vegetius advised that "[f]amine makes great[er] havoc in an army than the enemy, and is more terrible than the sword."[70] Simply stated, one moved an army into an area and let nature take its course. Very quickly, all provisions and fodder would be devoured, leaving a food- and forage-free zone which an opposing army crossed only at great risk. If the enemy did chance passing through such a barren wasteland, he was inviting a devastating attack; he would have used his meager reserve provisions in marching through the empty area and, now facing his opponents, would be unable to forage. "History knows many more armies ruined by want and disorder," wrote Cardinal Richelieu, "than by efforts of their enemies."[71] Vegetius reaffirmed this. "The main and principal point in war is to secure plenty of provisions," he advised, "and to destroy the enemy by famine."[72] When an army went into winter quarters, its cantonments were expected to be positioned on enemy soil. This deployment had twin benefits: valuable enemy provisions were consumed and the state saved considerable funds, no small thing when the upkeep of a nation's armed forces ingested some 40 to 50 percent of national expenditures even in peacetime and upwards of 80 percent during war.[73] Fighting an aggressive defensive war in the 1750s, which Frederick character- ized as the "defensive which turns into the offensive,"[74] he echoed Vegetius, stressing that the "greatest secret of war and the masterpiece of a skillful general is to starve his enemy. Hunger exhausts men more surely than courage," he advised his generals, "and you will succeed with less risk than by fighting."[75] When the enemy was more con- cerned with finding food than fighting, the propitious moment for battle had come.

But in order to march troops into an area so they could "outeat" the enemy and to maneuver them rapidly into battle required unearthing an ancient art that had been lost for centuries—marching in cadence. Rediscovering ancient lessons on the art of war, however, was not only a seventeenth- or eighteenth-century phenomenon. Very likely the ancient Romans read in Thucydides that the "Lacedaemians [marched] slowly and to the music of many flute-players placed among them, . . . in order that they might march up with even step and keeping time without breaking their order, as large armies are apt to do in going into battle."[76] Whether the Romans borrowed the idea of cad- ence from the Spartans, the concept was lost over the centuries. Mar- shal de Saxe of France may or may not have been the rediscoverer, but, in any event, he was its leading proponent. Since Roman times, armies were always accompanied by musicians, and Saxe wondered why. Was it to confuse the enemy? To enthuse one's own troops? Or did the Romans have another reason? Saxe discerned that the Roman legions employed drums and other instruments to keep time; increas- ing the time or tempo stepped up the speed of the march or charge. Now generals could experiment with dividing their forces, knowing that in so many hours one unit would be able to rejoin the other if it moved at a certain rate of march. Instilling march discipline cut down on straggling and desertion and, perhaps most significantly, allowed for the development of formational and intraformational maneuvering on the battlefield. For instance, instead of taking several hours, the deployment of marching troops into a line of battle could be accom- plished with a few, crisp, well-chosen commands.[77] As with the redis- covery of discipline or the introduction of the potato to European agriculture, this seemingly insignificant—to modern eyes—advance in the art of war actually had a major impact on both strategical and tactical operations, for it increased mobility and the control which a commander exercised over this troops. Cumulatively, these far-reaching advances transformed martial thought.

This intellectual advance in strategic thinking has often been misinterpreted. When armies joined in battle, destruction of the enemy as a cohesive force remained the primary objective. The subtle change which occurred was with the introduction of attrition not as a total strategy but as a means of inflicting casualties to weaken and outmaneuver an opponent; then, when one commander believed that conditions were favorable, the battle could be fought with a better chance of one's side winning. To use a sporting analogy in explanation, in a boxing match, one boxer pummels the other's midsection. Since both pugilists are well conditioned, the aim is not for the puncher to win this way but to tire his opponent, forcing him to lower his guard, thereby opening the way for a knockout blow to the head. Among the leading intellectual lights of the period writing on the art of war, Saxe's words, especially, have been misquoted or misused by historians specializing in other wars and periods to validate their own positions, or by those who employ Clausewitz as their guide to the past. "I do not favor pitched battles, especially at the beginning of a war, and I am convinced," go Saxe's often-quoted words, "that a skillful general could make war all his life without being forced into one."[78] Maneuver and "small engagements will dissipate the enemy," he advised, or in other words, attrition. "Nothing so reduced the enemy to absurdity as this method, nothing advances affairs better." Rarely quoted, however, are the words that followed this passage, which clearly show the Vegetian and classical influence on Saxe, which summarize much of the new strategic thinking, and which prove antithetical to some historians' portrayal of Saxe as a pseudo-proto-Jominian. "I do not mean to say by this that when an opportunity occurs to crush the enemy that he should not be attacked, nor that advantage should not be taken of his mistakes. But," the victor of Fontenoy added, "I do mean that war can be made without leaving anything to chance."[79] These were words of advice that Washington quoted or paraphrased time and again in orders and letters to his subordinates, and this Saxe, the Saxe of reality and not of modern historical misinterpretation, was one of the major influences on Frederick. It was obvious why. Fortune played too great a role in battle for an army (or a nation) to risk all on one hand of cards unless it had first stacked the deck by sapping the morale, provisions, and manpower of an opponent. "War is decided only by battles," wrote Frederick, "and it is not finished except by them. Thus they have to be fought, but it should be opportunely and with all the advantages on your side."[80]

Concurrent with (and, to a large measure, as a result of) the revolution in strategic thinking was a gradual sophistication in tactics. Field armies were streamlined as the massed phalanx-type formations devolved into smaller, more manageable autonomous units (like Roman maniples) for maneuver and into linear formations for battle. This stemmed, in no small part, from a strategic desire to increase mobility and from technical improvements in weaponry. Gustavus Adolphus reduced the weight and size of cannon, thereby creating the first true field artillery. The unwieldy matchlock evolved through several variants into the lighter, easily manufactured flintlock musket, which quickly became the standard infantry issue in the late seventeenth century. With an attached bayonet, it combined the pike's anticavalry defense with the musket's firepower. A further refinement occurred by 1700 with the European-wide shift from the plug bayonet (plugged into the muzzle, it precluded reloading) to the ring bayonet. At Blenheim, with only minor variations, Marlborough's troops were armed exactly as their great-grandsons serving under Wellington would be. On the battlefield, changes were slowly initiated—attack in echelon, nascent columnar formations, linear formations for added firepower— that would be perfected by Napoleon.[81]

Nevertheless, the range and inaccuracy of muskets, officerial perceptions of soldiers, and the command, communications, and control system of the period ensured a style of warfare that remained closer to the Imperial Roman army than to that of Imperial Germany. Doctrine actually forbade aimed fire; instead, fire by unit or line (volley fire) was the order of the day. After perusing many eighteenth-century English drill manuals, one historian observed that few illustrations pictured a soldier aiming while firing; the musket was firmly planted against their shoulders, but their heads remain erect, not sighting down the barrel.[82]

George Grant noted in his *The New Highland Military Discipline* (1757): "Any Commander that desires His Men to hold up their Heads when they fire . . . was never a Marksman himself; and in such Case, you may set Blind Men a Fireing as a Man that can see."[83] But this doctrine was not as foolish as it might appear to modern eyes, since doctrine was subordinate to the technology of the day. The eighteenth-century smoothbore musket—fired in volley in the heat, smoke, and noise of battle by drill-deadened, frightened men treated and loaded worse than packmules—geometrically lost accuracy over forty yards, hence regiments fired volleys, like a giant shotgun, figuring that enough concentrated lead would hit something. In Humphrey Bland's *Treatise of Military Discipline* (first published in 1727 and reissued many times), the military bible of revolutionary Americans, he suggests 60 paces as the *maximum* range of fire.[84] Several eighteenth-century field tests bore out his view. For instance, Frederick the Great trained his troops to fire rapid, not accurate, volleys, though one questions the supposed Prussian rate of five to six shots per minute on the battlefield.[85] At one test under the optimum conditions of a firing range, Prussian soldiers supposedly fired volleys at a six-foot-high sheet from 75 yards, achieving 60 percent hits; at 225 yards, this percentage dropped to 25 percent.[86] That the canny Prussians inflated the number of their hits is suggested by comparing their results against those of an English test in 1779. At 70 yards, "a battalion of excellent Norfolk Militia" hit their target only 20 percent of the time.[87] In another English test, a marksman fired a standard issue smoothbore "Brown Bess" musket at a one square foot target from Bland's suggested distance; he achieved 100 percent accuracy. Moving to 100 yards, however, this sharpshooter hit a *four* square foot target only 57 percent of the time. By comparison, a longbowman, firing at the second target also from 100 yards, hit it with 74 percent of his arrows.[88]

Military doctrine and poor-quality weapons were part of the problem, but additional factors must also be taken into account. For instance, among the problems affecting accurate and sustained fire on the battlefield were such things as poor-quality or improperly stored powder, dampness seeping into the firing mechanism, barrels and flints fouled by prolonged firing, poor-quality flints, and misshapen balls. Then, too, the human element must be allowed for.

Eighteenth-century battlefields were Dante's *Inferno* brought to life.

Black-powder weapons quickly filled the air with thick, cloying smoke. Shrieking horses, disembowelled by cannon fire and trailing their intestines, lent further discord to the noise, the "abattoir reek of split-open bodies, the foxy stench of bloody hair, and the roast-pork smell of gunners who had been blown up by their ammunition wagons."[89] Untested troops instinctively recognized this as hell, and veterans, remembering the grisly details of the last fight, were hardly reassured. What was called "cannon fever" or, now, battle fatigue sent thousands of men skulking along the fringes of the battlefield, seeking haven in spite of threats from officers and NCOs. Young subalterns carrying orders and information dashed about the field, often getting killed, losing their way, or forgetting their orders. In the firing line, the noise was deafening, the enemy unseen, and men often loaded and reloaded their weapons like automatons, packing four, five, or six charges down the barrel until, when fired, it exploded "like a bangalore torpedo."[90] Essential to loading a musket, ramrods were broken, bent, left in the barrel to be fired down range, all rendering the weapon unusable. No wonder that one historian has estimated that no more than 0.2 to 0.5 percent of all balls fired in volleys struck their targets.[91]

The overall effect created a battlefield that was much smaller and more confined than those of the Napoleonic era, thus increasing the need for both disciplined tactical organization and tactical maneuver. Once an army had maneuvered another onto a field of its choice and an order of battle set, the armies sometimes exchanged volleys and cannon fire, seeking not so much to damage one another as to test and to break each other's will. For actual assaults, however, one side had to close upon the other. Saxe posited that attacking troops should accept the defense's volley, then launch a bayonet charge at the quick step while the enemy frantically tried to reload, the attackers firing their weapons only in the following melee. (As Russian marshal Suvorov said, "the bullet misses, the bayonet does not.")[92] This created a problem for the defense: when to fire. The first round, loaded in the relative calm of prebattle with a clean barrel and sharp flint, was indeed, as Christopher Duffy describes it, a "precious resource." The Marquis de Quincy, writing in 1726, urged that troops should be instructed to hold their fire and suffer that of their enemy. "In normal circumstances a battalion is beaten once it has opened fire, and the enemy still has all its fire in reserve."[93] Frederick countered with this dictum: "Infantry relies upon firepower for the defensive, and the bayonet in the attack."[94] Until most of his veterans were killed off by the mid–Seven Years' War, Frederick had them attack with shouldered arms, so scornful was he of volley fire.[95] At twenty paces, "or better still, within ten," Frederick wrote, the attacking troops should give "the enemy a strong volley in the face. Immediately thereafter they should plunge the bayonet into the enemy's ribs, at the same time," he added, somewhat unnecessarily, "shouting at him to throw away his weapon and surrender."[96]

The origins of these tactics and the similarity with Roman warfare are obvious, whether they were consciously or unconsciously copied. A historian of the Roman way of war, F. E. Adcock, employing an interesting and illuminating analogy, described Roman battle tactics as the same "method advocated by Stonewall Jackson." Jackson summarized his tactical ideal thusly: "My idea is that the best mode of fighting is to reserve your fire till the enemy get—or you get them—to close quarters. Then deliver one deadly deliberate fire and charge."[97] Looking forward, Jackson's comments suggest that tactical innovation remained somewhat moribund through the American Civil War, in spite of the general usage of rifled muskets;[98] looking backward, it reflects how truly closer eighteenth-century battlefields were to the ancient past than to the twentieth century.

In his comments, Jackson, a student and teacher of military history, summed up much of the tactical doctrine of eighteenth-century warfare; in fact, he could have quoted from two of George Washington's favorite militarists with equal facility—Marshal de Saxe and Humphrey Bland. Bland, in particular, was quite influential on revolutionary American military thought, and his was possibly the first military book that Washington and many of his contemporaries read. Unlike many works of the period, Bland not only taught the evolutions or manual of arms but filled his treatise with commonsense military knowledge and clear tactical advice. For instance, Bland suggested that in an attack, at first the line of troops should march slowly in order to keep order and so that the "Men [were] not out of Breath when they come to engage." He advocated the Roman method of attack as did Saxe, Frederick, and, later, Jackson. If, after marching up to the enemy's position, his men had not been fired upon, an officer should have them deliver a volley, then immediately launch an attack "under the Cover of the Smoke, before [the enemy] can perceive it." The shock of a volley delivered at close range followed without delay by a bayonet attack should, Bland noted, ensure a successful assault. But, he cautioned, if you delayed the attack after firing your volley and gave "them Time to recover from the Disorder yours may have put them into, the Scene may change to your Disadvantage." Bland also concurred with other military men and writers, saying that "it being a received Maxim, that those who preserve their Fire the longest, will be sure to Conquer."[99]

This would be the general tactical doctrine which Americans borrowed heavily from to fight their Revolutionary War, adapting what they could or what they wanted to fit their needs. The essential problem faced by Washington and his subordinates in implementing this doctrine would be the absence of knowledgeable company-level officers and, especially, noncommissioned officers and disciplined troops. For reasons to be discussed in subsequent chapters, American political leaders in the early years of the war vehemently opposed the long-term enlistments so essential to building a disciplined army. Not until the later years of the Revolution did Washington have a core of veteran junior officers and NCOs around which to build an army and to fight the British regulars on anything like an equal basis.

For Europeans, however, and particularly the French, the aftermath of the Seven Years' War saw a great deal of tactical and overall innovation in the art of war. Following a war, any nation's military, victorious or not, should reassess the effectiveness of its doctrine in relation to the conflict just ended and the conflict to come. Defeat, especially, should force a nation's policymakers and military officers into doctrinal reappraisal which, in turn, should lead to reform. After their disasters of 1756–63, the French hotly debated what went wrong and what changes should be made in their doctrine. Following field trials in Normandy (1777–78), French expeditionary forces in America employed some of these innovations, effectively laying the groundwork for the successes of the Revolutionary and Napoleonic wars.[100] "With mapping, skilled staff officers, written orders, and a divisional structure," William McNeill writes, "the French created a framework capable of being fleshed out by the huge number of troops brought into service by the [French] Revolution." [101] The impact of this maelstrom of debate—books and pamphlets—was little felt by revolutionary Americans, however, for few of these works were translated and French-speaking and -reading American general officers were rare. General themes and some practical advice were no doubt transmitted by foreign officers on service in America, but as to their overall influence on what revolutionary Americans knew about war, it must be considered minimal.

Other, earlier Americans developed much of their practical knowledge of warfare from the lessons of the past and from Europeans such as Saxe and Frederick, just as the great Stonewall Jackson would do. But unlike most Europeans (especially the English) who mechanically copied Frederick's methods but failed to display Frederick's judgment, leadership, and flexibility, Americans borrowed only what they needed. These lessons were altered by the Americans' actual experience with war, their perceptions of these experiences, and necessity. It was not that Americans were especially astute in developing their military; rather, they had little choice. For as Europeans began rationalizing and professionalizing warfare, the colonists had, as always, to make do with what they had.

CHAPTER 6

———

The American Experience

Thoughts of war weighed heavily on the minds of early English settlers in North America. At any moment a hostile fleet might appear on the horizon or the stillness of a dawn could be shattered by war whoops. These threats to the settlements' very existence were genuine, and prudence dictated that the colonists take measures to defend themselves. That they did so, that in fact they prepared themselves militarily before they even landed, speaks much about these people.

The early colonists were products of a tumultuous, violent epoch in European history. Although the England that they sailed from was relatively pacific, to the aspiring colonists weapons of war were essential tools: they would no more have crossed the ocean without hoes or Bibles than have left their blunderbusses, crossbows, and pikes at home. Their understanding of war derived from fundamental and ancient sources and was influenced greatly by the seemingly endless ferocity of sixteenth-century Old World religious and secular strife, not the still-to-come Age of Reason. In the New World their ideas about war and the military were altered by and adapted to the exigencies of survival, circumstance, time and space, and their opponents. The transformation occurred so naturally and so smoothly that colonists scarcely perceived that they were modifying their Old Country ways.

The development of what became the American way of war was a continuously evolving process. Old World models were transfigured and shaped to fit practical colonial needs, needs dictated in large part by New World experiences. European advances in the art of war were eagerly studied, but not dogmatically followed in America, for that would have been impractical. As each colony developed something of its own character, the basic military establishment—the militia—mirrored the colony's evolving needs, hopes, fears, and growing complexity. With time, the children and grandchildren of the early settlers became less like their European cousins; no longer Englishmen, neither were they yet part of an overarching American culture. Rather, they had become provincial or colonial hybrids with differing institutions, traditions, concepts, identities, and ways of war.[1] When the professional British military began serving regularly in America beginning in the late seventeenth century, considerable discord ensued between these similar but different peoples. By that time, an indigenous colonial military culture was already well established, so the martial cultures of these two divergent peoples clashed. The colonists learned much about military matters from the regulars, but not all the lessons were positive. From this service, the manner in which the colonists viewed the regulars would be forever altered, and whether these impressions were wholly valid does not change the fact that they were widely and deeply held. Moreover, in response to the British military presence, the colonists' perceptions of themselves changed and began to further shape the idea of an American people, an American response, and an American military approach. These changing attitudes had much to do with the alacrity with which Americans dropped their plows and picked up their muskets in 1775.

Military considerations played an important, if varying, role in America from the founding of each colony. Before leaving Europe, colonial leaders recognized that the possibility of armed conflict in the New World was indeed real; omnipresent threats from external and indigenous enemies necessitated military preparedness. This need was clearly understood and unquestioned by the soon-to-be colonists. For it must be remembered that the decision to transport themselves, their families, and their possessions across the Atlantic to seek out commercial opportunities and to create new homes in the wilderness was not conceived on a whim. After all, the English colonies, as Samuel Eliot Morison sagely noted, were "founded consciously, and in no fit of absence of mind."[2] These colonists were intelligent, thoughtful people who prepared long and well prior to boarding ship. They certainly familiarized themselves with the considerable body of extant "promotional" or "travel" literature on the New World, for knowledge was perhaps their strongest weapon, and, having done so, they had a reasonably clear understanding of what they would need and what they might face.[3] Furthermore, they knew that England could offer little assistance; late sixteenth- and early seventeenth-century Britannia barely ruled the Channel and was only a shadow of the naval power it soon would become. Therefore, chance alone did not dictate that among the early settlers were numbered veterans of the Dutch and Irish wars: in Massachusetts, they served in an advisory capacity; in Virginia, they were leaders.[4] Ironically, so thorough was their preparation in addressing their defense requirements that recent scholarly interpretations have colored the early transoceanic migrations and colonial experience in a martial hue.

The initial successful settlements (at Jamestown, Plymouth, and Massachusetts Bay) were not the products of cross-Atlantic military assaults on hostile New World beachheads but colonizing efforts by civilians. Some scholars, however, observing how strong precolonial military preparations were and how much a part of the colonial ethos entwined with military affairs, have overemphasized the military aspects of English colonization, likening these nascent colonizing efforts to "an amphibious assault" and an "armed invasion."[5] Certainly late sixteenth-century (when the first unsuccessful English colonies were founded) and early seventeenth-century royal policymakers had hoped that the Virginia colony, for instance, would become a forward outpost "for the easie assaultinge of the Spanyards West Indies" and a friendly port of call "for the relievinge and succoringe of all shipps and men of warr."[6] From a geostrategic viewpoint, establishing colonies to threaten the northern flank of Spain's New World possessions made good sense. But as has been seen, these hopes would remain stillborn, for no European nation had the capability—specifically the funding— to accomplish such a task. Even Spain, with all the gold and silver of Peruvian and Mexican mines flowing into Bourbon coffers, found it impossible to quash a revolt in the Low Countries. Unlike the Spanish conquistadores who carved out an empire by force of arms, English settlers generally aimed at colonization: the creation of new communities and commercial ventures, all in harmony with the natives. True, this difference ultimately mattered little to dispossessed Native Americans, and economic exploitation (differing in degrees) played a significant role in the establishment and development of the new colonies. And, to modern eyes, that some colonists clanked ashore struggling under the weight of body armor and blunderbusses speaks more of conflict than harmony. But to cross the Atlantic to a New World without defensive weapons would have been the height of foolishness, and generally speaking, the colonists were anything but fools. The English were colonists first and then, only by necessity, part-time soldiers. Thus, as civilian-colonists whose only thoughts were of self-protection, their basic military establishment was defensive in nature and modeled upon the organization they knew best—England's local militia.[7]

The idea of a citizen-soldiery, lineally descended through the Saxons from the ancient Germanic *posse comitatus* (the power of the country) or war band, was an integral part of English tradition. Therein every able-bodied "free man above the age of fifteen, and under that of sixty" was considered a potential soldier, ready to do his part for God, Monarch, and Country (but, by law, not overseas) as part of the militia trainband.[8] This tradition was strongly held, and at its heart was the militia system. But the colonists only transplanted the idea of the English militia, not the practice. They could not, for the militia of the tradition no longer existed.[9]

Through mid-Elizabethan times, the militia served the English Crown long and well, but even as the first ships weighed anchor for the New World, its military role grew ever more diminished as the regular army slowly became professionalized. Since Europeanization of England's army lagged behind continental armies, the militia lingered on, but by the seventeenth century, for all intents and purposes and with possibly the sole exception of the city of London's trainband, its military role was nil. As is often the case, however, the tradition, or, more correctly, the myth of the tradition, strengthened with the actual institution's demise, ironically becoming more influential than the actual militia had ever been.[10] This concept was especially true among two groups: those who later perceived a large, professional standing army based in England as a real threat to civil liberties, and those who migrated overseas. The dearly held custom transplanted to America represented a tradition in the classical mold of free people dropping scythes and shouldering weapons to defend home and hearth, of rallying behind a natural leader to fight off the invaders, and then, the battle won, of going home to resume cutting hay. Little wonder that the earliest panegyrics to Washington, Israel Putnam, and other revolutionary heroes were replete with Cincinnatian imagery. As in republican Rome, no need existed for a professional army so long as a virtuous, well-armed, free citizenry stood guard, or so the tradition went. (And, by the eighteenth century, colonial Americans were the most heavily armed people in the world; not only did colonial law mandate owning and maintaining a firearm, but through the Revolution most colonials still shot for the table.)[11]

The simplicity and straightforwardness of the militia tradition masked the development of what became a fairly complex organism. As with any of the institutions built by colonial Americans, the militia system substantially differed from colony to colony, and it evolved by altering its form and mission to conform to changing realities. Generalizations about militia, therefore, are difficult to make, but within the early colonial period lies the genesis of American military thinking and of American thinking about the military. Therein, the attitudes, practices, and conceptual conflicts of the Revolution and beyond may be discerned in their infancy.

Of particular import, and arising early on, was the love-hate relationship Americans had with their military. As historian Marcus Cunliffe posits, the American military ethos "involves a wide range of attitudes and assumptions," including "many incompatible ideas"; thus, the ethos which evolved was "somewhat discordant."[12] These Euro-American colonists truly were a people of paradox. On the one hand, war was as integral a part of society as family or religion, so the need for a military arm was never questioned.[13] Colonials quickly responded when their communities faced immediate peril (such as in Virginia in the 1620s, New England in the 1630s and 1640s, and South Carolina in the 1710s) or when they fully understood why a particular action was necessary (the William Pepperrall expedition to Louisbourg, as one example). Those who did not come to arms for philosophical or religious reasons—Quakers and Anabaptists, for instance—were considered heretics.[14] Generally, colonists enjoyed the trappings of military service, the joviality of muster days, the parades, the pomp, and the enhanced sense of oneness, of community. Officerial rank was eagerly vied for since it was a fairly easy means of achieving status: once elected or selected, a man was "Colonel Washington" or "Captain Stark" for life (or until the next wartime promotion).[15] As in any society, some colonists actually found an avocation in wartime service. In war, such men rose to the forefront; they were the natural leaders, the John Masons, John Underhills, Benjamin Churches, and John Smyths, the true fighters for whom the danger and excitement of combat provided outlets for their inherent warrior ethos. These fighters did not necessarily make good soldiers, but in war, their actions inspired and lent courage to their less martial colleagues.

On the other hand, while colonials read a great deal about war and enjoyed things military, most generally lacked this truly warlike spirit (although after a few glasses of rum or port, most thought that they did), and the disciplined regularity any military requires—even the militia—was anathema to them. With exceptions, in the forest they remained civilians. For instance, Benjamin Church rebuked one unit for smoking while waiting in ambush. "But Capt. *Fullers* party, being troubled with the Epidemical plague of lust after Tobacco, must needs strike fire and Smoke it; and thereby discovered themselves."[16] For the most part, being a militiaman was as much a social function as membership in the Congregational or Anglican churches. Longfellow recalls the fate of most colonial weapons of war when he describes Miles Standish standing—

> . . . Ever and anon to behold his glittering weapons of warfare,
> Hanging in shining array along the walls of his chamber—
> Cutlass and corselet of steel, and his trusty sword of Damascus.[17]

Experience soon taught them that their carefully transported body armor and pikes, their European accoutrements of war, were good only for serving as wall decorations and links to martial myths. Most colonials never pulled their "trusty" swords down or if they did, they reshealed them as quickly as possible. Immediate threats demanded instant action, but then, when the immediacy of the danger was over, why linger about in camps, getting sick, being ordered about, when work aplenty waited at home. In the French and Indian War, British commander Lord Loudoun wrote the duke of Cumberland of these impatient Americans, "these Enthusiastical People," who "will undertake any rash thing, but if they do not get forward they immediately languish to go home," adding, "and when they grow Sick their hearts break and they Die."[18] To remain under arms after the threat had diminished or passed made no sense to practical colonials: seek out the enemy, fight them, and then go home. Later, when John Adams called for "a short and violent War" in 1777, he not only echoed Frederick the Great but also summarized an already long-held antimilitary attitude.[19] Colonials were always, at heart, impatient civilians, and as such they wanted a fairly immediate return on their investment of time, treasure, and blood.

When wars occur, most people desire a speedy resolution of the conflict, but from the decline of Rome until the late eighteenth century, few nations had sufficient economic-military power to score a decisive knockout in battle. Wars dragged on for years both on the Continent and in Europe's overseas possessions where, in particular, fires lit by European sparks smoldered long after the original blaze had been extinguished—much to colonial dismay.[20] Sometimes, however, wars were protracted by conscious strategic design born of necessity, not always understood by "cabinet practitioners," as armchair generals were styled in the eighteenth century.[21] Weak nations or aspiring nation-states fighting powerful opponents had to wage war with every scrap of ingenuity available to them, and time—outlasting and sapping their opponent's will—was often their best (and only) ally. Fighting for time, however, was not a strategy of attrition—although attrition played a significant role. This operational strategy, employed by the weak against the strong from time immemorial, forced a direct confrontation of the characters and wills of both national combatants, a psychological single combat such as that between the ideals and objectives championed by Britain and those of the united colonies from 1775–1783. The longer the weaker side persevered, its claim to legitimacy grew, its amateur generals and soldiers became veterans, and Britain's goals became harder to accomplish. Thus, following the defeat on Long Island, was born Washington's prudent strategy of September 1776 "to protract" the war, to "avoid a general Action, or put anything to the Risque, unless compelled by a necessity, into which we ought never to be drawn."[22] Here the influence of Frederick's and particularly Saxe's operational art on Washington was readily apparent. His deliberate strategic decision, along with his subsequent refinements of trading space for time—"luring the enemy in deep," to use a modern phrase,[23] until the time was ripe to move "to beat them up"[24] —disquieted impatient congressmen, and Adam's call for "a short and violent War" embodied their irritation. Long campaigns and long wars were not the American way in colonial times or thereafter.[25]

This lack of patience may be seen even in the earliest colonial days. The universal military training mandated by law in each colony portended the concept of "a nation in arms," but in reality, interest in mastering the manual of arms soon waned.[26] Mastering the seventeenth- or eighteenth-century manual of arms or evolutions required the discipline of endless repetitions, consuming time the colonists found themselves unwilling to sacrifice. Weekly militia drills gave way to monthly, then tri- and biannual musters, and the number of occupational exemptions from duty increased steadily.[27] Muster days became community social events, reminiscent of medieval fairs, with speeches and sermons, games, copious refreshments, and even some drill which one participant described as an "admirable burlesque of everything military."[28] In another Old World muster day tradition carried over the New, American militiamen scrupulously copied their English cousins who, contemporaries noted, at their annual or semiannual muster days proved more interested in drinking than drilling. "I could wish that our *Militia* instead of celebrating their Feasts to *Mars*," wrote Thomas Venn and John Lacy in 1672, "did not too much to *Bacchus* with carousing and drunkeness."[29] Even on the rare occasions when sobriety was the order of the day, little of military value could be accomplished with such infrequent, haphazard drilling. Every generation of colonials experienced a renewed enthusiasm for militia training, usually in response to a crisis, but when the crisis passed, so did the enthusiasm. This general decline of interest in actual service (corresponding, oddly enough, to increased study of the art of war), especially in the older, seaboard settlements, came about for two reasons.[30]

First, as the frontier pushed westward and local military threats declined, the demand for full mobilization decreased. Along the ever-changing frontier, the continuing need for military skills or at least a warlike *mentalité* was obvious. In the most settled areas, by contrast, basic military skills among militiamen atrophied at about the same rate that the illusion of their military prowess increased. But even when the coastline and the frontier were literally one, typical militiamen bore little resemblance to the mythological sharpshooting Indian fighters; Amerindians too regularly ambushed blundering militia units. The militia system, however, was not designed to produce military units ready for combat, but to ensure that men were armed and had a modicum of training;[31] generally, on the latter count, it failed miserably. In 1671 Virginia governor Sir William Berkeley optimistically reported to the commissioners of plantations in London that he could field eight thousand cavalry, but he was less sanguine about their proficiency.[32] In the French and Indian War, when Lord Loudoun came to America, he initially labored under the misconception that all colonial militiamen were skilled woodsmen and Indian fighters. But, as historian Stanley Pargellis noted, to his chagrin Loudon "discovered that the average provincial soldier knew less what to do if he fell into an ambush than a British regular, for [the militiaman] had never been trained, either in the discipline of arms or in frontier warfare."[33] Regarding weapons, unlike their European civilian contemporaries, most colonials knew how to load and fire a musket, but they traditionally employed aimed fire, not volley fire, much to the disgust of British officers. But what was doctrinal heresy to Europeans made sense to practical colonials. Shot and powder were expensive, and muskets were ineffective beyond the range when one could see the whites of an opponent's eyes; so until they had access to the seemingly unlimited (to them) Continental army powder and shot, most colonials were circumspect in their shot selection. But possession of a weapon, ability to use it, and hunting small game made a man neither a marksman nor a soldier (although Americans thought that they did), and what finally broke the power of Amerindian resistance were organized campaigns by regular soldiers—first British, then American—not disorganized backwoodsmen. Yet, as John K. Mahon notes, "folklore has enshrined the sharpshooting frontiersman as the conqueror of North America."[34] The myth grew to mammoth proportions during the Revolution when a few small companies of genuine sharpshooting frontiersmen from the Virginia and Pennsylvania backcountry (Morgan's and Cresap's riflemen, respectively) using rifled, not smoothbore, muskets earned the respect of British soldiers for their accurate long-range fire.[35] The talents of the few soon extended their attributes to the many just as it had in colonial times, and over time, the myth turned benchwarmers into stars.

Second, shortly after its creation, the colonial militia bifurcated. One branch was the general, universal service militia that became, by the mid-seventeenth century, a home guard whose role was more social and political than military: men could indulge themselves in their taste for military life without the harshness and boredom of campaigning. This branch of the militia with its clubby, political atmosphere produced that strain of democracy long associated with colonial militia. In trying to understand this division of the militia, modern historians sometimes ascribe to it roles that were simply beyond levels of colonial sophistication. This militia branch provided little that passed as basic military training even by seventeenth- or eighteenth-century standards, nor did it act as something of a contemporary replacement depot for units in the field. In fact, from a practical colonial perspective, sending the homeguard militia into the field made no sense, militarily or economically. For actual campaigning, colonial magistrates and legislatures found it less disruptive to a colony's economy, militarily advantageous, less distasteful, and, particularly important to thrifty New England Puritans, cheaper to field units of volunteers—some of whom, admittedly, were "volunteered," that is, drafted.

In part, the system borrowed from English practice; unless an emergency threatened, the "better" sort of people left military service to the "meaner" sort. This convention had a twin benefit for English magistrates in that they could meet military quotas and, at the same time, disburden "ye Parish of rogues, loyterers, pikars [petty thieves], and drunkards, and such as no other way can live."[36] Elizabethan soldier, playwright, and poet Barnabe Rich affirmed the magistrates'

habit of pressing "any idle fellow, some dronkerd, or seditiouse quari-
ler, a privy picker, or such a one as hath some skill in stealing of a
goose."[37] The late sixteenth- and early seventeenth-century English
practice of impressment for military service was immortalized in *Henry
IV*. Therein, the noted recruiter Sir John Falstaff confessed that he
had "misused the king's press damnably." He characterized his pressed
men as "the cankers of a calm world and long peace," but he took
umbrage when another made light of their appearance. "A mad fellow
met me on the way [back to camp]," he huffed, "and told me I had
unloaded all the gibbets, and pressed the dead bodies." Nevertheless,
as Falstaff acknowledged, his men were "food for powder; they'll fill a
pit as well as better."[38] Colonial American magistrates and legislators
did not rob the gibbets, sending "scapegallows" to war, although the
attitude of the "better sort" was not dissimilar.[39] The volunteer branch
of the colonial militia was generally made up of young men with
neither land nor families of their own. Communities as a whole or the
colonial legislatures shared in maintaining these volunteer units, offering land bounties, for example, in exchange for service in a campaign
—payable, of course, upon completion of the service. This contractual
form was scrupulously adhered to by both parties, including what the
volunteers judged as fair treatment—something British officers never
could fathom—or the volunteers went home. From this branch of the
militia, not the general militia, came the special companies led by
warriors such as Church and Underhill, raised for "good ruff worke,"[40]
and the contingents of colonials who served alongside the British in
the colonial wars—an important point that is too often ignored.[41]

The dual or bifurcated militia system, though not defined as such by
the colonials themselves, proved to be a practical arrangement for the
type of war fought in the colonies until the Revolution. Being volunteers with a land bounty awaiting them, the men were a bit more
enthusiastic about serving, and the colonies suffered minimal economic
and social disruption while they were off campaigning. Herein, however, lay the genesis of two American conceptions regarding the military which not only affected Revolutionary War military policy but
remained as legacies through modern times. (Both will be discussed in
greater detail in part III, and both came about from the bifurcation of
the militia.)

The first may be described as a slowly evolving change in attitudes. Although all white males[42] between sixteen and sixty (this varied somewhat from colony to colony) were considered as militiamen, the reliance upon volunteer units and the disintegration of the homeguard militia as an active and practical defense force fostered a separation between the community and its military. The actual volunteer soldiers were welcomed back to the community after their service; they were, after all, not regular, professional soldiers but colonial "Willies" and "Joes," neighbors again once they had turned in their uniforms for mufti. In fact, their land bounty provided them with the property to become full-fledged members of the community (one reason Continental soldiers later fought so bitterly for their back pay, and a point ignored by congressional and state legislators wedded to radical Whig ideology). But the concept of the "military" gradually delineated itself in colonial minds, even among seventeenth-century Pilgrims. When "the military system of Plymouth became more complex," colonial historian Douglas E. Leach writes, "the old group spirit and high morale of the early days correspondingly declined."[43] War increasingly became the "other guy's business," and in spite of innumerable militia exemptions, economic factors, high birth rates, and immigration continued to furnish a ready source of "other guys." As John Shy summarized, "every man's duty easily became no one's responsibility."[44] When the volunteers' contractual obligations were fulfilled, the units disbanded and little thought was given to the military until the next war, when the cycle repeated itself and the separation increased. The end of a truly universal military obligation—although the myth that every American male was ready and able to serve only grew stronger—would have an important and lasting effect on American conceptions of war.[45]

The second legacy was one of the great attainments of colonial and revolutionary America, actually anticipating events in England and preadapting colonial minds to eighteenth-century radical Whig ideology. This concept was civilian control of the military (which will be detailed later). To the colonists, the volunteer branch of the militia had all the advantages of a regular, "standing army," except that the "soldiery" remained under civil control, an important point with far-reaching implications. Civilian control of the military may be said to have begun, one historian suggests, when Captain Miles Standish was appointed by the civil authorities to head Pilgrim defensive efforts at Plymouth in 1621 (before that time, he had only served in an advisory capacity), but it developed into a tradition and hardened into an integral part of colonial society's relationship with its military.[46] When the volunteers contracted to serve the community for a specified length of time, the community in the form of its civilian council or legislature thus not only tied the military to it by legal and moral (and pietistic, for all volunteers took an oath—no small thing) means, but at the same time reinforced its own position as an official governing body. War— and enlisting men to serve in combat has a little something to do with war—is a legitimate act of a state, a *conditio sine qua non* of sovereignty. These perceptions would not be fully developed until the mid-eighteenth century, but even in colonial times they would have a major influence on developing American conceptions of war. In fact, when late seventeenth-century royal governors sought to impose a more military mien on the colonial way of governance, their ideas not only clashed with already long-held colonial practices and traditions but, to a large measure, helped further refine and define these concepts in colonial minds.

By controlling the purse strings, colonial councils and then legislatures scrupulously guarded against usurpation of civil control of the military (and those of the colonies) by royal governors when post-Cromwellian England began to take a more active interest in her New World possessions. Many of these late seventeenth-century governors were army officers (some 85 percent) who sought to manage the colonies along military lines.[47] An interpretative thesis advanced by historian Stephen Saunders Webb suggests that English policymakers in this period, by naming military men to royal governorships, were attempting to turn the colonies into military outposts or garrison-states. The desire and the will might have been there, but, again, the might required to impose that will was sorely lacking; economically, politically, socially, and militarily, England was simply wanting in all the essentials necessary for such a task, particularly in trying to make significant alterations in the already well-established sociopolitical culture of the North American colonies. In fact, attempts at imposing military rule by royal governors in New York and Massachusetts led to minor insurrections. In other colonies, North Carolina, for instance, "too much military authority was given to the governor. In consequence," one authority notes, "the quality of the militia system was determined . . . by the caliber of the governor," which was not always large.[48] The governors' efforts generally failed because of colonial fears of both a professionalized military and excessive concentration of power, because of their inability to wrest appropriations from the legislatures (policy is, after all, what is funded),[49] and because American colonials were not easily regimented. Governance—civilian or military—as perceived by colonists long steeped in biblical and political-philosophic thought depended upon a personal concord of the governed with their governors. Perhaps not as well articulated as John Locke's theory, the concept of a covenant or compact in its general religious-political-legal sense was well understood by colonists outside of New England. If royal authority overstepped its legal and moral grounds, it was meant to be questioned, then and later. "[A] licentiousness, under the notion of liberty, so generally prevails," lamented Cadwallader Colden to Lord Halifax in 1754, "that they are impatient under all kind[s] of superiority and authority."[50] Also, a sense of possessiveness or pride existed among the colonists regarding their infant institutions. Out of a wilderness, after all, they had established a new society, erected systems of government, and delineated the military's role in their society, all on their own, and English efforts to run roughshod over these colonial institutions were viewed with a displeasure that would grow to anger.[51]

An essential part of the evolving colonial and new American system —civilian control of the military—was a prerogative that was zealously protected, even more so following the governors' attempts to gain control. In the northern colonies control was exercised on the town level, where councils sought to control most aspects of human behavior; in the southern colonies, militia fell under county, then colonial jurisdiction. In 1638, for instance, when Bostonians innocently wanted to create a volunteer artillery company, fears of Praetorianism among the Bay Colony's leadership caused immediate controversy. The suspicious magistrates objected vociferously, noting "how dangerous it might be to erect a standing authority of military men, which might easily, in time, overthrow the civil power."[52] They eventually relented, but only after carefully determining that the commonweal would not be harmed. Even the democratic election of militia officers, a system that later drove Washington to curse, offended the sensibilities of John Winthrop, who perceived that vying for office encouraged unbridled ambition (Caesarism) and that too much democracy could prove harmful, a belief equally shared by Washington.[53] If the competition and factionalism continued, Winthrop caustically remarked, then the people of Massachusetts should "take up the rules of Matchiavell, and the Jesuits, for . . . a kingdome or house divided cannot stand."[54] Unanimity existed over how the military would be employed, but doctrinally it differed radically from what was occuring across the ocean. For as attempts were made to rationalize seventeenth-century European warfare, war in the New World increased in ferocity.

It is often forgotten, but the initial settlement of America took place concurrently with the Thirty Years' War (1618–48). In turn, this war was immediately preceded by the bloody wars of religion (which it partially encompassed) and followed by—of especial interest to the colonists—the turmoil of the English Civil War. Thus, the practical concepts of war and warfare held by colonials when they set foot in the New World (the current doctrine, so to speak) were not derived from an enlightened, rational age but from a period of extreme and seemingly endless violence. Attempts at a rationalization of warfare to curb the military excesses loosed in the Thirty Years' War came later, in the Age of Reason. This principled form of warfare, though certainly not unknown to the early settler in general terms, would only begin to have its minimal impact on European war by the late seventeenth century.[55] When colonial European and Native American relations changed from harmony to conflict and war threatened the settlements' very existence, the colonists did not ignore the influence of European war as some have suggested, devolving into a primordial barbarism.[56] Rather, in the manner in which they actually fought— albeit brutal by modern standards—the colonists were very much in accord with current European ethics and practices.

The hardy men and women who pitched and yawed across the ocean in small, leaky ships were tough products of violent times: death and suffering from childbirth, disease, and violence formed a part of everyday life. This point is essential to grasping their seemingly paradoxical nature: while their remarkable attainments in creating communities and adapting political and educational systems to the wilderness elicit deserved admiration, these same sensitive, literate people executed their fellow colonists for shirking work and for practicing witchcraft. To a large measure, this dichotomy reflects a modern perspective, as does, to an extent, labeling the colonists as paradoxical in character. Yet, within themselves, these seemingly incompatible, discordant themes (gentleness versus brutality, education versus superstition) were harmonized by the reality of their existence and times.

In a period when life expectancy was little more than half of what it is today, as was the case in the Chesapeake region, human life did not hold the same value it does in modern times. Death and dismemberment (or both) were common punishments for crimes, and running a redhot poker through a blasphemer's tongue met with general approval.[57] Only the physically and morally strong survived crossing the Atlantic, building shelters and creating farms, and the seasoning required to withstand New England winters or Chesapeake and Carolina fevers. The colonists came to the New World thinking that they could convert the Native Americans not only religiously but culturally, and while a great deal of intercultural exchange took place, violent clashes between the cultures also occurred.[58] When this happened, these tough people, appalled that Amerindians waged war on them regardless of gender or age, gave no thought to turning the other cheek.[59] The colonists were Old Testament Christians and their God was "Yahweh, a mighty man of battle."[60] They were believers in an eye for an eye and then some, and with God at their side, they answered Amerindian terror with a small-scale version of "total war" in the forests.[61]

That course of action was their only prudent choice if they wished to survive, for like many other primitive peoples worldwide, Amerindians were superb guerrilla fighters. Their tactics of stealth, surprise, and terror, combined with a consummate knowledge and use of their native terrain and a strong warrior ethos, made them fearsome enemies, especially to unskilled, ill-disciplined, civilian-militiamen whom they routinely outwitted and butchered. "[T]hey are lustie Souldiers to see to and very strong, meer *Hercules Rusticuses*," wrote one colonist in 1675 describing the native foe, "their fights are by Ambushments

and Surprises, coming upon one another unawares."[62] In the early
years of settlement, the colonists were generally burdened by arms
and equipment more suitable for a European high-intensity warfare of
set-piece battles than the low-intensity, guerrilla-like conflicts of America.
Even after colonists mounted their armor and blunderbusses on their
walls and adopted light muskets and certain Amerindian tactics, the
typical militiaman was still no match for the skilled native warriors,
although on occasion colonial ingenuity rose to the fore.[63] Discovering
a path used by raiding Amerindians, some colonists took three doors
and drove nails "as sharp as awl blades" though them, and placed the
doors on the trail. At least for one night, these Puritan "pungi stakes"
prevented a surprise attack.[64] For the most part, however, frustrated
by Amerindian guerrilla tactics, their refusal to stand and fight, and
having strong motives for revenge, colonials had little alternative in
their fight for self-preservation but to try and destroy the Indian as a
people.

   This strategy, born of equal parts vengeance, self-preservation, and
fear, actually reflected a great deal of courage on the part of the
colonials. Taken separately, the Amerindian and the New World forest each loomed menacingly in the colonial mind; together, they made
every crossing of the treeline a sphincter-tightening adventure for the
colonists. Such was their fear that only the most dire threat to their
very existence would make them venture from behind wooden pali-
sades. From a modern historical perspective, the threat may seem to
have been overblown, but to the colonists it was very real indeed. In
Virginia and in New England, colonists began attacking native villages, "Cutteinge downe their Corne, burneinge their howses, and
Sutch lyke," killing men, women, and children.[65] To be sure, racial
and cultural animosity and religious fervor probably fueled their actions; to many colonials these native warriors were "salvage & brutish
men," "cruell, barbarous & most trecherous,"[66] and later even their
almanacs urged them on: "March out brave Soldiers, now the Season's
good,/And make your Hatchets drunk with Indian blood."[67] Moreover, the colonials' very amateurishness and lack of discipline offered
no check on their vengeful fury, for while even disciplined troops can
lose control in the heat of battle, ill-disciplined, untrained troops—
usually the first to run when fired upon—are generally the most cruel,

especially with noncombatants and prisoners of war. But colonial attitudes and the way they waged war against the Amerindians primarily stemmed from two influential examples, one indirect and the other direct, and both rooted in the colonists' European heritage.[68]

Brutality and violence go hand in hand with war; after all, when reduced even beyond any Clausewitzian dictum, war is people killing other people. Politically, once a nation imposes its will upon another, the war is over. Put another way, when one nation's troops have killed enough of the enemy's troops, the enemy gives up. Brutal, but simple. Until the wars of religion, warfare in Europe had for the most part been between like societies, so rules of slaughter were mutually agreed to by opposing sides. These niceties were totally ignored, however, in two instances: when Christians fought one another over religious differences and when the Europeans waged their holy wars against non-Europeans (against Moslems, for instance, every war was a holy war) or those Europeans who were considered uncivilized. Then, warfare degenerated to its lowest form, pure slaughter with no quarter allowed.[69] With the threat of Turkish invasion hanging over Europe through the late seventeenth century and the ongoing religious strife, warfare of this sort had become all too commonplace, and it became yet another tradition of Western civilization carried over to the New World. But more specifically, the policy colonials employed, the strategy, the tactics, and even their attitudes toward people different from themselves, were influenced by and, to a large measure, borrowed directly from English pacification measures successfully tested in Ireland.

For specific examples and guidance on how to defeat their wily aboriginal opponents, the colonists borrowed a page from the way of war that they knew the most about—sixteenth- and early seventeenth-century English warfare in Ireland. Admittedly, on the surface this sanguine method of pacification or colonization appears bereft of any thought, for the brutality and terrorism employed by English commanders in Ireland certainly matched or exceeded the worst of the Thirty Years' War. In reality, however, the strategy was carefully planned and methodical, one born of frustration and need, reasons all to familiar to the threatened colonists, some of whom had considered colonizing Ireland before deciding on America. After all, for people at home in the classical period, for whom historical precedence meant useful knowledge, thinking in time was nothing knew. Faced with an opponent who in many ways resembled the "wild Irish," the North American colonists, partially led and advised by veterans who had learned war in Ireland, adopted a method of warfare which fitted nicely with their own overarching need for self-preservation.

The impact and influence of sixteenth- and early seventeenth-century English colonization efforts in Ireland upon the colonial ventures in North America were considerable.[70] In so many ways, Ireland was both the proving grounds and the inspiration for the successful colonization of North America. Many of the leading lights behind seventeenth-century English colonizing efforts in the New World either were involved in Irish colonization efforts or had fought there. Those among the Virginia Company, to cite but a few, included Lord Baltimore, Lord George Carew, Lord Arthur Chichester, and Sir Dudley Digges, and in New England, Indian fighters such as Fernando Gorges and John Mason earned their spurs in Ireland.[71] The contemporary literature generated by English attempts to colonize Ireland and to subdue the Irish was vast, and it strongly influenced the preconceptions of and the behavior toward Native Americans by seventeenth-century Anglo-colonists.[72]

Anyone reading the travel literature of the period—as the future colonists avidly did—is struck by the analogies between the wild Indians and the wild Irish. These similarities were such, noted historian Howard Mumford Jones, "that the English experience with one wild race conditioned their expectation of experience with another," a telling point.[73] Admittedly, much of this literature was embellished to ensure greater book sales or to entice aspiring colonists, but this "false advertising" actually heightened its impact on readers. Typical of this literature was the Englishman George Turberville, writing in 1568, who compared the wild Irish with the wild Russians:

> Wild Irish are as civil as the Russies in their kind,
> Hard choice which is the best of both, each bloody, rude, and blind.[74]

Writers spent considerable words delineating between correct English morals and those of the Irish and Amerindians. "[T]he wild Irish," wrote a contemporary of Henry VIII, "as unreasonable beasts, lived without knowledge of God or good manners, in common with their goods, cattle, women, children, and every other thing," adding that "in such wise that almost there was no father which knew his son, nor no daughter that knew her father."[75] Daniel Gookin, writing in 1674 about the Native Americans, was not alone in suggesting that they acted much the same as the Irish, the men divorcing their wives frequently to take up with others, and their wives doing the same thing.[76] Even by 1560, as historian David Beers Quinn writes, the "use of the Irish as the standard of savage or outlandish reference was well established," and in reading the travel material, one may substitute "Indian" for "Irishman" (and vice versa) and find almost identically written descriptions of Native Americans (Indians wore clothes like "Irish trouses," "Irish mantles," and their mournful cries over someone's death were likened to "Irish-like howlings" [keening].[77] In Virginia, one contemporary wrote that the Native Americans sleep "stark naked on the ground from six to twenty in a house, as do the Irish.").[78] In fact, since the Irish were long considered barbarous and wild in English literature, they provided English writers with a model for describing these new wild people, the Amerindians. After all, writes historian James Muldoon, the "Irishman with his long, flowing hair, outlandish clothing of skins or roughly woven cloth and unintelligible language, was as exotic a creature in the streets of London as a native of China or America would have been."[79]

In the sixteenth century, common knowledge held and long experience showed that Englishmen settling in Ireland soon succumbed to the inviting leisure-oriented, free and easy lifestyle of the Irish, becoming more Irish than the Irish; this fear had its corollary among the colonists who were so fearful of colonists "going Indian" that they generally refrained from utilizing Indians to fight Indians.[80] In Virginia, those colonists who "went native" were treated "in a moste severe manner" by Sir Thomas Dale, a veteran of the Irish wars. He "cawsed [some] to be executed, some he appointed to be hanged, some burned, some to be broken on the wheels, others to be staked, and some to shott to death."[81] Well aware of the problems encountered by the Virginia colony, New England settlers sought, at once, to proselytize to the Americans and to prevent all but officially sanctioned exchanges between the two cultures. Thomas Morton, who wrote in 1637 that the natives "are accustomed to build them houses, much like the wild Irish,"[82] so exercised Plymouth's leaders by his hedonistic cavorting with the natives that they whipped him and drove him from the colony. Such were Elizabethan fears of Englishmen metamorphosing into Irishmen that an ordinance of 1571 outlawed many aspects of Irish culture, from manners and customs even to clothing; by halting Irish customs by fiat, it was also hoped that the natives would become more like their masters.[83] But it was the English military experience in Ireland that not only had the greatest influence on colonial-Native American relations but also highlighted the essence of both conflicts.

To the English in Ireland and America, the inherent difficulty with the Irish and the Amerindians was certainly exacerbated by racism, but at its heart were cultural differences; it was, in fact, the age-old struggle between herding and hunting peoples and farming peoples, the latter seeking to impose their will on the strongly resisting former. In Ireland, English efforts to somewhat peaceably eradicate Irish culture and transform the native herdsmen into English-like—but never fully accepted as "English"—tillers of the fields failed miserably. Fierce Irish resistance, and particularly a hit-and-run style of war, created frustration and fear among the English who, in turn, responded savagely. For the sixteenth-century English, Ireland, one contemporary noted, "may well be called the Englishman's grave,"[84] yet, while many English lost their lives in combat, terrorist raids, and reprisals, the Irish toll was uncountable.

Extreme brutality became the norm in English attempts to suppress Irish resistance, and no safety existed in age or gender. English commanders of the late sixteenth century starting with Sir Humphrey Gilbert (who, too, had close ties to American colonization) concluded that the Irish lifestyle and culture was so intertwined with the Irish way of making war that the only way to resolve the conflict was to attack the Irish people themselves, not just the warriors. In modern terms, the phrase "cultural genocide" might be an accurate descriptor. After all, Irish life, culture, and warfare revolved around their "pastoral, transhumant way of life" and their herds of cattle or creaghts; wealth was not only measured by these cattle but the creaghts provided Irish warriors with a supply system that could follow them anywhere and one that the Irish fought for "as for their altars and families."[85] Thus, when Gilbert "killed manne, woman, and child, and spoiled, wasted, and burned, by the grounde all that he might," he effectively cut off the warriors from all support, including moral. "First the men of warre could not bee maintained without their Churles, and Calliackes [old women], or women, who milked their Creates [creaghts], and provided them with victualles, and other necessaries. So," he continued, "that the killyng of their [supply network] by the sworde, was the waie to kill the menne of warre by famine," warriors whose skill at evading the English until they could be ambushed was well-known.[86]

Like others before him, Gilbert intuitively recognized the psychological value of terror. He cut off the heads of the Irish men and women who were killed each day, and "laid [them] on the ground, by eche side of the waie leadyng into his owne Tente." When local people came to plead with him to spare their homes or families, they had to pass up this grisly pathway, this "lane of heddes, which [Gilbert] used *ad terrorem*, . . . [for] did it bryng greate terrour to the people, when thei sawe the heddes of their dedde fathers, brothers, children, kinffolke, and freends."[87] Gilbert was not alone in this practice. One of his fellow officers reported that he was able to identify formerly unknown Irish rebels because "I have their heads in camp," a surefire means of identification.[88]

Gilbert's strategy had a short-term, localized effect, but pacification of Ireland remained incomplete, and the cycle of war continued until Charles Blount, Lord Mountjoy, employed a similar policy on a much broader scale. Before Mountjoy's arrival, the English had undertaken a war of posts—mutually supporting strongpoints—but this strategy failed to interdict the highly mobile, marauding Gaelic warriors. "[T]hose holds and garrisons being ever weak and wretched," a writer noted disgustedly in 1599, "and serving just to as much purpose, as he that should endeavour to catch the wind in a net."[89] Pursuit was futile and often deadly, for the Irish were masters at melting into the woods or bogs, "knowing [that the English] cannot or indeed dar not follow them."[90] In words as easily applicable to seventeenth-century colonial frustration with Amerindian tactics, one contemporary wrote: "For we see by manifold experience, what madness it is for a . . . General to lead royal forces against naked rogues in woods and bogs, whom hounds can scarce follow, and much less men." The Irish, like the Amerindians, were perceived as not being like other men, but more like animals, or subhumans, subsisting on grass and shamrocks in any weather with neither clothing nor shelter to cover them. "It is impossible to defeat them at once, than to destroy so many wolves and foxes; the [Irish] may be effected by tract of time and means convenient, but not to be attempted by plain force in the open field," for they had "dens, coverts and labyrinths inextricable, for their succors."[91] The frustration of Increase Mather in 1675 about Amerindian guerrilla tactics was equally applicable to any English commander in Ireland of the 1590s. "Every swamp is a castle to them, knowing where to find us; but we know not where to find them." Or the complaint of the New England preacher: "[The Indians] doe acts of hostility without proclaiming war; they don't appear openly in the field to bid us battle."[92] In Ireland by the time Mountjoy arrived in 1599, the fear engendered by these warrior in the minds of the English soldiers was such that "they had as lief go to the gallows as to the Irish wars."[93] Mountjoy opted for a famine strategy that was in fact a scorched earth policy to force the mobile Irish into set-piece battles, in which English firepower and discipline stood a better chance. This was Gilbert's strategy writ large. The policy was officially approved, for it was thought that "[w]hen the plough and breeding of cattle shall cease, then will the rebellion end."[94] Mountjoy and his deputy, Sir (later Lord) Arthur Chichester, relied on the twin tactics of deforestation and destroying the Irish supply system, burning homes and villages, and slaughtering both the Irish and their livestock indiscriminately. "We spare none of what quality or sex soever," Chichester reported, "and it hath bred much terror in the people."[95]

The effect of this strategy was soon felt on the Irish, and contemporary descriptions of these sordid events further reinforced the literary theme of Irish barbarism and savagery. Chichester, reports Fynes Moryson, writing in 1617, "saw a most horrible spectacle of three children . . . all eating and gnawing with their teeth the entrails of their dead mother." Old Irish women (*calliackes* or *cailleachea*) were accused of luring young children to campfires, then killing and eating them.[96] Accusations of cannibalism, the depth of savagery, were common in the English literature on Ireland and were incorporated into later descriptions of Amerindians. The Native Americans were described as cannibals just like the "Heathen-*Irish*, who used to feed upon the Buttocks of Boyes and Womens Paps; it seems it is natural to Savage people to do so."[97] That the Irish reciprocated with terror for terror upon English soldiery and civilians there can be no doubt, just as the Amerindian way of war spared few colonials. But in the description of Irish atrocities committed against the English one may substitute "Indian" for "Irish" and observe the similarities. "[I]nfants were taken from the nurses' breasts, and the brain dashed against the wall; the heart plucked out of the body of the husband," went one account of Irish terrorists, "in the view of the wife, who was forced to yield the use of her apron to wipe off the blood from the murderer's fingers."[98] Just as the idea of colonizing Ireland played no small part in the settlement of the North American colonies, so, too, did these widely circulated descriptions influence the colonists' attitudes toward the Native Americans in both peace and war. The cruel but effective strategy of Mountjoy was carried across the Atlantic where it continued as the primary strategy against the Amerindians (through the nineteenth century).[99] For as Howard Mumford Jones suggested: "The doctrine that the only good Indian is a dead Indian first took shape in the belief that the only good Irishman is a dead Irishman."[100]

Wars against the Amerindians were heavily mythologized in the colonial psyche, and subsequently, the myth and the practice were assimilated as part of the American military tradition. Conveniently forgotten or ignored was the fact that the most successful punitive raids on the natives' villages and crops were carried out by carefully organized expeditions, especially in the eighteenth century, first by British and then by American regulars.[101] And even then these units were often bloodied in combats with the native warriors unless the invaders were accompanied by other Amerindians. Nonetheless, the success of these punitive expeditions against unfortified villages and of the bifurcated militia system had enormous implications for the American way of war in the Revolution and even beyond. In colonial minds, the correctness of the choice of militia as the primary military establishment and the employment of basically untrained, ill-disciplined volunteers for expeditionary forces was affirmed. By 1775, both mythology and, to an extent, brutality toward nonwhites were well-entrenched features of America's military culture. As early as the late seventeenth century, however, colonists had begun to receive a taste of a different type of war, a European warfare distinctive by its discipline, organization, and pace as English forces began serving regularly in America. This would add to colonial knowledge, but again would only affirm the superiority of the militia tradition.

The colonists learned a great deal from serving alongside their cross-Atlantic cousins, but as illuminating as these experiences were, to colonial eyes the British military was often cast in a poor light. From the late seventeenth century, European power struggles regularly spilled over into the New World. Colonists found themselves fighting wars in which their sons were killed and societies disrupted for reasons that were never clearly understood; these were the king's wars, after all, not theirs, although in many cases colonists bore the brunt of Old Country policies.[102] John Talcott of Connecticut summarized the feelings of many colonials when he wrote Sir Edmund Andros in 1687, hoping that "we may not be engaged in a bloody war for ye may'tey-'ing [maintaining] litigious boundaryes twixt England and French . . . for the sake of a bever trade."[103] Whitehall and Versailles manipulated the Indians (who, in turn, shrewdly played the Europeans off against one another), pitting one tribe against another and against their enemies' colonial populations. Once motivated to war however, these warriors proved difficult to control. In enlightened Europe, where nascent international law combined with depleted treasuries to have some effect at least in ending wars, treaties meant a cessation of hostilities. In America, wars often ran together, forming a seemingly endless low-intensity conflict with no beginning or end, only intermittent pauses. Talcott, a veteran of the Indian wars, lived in fear of another, "[t]he old proverb being true, the burnt child dreads the fire."[104]

European treaties, and Old World political-diplomatic machinations in general, confused and angered colonials. Unschooled in geopolitics and balances of power—but soon to learn—colonists could not grasp why they should surrender a Louisbourg, captured at the cost of colonial blood, to exchange it for a Madras in India, simply to satisfy treaty stipulations drawn up in Europe.[105] Growing more politically sophisticated in the 1750s and 1760s and becoming versed in the radical Whiggery of *Cato's Letters*, colonials would come to regard the giving up a Louisbourg as further proof of ministerial duplicity and corruption. Writing of earlier "ministerial" wars, equally applicable to the present in colonial minds, *Cato's* authors described them as "Ridiculous, expensive, fantastical wars, to keep the Minds of Men in continual Hurray and Agitation, and under constant Fears and Alarms." Peace, Trenchard and Gordon suggested, would only come at the whim of ministers who delivered up strongholds to the enemies for trifles to enhance their "domestick Designs."[106]

Colonists, who still considered themselves loyal subjects of the Crown, also could not understand why the English treated them so shabbily, not as fellow Englishmen but as inferiors. "The Americans," General James Wolfe charged, "are in general the dirtiest, the most contemptible, cowardly dogs that you can conceive," and his attitude was not unusual.[107] The English haughtily ignored established colonial practices, tried to run roughshod over the legislatures, and generally derided colonial military experiences learned over time at great cost. Some thirty years after Edward Braddock's costly defeat in the Pennsylvania woods (1755), George Washington still lamented the Britisher's failure to heed his advice. Serving on Braddock's staff as a volunteer gentleman, Washington tried to educate the veteran of the Dutch wars "to the mode of attack which, more than probably, he would experience from the *Canadian* French, and their Indians on his March." Braddock was so dogmatically wedded "in favr. of *regularity* and *discipline* and in such an absolute contempt were *these people held* [French-Canadians and Indians], that the admonition was suggested in vain."[108] Colonials were considered riff-raff by many officers and were assigned the most menial tasks. What was even more demeaning, the highest-ranking colonial officer had to obey orders from the youngest subalterns bearing royal commissions, commissions denied to almost all native-born colonials, a situation so frustrating to young Washington that he resigned and returned to planting. In part, English attitudes mirrored what J. A. Houlding called a national and cross-class "contempt for foreigners," which included the colonists.[109] Also, for Englishmen from the late 1600s, foreign service of any sort "was universally loathed," and "Scots and Irish [soldiers] were sent out in [their] place."[110] Of course, to be fair, English officers treated all auxiliary, non-English troops alike, be they Highlanders, Irish, Germans, or colonials; that is, as expendables.[111]

Colonials possibly could have accepted this abuse had the English not been so prone to failure, for victory is the greatest salve of all. But over eighty years of Anglo-American combined operations were marked by one fiasco after another, and colonial opinion of English military ability declined steadily. Even Wolfe's triumph at Quebec never blotted out memories of Braddock's ill-fated campaign or the slaughter of General James Abercrombie's men at Ticonderoga (1758). A song from 1776, "The King's Own Regulars," kept the remembrance fresh.

> To Monongahela, with fifes and with drums,
> We marched in fine order, with cannon and bombs;
> That great expedition cost infinite sums,
> But a few irregulars cut us all into crumbs.
>
> It was not fair to shoot at us from behind trees,
> If they had stood open, as they ought, before our great guns, we should
>   have beat them with ease,
> They may fight with one another that way if they please,
> But it is not *regular* to stand, and fight with such rascals as these.[112]

The virtues—dogged determination, stubbornness, and iron discipline —that enabled England to suffer defeat after defeat but ultimately win wars were not especially admired by colonials. To them, the English were pigheaded, intransigent, and, with a few notable exceptions, incapable of adapting their dogmatically held doctrines to the exigencies of war in America.

Admittedly, several English and foreign-born officers in royal service perceived that war in the colonies little resembled that on the European continent.[113] "To act in a country cultivated and inhabited, where roads are made, magazines are established, and hospitals provided," wrote the Swiss-born Henry Bouquet, "where there are good towns to retreat to in case of misfortune," was a way of war in which surrender meant being accorded the honors of war. Not so in the New World, he advised. There, war is "a rigid contest where all is at stake, and mutual destruction the object." America, wrote Bouquet who, along with General John Forbes, encouraged a young Virginian named Washington to read and study the art of war, was a "vast inhospitable desart, unsafe and treacherous, . . . where victories are not decisive, but defeats are ruinous; and simple death is the least misfortune which can happen" to a commander.[114] But the Bouquets, George Howes, and Wolfes who learned from their martial experience in the New World, who combined the discipline, firepower, and organization of the European art of war with the stealth, mobility, and flexibility of thought and action so necessary in America, who led the combined Anglo-American forces to victory, these officers quickly saw most of this knowledge lost to the "friction of peace" between the end of the French and Indian War and the Revolution.[115] Moreover, in terms of influence, the martinents who ignored the vagaries of American weather, keeping their troops in high-stocked woolen uniforms in the summer heat, bearing loads more suitable to a mule's back than a soldier's, and sending them against entrenchments in frontal assaults, became synonymous with English officers in colonial minds, eighteenth-century versions of "Colonel Blimp." "I compute An *English* soldier stands encumbered with a Weight of about Forty or Fifty Pounds," commented New Yorker Archibald Kennedy, "while that of a *Frenchman* or *Indian* is not about twelve or Fifteen. What service," the practical colonist asked, "can be expected from Men thus encumbered."[116] The English military showed itself to be human by its various blunders, which lowered colonial regard for the superiority of British arms while inflating their opinion of their own military capabilities.[117] As one Rhode Island clergyman noted, the Americans' sin of pride was the first reason for Braddock's defeat—sin or transgression of God's law served as a general explantion for calamities—and the second was that the British army was not trained "in the superior 'American Way of Fighting.' "[118]

The Americans' comprehension that a chink existed in the English presumption of superiority was an important, yet often overlooked, aspect of pre–Revolutionary War Anglo-American relations. After all, Americans had long felt a sense of inferiority to their cousins in the Motherland. Experiences or milestones of young adulthood color how a person thinks about subsequent events; consciously but especially unconsciously, attitudes and reactions fall into patterns, and those impressed early on malleable minds have the greatest consequences. One might argue that the most recent lesson has more of an impact, but, in the military where the lieutenants and captains of one war might not fight again until they are colonels and generals, the most recent lesson is usually the first. What a young officer learns during his first command or in his first war remains with him as he rises in rank and command.[119] For instance, Wellington's victory at Waterloo had less to do with the "playing fields of Eton" than it did with the hot, dusty plains of India, Portugal, and Spain, where the future Iron Duke learned his trade. What young American officers learned fighting in Mexico in 1846–48 was hard to put aside in 1861, and, for a more modern example, America's junior officers in World War II's European theater, in spite of subsequent service in Korea, never fully adapted to the special contingencies of a war in Asia's jungles. Another obvious illustration was George Washington, who, at a young age even by eighteenth-century standards, commanded Virginia's forces in the French and Indian War. Washington learned a great deal—both positive and negative—about tactics, combat, and the personalities of his future opponents, but even more importantly, he learned about human nature and will and what it took to field and maintain a military force in mid-eighteenth-century America with all its inherent limitations. The lessons he grasped, the ideas he perceived, and the invaluable practical knowledge he gained, all germinated in his mind in the decade and a half before the Revolution to bear amazing fruit when he was again called to arms. His circumstances and the breadth of his experiences were unique, but he was not alone in learning about warfare while fighting a war.[120]

A substantial number of colonial volunteers served with British forces in various wars and expeditionary operations, especially the war of 1754 to 1763. Attitudes formed, concepts developed, and experience gained in that war had direct and practical repercussions on how Americans perceived war throughout the revolutionary period. Serving alongside the British, living in the same camps, sharing the same miserable rations, slit trenches, and conditions, colonials came to know their future enemies, and surely they compared themselves with them: not as potential opponents, but as men. However they may have viewed native Englishmen before, after living together with them day after day in a totally British military environment they developed an increased sense of self-worth. Perhaps they had stood in awe of the British army earlier, naturally gawking at the precise organization, uniformed discipline, and the whole regalia of an eighteenth-century professional European army, but now they could not be overawed.[121] And another point worth noting, to these veterans the British army was little more than a tool of the Crown, a blunt, unthinking instrument of drill-deadened men and haughty officers that could pummel a colony's liberty into dust at the command of a king advised by corrupt ministers. Whether or not this accurately depicts the British army in the 1750s and early 1760s matters little, for among Americans this widely held perception counted for much. When anti–standing army republican propagandists began their pamphlet wars, images of vast columns of redcoated regulars remembered from youthful campaigning served to remind these men that what the writers warned of could come to pass.[122] As historian Fred Anderson commented about the veterans of the French and Indian War who became the middle-aged colonels, generals, and political leaders of the Revolution, "on the whole they were less likely than their fathers to remember the war favorably and were unlikely to be well disposed toward the redcoats with whom they had served. The Seven Years' War," he concludes, "had been, in effect, the greatest educational experience of their lives."[123] After their French and Indian War experience, cries that "the British were coming" would not send them scurrying away but forward to battle.

These lessons were improved upon, however, by much practical knowledge. Many colonials had enthusiastically kept abreast of changes in European warfare by reading military works as quickly as they were imported. Campfire or mess tent conversations with British officers showed the colonists, especially in the French and Indian War, that they read the same works as the professionals.[124] Although cerebral English officers rarely engaged in the polemical disputes of their French contemporaries, some native-born English officers and the many foreign officers serving the Crown did have, as one noted, their own "Military Literary World."[125] Dispersed all over the United Kingdom and posted overseas from the late seventeenth century, British officers could not congregate in salons as did the French, but as a survey by historian Ira Gruber of the personal libraries of English officers demonstrates, quite a few individuals stayed abreast of the current literature on the art of war. The most popular titles, this survey suggests, not only reflected the neoclassical age but the continued importance and value of the ancients' art of war. The Marquis de Feuquieres's *Memoirs*, Saxe's *Reveries*, Machiavelli's *Art of War*, and Turpin de Crisse's *Art of War*—a favorite of Bouquet and Forbes even before it was translated into English in 1761—were among the most popular of these classically based works, but the most important were Polybius's *History*, Caesar's *Commentaries*, and Vegetius's *De Re Militari*, translated in 1760 as *Military Institutions*. From such reading, as was noted earlier, the colonial understanding of the current European art of war was permeated with ancient knowledge. Of course, as Gruber cogently and correctly notes, the often contradictory messages of these works would add to the indecisiveness of English commanders during the Revolution. William Howe, whose assignment before sending his troops marching directly up Breed's Hill in a frontal assault on entrenched rebels was commander of the English light infantry, repeatedly vacillated, Gruber writes, over whether to seek "a decisive battle or to apply steady pressure [on Washington's army] through a series of flanking maneuvers, sieges, and skirmishes." Howe's replacement, Sir Henry Clinton, also "continued to exhibit a preference for conflicting strategies."[126] Governed by necessity and war-long shortages of troops and supplies, American officers, on the other hand, quickly learned that for them, indecision meant defeat.

For many colonials, however, their first tour of actual service stimulated them (and through them, others) to engage in further study of the art of war as veterans trying to put their experiences into perspective. Having been with a real army in the field, learning the basic day-to-day functions and jargon, they now read military works not as civilians but with the studied—and jaundiced—eyes of veterans. Upon a rereading, their old favorites Rollin, Vertot, and Plutarch took on new meaning. Veterans gobbled up the classics and read the recently translated works of Frederick, Saxe, and Vegetius as avidly as a young Corsican would in the 1780s. They analyzed these works, gleaning general themes and ideas and applying them to what they had experienced. The broad lessons of war in classical times mingled with the classically influenced contemporary European writing and what they knew and understood about war in the New World, as may be seen in the military titles published in America and those that they imported.[127]

This heightened interest in military affairs would pay unexpected dividends in 1775. During the French and Indian War, in sheer numbers never had so many colonials been under arms before. Returning to their communities, these demobilized soldiers found themselves discussing their experiences and reading with likeminded veterans, some meeting in loosely organized groups. Great Britain's decision to maintain a force of regulars in the colonies after the cessation of hostilities and the political and commercial turmoil created by the Stamp Act, however, increased colonial attention to martial affairs and a demand for additional books on the art of war. As more books on military history and theory became available, they were avidly read by increasingly large numbers of civilian military enthusiasts in the 1760s and early 1770s such as a Rhode Island anchorsmith named Nathanael Greene and a Boston bookseller, Henry Knox. When war broke out, it was from this assortment of amateur militarists, history buffs, and veterans of varying experience that the movement selected its military leadership. For reasons including health, age, and incompetence, some would be found wanting. But after many trials, no small number of errors, and learning war through war, the well-read amateurs who remained under arms evolved into veteran officers. These men, Washington's lieutenants, became the generals and colonels who led their troops to victory over some of Europe's finest professional soldiers.

Thus, by 1775 the practice of war in the colonies had become an often-paradoxical amalgam of ferocious brutality with enlightened rationality, of undisciplined, democratic citizen-soldiers with a classically influenced recognition of the need for disciplined troops, of myth and reality, and of a solid and substantial knowledge of the current art of European high-intensity warfare with an increased understanding of the requirements of war in America. When war came in 1775, colonial military leaders initially tried to emulate European doctrine and organization, especially that of the English. At first they shocked the British, but once the element of surprise was gone these American amateurs fared poorly against their professional British and German counterparts. With inadequate time, money, and societal backing to create and develop a Europeanized revolutionary army trained to Continental warfare, and in the field facing a superior foe, practical Americans devolved upon the way of war that they knew best, borrowing from European doctrine and their own colonial experience what they could use to fight an American war in defense of their new nation. In doing so, they ensured their independence.

PART III

The Intellectual Origins of American Conceptions of War

WAR has been the source of untold devastation, and it has spawned ideas that have altered the course of human events. For ancient peoples, war was a organic part of life, a phenomenon of nature like floods, famine, and disease, only occurring with greater frequency. The Hebrews of the Old Testament were chronically at war, and so, not surprisingly, the Bible addressed war in all its aspects. Much of the literature, poetry, religion, and history of classical Greece involved martial themes; sometimes to such an extent that the wisdom of the art of war overpowered the message of the poet.[1] In republican Rome, war became part of the very fabric of society and government. Because war and all its components were such an intrinsic part of their cultures, the ancients wrote long and deeply about it. As with so many classical and biblical ideas, ancient attitudes toward war were incorporated into the intellectual milieu of the seventeenth and eighteenth centuries.

In that milieu, war became the locus of significant study by some of the greatest minds of Western civilization. Realistically acknowledging that not all wars were evil, these great thinkers sought to curb war's destructive power, limiting it to the battlefield and seeking to harness its mighty energy for possibly the betterment of humankind or, at least, to ensure its survival. Because many of these eminent minds— and lesser lights as well—attained their initial knowledge and ideas from identical sources and built upon one another's accomplishments, it is hardly surprising that similarities existed in their conceptions of war. Their works, collectively, might be characterized as a humanistic effort to limit war by law and philosophy, and their writings joined with the Bible and the classics as keystones in Western intellectual achievement. As such they were stowed in the cultural baggage offloaded by early colonists on New World shores.

The Bible, the classics, and the great humanistic works helped shape colonial society, culture, and, to a large extent, American conceptions of war. The knowledge and the lessons transmitted to historically conscious Americans, when combined with long-held British traditions and the overall colonial experience, helped predispose colonists to accept enlightened ideas of the late seventeenth and early eighteenth centuries. While the post–Thirty Years' War resurgence in attempts to impose rational limits or controls on war generally was less than effective, the Grotiuses and Vattels not only borrowed heavily from ancient and modern sources but they also fostered an expanded interest in thinking about people and war, war and society, and society and the military. Colonial Americans eagerly followed these arguments, since they remained very closely attuned to the intellectual revolution in Europe, but in general terms they were already quite familiar with them.

This, too, proved much the case when in post-Cromwellian England oppositionist libertarians and radical Whigs began developing what came to be known generally as republican ideology. A central tenet or manifestation of this ideology was its vehement opposition to maintaining a standing, professional army in England. Strongly worded demands and well-crafted arguments in favor of civilian (parliamentary) control of the military and reliance upon a well-trained citizen-soldiery (instead of a professional military) were very popular among colonists, for whom the Englishmen appeared to be summarizing in well-written essays views already known and, in fact, practiced in the colonies. For among the colonials, these writers found a wide audience morally, philosophically, politically, and ideologically attuned and ready to receive their message. As with anything ancient or European, however, colonists adapted the libertarian propaganda and wisdom to fit their requirements, and the colonists had needs of their own.

For American colonial society was no longer a babe wrapped in swaddling nor even a spunky toddler, but a youth with a mind all of its own. Born of European parentage, it had been suckled on ancient classical and biblical teats renourished and lactating anew in a fertile environment. It had taken its first, often painful steps in this new land, and while it stumbled a bit, American society was nevertheless developing its own identity. It recognized, accepted, and turned to its parent society for guidance, but as separated children grow apart from a parent, so does the parent grow away from the offspring. By the time American society moved into its figurative adolescence and England sought to impose her will, parent and child were at odds, and memories clashed with realities.

Time and distance had fogged the colonists' perceptions of their former homeland: institutions and ideas highly regarded in the colonies had radically changed or were long out of fashion in Britain. The colonists' growth and maturation as a people—ignored by England—paralleled a similar evolutionary process among their contemporaries in the Motherland, but time and space affected colonial interpretations of cross-Atlantic events. England had undergone two revolutions and twelve years of military rule which left an indelible scar on its national psyche. Many of the resultant subtle alterations in the British political economy were not so much unknown by the colonists as misperceived by them. The political and philosophical ideal of England that Americans looked to was not imperial Britain of the 1760s and 1770s but one from an earlier time; hence, deviations (real or imagined) from this ideal were magnified in colonial minds, usually negatively.

From the same roots, the colonies and Mother country had bifurcated by the mid-eighteenth century, leading to substantially opposing positions and to cultural and political conflicts between these two similar, dynamic societies. Trenchard and Gordon had forecast this in *Cato's Letters*, in words the colonists knew well: "No Creatures suck the Teats of their Dams longer than they can draw Milk from thence, or can provide themselves with better Food: Nor," they added, "will any Country continue their Subjection to another, only because their Great-Grandmothers were acquainted."[2]

CHAPTER 7

War in the
Colonial Mind: Sources

War was a chronic preoccupation of the colonial American consciousness. The constant threat of Amerindian and later combined French and Indian raids from the west and north (those "Fiery Scorpions of Canada," wrote Cotton Mather in 1690) made practical considerations about war, warfare, and the military a necessity.[1] Coming as they had from a relatively peaceful England, the early settlers of the Chesapeake and New England regions relied upon advisors who had learned about war campaigning in Ireland and on the Continent to teach them the fundamentals of self-defense. These colonists could hardly be considered warlike or even of having a warrior ethos; in fact, the seemingly endless continental wars were motivating factors in their decision to emigrate. Nevertheless, if attacked, or even if they believed themselves threatened, the colonials responded with fierce brutality, waging "total war" against their native opponents.

On the surface, their behavior might appear to have been uncharacteristic for gentle Christian people and military novices, but in fact they were acting ethically, within their religious, moral, philosophical, and cultural tenets and in accordance with the general philosophy and traditions of European society at that time. Efforts to rationalize and bring reason to Western warfare were, after all, a late seventeenth-century phenomenon; colonial warfare, on the other hand, reflected its late sixteenth to early seventeenth-century origins. Although some historians still blanketly impose the "war as a chess match" metaphor upon seventeenth- and eighteenth-century European warfare, characterizations applicable to the fourteenth and fifteenth centuries were no longer valid as descriptions of post-Reformation warfare. Instead of war as something of a large-scale medieval tournament, jousting over minor possessions or points of honor, wars became vicious, bloody confrontations over ideas of religion or to satisfy a monarch's territorial lust. What had been the controlled action of one state against another for political ends dissolved into martial anarchy. War expanded from the battlefield until it encompassed the entire landscape, and noncombatants suffered along with soldiers. When a French commander in one of the religious wars was asked how his men could separate the heretics from the faithful in one town, his brutal answer paid homage to both military realism and King Solomon. "Kill them all," he ordered, "God will know which are His."[2] But in a sense, the controlled violence of war has always been a euphemism for controlled savagery, and the fine line between civilized, justified war and anarchistic violence such as that which swept Europe in the aftermath of the Reformation was easily crossed if these controls were loosened.

From the earliest times, people have instinctively recognized this, and have sought not so much to stop war as to diminish or minimize its destructive power. Rules of a sort, or codes, evolved to govern conflict between like peoples, and war was incorporated into society, making it an integral part of a nation's essence. Over time, aspects of this were refined as people continued their attempts to civilize war: at once, the most futile of undertakings and yet, if even minimally successful, the most rewarding of enterprises. A rich legacy of thought evolved from these efforts to become part of the intellectual and philosophical foundation of Western civilization; as such it was well known to seventeenth-century colonists in the New World. Many colonial ideas on military affairs were borrowed whole or in part from this heritage, but their overarching source for rules of personal and community conduct came not from classical but biblical directives. Yet this mixture of classics and Bible created few conflicts in the colonial mind, for the biblical view of war blended with the secular.

Humankind had long since accepted war as part of the natural order
and adapted itself accordingly. Recognition of this does not suggest
that people preferred war over peace; nor is it implied here that
humans are inherently warlike, although the historical inability of
humankind to achieve peace makes the point arguable. But war was an
inevitable part of life and should be treated as such. Peace was much
preferable to war, but so was a moderate rain shower to a destructive
flood, yet both occurred and humankind was as incapable of stopping
one as it was the other. As Herodotus had Croesus say: "No one is so
foolish as to prefer war to peace in which instead of sons burying their
fathers, father bury their sons, but," he added, bowing to the inevitable, "the gods willed it so."[3] Among the ancient Greeks, birth was
balanced by death, happiness by sadness, and peace by war. (Or, for
the ancient Hebrews and colonial Americans, "To every *thing there is* a
season, and a time to every purpose under heaven: . . . A time to love,
and a time to hate, a time of war, and a time of peace.")[4] For Pericles
(495–429 B.C.), harmony in life was symbolized by the "taut bow and
lyre." But, the Athenian leader suggested, one should be ever-watchful
to maintain this balance, lest they become as the Spartans and let war
dominate society.[5] From the beginning of human life, people have had
to fight for self-preservation (which, ultimately, is the moral justification for war), while at the same time battling to keep war and the
military from controlling their lives. As will be seen, both tasks proved
difficult.

War was one of the goads that prompted prehistoric humans toward
civilization. It seems quite likely that a desire for mutual security lay
behind the motivation for the decision of early men and women to join
with others in bands and communities. In doing so, individuals had to
subordinate themselves to the whole, something they have never quite
gotten over. This exchange, however, proved to be mutually beneficial: sacrificing some individuality, the newcomer shared in the security and other advantages that the community provided; and the community's security was enhanced with the addition of this person who,
if a man, was expected to aid in what amounted to his own defense. In
other words, a pact, a bond, a compact was formed, and membership
in the group was predicated by what was tantamount to military
service. But this warrior who stood lonely guard huddled behind a

thorn corral was not a full-time defender, for the community could ill-afford to lose his work. Accordingly, as these community member-warriors tended fields or flocks, hunted or gathered, their clubs or spears were always handy, ready to defend their people if called upon, even to the extent of giving up their lives. This was the essence of community membership.

As societies developed and became more sophisticated, security needs grew more imperative; so important did they become that war and all its associated components were integrated into the societal whole, becoming inseparable. Among primitive and some not so prim-itive societies, community defense merged with religion, such was the status afforded the warrior class. Both male and female gods were portrayed in martial garb, and gods of war ranked high on the religious totem, thus sanctioning war on an even loftier plane. Whether or-dained by the gods, nature, or God, war was part of life. In words that perhaps inspired Vegetius's famous dictum, "He, therefore, who desires peace, should prepare for war,"[6] Pericles lectured the pleasure-loving Athenians. In an early and still-used rationalization for the strategy of deterrence, Pericles explained to his fellow citizens that they must realize "that war is inevitable, and that the more willing we show ourselves to accept it, the less eager will our enemies be to attack us." And, he added, now exhorting his listeners, "it is from the greatest dangers that the great[est] honours accrue to a state as well as to an individual."[7]

Pericles combined a demand for personal sacrifice for the state with a call to glory, emblematic of how strongly analogous for a Greek were the twin duties of citizenship and defense of the city. Thus, the true patriot would suffer any sacrifice, even death, just as his ancestors had in order "to hand down [the] empire undiminished to posterity."[8] In calling upon these citizen-soldiers to emulate the ancients' courage, discipline, and virtue, Pericles followed the advice of Socrates, who had told him: "As we want [the people] to strive for pre-eminence in virtue, we must show them that this belonged to them in the old days," adding that "by striving for it they will surpass all other men."[9] In order to deal out and face death on the battlefield, men had to be assured that their sacrifice would gain them a measure of immortality. A modern cynic might proscribe this simply as a superficial motivational technique to get people to fight. Although there is some truth in this observation, to fight, to kill, and to die for one's community (be it tribe or nation) delves into the essence of human society, of humankind. Collectively it is defense of one's community; individually, it is defense of one's hearth and kin, the most human of all needs: the struggle for survival. Thus, death in battle was sanctified as the most honorable of all sacrifices, and, as part of the unstated compact, the state promised to honor its fallen heroes and to take care of their families. "Lo, it is no dishonorable thing for him to fall fighting for his country," Polydamas admonished the Trojans, Homer (eighth century B.C.) reports, "but his wife and children after him are safe, and his house unharmed." Euripides (479–406 B.C.) echoed this refrain when, in the *Madness of Hercules*, the chorus chanted:

> Thy friend, who once mid toils of battle-peers
> Shoulder to shoulder, did not shame—
> When thou and he were young, when clashed the spears,—
> His country's glorious name.[10]

Later, the Roman poet Horace (65–8 B.C.) would summarize this as "dulce et decorum est pro patria mori" (it is sweet and fitting to die for the fatherland).[11]

Then and now, the ultimate sacrifice so many have paid for so many nations brings forth both admiration and sadness, and it bespeaks much about humankind that little other than war so stirs a people. "There's nothing like war for bringing out courage," notes historian Henry Steele Commager with succinctness, "there is nothing like an emergency for bringing out ingenuity; [and] there is nothing like challenge for bringing out character."[12] Pericles's call to glory was not the first use of this rhetorical skill, nor the last. For veterans, however, war was many things, but throughout history, few have thought it glorious. "Our military glory looks very fine, seen from a distance," Frederick the Great acknowledged, "But if you had witnessed the distress and hardship with which it had been acquired, in what physical deprivations and struggle, in heat and cold, in hunger, filth and destitution, then you would have learnt to think quite differently about this 'glory.' "[13] William Tecumseh Sherman, no shrinking violet on the battlefield, summarized a long-held belief in a speech before Federal veterans in 1880: "There is many a boy here today who looks on war as all glory, but, boys, it is all hell. You can bear this warning voice to generations yet to come," adding, however, with patriotic resignation, "I look upon war with horror, but if it has to come I am here."[14] In this, both the Prussian and the Yankee echo a sentiment of Pindar (or Pindarus, 522–438 B.C.), a pre-Periclean Greek. "To the inexperienced war is pleasant, but he that hath had experience of it, in his heart sorely feareth its approach."[15]

Yet Pericles, for all his stirring and patriotic words, saw war only as a last resort. For the Greeks of his time, excluding the Spartans, war was a necessary evil, ranging in intensity from raids and a means of settling simple differences to all-out wars of domination. For those who can avoid it or have no stake in the matter, "war is the greatest of follies," Pericles said. "But," he added in words that carry a similar cadence to those of Jefferson's in the Declaration of Independence, "if the only choice between submission with the loss of independence, and danger with the hope of preserving that independence, in such a case it is he who will not accept the risk that deserves blame, not he who will."[16] After all, as Lycurgus (ninth century B.C.?) had noted earlier, "That city is best fortified which has a wall of men instead of brick."[17] Their devotion to virtuous duty and "zest for liberty" in defending themselves earned these Greeks the encomia of colonial Americans some two thousand years later.[18] For the Greek victories over the Persians at Marathon and Salamis were remembered by eighteenth-century republicans on both sides of the Atlantic as the victories of a citizen-military over a professional force. So strongly and widely held was this memory that one nineteenth-century Englishman wrote: "The battle of Marathon, even as an event in English history, is more important than the battle of Hastings," such was its consequence to Western culture.[19] Although what colonials knew of the battle was based on Herodotus's greatly inflated figures, and though they ignored the fact that the Greek citizen-soldiers were in fact hardy, well-trained veterans of innumerable conflicts, their perception nevertheless validated republican preference for the militia, affirming radical Whig theory in their minds.[20] Eighteenth-century Americans, to reiterate, read broadly but were selective in their use of history.

The ancient Greeks were incessantly engaged in some sort of military activity,[21] and in doing so, developed strong ideas about the role that a military played in their society. Generals *(strategoi)* were never allowed too much individual power, and they had to answer to civilian control in the field and after significant actions. Both Spartans and Athenians dispatched civilian supervisors to accompany their forces on campaign, and Greek commanders were not only expected to defeat the enemy but to do so according to certain standards. A general might win the most glorious victory, but if he broke this code of conduct, he was subject to trial and, if convicted, death. Pericles's son, for instance, was among a number of Greek generals who were tried and executed for failing to recover the drowned bodies of Athenians in spite of achieving a significant naval victory off of Lesbos.[22] Presaging or, perhaps, the source of Voltaire's snide comment that English admiral John Byng was executed in the Seven Years' War to "encourage the others," Athenian policy often had the opposite effect. They not only lost good leaders, notes historian Arther Ferrill, but encouraged passivity in command; witness the disastrous Athenian campaign in Syracuse as an example.[23] Along with governing how wars should be fought by their commanders, the Greeks also attempted to place limitations upon warfare.

One way, suggested by Plato (427–347 B.C.) in *The Republic*, was for like peoples (in this case Greeks) to wage war among themselves according to some basic rules. His proposition can in no way be considered as an attempt to stop war: for Plato that would have been tantamount to folly. For instance, when Greeks fought barbarians it was because they were "enemies by nature," but even at war "Greeks . . . are still by nature friends of Greeks." War against people other than Greeks was accepted as a natural event, but intra-Grecian war was attributed to Greece's being "sick . . . and divided by faction."[24] To a large extent, Plato's admonitions addressed this problem of factionalism among his fellow Greeks. Internal discord proved to be Greece's Achilles' heel, so to speak, against both the Macedonians and later the Romans, a fact not unnoticed by either Tacitus (A.D. 55–117) or Americans of the revolutionary generation. As Tacitus wrote: "Nec aliud adversus validissimas gentes pro nobis utilius quod non consulunt" (Against these very powerful tribes there was no circumstance more useful to us than their failure to plan in common.).[25] The Greeks, Plato advised, must unify to fight the common enemy. As a thoughtful means of limiting mutual slaughter and destruction among his fellow Greeks, Plato proposed several rules of war. Greek prisoners of war should not be sold into slavery, Greek casualties should not be robbed, and a fallen Greek's weapons and armor should not be stripped from him and offered up at temples or shrines, which was a long-held custom.[26] Practices such as these only fueled revenge and further conflict. Plato hoped that Greeks would adopt his measures, "while treating barbarians as Greeks now treat Greeks."[27]

In his attempt to limit brutality, barbarism, and war in general among the classical Greeks, Plato delineated warfare into two types which would remain as legacies of Western civilization through the eighteenth century: that is, war between like peoples and war between unlike peoples. When Greek fought Greek, a code should be followed to limit bloodshed; among unlike peoples, all restraints could be cast off. Plato (among others) also made the citizen-soldier the epitome of virtue and manliness in his *Republic;* brave soldiers should be allowed to father many children, both as a reward and to furnish the state with additional defenders. Less odious were his suggestions about this virtuous citizen-soldiery's military proficiency. Citizen-soldiers, as opposed to a professional military, were central to Plato's republican concept, yet he would have been horrified at the way eighteenth-century radical Whigs in America twisted his ideas, seeking to instill by ideological transmutation what could only be accomplished, as Plato knew, over time by discipline and drill. For Plato, constant rigorous training was the only means of achieving and maintaining a knowledge of arms, especially for a citizen-army. "[A]re we to believe that a man who takes in hand a shield or any other instrument of war springs up on that very day a competent combatant in heavy armour or in any form of warfare?" he asked rhetorically. Why was it, he inquired, that people believed that soldiers could be created overnight by merely handing them arms, when the same people would laugh at the idea that giving an untrained person a brush or chisel turned him into an artist.[28] These Platonic perspectives were ignored by those in the eighteenth century trying to build another republic in the wilderness. But his fundamental concept of a citizen-soldiery as integral to a free society was one of many ideas that continued strong as the balance of Mediterranean power shifted from the Aegean to the Tiber.

Perhaps even more than the Greeks, war was a necessity and a major influence upon society during the development of the Roman Republic.[29] Romans recognized that they could not stop or even control war; therefore they harnessed its energies for the common good.[30] Thus, they thought of war not only as inevitable but in many ways as desirable. War unified peoples of disparate natures and factions. It cleansed a nation of sloth and moral laxity by introducing discipline. War and its challenges were seen as bringing out the best in a nation's character. Sallust, who was widely read and quoted by American colonials, declared that war invigorated the Republic and ensured its survival. "By two principal Means," he wrote, "Valour in War, and righteous Conduct during Peace, [the early Romans] supported their own Reputation, and that of the common Weal."[31] Selfless sacrifice and public service, whether as centurion or solon, were virtues among republican Romans. "It is glorious to serve one's country by deeds; even to serve her by words is a thing not to be despised," wrote Sallust, "one may become famous in peace as well as in war."[32] Sentiments such as these were common to Roman writers popular among the colonists. "It is our duty, then," wrote Cicero, "to be more ready to endanger our own than the public welfare and to hazard honour and glory more readily than other advantages."[33] To the Romans, war was central to the republican ethos.

In the early Roman Republic a citizen's service in the legion was not a duty but a right and a privilege. Only landholding freemen could be citizens, and only citizens could bear arms for their country. The Greeks had spoken of *eleutheria* (living as one pleases); this concept was unknown to republican Romans for whom *libertas* meant "freedom to do such things as are permissible."[34] From youth Roman children— and particularly the boys—were inculcated with the Roman virtues of obedience, duty, honor, and discipline. Their education and sports trained their minds and bodies "so that the whole youth of Rome were accustomed to support the rudest fatigues."[35] They learned that the "noblest heritage . . . is a reputation for virtue and worthy deeds; and to dishonour this must be branded as a sin and a shame."[36] In Cicero's words, sound moral principles applicable to parental and political as well civic guidance were artfully blended. Youth, he posited, must be "protected against sensuality and trained to toil and endurance of both mind and body, so as to be strong for active duty in military and civil service."[37] Also, the Romans' religious beliefs encouraged them, so that when they entered their names on the draft rolls, they were prepared for legionary duty in every respect. In the early Republic, those who failed to register were despised as traitors and sold into slavery.[38] Later-day republicans who sought inspiration, precedence, and validation from the golden age of Roman patriotism and virtue would also make a citizen-soldiery pivotal to their ideological schemes. But they looked to the myth, not the reality.

The early republic was agrarian, primarily composed of hardy small farmers and landholding peasants who maintained their proficiency at arms with constant drilling and training and, because Rome pursued an aggressive foreign policy, from regular service in the field. New levies were merged with veterans in small ratios so that when a legion was mobilized, it could march out ready for battle. When assembled, these citizen-soldiers swore an oath, not to the state, but to their legionary consul. By this oath, a serious religious matter, they acknowledged their duty and pledged themselves to strict obedience, or in other words, martially disciplined subordination, a point ignored by eighteenth-century republican zealots.[39] Equally important to the high state of military preparedness of these farmers (and equally ignored by their latter-day disciples) was the ability of the state to feed and maintain them in the field. Reliance on a citizen army, it should be added, was based upon reasons other than necessity. Romans were well aware that a powerful military personality at the head of a legion posed a threat to the republic; by making every citizen a soldier, they created a bulwark against despotism. By rotating different legions on active duty, they ensured that the military was not kept together long enough to breed dissent or to be wooed by an ambitious leader.

As with the Greeks, the Romans exercised civilian control over the military, and civilian oversight was the function of plebeian magistrates. After all, the problem posed by Juvenal (A.D. 60–140) in his famous question, "Quis custodiet ipsos custodes?" (Who will guard the guards themselves?) existed even before the poet.[40] Other republican forms of insurance against a coup d'état were politically expedient but militarily unsound: the dual consulship, which divided power but also split command; the annual selection of consuls, which precluded continuity in command and required the new consul to learn on the job; and the provision that no man could serve as a consul more than one year in ten, which deprived the state of invaluable experience and skills.[41] Military competence was required of a consul, but it was not considered paramount. More importantly, consuls were expected to "know how to join the Dignity of the Commander with the Modesty of the Citizen. Qualifications too shining," noted the Abbé de Vertot, in words applicable to modern times, "were even suspected, in a State where Equality was looked upon as the Foundation of public Liberty."[42] Again borrowing from the Greek practice, a commander's success was measured more by his adherence to republican principles than by his victories. "The General of an Army, though the Battle be lost, yet [is] worthy of Commendation," wrote Seneca, "if he has discharged all the parts [duties] of a prudent Commander."[43] Excellence was demanded, but the slightest hint of personal ambition or self-aggrandizement caused republican hearts to flutter. For "those fierce Republicans could not bear even to be served with superior Talents, that might even have the least Prospect of subjecting them."[44] For instance, after his disastrous defeat by Hannibal at Cannae, Terentius Varro was praised by the Senate for his adherence to republican principles, not executed as he would have been in Greece.[45] From the fourth century B.C. to the end of the Republic, the ideal consul or military commander was based on the Cincinnatian model—just as in 1775. "There is nothing certainly nobler or greater, than to see a private person, eminent for his merit and virtue," wrote Rollin, describing this paragon, "and fitted by his excellent talents for the highest employments, and yet, through inclination and modesty, preferring a life of obscurity and retirement." Such a man would "sincerely refuse" any offer made to him, even that of ruling over his country in time of crisis, and would only "at last consent to undergo the toil of government, upon no other motive than that of being serviceable to his fellow citizens."[46] Whether or not he studied these words, George Washington surely molded his character in preparation for a similar part. And essential to the role, he understood, was a military under, not above, civil control. This subordination of the military to the republic ("cedant arma togae" [let arms yield to the gown] in Cicero's words)[47] served Rome well until military success began weakening Roman resolve and would be most influential on Western society, especially in the eighteenth century.

As later Roman historians and writers perceived it and, through them, seventeenth- and eighteenth-century republicans understood it, the decline of the Republic began in the victorious aftermath of the Punic Wars. Small and poor, surrounded by enemies, Rome had to rely upon organization, self-discipline, and obedience to carry out her aggressive foreign policy. Discipline meant sacrifice, and constant warfare left Roman citizens impoverished but tough and warlike. For these early Romans had "made a Virtue of what was the mere Effect of Necessity, and Men of Courage looked upon this equal Poverty of all the Citizens as the Means to preserve their Liberty from Usurpation."[48] Particularly during the Second Punic War, when Hannibal rampaged up and down the Italian peninsula, the people disciplined themselves to the sole objective of defeating their cross-Mediterranean rival. By the conclusion of the Punic Wars, however, "Peace and plenty, things desirable to others, were a burden and a plague to [the Romans], who had formerly endured fatigue, dangers, straitening and distressing circumstances, with ease. Accordingly," Sallust wrote, "first the love of money, and then of power grew upon them: these were in a manner the source of all evils."[49] Peace, the joy of newfound prosperity, and the absence of significant rivals allowed Romans to sample luxury for the first time, and they reveled in it. Earlier, the "Common Dread of Enemies abroad perserved decent Demeanour in the whole Community," he noted, "But, as soon as that Dread forsook the Minds of Men, then instantly rushed in Ambition and Debauchery, Excesses which Prosperity delights in."[50] Or as Juvenal moralized, "When Riches grew to be necessary, the Desire for them, which is the Spring of all Mischief, followed."[51]

The morally political themes of these writers and of eighteenth-century popular historians would have great impact on prerevolutionary Americans, coloring their perceptions both of England and of themselves. "Liberty, so dear to the first *Romans* . . ." and to Americans, "was guarded by Poverty and Temperance," wrote the Abbé de Vertot, "Love of their Country, Valour, and all other Virtues both Civil and Military, were found always to attend it."[52] During the Punic Wars the people had clamored for "a State of Peace and Repose;

now that they had obtained it," wrote Sallust, it "proved more destructive and calamitous" than war.[53] War unified these disciplined people, and luxury was unknown and unnecessary. But upon the coming of peace, ". . . Poverty, which had been the Mother and Nurse of Virtue, grew insupportable."[54] Colonial Americans took heed from these words, and when they read the following in *Cato's Letters*, they surely altered it to fit their needs, substituting *English* for *Roman*, just as the writers had originally intended: "The *Roman* Virtue and the *Roman* Liberty expired together; Tyranny and Corruption came upon them almost hand in hand."[55]

As Trenchard and Gordon indicated, the changes in Roman mores gradually affected the Roman conceptions and practice of war and ultimately, two thousand years later, those of the revolutionary Americans. Where before the Punic Wars Roman legionaries were predominantly drawn from the yeoman class, following the Marian reforms in the second century B.C. landless peasants came to dominate the ranks. Service, duty, discipline, and obedience, the old Roman virtues, were no longer in vogue among the general populace. Equally applicable here were the words of historian John Shy, describing a similar lack of spirit among colonial Americans, wherein "every man's duty easily became no one's responsibility."[56] The concept of the agrarian citizen-soldier as the epitome of Roman manhood was replaced by that of the gentleman who dabbled in war if he took the field at all.[57] Soon, even while the Republic still existed in name, the landless peasants drifted from the discipline and hardship of army life to swell the ranks of the mob, and they were replaced with non-Roman Italians and Romanized Celts, although, it should be added, with no drop in military efficiency or performance. To an large extent, however, the altered composition of the legions naturally followed changes in the military's mission. Whereas previous wars were fought on the Italian peninsula or for short periods of time in the provinces, now Roman hegemony extended around the Mediterranean basin. For a citizen-soldier, serving near home or abroad for a year or two was a duty; to be stationed overseas indefinitely was punishment. As the size of Roman territory increased, the number of Romans in actual service decreased proportionately to the number of Romanized locals levied or enlisted for duty. In part this no doubt stemmed from the fall of military service into disfavor among Romans, but many "barbarians" saw the military as a means of bettering themselves and, eventually, gaining Roman citizenship.[58]

Yet later Romans writers and late seventeenth- and eighteenth-century Euro-American libertarians and Whigs generally ignored these geostrategic realities (and the question of why men served), dwelling instead on the decline of Roman virtue. As one American (of many) in 1774 described this period, analogizing circumstances in England with those of Rome, Rome's "ambition was sated. She sat down in indolence to enjoy the fruits of conquests," and in doing so, "[l]uxury and dissipation ensured." The Roman discipline, obedience, and hardness had softened, and "Rome, from being the nursery of heroes, became the residence of musicians, pimps, panders, and catamites."[59] Thus to Roman and latter-day republican thinking, liberty and a nonprofessional citizen army were inextricably linked; militia was forever the bulwark against corruption and tyranny.

While the Republic still lived and immediately after its fall, writers were already harkening back to the "good old days," lamenting their passage and seeking, as Vegetius would some five centuries later, to rekindle the greatness that was Rome's. It is ironic, of course, that these lamentations for a return to the virtuous, halcyon days of the past were written even as Roman power and influence continued to expand on all fronts. The very affluence and easy life-style the poets and political writers bemoaned provided them with the luxury of time to think and write. Also, the Rome they looked back to no longer existed. By the end of the Republic, Rome had become a huge city and the sophisticated center of a vast economic system with the benefits and ills of both. For many, however, the ongoing wars of conquest were no longer perceived as merely defensive or even preemptive as they had been in republican days, but aggressive wars for domination. Livy (59 B.C.–A.D. 17) hailed the citizen-soldier ethos, and compared the Roman virtues of earlier times with the degeneracy of spirit in his own. The epic poem of Virgil (70–19 B.C.), the *Aeneid*, has been studied not only for its literary worth but specifically as an epic of war.[60] Of course, as one scholar cogently observed about Virgil, writing about war and "reveling in blood are not necessarily concomitant."

For Virgil "tristia condere bella" (wrote of the sadness of war), and did not extoll its virtues.[61] "The love of war," to this half-Roman, half-Celtic bard, "is madness, criminal folly" ("insanus amor duri Martis"), especially since the state had been militarized and wars now were fought for the sake of conquest and glory alone.[62] But neither Virgil nor his characters were pacifists; the *Aeneid* does begin with the famous line, "Arma virumque cano" (arms and the man I sing). But battle, he argued, should be joined only when there was no other recourse and the fight was just; then, Virgil's characters fought and fought to win. Rome's mission—to Virgil—was not simply to conquer but to civilize, "to rule the peoples, and crown peace with law; to spare the conquered, and beat down the proud."[63] In other words, war itself was accepted as a matter of course, but now some Romans questioned whether specific campaigns even needed to be conducted and what the justification was for them. These concepts had been elaborated upon earlier by Cicero (106–43 B.C.). The works of this statesman and philosopher, coursing through Western civilization and across the Atlantic, would be especially influential on colonial Americans' conceptions of war.

Cicero has been portrayed as transforming the ancient concept of a just war into a "code for conquerors—and ethic for empire,"[64] but that is a modern interpretation. For those who followed Cicero's writings, his was an attempt to bring law and order to war, an effort to civilize an aspect of human interaction prone to barbarism. If law, and thus order, could be applied to war, then in effect war would be limited or controlled to an extent. What Cicero did was to codify earlier and current ideas about what constituted a just war; or, to put it another way, he indicated when it was morally, philosophically, and politically justifiable to go to war. In this he joined ancient ideals with a realistic appraisal of current Roman realities. First and foremost, war was the exclusive domain of the state. As with all talents, military and otherwise, citizens were allowed to develop and hone their skills under the state so "that she may appropriate to her own use the great and more important part of our courage, our talents, and our wisdom." What remained for private use was "only so much as may be left after her needs have been satisfied."[65] Service to the state was, to Cicero, an accepted provision of citizenship, the natural way of things, and was not limited to emergency circumstances.[66] To educate and train one's mind and body in every way which might better the state was "the noblest function of wisdom, and the highest duty of virtue," as well as the "best proof of its possession."[67] For Cicero, "military commands and consulships are to be classed among things necessary rather than things desirable," adding in what surely was a swipe at his contemporaries Crassus, Pompey, and Caesar, that "they are to be undertaken from a sense of duty and not sought for profit or glory."[68]

Thus, to Cicero, war, making war, and deciding how wars were to be fought were functions only of the state, and as such must follow certain specified guidelines. In this he freely admitted to borrowing concepts from others, and he was much influenced by Marcus Cato (234–149 B.C.).[69] Cato was so strict in his adherence to the law that, as Cicero recounted it, when Cato's son was discharged from an army which remained in the field, Cato warned him "to be careful not to go into battle; for, [Cato said], the man who is not legally a soldier has no right to be fighting the foe."[70] His words also may be seen as a stricture against two of the most dangerous types of war: civil wars and wars fought over ideas, religious or secular.[71] Disputes could only be settled in two ways, Cicero wrote, by discussion and by force. Since "the former is characteristic of man, the latter of the brute, we must resort to force only in case we may not avail ourselves of discussion."[72] Here Cicero implicitly assented to the concept of war as a natural event, and he openly acknowledged its barbaric nature. In the very act of taking up the gladius against an opponent, civilized or barbarian, Romans figuratively (and sometimes literally) regressed into savagery. Diplomacy must be first resorted to for resolving differences, an attempt at placing a control on war, for only an uncivilized brutish people would initiate hostilities unannounced.[73] If diplomacy failed, then war as just conflict resolution was the next step, but only after certain civilities were carried out. For "no war is just," wrote Cicero, "unless it is entered upon after an official demand for satisfaction has been submitted or warning had been given and a formal declaration made."[74] Of course, all of these martial amenities were only for wars between Romans and other like peoples. This was the Greek way, but in spite of Cicero's remonstrances, rarely was it practiced by the Romans though not necessarily for philosophical reasons. In Cicero's time and thereafter, Rome fought few like peoples; they had already conquered them. By Cicero's death in 43 B.C., they were advancing the frontiers of what soon was officially the Empire, not of provinces.

Cicero addressed other issues regarding war and warfare. Once victory was achieved, magnanimity was the order of the day; Romans "should spare those who have not been blood-thirsty and barbarous in their warfare." They should "show consideration" to those whom they have conquered, and he specifically urged "protection" of prisoners of war and agreed with the principle of officer parole. By these ideas, Cicero demonstrated an understanding of sound pacification: honorable treatment of a defeated people curbed revenge as a motive for rebellion, thus allaying a costly and protracted guerrilla insurgency.[75] Differentiating between types of conflicts, he suggested (perhaps bowing to the inevitability of human nature) that war could be considered just if waged even "for supremacy and when glory is the object," but this type of war had to adhere to the same rules as above. Sometimes duty, circumstances, and the preservation of the army or of Rome demanded that Romans fight barbarians in the barbarian way, which was not particularly desirable but preferable to "slavery and disgrace." Here he implied that the concept of a just, humane war did not apply to war with unlike peoples. Overall, however, Cicero believed that: "Bellum autem ita suscipiatur, ut nihil aliud nisi pax quaesita videatur" (War, however, should be undertaken in such a way as to make it evident that it has no other object than to secure peace).[76] Some of his tenets and ideas appear to be philosophical hairsplitting, creating rationalizations instead of a code to mask the impotency of attempting to control what could not be controlled. Yet, through his writings, he fashioned a philosophic structure which subsequent great thinkers built upon in their efforts to limit war and military power.

From the late days of the Empire up through the eighteenth century, the theories of just war and conceptions of controlling martial violence were incorporated into the general framework of Western thought. Beyond the effort to limit war lay an attempt to create an overarching or universal (to Christian nations) set of guidelines governing interactions among nations, a form of international law in which—until the Reformation—the Church served as final arbiter, with excommunication its cudgel of last resort.[77] Ambrose, Augustine of Hippo, Aquinas, and other giants of Western intellectual achievement built upon concepts of war delineated by biblical and classical ancients.[78] Although differing in certain respects, the general themes enunciated by these intellectuals and theologians became integral parts of Western culture and the Western way of war, remaining so even after the Reformation. In fact, these ideas may be discerned in the fundamental rules of international behavior as codified in the seventeenth century by Hugo de Groot (Grotius) and, a century later, by Emmerich de Vattel, among others.[79] Briefly summarized in very general collective terms, these ideas were: only the state can legitimately make war; any war authorized by the state, therefore, was legal but not necessarily just, although this remained a gray area; all defensive wars, including preemptive strikes against real threats, were just and even aggressive wars could be just at times; civil wars and wars fought for religion were not legitimate and thus were prohibited, except if one's cause was just; and in wars against non-Christians, whether specifically fought under the guise of religion or glory, no rules applied, except that the wars be called for by either state or papal authority.[80]

In part, these concepts were borrowed from the past, but they reflected the realities of war, warfare, and society over the centuries in which they were developed. St. Augustine (A.D. 354–430), writing as the Roman Empire crumbled and about the same time as Vegetius, posited that state-authorized defensive war was just, based as it was on the natural right of self-preservation. Augustine's was not a passive Christianity, for he also believed that an aggressive (offensive) war could be carried out by the state to avenge injuries.[81] This theme was further refined in the thirteenth century by St. Thomas Aquinas in *Summa Theologica* and in the canon law compiled by Pope Gregory IX, helping to define what constituted a *jus ad bellum* (the right to make war) and a *jus in bello* (what was right in battle).[82] Aquinas affirmed Augustine's views, and wrote that, above all, qualification as a just war was dependent upon state authorization; as with most of these great minds, Aquinas found the very idea of popular rebellion abhorrent.[83] "I shall make it plaine; That Warres Preventive upon Just Feares, are true Defensives, as well as upon Actuall Invasions," wrote Francis Bacon (1561–1626), "and againe, that Warres Defensive for Religion (I speake not of Rebellion) are most just," adding "Though Offensive Warres, for Religion, are seldome to be approved, or never, unless they have some mixture of Civil Titles."[84] Their genuine fear of popular uprisings arose, to a large measure, from a concern over destabilization. That is, if the "people"—whoever they might be— rebelled and toppled the existing government, they would be easy prey for a military leader or a powerful tyrant, or, worse, they might dissolve into barbarism. Quite possibly, for these great thinkers, the dampening effect of the latter was the most threatening of all.

In Sir Thomas More's (1478–1535) *Utopia* may be found a synthesis of sixteenth-century concepts of a just war, but writing at the same time as Machiavelli (1469–1527), More, too, addressed the realities of war and geopolitics in Renaissance Europe. His not-so-fictitious Utopians regarded war "with utter loathing," believing it "an activity fit only for beasts" or mercenaries who were, generally speaking, pretty much the same in their minds.[85] More's "war of beasts not of men" metaphor has roots in antiquity (see Cicero above), and from a reli- gious-intellectual standpoint (the beast as the devil) is the basis for trying to curb war's excesses. Erasmus (1466–1536), who begins his work with the above-cited quote from Pindarus, indicates that it was common usage by employing in a similar fashion: "To clash with violence is characteristic of beasts and gladiators whom I class with beasts." (Later, in the eighteenth century, Voltaire applies it in a natural law fashion. "Men must have corrupted nature a little, for they were not born wolves, and they have become wolves.")[86] Since the Utopians were a wealthy, trading people and preferred to spill blood other than their own, they made use of hirelings, particularly for overseas conflicts. This parallels the common English and continental European practice of employing nonindigenous soldiers to do a nation's dirty work. The Utopians did this with few qualms, "thinking that they would be the greatest benefactors to the human race if they could relieve the world of all the dregs of this abominable and impious people."[87] One wonders if More was not referring to the Scots, Irish, and the sweepings of English gaols who fulfilled this role for the Crown; even in More's time, the preference existed for sending "ex- pendables" rather than Englishmen overseas. More's words would have pleased Machiavelli, who held mercenary soldiers in contempt and ridiculed them by claiming that they fought bloodless battles.[88] To a degree, borrowing from Vegetius and others as More did, *The Prince*'s author pursued the concept of patriotic military service (the essence of *virtu*) as an alternative to the ambitious, intriguing *condottieri* (mercenaries) who came to pose a real threat to Italian civil authority.[89] Machiavelli would have been pleased to find that in spite of their predilection for hiring mercenaries, Utopian "men and women alike assiduously exercise themselves in military training . . . lest they be unfit for war when need requires."[90] Here was More's homage to the English militia which, at the time, still retained a certain military value.

Using *Utopia*, More outlined his theory of what constituted a just and unjust war, and therein may be seen the direct linkage between his thinking and that of the Romans and even the Greeks. Utopians went to war only if invaded, to protect their territory or that of their allies, or "to requite and avenge injuries previously done to them"— but only if they, as the state, "approved the war" and had exhausted all diplomatic channels. Just war included preemptive attacks, for Utopians neither wanted war on their soil nor wished to bring foreign mercenaries within their midst—the latter being another central theme of seventeenth- and eighteenth-century English libertarians and Whigs. If a Utopian "is wrongfully disabled or killed anywhere [in the world] . . . [the Utopians] cannot be appeased but forthwith declare war." More's fictional characters, when forced into war, made particularly nasty opponents. The Utopians recognized that "the common folk do not go to war of their own accord but are driven to it by the madness of kings."[91] Therefore, from the moment war was declared, they offered enormous sums to ensure the assassination of the enemy ruler, believing that in killing the head the body would die. Assassinating opposing rulers, the Utopians felt, "reflects great credit," first, on their wisdom, because killing one person would conclude the war without costly battle, and "secondly on their humanity and mercy" for by eliminating one guilty party, they saved countless innocents.[92] Certainly Machiavelli would have approved. As he wrote in *The Prince*, when "it is a question of the safety of the country, no account should be taken of what is just or unjust, merciful or cruel."[93] In a very large sense, his realpolitik dictum reiterates the law of self-preservation much evident in the literature of the period, a real need which overrode all these philosophic constraints. More's Utopians agreed, for if assassination did not work, they had no compunction against "sow[ing] the seeds of dissension broadcast and foster[ing] strife" among the common people, raising dreaded rebellion among their opponents to advance their ends.[94] If wars must be waged, they were meant to be won, a point well understood by the early colonists.

As the Utopians' attitudes toward mercenaries and assassination show, life was cheap, especially the lives of unlike peoples. For instance, the crossbow was proscribed by Pope Innocent III at the Second Lateran Council in 1139 as being too lethal for use against Christians, but little was said about its use against infidel Moslems or even European barbarians.[95] Fourteenth- through sixteenth-century "fringe" Europeans such as the Irish who remained (quite literally) beyond the Pale, "were so farre out of the protection of the Lawe, as it was often adiudged no fellony to kill a meere Irish-man in the time of peace."[96] Overall, Church attitudes toward weaponry and warfare rarely hardened into dogma. The shedding of Christian blood by the sword was abhorred, yet when the Archbishop of Mainz killed nine men with a club, nary an eyebrow was raised.[97] The introduction of gunpowder weapons created some confusion in superstitious Europe over whether they were the devil's spawn (hence, "son of a gun" meant "son of the devil") or, as John Donne thought, an invention of the devil with benefit for man.[98] But this point was moot when fighting non-Christians or, from the twelfth century onward, "heretics, schismatics, and excommunicants."[99] Among such, except for individual chivalrous gestures, no rules applied other than the war must have papal or civil approval, making it, at least, a *de facto* crusade. As John U. Nef cogently noted, religious or holy wars—like later ideological wars—sanctioned any butchery on their behalf.[100] But this is a point worth exploring, for what are holy wars if not wars of ideology?[101] Although spoils may be gained in a holy war (in Augustine's words, "the struggle of good men against wicked men,")[102] its primary objective—if not merely a justification for simple conquest—is to defend one's ideas or beliefs against another or to impose one's ideas or beliefs upon another. As Hans Delbrück reminds us, the "mystical-transcendental trait of mankind is capable of developing a gigantic force," but, as he also notes, harnessing this power to military ends is extremely difficult.[103] He could have added that once set in motion and directed, an energy this powerful could turn the world upside down, a fact of which the great thinkers were only too well aware. During and immediately following the Reformation, this gigantic force was in fact unleashed, but its power was diffused through factionalism. Yet even dispersed, such was the destructive power of these wars over religious ideas that all Europe was torn asunder and reshaped; and, less than a century later, the concept of Christian holy war would have a direct influence on early Americans in their wars for survival and, later still, revolution.

Because of his centrality to the Reformation and its resultant upheavals, Martin Luther's (1483–1546) views on war are worth noting. As with other great thinkers of the period, Luther thought war an evil necessity. Without armies, there would be no peace, he wrote. A just war, therefore, "is only a very brief lack of peace that prevents an everlasting and immeasurable lack of peace, a small misfortune that prevents a great misfortune."[104] Defensive wars fought for the preservation of self and one's religion, Luther believed, were the only truly just wars. "It is not right to start a war just because some silly lord has gotten the idea into his head," he wrote, adding that "whoever starts a war is in the wrong."[105] Princes who start wars for glory, gain, or vanity were "fools." "God restrains such princes by giving fists to other people, too," he warned, "Thus one sword keeps the other in the scabbard."[106] Consequently, "[n]o war is just," he wrote, "even if it is a war between equals, unless one has such a good reason," and the only good reason was "lawful self-defense." Citing biblical precedents, Luther noted that even a righteous people fighting for a righteous cause would be defeated if they initiated hostilities.[107] Wars of rebellion, on the other hand, even against tyrants, were an abomination. Tyrannical rulers were bad, he acknowledged, but the alternative was mob rule. "A mad mob is a desperate, accursed thing. No one can rule it as well as tyrants, who are like the leash tied to a dog's neck." Here, as he often did, Luther borrowed from Aesop to make his point. A country ruled by a tyrant was like a beggar with many wounds. "Flies got into them and sucked his blood and stung him. Then a merciful man came along and tried to help him by shooing the flies away from him. But the beggar cried out and said, 'What are you doing? Those flies were almost full and did not worry me so much; now the hungry flies will come in their place and will plague me far worse.' "[108] Luther in his *Warning to His Dear German People* (1531) did condone civil disobedience and rebellion in one circumstance: when a ruler either transgressed the gospel by trying to reimpose Catholicism or if the prince ordered the faithful to arms against their fellow Luterans. In order to rationalize this seeming inconsistency, Luther juxtaposed his theory of just war on Christian holy war. "For in such an instance, when the murderers and bloodhounds wish to wage war and to murder, it is in truth no insurrection to rise against them and defend oneself."[109] Luther certainly was no advocate of war, but if the faith was threatened, he was characteristically realistic about military readiness and straightforward as to how war should be waged. Be prepared, "[b]e men, and test your armor. Then you will not have to think about war to fight," he wisely suggested. "The situation will be serious enough, and the teeth of the wrathful, boasting, proud men who chew nails will be so blunt that they will scarcely be able to bite into fresh butter."[110] After all, as colonial New Englanders and Virginians understood, in a righteous cause, "it is not man, but God, who hangs, tortures, beheads, kills, and fights. All these are God's works and judgment."[111]

Other concepts of war spawned in ancient times remained current through the colonization of America as part of the overall Western conceptualization of war, though not necessarily as part of Christian theology. Machiavelli's influence, for instance, was felt on later writers such as the French essayist Montaigne.[112] Drawing from both Machiavelli and ancient sources, Michel de Montaigne (1533–1592) sought to resurrect the Roman virtues, including a citizen-soldiery. "Whoever is prepared to bear valiantly the accidents of everyday [sixteenth-century] life," he wrote, "would not have to swell his courage to become a soldier."[113] Montaigne urged defense of France, but he understood constant foreign adventuring as sapping the virtue and treasure of his nation, which might lead to internal dissension; therefore he cautioned against constant war for political or royal aggrandizement. Like Aquinas, Luther, Bacon, and many others, Montaigne disavowed popular rebellion and civil war. "A monstrous war! Other wars work outwardly, this also against itself, biting into its own vitals and destroying itself with its own poisons." In rebellion, all "discipline flies from it. It comes to cure sedition, and is full of it." Even tyranny was better than civil war in Montaigne's estimation.[114]

Another perspective was offered in the late seventeenth century by John Locke, whose works were carefully scrutinized by colonial Americans, particularly those who launched the Revolution. Locke took an enlightened position, arguing for the natural law of self-preservation. As it was "man's first care and most natural desire" to be safe, then the first end of government (established by contract between ruler and ruled) was "to secure the members in their lives, liberties, and possessions."[115] Locke's perspective was new, but the concept originated in antiquity. Luther, too, had addressed this issue. "Worldly government has not been instituted by god to break the peace and start war, but to maintain peace and avoid war. Paul says in Romans 13[.4] that it is the duty of the sword to protect and punish, to protect the good in peace and to punish the wicked with war."[116] Government's (the ruler's) first duty was to protect its people (the ruled). "That is [the prince's] office, that is why he has the sword."[117] Borrowing a concept possibly derived from Pericles, Vegetius, or any of a dozen others, Locke wrote that since security of the people was such a key function of government, then a nation's military should not be merely equal to that of potential enemies, but superior.[118] Filled with patriotic troops, such a superior force would deter enemies and keep the peace while at the same time posing no threat to the commonweal. In words much quoted by revolutionary Americans but equally applicable to their colonial grandparents, Locke summarized a great deal in this simple statement of war under natural law: "I should have the right to destroy that which threatens me with destruction."[119]

The Lockean perspective, so clearly restating the fundamental law of self-preservation going back to the origins of humankind, condensed the problem philosophers and legal minds had in implanting just war theory on real warfare. Just as seventeenth- and eighteenth-century nations did not have the socioeconomic and military wherewithal to conduct a total war, neither did they have sufficient civilian and military bureaucracies, clearly defined chains of command, civilian oversight, adequate systems of military justice, or, most importantly, the desire to enforce any rules of war save the most general.

The ideas of Grotius, Robert Bellarmine, Baron de Montesquieu, and Vattel were well known in Europe and America, and their legalistic arguments particularly appealed to politically conscious colonials. Through the eighteenth century, however, the actual impact of these concepts on war and how wars were fought was minimal. Officers who were captured or had surrendered were paroled on their word of honor that they would refrain from participating in the war (even to reporting troop movements) until they had been exchanged. Prisoners of war were exchanged on an even basis, and certain battlefield formalities were followed. During the American Revolution, however, because the colonists were rebels in British eyes and English officers loathed considering former shopkeepers and farmers as brother officers, many of these niceties began to be ignored. The British took particular offense at the sensible practice of American sharpshooters (especially Morgan's riflemen) in singling out officers as targets, and while officer parole and exchange continued, thousands of American prisoners of war rotted and died in English prison ships and jails.[120] "Altogether the eighteenth century offers no exception to the general rule that 'war is hell,' " writes Christopher Duffy. "Its reputation for moderation comes from the fact that atrocities in other times were generally worse, and," he adds, "that the civilian peoples were most often incidental victims of careless brutality than the deliberately selected targets of military operations."[121] The ideas and writings of these great thinkers had an important direct and indirect influence on the prerevolutionary generation's thinking about war and the military, but not much on its practice. For the early colonists, however, while they looked to Europe for ideas, they took their marching orders from a Higher Authority.

The centrality of the Bible to Western culture and thought has been often overlooked by historians, but to colonial Americans the Bible— for them, the revealed word of God—was the source of directions in war as in all aspects of their lives.[122] Such was their genuine empathy for the ancient Hebrews that many of them, too, assumed the persona of Chosen People. To be sure, they knew and understood the law of nature as handed down from classical times, and they valued both intellect and piety, but for seventeenth-century colonials, the word of God was paramount.[123] Even their laws acknowledged this: "The Lord is our judge, the Lord *is* our lawgiver, the Lord *is* our king; he will save us."[124] God gave them hegemony over the land ("heaven, *even* the heavens, *are* the Lord's, but the earth hath he given to the children of men"),[125] including the native inhabitants, as He had provided for the Hebrews arriving at biblical Canaan. "Ask of me," one colonist wrote, quoting from Psalm 2.8, "and I shall give thee, the heathen for thine inheritance, and the uttermost parts of the earth for thy possession."[126] This belief had been reinforced even before disembarkation when God employed natural calamities to help facilitate colonial settlement—just as He had employed natural forces to guide the Hebrews from Egypt and across the desert (where they marched, "in good order, in *Rank* and *File*," led by Moses, the "Captain General of the Hosts of Israel").[127] Contact with early seventeenth-century European explorers (and, perhaps ever earlier, fishermen) introduced previously unknown diseases to the Native Americans, wiping out whole villages and tribes. But to the colonists, it was the "hand of God [that] fell heavily upon them, with such a mortall stroake, that they died in heapes." So many bones and skulls were scattered near the now empty towns of New England that to one settler writing in 1637 "it seemed to me a new found Golgatha."[128] Most acknowledged that the cause of death was "an epidemical and unwonted sickness" that struck in 1612 and 1613, but they all understood that "divine providence made way for the quiet and peaceable settlements of the English."[129] Yet, because He had not killed off *all* the natives, the colonists remained aware that God had also retained some as a means of retribution.[130]

Among Europeans of the period, common knowledge held that breaking God's law resulted in divine punishment, whether individually or to a people or nation in general. Natural catastrophes such as floods, droughts, famines, pestilences, or wars were God's way of chastising sinners, and, because of humans' inherently sinful and corrupt nature, these misfortunes occurred with great regularity. In particular, war was commonly perceived, Barnabe Rich noted in 1604, as having been "ordained by the Almightie himselfe, as a scourge upon the people, to make them feele and know their sinnes."[131] Or, as one New England minister preached, "Wars are visible sad Instances, awakening dreadful Demonstrations, of the deep Corruption of human Nature."[132]

Certainly, among New England Puritans, in whose theology the concept of a special covenant with the Almighty was integral,[133] breaking this compact resulted in the withdrawal of God's blessing, bringing punishment upon them oftentimes in the form of Native Americans. The slaughter that initiated and closed King Philip's War (1675–76) and left the colonial frontier devastated had been caused, according to Cotton Mather, by the *"Degenerate Estate* of the *present Generation in New England."* These "Second generation worldings," he wrote, "by departing from the pure faith of their fathers, had brought upon themselves war and defeat, starvation and pestilence."[134] It was those "Bad-Livers . . . that bring whole Armes of *Indians* and *Gallic* Blood Hounds in upon us; tis *you,"* he accused, "that clog all our *Councils* with such Delay and Slowness, as terrifies us in our most Rational Expectations."[135] Luckily, God had come to the rescue. "The marvellous Providence of God immediately extinguished that *war,"* Mather wrote in *Magnalia Christi America,* "by preparing the *New-English* arms, unto the utter subduing of the Quarrelsome nations and affrightening of all other natives."[136] As the Chosen—and like their Hebraic counterparts—Puritans believed that not only did God punish them with these "Arm[i]es of *Indians* and *Gallic* Blood Hounds" but He tested their faith by fire and tomahawk; if they passed the test and kept the faith, redemption was possible. Thus, they could accept Amerindian raids with what one called "the most Lively and Awful Sense of Divine Rebukes," and then, countenanced by God and just war theory, immediately dispath volunteer militia on a holy mission of revenge.[137]

But for non-Puritan colonists, too, trials and tribulations from God were part of humankind's lot, for all people were inherently sinful and wicked. Although they believed that they did, New England covenanters did not hold a monopoly on these concepts. Even through the American Enlightenment and past the Revolution, a providential explanation for natural calamities or propitious events was the rule among all colonials and contemporary Europeans. After all, to a people whose parents and grandparents had seen a Spanish armada wrecked by divine winds, an especial relevance existed.[138]

To a large measure, the colonists' initial and subsequent relationships with the native Americans were dictated by Scripture. At first, recounted a minister in 1738, they "sought their and the *Natives Peace,* did all they could to *teach* and *win* and *save*'em: But when *Hatred* was return'd for their *Love* and *Enmity* for their offer'd *Friendship*," he declared, the colonists "resolutely *defended* themselves, and pursu'd their Invaders."[139] In part, this proffered olive branch stemmed from attempts to Anglicize and convert the Indians both religiously and colturally, practical efforts to make the transition to a new life harmonious, and, harkening back to ancient wisdom, diplomatic endeavors to preempt potential conflict. Yet there was not a man or woman among the early colonists who did not recall God's admonition to the Israelites upon entering Canaan: "When thou comest nigh unto a city to fight against it, then proclaim peace unto it. And it shall be, if it make thee answer of peace, and open unto thee, then it shall be, *that* all the people *that is* found therein shall be tributaries unto thee, and they shall serve thee."[140]

As with the revolutionary generation's use of the classics, early colonists did not employ Biblical quotations *ex post facto*, placing a scriptural imprimatur on deeds already done; the Bible was such a part of their way of life, their thinking, their essence, that there is nothing comparable a modern scholar can draw upon to analogize its importance. Through their own reading and through ministerial interpretation, the Bible addressed every aspect of their lives—temporal, spiritual, or metaphysical. Thus, when the Native Americans knocked the olive branch from one hand (from a colonial perspective), the other was already drawing a sword from its scabbard as Scripture advised. Unable to bring the highly mobile Native Americans to bay, the colonists sent volunteers to launch surprise attacks on enemy encampments, less an adoption of Amerindian tactics than a reprise of Gideon's bold attack on the Midianites.[141] In sacking Native American villages, slaying men, women, and children, colonists simply followed God's directive to the Hebrews upon entering Canaan if their offers of peace were rebuffed, to "save alive nothing that breatheth." They were ordered to "utterly destroy" those who lived in their "inheritance," for they might contaminate the Chosen.[142]

To a people guided in learning about war by the English experience in Ireland, who believed that the Bible was the word of God, who looked to Europe and saw only savagery in war, and who were, above all, governed by self-preservation, such direct orders were clear and precise. True, these colonists were Christians who looked to the New Testament and Christian theology to justify their going to war. And, for them, Jesus Christ "came as a great General, a mighty Man of War . . . at the head of all the *Train-bands* of Heaven."[143] But the New Testament's overall message of love, peace, and brotherhood lacked the martial flavor and specific military advice the practical colonists needed. When it came to actual battle, their God was an Old Testament "man of warre" and "his name was *Jehovah*."[144] The wars of self-preservation and conquest that the Hebrews fought under God's direction were brutal affairs. Men were slaughtered, women and children sold into slavery, and body counts were made by totaling the enemy's amputated foreskins or hands (thus, the expression "they are in our hands").[145] In America, the colonists adopted a like way of war, also identical—perhaps not so coincidentally—to that of the English in Ireland, except for the way they counted enemy dead. Some colonists initially copied Sir Humphrey Gilbert and others and collected enemy heads,[146] but this burdensome practice most likely led practical colonists to adopt the Amerindian custom of counting scalps, which were less cumbersome. Reduced to its essence, the primary lesson of Old Testament warfare, notes biblical scholar Peter Craigie, is that if "war is to be waged at all, it must be done thoroughly. There are no half-measures in war; it is not a game to be played casually," either in the Old Testament or in the New World.[147] The brutality of such a way of war is self-evident, yet as God's warriors in a righteous cause, colonists had moral, religious, cultural, historical, and legal justifications for their actions.

For them, the concept of a just war was more than a theoretical argument, it was a key element of their conceptions of war and, in part, of their idea about the role of a military in their society. War was a necessary evil; it required official sanction by legally appointed or elected magistrates (the state); only wars fought in defense of the faith or under God's direction were just; and while offensive war was an abomination, a preemptive defensive war was acceptable if a real danger of attack existed. Excluding some Quakers and other pacifistic sects,[148] even the least militant colonists recognized that self-preservation made defensive war (even an aggressive defensive war) justified. As Thomas Hobbes summarized, "convenants, without the sword are but words, and of no strength to secure a man at all."[149] Roger Williams, who pleaded with John Winthrop "to prevent [hostilities] by loving Mediation or prudent Newtralitie,"[150] also advised that "all men of Conscience or Prudence, ply to Windward & wisely labour to mainteine their Wars to be defensive."[151] Increase Mather believed that "the light of Nature directs man unto a *Defensive War*." Of course, any war called by God was just, including offensive wars in defense of the colonists' "Liberties, Properties and Possessions." Since "God has put a principle of self preservation into his Creatures," Mather wrote, any war fought to preserve life and the faith was just. "Only it is to be remembered that an *Offensive War* is not to be undertaken," he cautioned, "but with the Consent and Authority of the Magistrates." For "It is not for private persons to revenge without direction from God or his Vice-Regents."[152] This theme, that the only truly just and legal war is one which has been authorized by God or the state, came down to seventeenth-century America from its ancient biblical and classical past as an integral part of Western conceptions of war, and within it may be found the origins of civilian control of the military.

In the Old Testament, the decision to go to war or not was God's alone. No matter how seemingly righteous the cause, if God, speaking through His prophets or appointed representatives, did not authorize a war, the Israelites would be defeated. Although the Hebrews constantly tested God (and lost), Yahweh established the primacy of the annointed leader or leadership before they reached the Promised Land. When Moses came down from Mt. Sinai bearing the tablets of the law, he found his people cavorting in idol worship. God, through Moses, ordered the Levites to put three thousand men to death. To John Calvin, the Levites were the precursors of his Protestant Elect, "a special group of men to whom God had given special privileges and commands," writes Michael Walzer, "but they were also symbols of the coming generations of holy warriors."[153] Here would be the precedent, notes another scholar, for the Protestant Elect to participate "enthusiastically in *war* against evildoers," a fact New England magistrates knew well.[154] Also affirmed in his bloody confirmation was the superiority of the civil over the military which, in turn, legitimized the military's actions. "It is not for the pious to afflict and hurt," wrote Calvin, "yet to avenge, at the Lord's command, the afflictions of the pious is not to hurt or to afflict." Borrowing as much from Augustine as from the Bible, Calvin noted that only the duly appointed magistrates (or Elect) "have a mandate from God," *ergo*, only the magistrates can legitimize or justify going to war, thus making war a legitimate act of the state.[155] Another divine confirmation of the power of the magistrates stemmed from the biblical *herem* or ban. God, through His legitimate representative Joshua, had ordered a village sacked, all inhabitants slaughtered, and forbade all plundering. One soldier concealed a necklace, and God directed Joshua to execute the soldier, his family, and his livestock, and "all Israel stoned him with stones." Failure to carry out God's (the magistrate's) command also resulted in the loss of Saul's crown.[156] Thus the power of colonial magistrates was confirmed by the highest authority, a power that they would not let English governors or officers arrogate from them easily.

The colonists' armed sorties against the powerful Amerindians, though fueled with religious zeal, were not undertaken without some qualms. The colonists confronted a moral dilemma modern Christians still face: reconciling tenets against killing with the necessity of taking life on the battlefield. Or, as one scholar wrote, how to harmonize God the warrior of the Old Testament with the God of love in the New.[157] As usual, colonial ministers helped to guide colonists through these difficulties. The Sixth Commandment which forbade killing was interpreted thusly: "THIS *Precept doth not interdict Christians the Liberty of making War, upon their Offensive Neighbours.*" This same preacher then quoted from Luke 22.36, seeking validation from the New Testament. *"He that hath no sword, let him sell his garment and buy one."*[158] A "Souldier must love his enemies as they are his enemies, and hate them as they are gods enemies."[159] In doing God's work militiamen should not enjoy killing other people, but "Obedience to your great Commander shou'd be always delightful to you."[160] Since God "comes Himself as the Generalissimo into the Field with his people," their actions were sanctified by His presence.[161] So, in fighting the good fight, "the *Sword* is, as it were, *consecrated* to God," one minister preached in Virginia, "and the Art of WAR becomes a Part of our *Religion*."[162] "Blessed *be* the LORD my strength, which teacheth my hands to war," another quoted from Psalm 144, "*and* my fingers to fight."[163] Standing shoulder-to-shoulder with the colonists was the "Lord our God for to helpe us and to fight our battells"; they should not fear death.[164] After all, *"[f]or a souldier to die in the field in a good cause, it is as for a preacher to die in a pulpit."*[165] In a righteous cause as approved by God through the authorities (the state), Christians were morally, ethically, and legally expected to pick up arms, fight, and kill. Thus could Lion Gardener exult when the volunteers "returned with victory to the glory of God, and honour of our nation, having slain three hundred, burnt their fort, and taken many prisoners," and another colonist rejoiced that the "name of Pequits (as of *Amaleck*) is blotted out from under heaven, there being not one that is, or, (at least) dare call himselfe a Pequit." Even Increase Mather felt pleased that so many Indians had been "Berbikew'd."[166]

For the most part, their ministers urged them on, accompanying them in battle and often joining in combat as had biblical prophets.[167] Like their English counterparts in Cromwell's New Model Army, colonial men of the cloth acted as combination chaplains and morale officers, performing roles much akin to that of a modern political officer in Marxist-Leninist revolutionary armies.[168] They reassured volunteer militiamen that the ideal and the ideas they were fighting for were just, for they were God's. When the Revolution came, the ministers continued rallying and motivating the troops, altering their jeremiads only slightly to square them with republican ideology.[169] Quoted time and again to prompt reluctant townsmen into enlisting was a favorite biblical verse of the Crusaders: "Cursed be he that keepeth back his sword from blood."[170] These ministers were more than just clerical drill sergeants, however, for they were a necessary link in the development of American conceptions of war. Well-educated and well-read in both the classics and popular literature, they refined contemporary and ancient just war theory to fit conditions facing their flocks, tossing in considerable practical military wisdom for good measure.[171]

Thus being a Christian was not incompatible with shouldering a musket and fighting God's foes. In a theme echoed over and over through the Revolution, being a Christian, a minister advised, in no way "deprives us of the Privilege of Self-Defense and Self-Preservation."[172] As Samuel Willard declared in 1699 in an artillery sermon entitled, "The Man of War": "Christianity is no Enemy to Souldiering . . . [for] the Christian Religion cannot otherwise be defended or secured against the invaders and oppressors of it, who are unreasonable men," he noted, adding, "and can be no other way disputed, but at the Swords point, and Canons mouth." "Beware," he must have thundered, "of embracing that cursed Machiavellian principle, that too much of Religion will make a man Pusillanimous."[173] And so "They pray'd and wro'd and fought," a minister sermonized, "plow'd and built, with their Guns and *Swords by their Side*."[174] Having had it drilled into their heads from childhood in sermon after sermon that God was at their side in all things, including battle, it was no wonder that colonial and later revolutionary Americans developed an inflated sense of their own moral and martial worth.

CHAPTER 8

The English Legacy

Ideas can be simple or complex. Those which gain the greatest popularity and have the most influence are ideas that, in spite of their complexity, have been simplified or made understandable to the largest number of people. Modification such as this is often accomplished, consciously or unconsciously, by reducing an idea or a series of ideas into something representative of their essence: by the creation of a symbol.

The concepts that as a whole have been called American revolutionary republican ideology resulted from several strains of intellectual inquiry, the rediscovery of sources going back to biblical and classical times, massive societal shifts which were felt but not fully recognized, and the exigencies of the times. In sum, the totality of revolutionary ideology with all its nuances, complexities, and debts to foreign and ancient thinkers was fully known and understood by relatively few of the prerevolutionary generation. Many grasped the general concepts of what Americans were against and what they were for, but the whole was so vast as to preclude most from a complete understanding. Therefore, symbolization occurred, and complex issues were reduced so that the Sasquatch of Americana, the elusive average person, could comprehend why rebellion appeared to be the only solution.

Two of these symbols were military in nature: the British army, as a manifestation of ministerial tyranny and everything loathed by freedom-loving colonists, and the militia, as an emblem of all colonial republican virtues and ideas. In a sense such a condensation greatly oversimplifies; there were additional symbols and much early American ideology was known in other guises. And yet, a redcoated British soldier standing on a cobbled Boston street and a ragtag group of farmers stumbling through the manual of arms were vivid, living representations of how bitter relations had become between mother country and colonies. To colonials, that solitary British soldier, standing ramrod stiff in his heavy woolen uniform with its rigid stock, brought home all the fine words of John Dickinson and oratorical flourishes of Sam Adams. He was tyranny in flesh and blood. All the revolutionary rhetoric that poured forth could not raise the visceral loathing that this single soldier could engender by his mere presence. He was a visible and tangible threat to life, liberty, and property, not a metaphorical allusion conjured up by a penman evoking visions of Caesar's legions marching through the streets. To be sure, republican propaganda heightened awareness, but the roots of hatred for this soldier and what he represented went deep: they were embedded in the Americans' heritage and ethos.

Similarly, the concept of a citizen-soldiery was an integral part of the republican mythos dating from antiquity. That in actual practice the myth never quite squared with reality was beside the point, for what colonial Americans believed was true had an impact on subsequent events. Their perceptions of themselves and of the changing political economy of Great Britain were manifestly affected by space and time. While colonists were generally aware of the vast social shifts Europe had undergone and was undergoing, living and growing across the Atlantic they could not fully comprehend the effects any more than most Europeans could. Their perceptions were clouded, and all they could see was that Europe, especially Great Britain, had departed from their ideal. The reliance of the Crown upon a regular professional army was, to colonial eyes, one of the most telling manifestations of tyrannical corruption. Standing as a bulwark against the corruptive changes, however, was that pure symbol of republican virtue, the colonial militia.

When the Continental Congress decided in 1775 to create its defense establishment in the volunteer militia mold, it based its decision not on republican ideology alone but also on long- and deeply held ideas that were part of the American essence. For the Congress, it would have been a total refutation of principle and tradition to have done otherwise. The wave upon wave of anti–standing army rhetoric which had rolled across the Atlantic from England since the late seventeenth century roiled colonial emotions and helped erode loyalty to the Crown. But while the arguments were fresh, persuasively written, and influential, they reached an audience that was strongly predisposed toward them. For Americans' conceptions of war and the role a military would play in their society had been formed long before.

As a people the English have made excellent soldiers; histories are replete with accounts of their valor from Hastings to Waterloo and beyond. When threatened from without or within, Englishmen knew their duty and responded to the call to arms, fighting with dogged determination until the conflict was resolved. "Our nation may boast, beyond any other people in the world," noted Samuel Johnson with pride, "of a kind of epidemick bravery, diffused equally through all its ranks."[1] Then, however, having done his duty, the Englishman wanted to leave the army and return home, for at heart he truly was a citizen-soldier. The English appeared to lack a martial nature. They did not have the warrior ethos of their neighbors to the north, the Scots, nor were they as habitually combative as the Gaels across the Irish Sea.[2] Although they enjoyed the trappings of the military and regularly sharpened their combat skills by turning training into games, England had no great desire or need before the mid-seventeenth century for a regular professional army. In fact, the opposite was true: Englishmen readily answered when God and country called, but a professional army on their soil was anathema to them.

   The English loathing of professional armies and professional soldiers was already a deeply held tradition when the seventeenth-century settlement of North America began; subsequent events only hardened this attitude. At its heart lay the concept of community defense solely by community members as a right of membership. Derived from the *posse comitatus* of the Germanic peoples, the idea crossed to England with the Angles and Saxons where, after time, it was mated with lessons gleaned from biblical and classical writings as a part of the

English political system. The concept of defense of England only by English citizens was incorporated into the Magna Carta, and it grew to be an ingrained part of the constitutional legacy of the English. "As soon as peace is restored, we will remove from the kingdom all foreign knights, cross-bowmen, serjeants, and mercenaries, who," it was noted at Runnymede in 1215, "have come with horses and arms to the detriment of the kingdom."[3] Regular soldiers (foreign hirelings in particular, but even indigenous troops) having no ties to the nation they defended, but owing allegiance only to their paymasters, were seen as threats to English liberty. St. Thomas More borrowed from this tradition in creating his fictitious Utopians, who "never lightly make war in their own country nor is any emergency so pressing as to compel them to admit foreign auxiliaries into their island."[4]

Another reason may be considered as environmental or even practical. England is part of an island, a large one to be sure, but an island nonetheless, and the insularity that afforded protection had much to do with the development of English conceptions of war and the military. The deeply felt, almost paranoid hatred and fear of regular or standing armies espoused in the late seventeenth and early eighteenth century by Fletcher, Trenchard, Gordon, and other radical Whigs and libertarians were uniquely English; across the Channel and North Sea, continental nations with land borders and menacing neighbors could not consider replacing their armed forces with a civilian-militia even as an intellectual exercise. Even if their armies were maintained solely for defense, national security demanded a strong military to dissuade hostile encroachments. For England, both deterrence and defense rested with the Royal Navy. If another nation attempted to invade England, and if its forces managed to slip past or defeat the Royal Navy, then all England could rally to the point of attack and drive the enemy into the sea. In 1588 the roads to the Channel coast were crowded with militiamen filled with patriotism and religious zeal to combat the threat to England posed by the Catholic Spanish. That the invasion did not take place, through Providential intervention, and that the defense was not put to the test mattered little.[5] Englishmen had done their duty for God, Queen, and country, and in the doing contributed to an already inflated militia tradition.[6]

While militia theoretically protected the home island, England had fielded and maintained regular forces on the Continent for decades, particularly in the Netherlands and France. As was their habit, the English relied heavily upon Scots and Irish to fill their ranks, but more than a few native Englishmen were pressed for overseas duty. These impressed men were not the yeoman farmers and stout militiamen of legend (for militia did not serve overseas) but, as described in an earlier chapter, "dronkerds," "privy pickers," and "seditiouse quarilers." "In England when service happeneth," wrote Barnabe Rich in 1587, "we disburthen the prisons of thieves, we rob the taverns and alehouses of tosspots and ruffians, we scour both towns and country of rogues and vagabonds."[7] Such men had little enthusiasm for military service, and, as Matthew Suttcliffe noted in 1593, "if they had their deserts, they were to be sent rather to ye gallowes, then to the warres for the most part."[8] As one contemporary described troops being sent to Germany in 1624, "Such a rabble of raw and poor rascals have not lightly [lately] been seen, and they go so unwillingly that they must rather be driven than led."[9] The Stuart kings wanted very much to be players on the continental stage. But, as their dreams of making Virginia a military outpost went for naught, their "inept and occasional interventions" had little effect on the Thirty Years' War.[10] When the troops returned home, disabled or disbanded, they were dumped upon society, left "In Red-coat rags attired, [to] wander up and down."[11] Or, as one poet described them:

> Wars now is worse, than walking horse,
> For like a hackney tied at rack,
> Old soldier so (who wanteth force)
> Must learne to beare a pedlar's pack,
> And trudge to some good market towne,
> So from a knight becomes a clowne.[12]

The veterans were victims of unpopular royal adventuring, not heroes of a patriotic war. Begging, starving, drinking, turning to crime and other forms of social disruption, these "old fogeys" were despised by a sixteenth- and early seventeenth-century English civilian populace.[13]

The impact of these veterans on English society colored the thinking of Englishmen (and soon-to-be colonists) about soldiers, professional armies, and the military in general. As noted, these veterans were not middle-class farmers or stalwart yeoman; they came from the meanest sort and the army they served bore no relationship to the small but disciplined British army of the post-Cromwellian period. Impressed against their will or having exchanged the gibbet for a soldier's life, they were employed overseas where rules and conduct were less restrained,[14] "where they think it foolish scrupulousness to use either tenderness o[r] conscience." There, as one sixteenth-century writer noted, they became "so venomous a brood to their native country . . . that they are rather to be vomited out of the bulk of the commonwealth than to be nourished by the same."[15] When they arrived back in England, with nary a thank-you from the government they had served, it was little wonder that many turned into footpads, highwaymen, and gin-addled alcoholics. "That great and wise Encouragement which the Ancients gave their Soldiers," one writer commented, "of providing for the Maimed, or Superannuated, by feeding and maintaining them, or by Rewards in Lands, is not practised among us."[16] An unenlightened social conscience did not perceive of these men as victims of war but as purveyors of unrest and vice, particularly the latter. Barnabe Rich, an ex-officer and one of the veterans' few defenders, described the civilian perception of these men in 1578 by recalling Agrippa's words: "that you desire to see a true Tyrant, a Prophaner, or a Murtherer, a Robber, a Rauisher, a Deflowerer, if you would haue all these seuerall conditions in one singular person," he wrote, "and if you desire to include all this matter in one word, it is comprehended in this one name Soldier."[17] As is often the case (with the Irish, Amerindians, and others), caricatures became stereotypes which, in turn, entered into the national consciousness. In part, civilians had a preconceived notion about soldiers, drawn in a large measure from the age-old conflict between "lazy, lower-class" soldiers and "hardworking, respectable" civilians. Among civilians, for whom militia muster and drill were synonymous with roisterous good times, even if soldiers drilled and marched all day (which they did not), they were not perceived as working or, at least, doing virtuous, civilian work. Whatever the cause, the veterans were seen as disruptive to society, and, as tangible evidence of the corrupting nature of both war and the military, were hated and feared by civilians who "condemn[ed] soldiership," and, wrote a contemporary, ". . . despise[d] the profession of arms as a vile and damnable occupation."[18] "Souldiers," another noted,

". . . are now looked vpon with a contemptfull eye," as corrupters of the moral fiber of the nation.[19] For most civilians, contact with these discarded veterans was the only relationship they had with the military, for during the early colonization of America, England enjoyed a relative peace at home.

Safety being ensured by the navy, the martial prowess of sixteenth- and seventeenth-century Englishmen declined to a miserable state. As described earlier, the myth of the militia's strength flourished even as its actual proficiency declined; training grew lax and muster days turned into riotous drunks. The "Trained Bands, especially in the Counties, rarely meet to Exercise, and then return at Night, where they feed well, and lie warm," the Earl of Orrery wrote.[20] The militia mythos, however, combined with peace to lull Englishmen into an exalted sense of their own security and martial abilities (not unlike Americans in 1775). "The danger of all," noted Lord Cecil, a veteran of the Irish wars, in 1628, "is that a people not used to war believeth no enemy dare venture upon them."[21] Peace at home, the Royal Navy, and geographic insularity made English conceptions of war different from those of their continental neighbors (England, Shakespeare wrote, "This fortress built by Nature for herself Against infection and the hand of war").[22] "Peace hast so besotted us, that as we are altogether ignorant [of military affairs]," wrote Cecil, "so are we so much the more not sensible of that defect, for we think if we have men and ships our kingdom is safe, as if men were born soldiers."[23] One Englishman disgustedly noted in 1579 that without the navy and the Channel, men would "know and value the soldier and lick the dust off the feete" of an army.[24] Many saw the militia as a cheaper, less dangerous, and less odious alternative, while some attributed the decline of martial spirit to moral laxity. "Our minds are effeminated, our martiall exercises and disciplines of warre," noted Rich, "are turned into womanish pleasures and delights."[25] Harkening back to Greek mythology, one contemporary noted that when Hercules had to choose between Virtue and Vice, he selected Virtue, "and I thinke sent the other into England, where at this present she is duetifully served."[26] To the thinking of most Englishmen, there was no need for a costly, seldom employed and potentially dangerous professional army as long as there was a well-trained citizen-soldiery. As Lord Burghley, Elizabeth I's chief advisor, noted, "soldiers in peace are like chimney's in summer."[27] But by the turn of the seventeenth century, a militia disciplined and trained in the art of war existed only in tradition and folklore, and the English military hearth was cold indeed.

Thus the conceptions of war carried across the Atlantic by colonists were much influenced by cultural myth, more than a hundred years of relative internal peace, a long-held hatred of soldiers and things military, and a healthy suspicion of royal intrigue. The classical notion that wars united a nation in a surge of patriotism was seen by the generation that furnished the first colonists as being no longer true. Pressed men and those saved from the gallows were not the virtuous patriots of ancient republics or Edenic mythologies. These "cankers of a calm world and a long peace" were but fodder for the king's wars.[28] Wars were the purview of kings, and royal adventuring and wars of glory resulted in little for the people, save burdening them with higher taxes and unruly veterans.[29] "As for fame and glorye, desyred but for worldly pleasure, doth vnto the soule inestimable harm," wrote Thomas More. ". . . Thys maketh battailes betweene these great prynces, and wyth much trouble to munce people, and greate effusyon of bloude, one kynge to looke to raygne in fyue realms, that can not wel rule one."[30] Wars did provide the nation with a chance to purge itself of the meanest sort and various undesirables such as the Scots and Irish, but not all were killed on the Continent. War corrupted those forced to serve and they, in turn, did little more than corrupt and disturb society upon their return.

In sum, the conception of war and all its components held by most Englishmen at the time of colonization was negative, and may be summarized in a few short lines with classical overtones written in 1590, lines well known to later Americans in both verse and theme. "Warre bringeth ruine, ruine bringeth povertie, povertie procureth peace, and peace in time increaseth riches," wrote Thomas Fenne, "riches causeth statelinesse, statelinesse increaseth envie, envie in the end procureth deadly mallice, mortall mallice proclaimeth open warre and battaile: and from warre again as before is rehersed."[31]

The English tradition of opposition to a professional military was firmly implanted in colonial minds, and circumstances and events both in the New and Old Worlds would only reinforce their beliefs. In the colonies, time, opponents, biblical and classical admonitions, terrain, and dozens of other practical and religiophilosophic reasons prevented the formation of anything resembling a professional standing army. As was discussed in an earlier chapter, the slightest hint of a military threat to civilian control sent colonial magistrates into paroxysms, decrying Caesarism, Praetorianism, or worst of all, the development of a regular, professional military force neither paid nor controlled by the people. And the last of these, the question of who shall rule, was at the immutable essence of colonial civil-military relations and ultimately of American republicanism. In the mid-seventeenth century, events in England turning on this question would have a major impact on American conceptions of war, both indirectly and directly.[32]

It all began with an attempt to institute an absolutist monarchy in England. The Stuarts, wishing to emulate the continental kings, posed a challenge to English constitutional liberties, and the upshot was civil war.[33] At the head of an absolutist monarchy was, of course, the king, but the body of absolutism combined a professional bureaucracy and a professional standing army. By modern standards, England's bureaucracy and army were small, even tiny, and unsophisticated, and yet, from a relative perspective, they were extremely efficient compared to what had previously existed. From a monarchical standpoint, the former was the means by which the king ruled, the skeleton of government as it were, collecting taxes and running the state on a day-to-day basis; the army was the muscle, the long arm of the king's foreign policy.

The professionalization of the civil and military functions of government turned the nobility out of office (and cut off their sinecures), fully divorcing the king from his people, who were now little more than tax-generating machines. Some saw this development as a great benefit to England, the beginning of a stabilization and standardization of government that would increase and protect trade; to give up a few liberties seemed a fair exchange.[34] For others steeped in classical learning and tightly bound to English traditions, however, the evolution of total power into the hands of one man backed by the full might of the state and an army loyal only to him was tyranny.[35] Law and the Constitution could easily be overturned, and the worst horror of all, a reintroduction of Catholicism, was not unlikely. Here was a genuine threat to life, liberty, property, and religion, a threat that could not go unanswered. From the same sources and heritage that had led their colonial cousins to make civilian control of the military an essential part of their polity, those in England realized that he who controls the money and the army wields absolute power.[36] Charles I increasingly sought to supersede Parliament's fiscal control of his military adventuring by taking full charge of the Treasury. But things did not work out as he had planned, and he lost not only his power but his head as well. Or, as Andrew Fletcher commented in 1698, the king "did indeed endeavour to make himself Absolute, tho somewhat preposterously; for he attempted to seize the purse, before he was Master of the Sword."[37]

When the chain of events culminated in an outbreak of hostilities between the forces supporting Charles I and those backing Parliament, the long "friction of peace" had taken its toll; there was little professional about either military force. Writing from the king's camp, Sir Edmund Verney observed, "I daresay there was never so raw, so unskilful, and so unwilling an army brought to fight."[38] As the small regular English army was scattered in garrisons and overseas, both Charles and his opponents relied upon volunteer militias that were singularly inefficient and unmartial. One contemporary described them as ". . . effeminate in courage and incapable of discipline because their whole course of life was alienated from warlike employment."[39] Moreover, after the initial zeal for war evaporated, neither side could recruit enough volunteers to flesh out its regiments, so both resorted to the press. Organization was sorely lacking, hunger and nakedness being common to both armies.[40] Without constant and rigorous training the militia of myth and tradition had disintegrated to such a state of ineffectiveness that in order to continue the war, the parliamentary side found it necessary to create an actual regular army. But the colonists overseas and their descendants who would face a similar crisis in the 1770s ignored the reason for the creation of this army—the total failure of the volunteer militia to accomplish its assigned mission—and concentrated instead on its subsequent actions.

Briefly summarized, the parliamentary forces were reorganized as the New Model Army in 1645 (thus introducing "new modelling" into the American revolutionary lexicon), but this was an army the like of which had not been seen since the Crusades. The analogy is appropriate, for while the New Model soldiers initially fought successfully for Parliament and England, they would come to fight for a higher cause, becoming Puritan holy warriors, an army of Saints.[41] "Religion was not the thing at first contested for, but God brought it to that issue at last," noted Oliver Cromwell, "and gave it unto us by redundancy, and at last it proved that which was most dear to us."[42] "God raised up some Heroes," a contemporary account went, ". . . to bring down the Mountain of Monarchary." These "heroes" had little choice, the author noted, for "if the Parliament had not opposed king *Charles*, God would have been revenged on them."[43] It should be noted however, that although the many chaplains who accompanied the army assured the troops that "God would have his Saints skilful in Martial order," the New Model Army remained a pale imitation of continental armies.[44] At Nasby (1645) and Preston Pans (1649), for example, Gustavus's introduction of field artillery during the Thirty Years' War was ignored, for none was used in either battle.[45] Nevertheless, these soldiers had already been engaged in a fight for what was tantamount to an ideological question. Now they were joined in an even stronger cause, a fight for an ideal, linked in a covenant with God just as their transatlantic contemporaries were.

But in England, the Covenanters deviated. Following the defeat of the royalist forces, Parliament sought to disband its victorious army with little thought to the individual soldiers. This action was in keeping with the normal English practice, deriving from a fear that the swords turned outward, defending Parliament, could easily be reversed. Some of the regiments were to be sent to Ireland, and the rest were simply told to go home; but none was to receive his back pay, which ranged from eighteen weeks' worth owed to the infantry to some nine months' worth to the horse.[46] As one contemporary noted, "those who pay the Souldiers, shall have obedience; but as the proverb is, No money, no Swiss: No money, no obedience."[47] Parliament, in effect, supplied the army with a "unity of resentment" that affected every man in it, and the army revolted and seized power.[48] Here was the stuff of later republican nightmares.

As the army saw things, Parliament, by breaking its covenant with the troops, was now as corrupt as the king it had overthrown, and thus only the incorrupt army could save the English people. "All wise men see that Parliament privileges as well as royal prerogative may be perverted or abused," read the Army Remonstrance of 23 July 1647, "to the destruction of those greater ends for whose protection and preservation that they intended, to wit, the rights and privileges of the people and the safety of the whole."[49] Fighting for and directed by God, the army was not overthrowing the government and usurping power but righting a wrong; after all, the pietistic soldiers—so the common wisdom went—were simply carrying out God's orders. "The Pretorian Cohorts advanced the Emperors at their pleasure; the Janizaries the Great Turkes; but our Army is so pious, there is no fear."[50] Parliament and England paid a high price for failing to meet their obligations: twelve long years of military rule and overseas war.[51] "Who could foresee that *Cromwell* would enslave those whom he was employed to defend?" asked *Cato* some sixty years later, "But there is no trusting of Liberty in the Hands of Men, who are obeyed by great Armies."[52]

But pay was only one of several demands made by the army. Another was manhood suffrage, which drove something of a wedge between the officers (who loathed the concept) and the enlisted men (who made it a major demand). This incipient strain of democracy gave pause to some who saw the army as a savior, and in part, it led to the elevation of Cromwell to be Protector in 1653 (for anything was preferable to democracy, the rule of the mob). His death six years later ultimately led to the restoration of Parliament, which set about trying, in a contemporary's words, "to bring the military sword under the power of civil authority."[53] Almost immediately the army expelled the sitting Parliament when that body sought to reexert its control by having all military commissions reviewed and passed on by it.

This second military takeover proved universally unpopular. The poet John Milton (1607–74), who had served the Protectorate, called the expulsion "illegal and scandalous." "I fear me barbarous or rather scarce to be exampled among any barbarians, that a paid army should . . . thus subdue the supreme power that set them up."[54] The army demanded autonomy, but with Cromwell gone there was no unanimity among officers and men. General George Monck (also Monk, 1608–

70) failed to join in the demands, saying that "soldiers received and observed commands, but gave none." Thus reaffirming parliamentary (civilian) control of the military, Monck led troops under his command toward London to reseat Parliament. Members of the anti-parliamentary faction begged him not to march against them, but Monck, probably after ascertaining popular opinion, replied: "I am engaged in conscience and honour to see my country freed from that intolerable slavery of a sword government, and I know England cannot, nay, will not endure it."[55] The mutinous army disbanded shortly thereafter, Parliament was reseated, and the Restoration was initiated. Civil-military relations, however, were inalterably changed.[56]

The years of military rule had an enormous impact upon English political thinking, and, as interpreted by the radical Whigs and libertarians, on prerevolutionary Americans. In spite of a great deal of justified negative imagery, Cromwell had restored England to greatness, and thus criticism of him was often tempered.[57] And, for better or worse, England now had a professional standing army on English soil. Compared to late seventeenth-century continental armies, it was small, tiny in fact, and not particularly martial in ability or spirit; the English consistently broke and ran before the unmilitary but fierce Highland warriors. But the army earned England a certain amount of international respect, especially when combined with the increasing might of the Royal Navy. Under the restored monarchy, the actions of Charles II and James II received close parliamentary and popular scrutiny, particularly their military policies. Calls to dissolve the army entirely were still heard, but international necessity precluded doing so. If England was to be a major power, it required a military force capable of projecting its will beyond naval reach. Because civil unrest was the bane of seventeenth- and eighteenth-century England, because smuggling cost the Treasury considerable tax monies, and because cross-border incursions by Scottish Highlanders were always a threat, military units had to be stationed on English soil. So strong, however, were the fears engendered by the Civil War and Protectorate that even these seemingly necessary deployments were regarded with mistrust.

The interpretation offered by zealous republicans, one that later fed the suspicious nature of their colonial readers, perceived this tiny army as the first step toward tyranny. Before the rise of absolutism and even following the Restoration, this interpretation goes, English governments did not raise enough revenues to make corruption worthwhile. When power became centered upon the king, his ministers, and their wealthy cohorts, noted these political pensmen (whose criticism of past events was but a thinly couched attack on the present rulers), the potential for corruption was increased: handing out offices for favorites and creating sinecures for their cronies in the army was absolutism's most obvious and odious symbol.[58] Certainly, under an absolutist or strong monarchical government, both bureaucrats and, indirectly, the military were dependent upon the king—and how well they performed their assigned duties—for their existence. Historical reality was a bit different from this interpretation, but one is more apt to remember what one wants to hear. Yet history need not be viewed through a republican prism to see that the king kept the troops, and the troops kept the king, all balanced on the people's backs.[59] "To comply with the People, [a tyrant] must give up his Power," wrote *Cato*, "to comply with his Soldiers, he must give up his People."[60] Thus professionals (especially the military) were inextricably wedded both in fact and in the people's minds with everything evil about excesses in monarchical power, thus, in turn, making the very term "professional" opprobrious.[61]

Having a professional army stationed on English soil alone raised eyebrows and fears, but how these troops were housed elicited considerable fury: they were quartered among the local households in the towns and counties in which they were stationed. From the late seventeenth century through the American war, the primary mission of the army stationed in England was civil, not military; that is, the army formed the national police force, chasing down smugglers (yes, there really were pirates at Penzance) and felons of all sorts, and maintaining civic order.[62] To accomplish these missions, the army was dispersed throughout the nation, which did little to increase its military efficiency. Quartering the troops in private homes was cheaper and prevented the men from gathering in barracks, those hotbeds of sedition,[63] but this positive note was nullified because neither reluctant landlords nor their unwelcome houseguests were pleased. Soldiers knew the low regard in which they were held, and even if they were on their best behavior—very unlikely—civilian animosity made itself known. Of course, householders did receive a welcomed government stipend for housing the soldiers, and much civilian protest occurred when this payment was slow or delayed. On the other hand, quartering was also seen as an additional tax or even as confiscation of property.[64] A standing army, however, was a boon to military contractors and bankers, and on the local level, sutlers, prostitutes, and liquor merchants were pleased to have a unit stationed nearby.[65] But to townspeople who loathed soldiers (soldier-baiting was a much beloved sport in England),[66] this was simply more corruption wrought by social parasites.[67] (Similar attitudes prevailed in America in the 1760s and 1770s, and when poorly paid soldiers took part-time jobs at low wages, they added another source of irritation.)

After James II had almost totally alienated the English people[68] and the Glorious Revolution of 1688 led to the accession, by request of Parliament, of William and Mary to the throne, the Bill of Rights and the Mutiny Act not only forbade quartering but also placed military appropriations and martial discipline under parliamentary control.[69] Power had been defined, and it rested with the people in Parliament, for, as was noted in *Cato's Letters*, "to pay well, and hang well, to protect the Innocent, and punish the oppressors, are the Hinges and Ligaments of Government, and chief Ends why Men enter into Societies."[70]

Inspired by the trauma their nation was going through or had undergone, writers and thinkers as diverse in their views as Hobbes, Harrington, Sidney, Moyle, Locke, Trenchard, Defoe, Bolingbroke, Gordon, and others borrowed from the classical and biblical past and from contemporary European writings to develop their concepts of what England's polity should be and to define the role of man to ruler and ruler to man. These strains of political philosophy followed many courses; some were parallel and built on the work of others, and some took diametrically opposite approaches. Yet they all sought to remake, to enlighten, and to redefine the English political character or essence. And in varying degrees, the role of a military in their society remained an ongoing theme in all their works. The specter of Cromwell was never far from the thoughts and writings of English political thinkers from the 1680s to 1720s.[71]

For prerevolutionary Americans, however, the diverse writings of such men provided a multitude of concepts from which to pick and choose. In youth and young manhood they gorged themselves on imported delicacies from the finest intellectual pantries of Europe, and their intellects and perceptions expanded accordingly. But instead of becoming corpulent and indolent of mind, they turned these calories into lean, sinewy muscle. They could not partake of everything, so they approached this heavily laden intellectual groaning board selectively, choosing from this and from that, finding especially palatable items that tasted like an old colonial favorite. Such was the case with the English antimilitary tradition, a linchpin of both English and American republican philosophies and as such a major influence on American conceptions of war in 1775.

The English antimilitary tradition was compatible with everything that colonial Americans were about. Their religious and secular education had inculcated them with the virtues of a citizen-soldiery, of men who dropped their shepherd's crook or plow and picked up their sling or gladius to defend Israel or republican Rome. If their homes or immediate communities were threatened, colonists would fight, but most avoided actual service in the volunteer militia, satisfying their martial urges in the local, homeguard units if at all. Nonetheless, the colonials' military establishment, no matter how scorned it was by the British, fully reflected the wants and needs of their society. Americans had survived and prospered in their new land without any regular army, for their militia served them quite well with little of the social disruption an army created. Following a campaign, the volunteer militia force dissolved. But instead of broken, dispirited men returning as a plague upon society, the disbanded volunteers were friends and neighbors who came home to retake their pew in church and resume their lives, probably never to take up arms again. Of course, since anything related to military service lent itself to corruption in the colonial mind, ministers strongly urged the volunteers to keep a sharp eye out for vice. Officers were advised to "Keep yourselves from *Effeminancy* and *Intemperance*, which has been the ruin of so many Soldiers."[72] Another warned young troopers that they were "entering into *the School of Vice:* for such the Army has generally been."[73] If by chance they had been corrupted even in their short service—hard to believe since the frontier presented few opportunities for sin, excluding the smuggled canteen of rum—redemption would soon follow the resumption of their normal lives, for the community demanded it. Because these men fought for their communities, liberties, and property, there was little cause to worry about sedition. Nevertheless, just as Goodwife Smith reported any deviationist tendencies among her neighbors, so did the magistrates pounce on anything that smacked of a usurpation of civilian control of the military.

Other aspects of American antimilitarism preconditioned colonials to republican ideology. Not only were armies seen as corrupting society with profanity, ungodliness, drunkenness, whoring, gambling, and thievery (what the army called foraging, civilians called theft) they were also extremely disruptive to the economy. As historian John Shy noted, to American farmers and townsmen, a military force was a "nasty and wasteful institution, which became especially troublesome when any of it was nearby."[74] (In the Revolutionary War, Washington lamented: "How disgraceful to the army is it, that the peaceable inhabitants, our countrymen and fellow citizens, dread our halting among them, even for a night and are happy when they get rid of us? This can proceed only from their distress at the plundering and wanton destruction of their property.")[75] Of course, this attitude did not stop these farmers and townsmen from doubling their prices on sales to the army. To thrifty Americans, it defied logic to pay high taxes during peacetime for soldiers to lie about, doing little except seeking out vice, and during wars the cost of armies saddled posterity with crushing burdens of public debt. Moreover, citizens who tried to obtain payment for a wagon or team "borrowed" by the military often received partial value if anything. For some this form of confiscation of their property was an unwarranted tax or thievery by petty tyrants; for others, it was just plain unfair. Either way, it won the military few friends.

So while colonial Americans fully understood the need for war and rarely shied away from a just fight, their incipient national character rebelled against anything that bespoke of militarism or a professional standing army, especially if it was nearby. Thus when controversy over the version of the anti–standing army question most closely associated with English libertarian and American republican thought developed from the late 1690s onward, colonials were not only well aware of its basic arguments but they were already quite favorably predisposed toward them.

This particular controversy was long in brewing. As indicated, traditional English antimilitary attitudes had been exacerbated by the years of the Civil War and the Protectorate. To have been burnt once was reason enough to be doubly conscious of fire, and even the legal protections wrought by the Glorious Revolution could not quell very real fears.[76] Events came to a head after the signing of the Treaty of Ryswick (1697), when King William argued against disbanding the army.[77] His action was immediately challenged in Parliament, and a heated pamphlet war broke out.[78] On the surface, the arguments of the antiarmy faction were fairly straightforward: maintaining a professional army (a "standing army") in time of peace was both unconstitutional and a threat to English liberties. "I say," stated Andrew Fletcher in 1698, "if a Mercenary Standing Army be kept up (the first of that kind, except those of the Usurper Cromwel, and the late King James, that Britain has seen for thirteen hundred years) I desire to know where Security of the English liberties lies, unless in the good Will and Pleasure of the King."[79] As *Cato* noted some twenty years later, "it is eternally true, that a free Parliament and a standing Army are absolutely incompatible, and can never subsist together."[80] In part an uneasiness arose from the presence of King William's Dutch guards.[81] Also, because of its police function, small numbers of troops were dispersed across the land in towns and villages where heretofore soldiers were a rarity; a few soldiers, highly visible in their red coats, provided the illusion of many, a most disturbing turn of events. But even after the question of the Dutch guards was resolved, the controversy raged, for what was at stake was nothing less than who would control the English government—the king and his ministers or the people through Parliament?

The standing army controversy became a metaphor for radical Whig-libertarian attacks on the power and rights of the king, which, in turn, increased factionalism in England. Some fifty years later, colonial Americans, and particularly those who became the leaders of the revolutionary movement, avidly read these arguments, finding in them precedents and fresh validation for their own concepts. What colonial readers missed or ignored, however, were subtleties that were, in fact, important features of the argument.

For instance, those who argued for a standing army were not advocating a return to "sword government" but trying to infuse law, tradition, and constitution with new realities. This faction, never as well known among colonists as their more obstreperous, radical cousins, were for the most part the moderate Whigs; in modern terms they could generally be described as pragmatists.[82] England had entered into that series of European conflicts which collectively have been called the Second Hundred Years' War (1689–1815). For the moderate faction, as Lawrence Cress documents, "standing armies were both necessary for and compatible with the survival of free institutions."[83] They were not warmongers—far from it, but they perceived English involvement in these balance-of-power struggles as a chance to expand English hegemony and influence with a resultant increase in trade. Great Britain, by the Treaty of Utrecht (1713, ending the War of the Spanish Succession), "had emerged as a Great Power, and if she wished to retain that status in the councils of Europe," J. A. Houlding notes, "she would be obliged to bear the expense of a more sizable military establishment."[84] What was even more essential, if the British withdrew into themselves behind the not entirely impregnable defenses of the Channel and fleet, Great Britain would not only be relegated to Lesser Power status but eventually could become susceptible to foreign (read French) invasion. To the moderates, Trenchard and the other antiarmy pamphleteers were naysayers, "Murmurers, Grumbletonians." They "always cry Wo, Wo, and frighten themselves and the World with sad Tidings." The pamphlet wars, commented moderate Whig Daniel Defoe, were contests between the "Men of Sense against the Men of Wit."[85]

No longer were the fleet, insularity, and the militia defense enough, the moderates argued, presaging Adam Smith; modern war had grown so complex as to demand full-time officers and soldiers (professionals) and to render the militia (amateurs) obsolete, except under the most dire of emergencies.[86] Whereas before individual courage had dominated the battlefield, now with threats from the Jacobites and other European nations, "Management is the principle Art of War," and a regular standing army was a necessity.[87] Militia simply took too long to train and discipline to be of value in modern, eighteenth-century war. Here army advocates had to tread lightly, for in disclaiming the value of militia they faced myth, tradition, and a strong lobby. (Also, appropriations for an army might lessen those of the navy, which had its own powerful advocates.)[88] Not generally understood in the colonies, however, was the fact that there was considerable intra-Whig faction fighting throughout this period, particularly following the ascendancy of the Hanoverian George I (1714). The devastating effect of the South Sea Bubble (1720) rippled through English society and political life, influencing Trenchard and Gordon to take quills in hand to begin penning *Cato's Letters*. What developed from this period was a fragmented, complex sociopolitical situation in England that was never fully appreciated nor understood in the colonies.[89]

The result, of course, was a compromise of sorts: a small standing army would be maintained, officered by gentlemen, and Parliament would control its pay, thus dictating its ultimate loyalty. By the turn of the century, the moderate Whigs recognized that militia alone stood no chance against the might of France or even a Jacobite army of Highlanders.[90] As England developed and became more and more economically dependent upon its increasingly far-flung empire, regular troops were needed to protect these valuable possessions. Troops garrisoned in Tangier, Ireland, the West Indies, and America posed little threat to Parliament, were cheaper to maintain,[91] and were hidden from budget–cutting cheeseparers and anti–standing army fanatics. By the eighteenth century, overseas regiments maintained small recruiting detachments in England and shell regiments in Ireland that could be fleshed out in time of war, facts unrecognized by Americans. But the primary mission of the small army in England was its police function: as a constabulary for the Customs Service and for crowd control.[92] (In the colonies, except for half-hearted nighttime patrolling to prevent slaves from congregating, American militia was not employed in a police role until the Revolution, when it became something of a revolutionary homeguard.) As historian J. H. Plumb has observed, "no nation rioted more easily or more savagely than England—from 1740 to 1830 angry mobs, burning and looting, were prevalent as disease."[93] From agrarian unrest to urban turmoil to proto-Luddism in the milltowns, the English were quick to turn to mob violence. The old social order, "rooted in paternalism," was altered by the presence of the constabulary-soldiery. Even though they quelled the disruptive rioting, the army remained "universally reviled" among the general public until the beginning of the nineteenth century, when it was finally recognized as essential to maintaining the social order.[94]

As radical Whig-libertarians saw things, however, there could be no compromise about a standing army, and they grew increasingly shrill in their demands. "Whether our Enemies shall conquer us is uncertain; but whether Standing Armies will enslave us, neither Reason nor Experience will suffer us to doubt," went the argument of one radical. " 'Tis therefore evident, that no pretence of danger from abroad, can be an Argument to keep up Standing Armies."[95] From this sort of rhetoric and for other reasons, the radical Whigs steadily lost adherents in England, but they gained them elsewhere. Their arguments in favor of militia now accepted the need for regular training of their proposed citizen force, to a degree. "I can see no reason why a country-fellow may not as easily learn to handle his arms, as to play at cricket," wrote the future Lord Liverpool in 1757.[96] But by the 1740s and 1750s, the continued social unrest among the lower class made putting arms in their hands less than desirable. Yet, it was to this small segment of the English political spectrum—a faction that by the 1760s and 1770s was little more than a fringe element—that prerevolutionary American republicans looked for ideas.

The extreme libertarian-radical Whig argument, as described in that colonial favorite, *Cato's Letters*, was totally antimilitaristic in a classical and traditional English vein: but reflecting and in keeping with much of the intellectual revolution sweeping Europe, the authors proposed a philosophic and idealistic vision that ignored European geopolitical realities and England's role as a major power.[97] *Cato*'s authors understood power; and history, both ancient and modern, taught them that he who controlled the army controlled the nation. If power was invested in one man or in several "without Controul [it] is never to be trusted."[98] From Cicero's *De Legibus* they adopted the formula that a general should only serve one year, a dubious proposition American radicals later proposed on several occasions during the Revolution. Trenchard and Gordon also lent their imprimatur to the republican

Roman concept of emergency dictatorship, thus paving the way, some fifty years later, for the Continental Congress (with considerable trepidation) to name Washington virtual dictator in 1776. But here, too, they specifically noted that this was an emergency measure for only a limited time.[99] Tyrants and standing armies were as one: a symbiotic relationship evolved among the tyrant, his corrupt and venal ministers, and the army.[100] "So that under a Tyrant," noted *Cato*, "there is no End of Tyrants: From him that sways the Scepter to him that carries a Musket, all are Tyrants, and every one for himself as far as he dare."[101] The proper monarch or ruler was in his position only by the consent of the people; he was obeyed because the people chose to obey him. "The Laws therefore of Tyrants are not Laws, but wild Acts of Will, counselled by Rage or Folly, and executed by Dragoons."[102] Thus the only way to stave off tyranny or to prevent a monarch from becoming a tyrant was through checks administered by the people, and one check was a subject dear to the hearts of colonial Americans, the militia.

For *Cato*, as for his colonial admirers, a citizen-soldiery was the only bulwark against tyrannical government. Before Cromwell's New Model Army, "Our Armies formerly were only a Number of People armed occasionally," stated *Cato*, "and Armies of the People are the only Armies which are not formidable to the People."[103] In free nations where ruler and ruled lived in harmony, no need existed for a professional army, for "every Man being a Soldier, or quickly made so, they improve in a War and every Campaign fight better and better."[104] Here was the classical influence of ancient Greece and Rome writ large and the selective reading of history which so influenced American republicanism. Militia armies could be raised for emergencies, *Cato* wrote, and then disbanded immediately after the crisis had passed.[105] Certainly, *Cato* argued, "his Majesty would have as many Men at Command as he has now," for "When the People are easy and satisfied, the whole Kingdom is his Army."[106] The "best security of a Prince amongst a free people," *Cato* concluded, "is the Affections of his people."[107] On the face of it, this argument is clear, but it must be considered within its context. Another fear of the antiarmy faction focused on the composition of the armed forces. The much-lauded militia of myth was composed of property-holders and yeoman farmers. A regular army, it was feared (with some justification), would be composed of the unemployed, jailhouse sweepings, and other undesirables; in sum, little more than mercenaries loyal only to their paymaster.[108] The "free people" *Cato*'s authors refer to are the freeman of the traditional myth. But Trenchard and Gordon were not simply seeking to reinstill virtue in England and forestall a resurgence of Cromwellian sword government by copying the Grecian and Roman republican citizen-soldiery. By carefully building their argument on ancient and modern principles and philosophies, including just war theory, the authors of *Cato's Letters* appeared to be making a strong case for an isolationist Albion.[109]

As *Cato*'s ideas developed over time, what had been an anti–standing army stance was combined with just war theory, so that only a purely defensive war was justified; any other military action—even preemptive defensive war—was tyrannical or corrupting. After all, as they stated in an almost Lockean manner, the "sole Ends of Men into political Societies, was mutual Protection and Defence; and whatever Power does not contribute to these Purposes, is not Government, but Usurpation."[110] Only being attacked sanctioned a just war. "Whoever puts himself in a State of War against me," *Cato* declared, echoing Augustine, "gives me a Right of War against him; and Violence is a proper Remedy for Violence, when no other is left."[111] Thus affirmed was the right to self-preservation. "But," sounding much like Montaigne, "to embark in Wars, and make Conquests at the Expence of the People, and not for the People, is a preposterous Way of protecting them, and of fulfilling the Duties of Reigning."[112] At the time *Cato's Letters* were written, England had gained little from her continental adventuring except a loss of life and much treasure.[113] Even defensive wars were terribly expensive, and, as the colonists already knew, extremely disruptive to the economy.[114] War meant that the navy would have to refit and operate far from home waters, possibly even ferrying an army which had to be raised, fitted out, and maintained. War meant raising taxes, civil disruptions, and further rioting. War involving an ally meant war for England, something *Cato* vehemently opposed. *Cato* advised avoiding entangling alliances at all costs, so that "we too shall at last in our Turn, consider only our own Interests, and what is best for ourselves."[115] And in the ultimate calamity, as war

meant increasing the standing army, it also meant increasing monarchical and ministerial power. War, to *Cato*, was only a breeding ground
for corruption and tyranny. *Cato* concluded one letter with the wish
"That all Nations would learn the Wisdom of the prudent *Sancho*,
who, when the Hero his Master madly attacked the Wind-Mills and
the Lions, stood at a safe Distance in a whole Skin. If their governing
Don Quixotes," he continued, "will fight, right or wrong, let them fight
by themselves, and not sit at home and wantonly sacrifice their People
against Wind-Mills and Fulling-Mills."[116]

For Americans of the prerevolutionary generation, there could have
been little that was startling or new in *Cato*'s attacks on standing
armies, for their previously existing conceptions of war were drawn
from the same sources from which *Cato* drew. To be sure, *Cato*'s words
clarified and defined colonial ideas, provided fresh insights and additional rhetoric, and perhaps most importantly, furnished an additional
bond to link these disparate peoples together, culling ideas from a
variety of sources and fashioning them into an all-encompassing ideological framework. But for matters of war, it only reinforced the strains
of antimilitarism and republicanism that extended far back across the
Atlantic into ancient times.

Afterword

The conceptions of war held by Americans in 1775 guided their military effort on the long road to independence. These concepts formed the context within which the war would be waged, defining the role that American armed forces would play in the Revolution and thereafter. That the ideas often clashed; that the mythologized traditions and lofty ideals of civilian policymakers proved unrealistic when the rebellion turned into a lengthy, debilitating, and disillusioning war; and that it was a long-serving and long-suffering group of ill-paid and poorly treated regulars, not the citizen-militia of hallowed tradition and republican ideology, who outlasted the British; all of this and much more heightened the impact that these conceptions had on American revolutionary military thought and action.[1]

The irony is, of course, that a people with a long tradition of being antimilitary, with impatience for long, costly wars, and with a visceral loathing for regular, standing armies ended up depending upon a small band of officers and men who had literally become, by the later years of the war and from learning war through war, professional soldiers.[2] That this lesson was immediately ignored and the citizen-soldiery enshrined as the saviours of the republic while the real heroes were cast aside and excoriated also points out how deeply embedded were these conceptions in the American psyche. That Americans have continued with this paradoxical arrangement says much about their character, then and now.

In all military aspects of the American Revolution, from the creation of the fundamental military establishment to the composition of the army to the inglorious treatment of veterans, the impact of Americans' long-held concepts of war may be discerned. This should come as no surprise, however, since any nation's or aspiring nation-state's armed forces and the role assigned to them represent the values, goals, and attitudes toward military affairs of the parent society. In the colonies, ideas and perspectives about war, warfare, and the military had been incorporated as integral components of colonial culture and society and, as such, of the embryonic American character. So widely known and commonly held were these ideas that they formed, to a large measure, indispensable strands in the cord which bound together contentious and dissimilar colonies and colonists. Moreover, these concepts had become entwined with the evolving republican ideology, blending the Revolution's objectives and the means of achieving them: the ideas that Americans fought for and the way they fought for them were one. Consequently, like their ancient Grecian, Hebraic, and Roman counterparts, staunch colonial republicans found that adherence to principle was primary; success on the battlefield mattered little if accomplished through nonvirtuous, unrepublican means.

Seemingly, herein lay the genesis of military defeat, yet for republican zealots it was a practical, virtuous prescription for victory. The Revolution and the way the war would be fought were experiments in the application of political theory to real life situations. But the evolving social, political, and philosophical ideas that as a whole have been lumped together as revolutionary ideology were, in fact, drawn from many sources, sources that frequently took diametrically opposing stands on the same issues. On the face of it, differences among political leaders were greater than any commonalities; adherents to one strain of this umbrella ideology looked at proponents of other aspects of it as deviationist. The controversy between the radical and moderate Whigs that had occurred in England from the 1690s through the 1730s was, to an extent, rekindled by colonists who concurrently were growing increasingly at odds with the Crown. What did unite colonists under their overarching though ill-defined ideology were the general themes upon which all could agree, such as their mistrust of ministerial government, "Liberty," "no taxation without representation," "Freedom," an abhorrence of expensive and dangerous standing armies in time of peace, and the preeminence of citizen-soldiers over professionals.

From the early 1760s, colonial republicans of all persuasions recognized the need for strength through unity. In their pamphlets and speeches they strove not only to enlighten their fellow citizens in matters of political theory but also to stress the absolute necessity for inter- and intracolonial concord. By juxtaposing ancient classical and biblical authors with the modern theorists of different persuasions whom colonists so admired, patriot pensmen and orators showed disparate but historically and politically conscious Americans that while contrasting shades of republicanism might differ on details, on general principles there was accord. So important was this newfound unity that the colonial representatives meeting as the Congress in 1775 and 1776 went to extraordinary lengths to ensure its continuation, for they feared discord and faction more than the British army. Delegates who might otherwise have stormed out of meetings or thrown up their hands in dismay now redoubled their efforts in the interest of harmony. Accordingly, when agreement was reached, such as on the creation of a military establishment and the composition of the army, they were loath to disturb it. Especially for those who constituted the revolutionary political leadership—the policymakers in Congress and those in the colonial/state legislatures who controlled the purse strings —any deviation from the revolutionary or republican way of war, no matter how dire the military exigency, would have been a refutation of the guilding principles of the Revolution and a harbinger of disunion.[3]

Illustrative of this were the actions taken by the Congress following the outbreak of rebellion in Massachusetts. As the responsibility for intercolonial leadership and policy making devolved upon their shoulders, the colonial representatives were forced by necessity to come to grips with this unforeseen military conflict. They had not wanted war, but, since the British "had made an unprovoked assault on the inhabitants" of Massachusetts, the colonists's actions in defense of their lives, liberties, and properties were justified by biblical, classical, and international law. Validated by historical precedence, fighting under God's ensign, and absolved from any hint of unnatural rebellion by nature's law of self-preservation, the colonists explained their actions to themselves and to the world as a whole when they issued their "Declaration of the Causes and Necessity of Taking Up Arms," on 6 July 1775.[4] Intuitively these republican stalwarts brought forth a military establishment based not so much upon the colonial militia model as upon the ancient, classical tradition of freemen rallying to drive out the invaders. A republican army, after all, was not only supposed to support and defend the Revolution and the united colonies but it had to be a living embodiment of the superiority of a virtuous citizen-soldiery, thus affirming and manifesting a central tenet of revolutionary ideology. Following in the historical footsteps of the Greek and Roman farmers who saved their republics on many occasions were those citizen-militiamen who entrapped the British hirelings in Boston.

Even as the congressmen debated the form of their armed forces, reports of additional republican successes poured into Philadelphia, attesting to the correctness of their views and coloring their thinking. From Georgia to New England virtuous colonists were forming companies, drilling, and readying themselves to drive the ministerial forces from their shores. These were heady times indeed for colonial republicans and, as historian Charles Royster describes it, a *"rage militaire"* swept the land.[5] Heroic classical allusions were updated to fit eighteenth-century American needs. One elderly New Jersey matron dusted off an old Spartan adage and sent young men off to war with the following admonition: "Let me beg of you my children, that if you fall, it may be like men, and that your wounds not be in your back parts."[6] Images of the British regulars fleeing before the guns of the Massachusetts militiamen, of the polyglot New England army slaughtering redcoats on Breed's Hill, of the last sails of the Royal Navy fading away as General Howe's army evacuated Boston, swept the colonies with excitement and intoxicated congressmen and the various legislators. God truly seemed to be on their side. To those for whom radical Whig ideology was the gospel and Trenchard and Gordon its prophets, here was validation, not from theory but from real experiences. By the early summer of 1776, the colonial political representatives felt confident enough to declare the compact between themselves and Great Britain null and void. A new nation was born, created by a virtuous citizenry who would rally to defend their lives, liberties, and property whenever need be.

Taken at face value, the appeal of a citizen-soldiery over a standing army on a European model was self-evident for republican colonists. From a practical standpoint, the militia system already existed, so there was considerable familiarity with it; it had, in colonial minds, proved its worth time and again; it was far less costly; and it dovetailed with republican ideals. Then, too, recent experiences in Massachusetts and other colonies appeared—to those distant from the action who received only the most glowing reports from their fellow republicans in the field—to have validated their decision politically, militarily, and ideologically.

The reality, however, was quite different, and for those who were commissioned with leading the "army" of citizen-soldiers and charged with defending their new nation, as well as those who were more practical in their understanding of war, politics, and society, the future was anything but bright.

The republican political leaders had, to a large measure, confused myth, tradition, and the surprising early successes of their "citizen-army" with the reality of war. For years, in pamphlets and newspapers and from street corners and pulpits, republican propagandists had warned their fellow citizens that the imposition of ministerial tyranny by a mailed fist posed a real threat to their liberties and properties. Standing as a bulwark against this danger was the ancient republican and traditional colonial defense—the militia. When the British were driven back by the Massachusetts militia just as was supposed to happen, the prophecies seemed fulfilled. It was no wonder that by the summer of 1776 the *rage militaire* began to ebb as many believed that the war was won, that Providence and republican virtue had triumphed over corruption and tyranny. In fact, the military situation was grim and worsening.

The initial American military response to British aggression had not been accomplished by any organized, well-trained militia but by simple farmers and tradesmen, a truly popular reaction linked to antecedents beyond the classical period and into prehistory. The community was attacked, the community defended itself: it was the natural law of self-preservation.[7] But those farmers and tradesmen soon began to drift home from their encampments. Their rage, patriotism, contrariness, or whatever had motivated them to stand up against British regulars soon waned in the face of the dreary routine of army life. They had done their bit, affirmed their patriotism and manhood, and now they had fields to harvest and harnesses to mend. In their place came the grandsons and sons of those who had filled out the volunteer militia units of prerevolutionary wars, the odd assortment of down-and-outers, the unemployed, adventurous, and the young that armies have always attracted.

These men bore no likeness to the ancient Greeks and Romans with whom they were regularly compared. The classical writers and the great thinkers of Western history who almost unanimously extolled the virtues of a volunteer citizen-soldiery or militia over paid regulars, all called for a "well-trained" militia. Their "militiamen" were both good citizens and disciplined, skilled soldiers; in fact, to be the former, one had to be ready and able to assume the role of the latter. For the most part, American militiamen had not even the rudiments of drill, and the disciplined subordination requisite to any military force was not only unknown to them but disparaged as antirepublican. As 1775 wore on, when even these men began leaving, Congress had to respond to Washington's pleas for replacements lest the army dissolve.

Congress faced a grave dilemma. Pure volunteerism was a failure; the men came into camp, stayed a short time consuming valuable food and forage, became bored, disillusioned, or homesick, and left, taking their muskets with them. Yet for zealous republicans Washington's calls for long-term enlistments (enlistments for several years or the length of the war) came uncomfortably close to being requests for a standing army. An evolving, more moderate Whig composition gradually emerged in the Congress, however, and dire necessity eventually led to some change. After considerable debate, Congress allowed troops to be enlisted for a campaign; but as Washington's army continued to disintegrate every year only to have to be rebuilt as the new campaign season began, Congress eventually increased the size of the military establishment and extended the term of service to the length of the war.[8] Washington was finally able to train and keep a solid core of veterans, yet this proved no panacea: wastage, reinforcements detached to other commands, and the inability of the states to furnish replacements forced him to be dependent upon short-term militia for the rest of the war.[9] But the action, nonetheless, has been hailed as a watershed of sorts. "Indeed," as historian Lawrence Delbert Cress notes, "once Congress and the states accepted the necessity of long-term enlistments, the public apparently had no trouble relegating the principal burden of military service to the poor and economically insecure."[10] Others have suggested that extending enlistments denoted a compromise of ideological principles.[11] What actually occurred, in fact, was nothing more than the reprise of a long-held colonial practice. Faced with a serious problem, Congress sought a practical solution and resurrected the volunteer half of the old bifurcated militia system. Letting the burden of fighting—other than in the immediate community—fall upon the socially and economically disadvantaged was a long accepted colonial practice: everyone's duty soon became no one's.

Some radicals did not perceive it in such light, nor did worsening conditions from their own side in the ever-lengthening war alter their deeply held attitudes. "The militia began, and I sincerely hope the militia will end, the present war," Benjamin Rush wrote John Adams (who came to favor extending the term of service) in late 1777, after Philadelphia had fallen and Washington's troops lay numb with the cold at Valley Forge. "I should despair, of our cause if our country contained 60,000 men abandoned enough to enlist for 3 years or during the war."[12] Rush had little reason for despair, for the lure of easy money from privateering and increased wages at home kept most Americans from joining the army. Returning veterans filled their ears with tales of the want of food, pay, clothing, and almost unbearable conditions, yet, for republicans of a radical Whig bent, even the poor half-frozen souls supping on gruel who made up the army conjured up fears of a standing army. In 1780, a year that almost witnessed the total collapse of the revolutionary movement, Yale President Ezra Stiles wrote his opposite at William and Mary, James Madison. "Arma cedant Togae [military power must be subordinate to civil authority] was a Maxim of the Roman Senate," noted Stiles, "but this is reversed with a Toga cedat Armis in the present unnatural War: unless Congress should assume the Toga."[13] Such was the army's "control" of Congress that in late 1780 Washington wrote Gouverneur Morris that "it would be well for the Troops, if like Chameleons, they could live upon Air, or like the Bear, suck their paws for sustenance during the rigour of the approaching season."[14] The bias against a standing army however, remained too strong for Washington to overcome, no matter how he tried, but his efforts always continued within the chain of command.

Civilian control of the military, a colonial practice of long standing and an integral component uniting both radical and moderate Whigs, remained inviolate throughout the war. That this occurred has been justly ascribed to the behavior of Washington and the model he created. To Washington, the preeminence of the civilian policymakers in Congress ("a due subordination to the supreme Civil Authority") was central to why the war was being fought.[15] To be sure, Washington and his lieutenants strongly criticized the policies that placed such a strong reliance upon short-term militia enlistments and despised their dependence upon local, homeguard militia to flesh out their lines. But Washington and other moderate Whigs in no way questioned civilian control; what confused and frustrated them was that the radical hatred of British standing armies in time of peace had been transferred to American forces fighting for the critics' independence. Washington understood the historical and philosophical fears Americans held toward a standing army in either peace or war. But those armies which had usurped civil power were not like the American revolutionary army. The armies who instituted sword government had none of the "ties, the concerns or interests of Citizens or any other dependence, than what flowed from their Military employ; in short," Washington wrote in 1778, this was because they were "Mercenaries; hirelings." American officers and men, the army of Congress and the people, he added, were "Citizens having all the Ties, and interests of Citizens." He could understand congressional prejudices against a standing army in time of peace, but the Americans' "policy to be prejudiced against them in time of *War*" left him baffled.[16]

The motives of Washington and other moderate Whigs in and out of the military in calling for long-term enlistments and the establishment of a regular army combined ideology and pragmatism. As great thinkers from ancient Greece onward feared, moderate Whigs were also genuinely apprehensive that a popular rebellion, once begun, might grow out of control, turning revolution into bedlam. Standing the radical position on its head, moderates perceived an organized, well-disciplined, regular army composed of virtuous citizens as a republican bulwark against a democratic mobocracy.[17] Then solely from a military perspective, Washington's experiences, observations, and reading led him to conclude that only a disciplined and organized force had any hope of success against British and German professional soldiers. Washington never sought to field an exact replica of a regular European army; not only was this practical veteran of Braddock's defeat too cognizant of the failings of such an army in America but he fully understood (better than anyone save, perhaps, his able lieutenants Nathanael Greene and Daniel Morgan) both the advantages and limitations of his fellow citizens at arms and the American military culture. But he was adamant in his desire to instill his citizen-soldiers with the discipline and subordination history had shown to be elemental to the effectiveness of any military force at any time, be it a regular army or guerrilla unit.[18] In order to do this, he required time, time to establish an organization, time for natural leaders to rise to positions of responsibility and mature as officers and, more importantly, noncommissioned officers, and time to turn civilians into seasoned soldiers. Faced with an army that kept melting away before his eyes, superiors who were reluctant to provide him with the tools he required, and a powerful opponent, Washington found his leadership and his Catoian resolve tested to the utmost.

Washington's pragmatic, moderate Whig position makes equally good sense to modern eyes as it did during the war, but the radical Whig viewpoint must be judged according to eighteenth-century, not twentieth-century criteria. The multifarious concepts and philosophies that are known as American republican ideology were essential to the making of the Revolution. Without the solidarity they provided, there may very well have been armed insurrections in several colonies, but it is doubtful that there would have been a Revolution or a United States. What was crucial to generating popular support for a unified revolutionary ideal, creating a climate of rebellion, and carrying the Revolution through the Declaration of Independence, however, proved inadequate for "the long, enervating, and disillusioning war" that followed.[19] Historian Lawrence Cress neatly summarizes the question American political leaders and policymakers were forced to deal with: "Was the discipline and military expertise required to defeat a professional British army compatible with the tenets of a republican revolution?"[20] Traditionally, the colonists had found long-serving volunteer units composed of men from the lower strata of society "more convenient and reliable."[21] Yet contraposed against this practical custom were equally longheld, historically justified fears that those who guarded the commonweal might easily turn their weapons upon it.

In a sense, the question highlighted the difference between war in the abstract and war in reality. Historically, firebrands who lead the charge for war temper their rhetoric upon burying a son, and those who vehemently argue against defense expenditures are often the first to criticize the military when ill-trained and ill-equipped troops are defeated. For many, however, coming face-to-face with the awfulness of war produces a recognition that while wars should be avoided, sometimes they cannot be, hence the Vegetian proscription, "qui desiderat pacem praeparet bellum" [let him who wants peace prepare for war] takes on a fresh meaning. For instance, future president James Madison, in the 1788 Virginia debates over ratification of the Constitution, argued that a "standing army is one of the greatest mischiefs that can possibly happen." Later, in his first Inaugural Address in 1809, he reiterated that Americans should always "remember that an armed and trained militia is the finest bulwark of republics." But by 1815, his position had changed. Addressing both houses of Congress, he firmly stated that "a certain degree of preparation for war is not only indispensable to avert disasters in the onset [of a war], but affords also the best security for the continuance of peace."[22] Apparently, the burning of the presidential mansion by British regulars in 1814 altered his opinion.

During the American Revolutionary War, the question was never fully resolved.[23] Radical republicans perceived any indigenous military force other than militia as a threat to liberty, and they saw any increase or professionalization of such an army as a refutation of the very principles over which they had gone to war. Washington and the moderate Whigs saw a regular army enlisted for the war as the most efficient and practical means of defeating the professional British army, but perhaps even more importantly, they regarded a regular army controlled by the Congress as a guarantor of American liberty against the anarchy of the people.[24] Conceivably, the factionalism that republicans of all persuasions so feared and which had its roots in the war was exacerbated by conflict emanating from irreconcilable differences over this question. But for the war, the burden of actual service came to rest upon those who carried on throughout the long war in spite of hardships created by their own revolutionary objectives, this "band of brothers"—Washington, his key lieutenants, and a hard core of officers and soldiers.[25] So closely related were these ideas to the core of their American character that even as these men criticized, protested, and threatened to resign, for the most part they continued serving and fighting for their freedom and that of their country.

The Americans' conceptions of war in 1775, drawn from a heritage and culture rooted deeply in the ancient past, were more than simply influences on the revolutionary way of war; they remain part of the American character through the present, a legacy of and a link to our Western heritage. It is an often contradictory legacy, befitting its people, of antimilitarism and a readiness to fight and die when freedom is threatened, of equally principled people going off to war and of those refusing to serve, of fighting for secular ideas with the zealousness of holy warriors, of democracy and discipline, of myth and reality, and of complaints, disagreements, and iconoclasm and a strict adherence to civil authority by the military. The true strength of this legacy may be seen even today.

Abbreviations

AHR   *American Historical Review*
AQ   *American Quarterly*
BIHR   *Bulletin of the Institute of Historical Research*
CJ   *Classical Journal*
CMHS   *Collections of the Massachusetts Historical Society*
EIHQ   *Essex Institute Historical Quarterly*
HTR   *Harvard Theological Review*
HLQ   *Huntington Library Quarterly*
HS   *Historical Studies*
JHI   *Journal of the History of Ideas*
JIH   *Journal of Interdisciplinary History*
JMH   *Journal of Modern History*
MA   *Military Affairs*
MQR   *Mennonite Quarterly Review*
MVHR   *Mississippi Valley Historical Review*
NCHR   *North Carolina Historical Review*
NEHQ   *New England Historical Quarterly*
NEQ   *New England Quarterly*
PAPS   *Proceedings of the American Philosophical Society*
PCSM   *Publications of the Colonial Society of Massachusetts*
PEQ   *Palestine Exploration Quarterly*
RUSI   *Royal United Service Institute Journal*
SJT   *Scottish Journal of Theology*
VMHB   *Virginia Magazine of History and Biography*
WMQ   *William and Mary Quarterly*

Notes

Preface

1. Charles H. Firth, *Cromwell's Army: A History of the English Soldier During the Civil Wars, the Commonwealth and the Protectorate*, 3rd ed. (London: Methuen, 1921; reprint 1961), vi.
2. B. H. Liddell Hart, *The Ghost of Napoleon* (London: Faber and Faber, 1933), 11.
3. Ibid., 11–12.

Introduction

1. Commission from the Continental Congress, W. W. Abbot et al., eds., *The Papers of George Washington: Revolutionary War Series*, 2 vols. to date (Charlottesville: University Press of Virginia, 1985–), 1:7. Hereinafter cited as *Washington Papers RWS*.
2. Undelivered First Inaugural Address: Fragments, W. W. Abbot et al., eds., *The Papers of George Washington: Presidential Series*, 3 vols. to date (Charlottesville: University Press of Virginia, 1983–), 2:159. Hereinafter cited as *Washington Papers PS*.
3. To John Augustine Washington, *Washington Papers RWS*, 1:19.
4. *Washington Papers PS*, 2:159.
5. See especially Forrest McDonald, *Novus Ordo Seclorum: The Intellectual Origins of the Constitution* (Lawrence: University Press of Kansas, 1985); McDonald, *E Pluribus Unum: The Formation of the American Republic, 1776–1790* (Boston: Houghton Mifflin, 1965; Indianapolis: Liberty Press, 1979); Gordon S. Wood, *The Creation of the American Republic, 1776–1787* (Chapel Hill: University of North Carolina Press for the Institute of Early American History and Culture, 1969; New York: W. W. Norton, 1972); Bernard Bailyn, ed.,

Pamphlets of the American Revolution, 1 vol. to date (Cambridge: Harvard University Press, 1965); and Bailyn, *The Ideological Origins of the American Revolution* (Cambridge: Belknap Press of Harvard University Press, 1967), among others. For a general work focusing on military aspects of this theme, Reginald C. Stuart's *War and American Thought: From the Revolution to the Monroe Doctrine* (Kent: Kent State University Press, 1982), esp. his early chapters, was invaluable.

6. Clifford K. Shipton, "Literary Leaven in Provincial New England," *NEQ* 9 (June 1936):203.

7. In doing this I recognize that there will be some repetition in subsequent chapters. I have tried to hold this down to a minimum, but some was unavoidable. *Mea culpa.*

8. Concepts drawn from Robert R. Palmer, "The Great Inversion: America and Europe in the Eighteenth-Century Revolution," in Richard Herr and Harold T. Parker, eds., *Ideas in History: Essays Presented to Louis Gottschalk by His Former Students* (Durham: Duke University Press, 1965), 4.

9. Trenchard and Gordon, *Cato's Letters: or, Essays on Liberty, Civil and Religious, and Other Important Subjects,* 4 vols., 6th ed. corrected (London: J. Walthoe, 1755; reprint ed., 4 vols. in 2, New York: Da Capo Press, 1971), no. 86, 3:174. Hereinafter cited as *Cato's Letters,* along with the number of the essay, volume, and page from this edition.

10. See James Kirby Martin's and Mark Edward Lender's excellent *A Respectable Army: The Military Origins of the Republic, 1763–1789* (Arlington Heights, Ill.: Harlan Davidson, 1982), esp. 23.

1. The Origins and Development of
American Conceptions of War to 1775: An Overview

1. Quoted in Alfred Vagts, *A History of Militarism: Romance and Realities of a Profession* (New York: W.W. Norton, 1937), 35.

2. In theory this point is perhaps arguable, but reality posits a telling point in rebuttal. There are many, however, who would fail to bring the military into the equation at all, belying their results. Writing in the 1930s, Alfred Vagts, no particular admirer of things military, explained that some try to ignore the military and its history "on the curious assumption that by ignoring realities the realities themselves will disappear," *History of Militarism,* 28. In medical parlance, this is called denial.

3. See chapter 5.

4. Walter Millis, *Arms and Men: A Study of American Military History* (New York: G. P. Putnam's Sons, 1956; New Brunswick, N.J.: Rutgers University Press, 1981), 13.

5. The most authoritative guide, Howard H. Peckham, ed., *The Toll of Independence: Engagements & Battle Casualties of the American Revolution* (Chicago: University of Chicago Press, 1974), 3, lists total casualties for the day as

Americans: 49 killed, 39 wounded, and 4 captured, and British: 73 killed, 193 wounded, and 22 captured or missing.

6. Edmund Cody Burnett, *The Continental Congress* (New York: Macmillan, 1941), 65–70, among others.

7. To James Warren, 21 May 1775, in Paul H. Smith et al., eds, *Letters of Delegates to Congress 1774–1789*, 15 vols. to date (Washington, D.C.: Library of Congress, 1976–), 1:364, hereinafter cited as Smith, *Delegates*. See also Robert J. Taylor et al., eds., *Papers of John Adams*, 6 vols. to date (Cambridge: Belknap Press of Harvard University Press, 1977–), 3:11.

8. See Edmund S. Morgan and Helen M. Morgan, *The Stamp Act Crisis: Prologue to Revolution*, new, rev. ed. (New York: Collier Books, 1963). Originally published in 1953 (Chapel Hill: University of North Carolina Press for the Institute of Early American History and Culture), this work remains vital and stimulating.

9. *Washington Papers PS*, 2:159. On the other hand, some high-ranking British officers were less than sanguine about the army's ability to put down the rebellion. General Edward Harvey, Adjutant-General of the royal army, commented on 30 June 1775, "that attempting to Conquer A[merica] Internally by our Ld. [Land] Forces, is as wild an Idea, as ever controverted Com[mo]n Sense." "Where's the Means?" he asked, "Not by Land, by Brit. Troops. The Fund is not Suff[icien]t, take my word for it. A Driblet is going over, what then?" Quoted in J. A. Houlding, *Fit for Service: The Training of the British Army, 1715–1795* (Oxford: Clarendon Press, 1981), 135–36. That same day he penned a note to William Howe, unaware that Howe's troops had already suffered mightily on Breed's Hill. "America is an ugly job, . . . a damned affair indeed." Quoted in John W. Fortescue, *A History of the British Army*, 13 vols. (London: Macmillan, 1910–30), 3:169.

10. *Washington Papers PS*, 2:159.

11. Michael Kammen, *People of Paradox: An Inquiry Concerning the Origins of American Civilization* (New York: Alfred Knopf, 1972; New York: Vintage Books, 1973).

12. On the latter aspect, see Edmund S. Morgan, *American Slavery American Freedom: The Ordeal of Colonial Virginia* (New York: W. W. Norton, 1975).

13. Cultural exchange and influence among Euro-Americans, Native Americans, and Afro-Americans was so extensive that delineating the origins of some traits and practices is impossible.

14. Quoted in Theodore S. Hamerow, *Reflections on History and Historians* (Madison: University of Wisconsin Press, 1987), 29.

15. For just a few examples, see Deut. 20.2, 10–11; Josh. 1.5; Judg. 2.10–15, 3.6–14; 1 Sam. 7.9–14; Ps. 46.1; and Jer. 11.9.

16. Richard E. Neustadt and Ernest R. May, *Thinking in Time: The Uses of History for Decision-Makers* (New York: The Free Press, 1986), 265.

17. Millard C. Lind, *Yahweh Is a Warrior: The Theology of Warfare in Ancient Israel* (Scottsdale, Pa.: Herald Press, 1980), 13.

18. For just a few examples, see Josh. 2.1–24 on the value of good intelligence and reconnaissance and 8.1–25 on the importance of a well-conducted ambush and surprise. In Judg. 7.9–24, Gideon employs guerrilla tactics, surprise, terrain knowledge, exaggeration of force, and various other stratagems to defeat the superior Midianite army.

19. Allardyce Nicolli, ed., *[George] Chapman's Homer: The Illiad, The Odyssey and the Lesser Homerica*, 2 vols., 2nd ed. (Bollingen Series 41) (Princeton: Princeton University Press, 1967), book 13, lines 570–75. See also Graeme J. L. Hall, "The Guerrilla as Midwife: The End of the Union (Ireland) and the Mandate (Palestine)," Ph.D. dissertation, The University of Alabama, 1988, 3.

20. 1 Sam. 8.6–19.

I. The Classical Inheritance

1. The depth of this scholarship may be measured, to cite but a few works, in Meyer Reinhold, *Classica Americana: The Greek and Roman Heritage in the United States* (Detroit: Wayne State University Press, 1984), with its excellent endnotes and bibliography; Richard M. Gummere, *The American Colonial Mind and the Classical Tradition: Essays in Comparative Culture* (Cambridge: Harvard University Press, 1963); John Eadie, ed., *Classical Traditions in Early America* (Ann Arbor: Center for Coordination of Ancient and Modern Studies, 1976); and Gilbert Highet, *The Classical Tradition: Greek and Roman Influences on Western Literature* (New York: Oxford University Press, 1957).

2. Old Wine in New Skins

1. This concept of an eighteenth-century Euro-American "cult of antiquity" is drawn from many sources, but see especially Harold T. Parker, *The Cult of Antiquity and the French Revolutionaries: A Study in the Development of the Revolutionary Spirit* (Chicago: University of Chicago Press, 1934); Meyer Reinhold, *Classica Americana*, 23–49; Gummere, *American Colonial Mind*, 1–2; Wilson Ober Clough, ed., *Intellectual Origins of American National Thought: Pages from the Books Our Founding Fathers Read*, 2nd rev. ed. (New York: Corinth Books, 1961), 4; J. Bronowski and Bruce Mazlish, *The Western Intellectual Tradition* (New York: Harper & Brothers, 1960); and David D. Van Tassel and Robert W. McAhren, eds., *European Origins of American Thought* (Chicago: Rand McNally, 1969), 1–122, among others.

2. See Durand Echeverria, "The French Image of American Society to 1815: Some Tentative Revisions," in Paul J. Korshin, ed., *The American Revolution and Eighteenth Century Culture: Essays from the 1976 Bicentennial Conference of the American Society for Eighteenth-Century Studies* (New York: AMS Press, 1976), esp. 257 and 260. See also Jeffrey Barnouw, "American Independence —Revolution of the Republican Ideal: A Response to Pocock's Construction

of 'The American Republican Tradition,' " in ibid., 31–73; Michael Kraus, *The North Atlantic Civilization* (Princeton: Van Nostrand, 1957); and Echeverria, *Mirage in the West: A History of the French Image of American Society to 1815* (Princeton: Princeton University Press, 1957).

3. Howard Mumford Jones, *O Strange New World—American Culture: The Formative Years* (New York: Viking Press, 1964), 106.

4. I. Bernard Cohen, "The Eighteenth-Century Origins of the Concept of Scientific Revolution," *JHI* 37 (April–June 1976):257–58; Samuel Johnson, *A Dictionary of the English Language: in which the Words are deduced from their Originals, and Illustrated in their Different Significations*, 2 vols. (London: W. Strahan, 1755). See also Henry Steele Commager, "Leadership in Eighteenth Century America and Today," *Daedalus* 90 (Fall 1961):644; William Gribbin, "Rollin's Histories and American Republicanism," *WMQ* 3rd ser., 29 (October 1972):611; Edmund S. Morgan, ed., *Puritan Political Ideas 1558–1794* (Indianapolis: Bobbs-Merrill, 1965), xxxvi, xxxviii; S. N. Nulle, "Julian in America," *CJ* 61 (January 1966):166; Clough, *Intellectual Origins*, 4; Charles F. Mullet, "Roman Precedents and the British Colonial Policy in 1770," *HLQ* 7 (November 1943):97–100; R[obert] Makintosh, *Comments on the Growing Breach between the American Colonies and England* (London: n.p., 1770); and McDonald, *Novus*, 5–7.

5. Commager, "Leadership," 663.

6. H. Trevor Colbourn, *The Lamp of Experience: Whig History and the Intellectual Origins of the American Revolution* (Chapel Hill: University of North Carolina Press for the Institute of Early American History and Culture, 1965), 189; Colbourn, "Thomas Jefferson's Use of the Past," *WMQ* 3rd ser., 15 (January 1958):57; Charles Mullet, "Ancient Historians and 'Enlightened' Reviewers," *The Review of Politics* 21 (July 1959):550; Gummere, *American Colonial Mind*, viii; Gummere, "Some Classical Side Lights on Colonial Education," *CJ* 55 (1959–60):223; Clough, *Intellectual Origins*, 15; and Reinhold, *Classica Americana*, 50–93.

7. Four decades after the Revolution, the sons and grandsons of these veterans would fight a war that in many ways harkened back to an earlier way of war, yet a war that technologically and strategically anticipated twentieth-century warfare. Confederate General Robert E. Lee, son of Revolutionary War hero Henry "Light-Horse Harry" Lee, is but one example. See Charles Royster, *Light-Horse Harry Lee and the Legacy of the American Revolution* (New York: Alfred A. Knopf, 1981); Thomas E.Templin, "Henry 'Light-Horse Harry' Lee: A Biography," Ph.D. dissertation, University of Kentucky, 1975; Douglas Southall Freeman, *R. E. Lee: A Biography*, Pulitzer Prize ed., 4 vols. (New York: Charles Scribner's Sons, 1936), esp. vol. 1; and John Morgan Dederer, "The Origins of Robert E. Lee's Bold Generalship: A Reinterpretation," *MA* 49 (July 1985):117–23.

8. Forrest McDonald and Ellen Shapiro McDonald, *Requiem: Variations on Eighteenth-Century Themes* (Lawrence: University Press of Kansas, 1988), 187.

9. For the purely military aspects of this, see chapters 4–6. See also Martin Van Creveld, *Technology and War: From 2000 B.C. to the Present* (New York: The Free Press, 1989); Brooke Hindle, *The Pursuit of Science in Revolutionary America, 1735–1789* (Chapel Hill: University of North Carolina Press for the Institute of Early American History and Culture, 1956); and K. L. Ellis, "British Communications and Diplomacy in the Eighteenth Century," *BIHR* 31 (May 1958), 159–67.

10. Alice M. Baldwin, *The New England Clergy and the American Revolution* (Durham: Duke University Press, 1928), 7, 10–11.

11. Morgan, *Puritan Political Ideas*, xiii, and for just a few examples, see Cotton Mather using Caesar's *Commentaries* in an analogy (235), and Elisha Williams equating Caesar and pontiff (". . . be he *Pope* or *Caesar* . . . ," 277). See also Michael Walzer, *Exodus and Revolution* (New York: Basic Books, 1985), 134; Richard M. Gummere, "Classical Precedents in the Writings of James Wilson," PCSM 32 *Transactions 1933–1937* (Boston: By the Society, 1937), 525; Benjamin Colman, *A Sermon Preached to the Honourable and Ancient Artillery Company in Boston, June 5, 1738* (Boston: J. Draper, 1738), 29; and Hull Abbot, *Mr. Abbot's Sermon Preach'd to the Artillery-Company in Boston, June 2, 1735* (Boston: S. Kneeland and T. Green, 1735), 26–27, among others.

12. Quoted in Baldwin, *New England Clergy*, 15.

13. Joseph Ellis, "Habits of Mind and an American Enlightenment," *AQ* 28 (Summer 1976):158.

14. Abbot, *Sermon*, 1.

15. Walzer, *Exodus*, 134.

16. Guenther Lewy, *Religion and Revolution* (New York: Oxford University Press, 1974), 33.

17. "Newes From Virginia," by Robert Rich, quoted in Albert Bushnell Hart, ed., *American History told by Contemporaries*, 10 vols. (New York: Macmillan, 1897), 1:287.

18. Morgan, *Puritan Political Ideas*, xxxii.

19. Exod. 18.18, 21; Walzer, *Exodus*, 127.

20. Walzer, *Exodus*, 127.

21. Julian P. Boyd et al., eds, *The Papers of Thomas Jefferson*, 22 vols. to date (Princeton: Princeton University Press, 1950–), 1:494–97, among others.

22. For source material on colonial and revolutionary-era education, see Ronald M. Gephart, comp., *Revolutionary America 1763–1789: A Bibliography*, 2 vols. (Washington, D.C.: Library of Congress, 1984), esp. 2:967–79.

23. Colman, *Sermon*, 25.

24. Nathaniel B. Shurtleff, ed., *Records of the Governor and Company of the Massachusetts Bay in New England*, 5 vols. (Boston: W. White, 1853–54), 2:203.

25. Morison, *The Founding of Harvard College* (Cambridge: Harvard University Press, 1935), 157. See the School Laws of Massachusetts, 1642 and 1647, reprinted in David Hawke, ed., *U.S. Colonial History: Readings and Documents* (Indianapolis: Bobbs-Merrill, 1966), 230–31.

26. " 'A Dissertation on the Canon and the Feudal Law,' No. 3," in Taylor, *Papers of John Adams*, 1:120. See also Henry F. May, *The Enlightenment in America* (New York: Oxford University Press, 1976), 35.

27. " 'A Dissertation,' No. 3," 120. This antidemocratic attitude among some New Englanders was reinforced by their reading of *Cato's Letters*. The authors, as was the case with most radical Whigs and libertarians, were fully against raising the expectations of the lower classes, and they questioned the value of educating the poor. "By taking Boys and Girls from the low and necessary employments of Life, making them impatient of the Conditions which they were born to, and in which they would have thought themselves to be happy, to be Sempstresses, Footmen, and Servant Maids, and to teach them to read Ballads?," no. 133, 4:245.

28. Charles Francis Adams, ed., *The Works of John Adams, Second President of the United States, with a Life of the Author*, 10 vols. (Boston: Little, Brown, 1850–56), 5:495.

29. Along the ever-shifting frontier or colonial backcountry, especially in the South, from the mid-seventeenth century there were large numbers of Euro-Americans for whom survival, not formal education, was paramount. While their cultural ethos came to dominate the region, because of their isolation they had little impact on mainstream (i.e., coastal) colonial life and culture up to the Revolution. See Grady McWhiney, *Cracker Culture: Celtic Ways in the Old South* (Tuscaloosa: University of Alabama Press, 1988), esp. its fine bibliography.

30. The "Virginia Act for Training of Poor Children," in *The Annals of America*, 24 vols. (Chicago: Encyclopedia Britannica, 1968), 1:342.

31. R. G., *Virginia's Cure: or an Advisive Narrative concerning Virginia* (London, 1662), quoted in Hart, *American History*, 1:296.

32. Adams, *Works of John Adams*, 5:494–95.

33. Ibid., 3:400.

34. Edwin Oviatt, *The Beginnings of Yale (1701–1726)* (New Haven: Yale University Press, 1916), 54.

35. *Nevv England's First Fruits; In Respect, First of the Conversion of some, Conviction of divers, Preparation of sundry of the Indians. 2. Of the progresse of Learning, in the Colledge at Cambridge in Massachusetts Bay* (London: R. O. and G. D., 1643), 12.

36. May, *Enlightenment in America*, 33–37; Louis B. Wright, *The Cultural Life of the American Colonies, 1607–1763* (New York: Harper & Row, 1957), 99; Daniel J. Boorstin, *The Americans: The Colonial Experience* (New York: Random House, 1958), esp. 175 and 169–99; Wesley Frank Craven, *The Southern Colonies in the Seventeenth Century, 1607–1689* (Baton Rouge: Louisiana State University Press, 1949; reprint 1970), 291–92; and Louis Shores, *Origins of the American College Library* (Nashville: George Peabody College for Teachers, 1934), 3, who discusses the failed attempt to create the first colonial college—"Academia Virginiensis et Oxoniensis"—far from potential Indian attack.

Several colleges were specifically created to train indigenous American ministers, for reasons that stemmed equally from need and fear. Dread of an Anglican bishopric grew quite strong in the eighteenth century; in fact, many of the same arguments against the royal imperative in things political were used against installation of a British bishopric. See Carl Bridenbaugh, *Mitre and Sceptre: Transatlantic Faiths, Ideas, Personalities, and Politics, 1689–1775* (New York: Oxford University Press, 1962), esp. 230–87.

37. See Samuel Eliot Morison, *The Intellectual Life of Colonial New England* (Ithaca: Cornell University Press, 1936; New York: New York University Press, 1956), 57–112; Reinhold, *Classica Americana*, 25–27; "Education in Colonial Virginia," *WMQ* 1st ser., 6 (January 1898):171–87; and Thomas Jefferson's suggested curriculum and ideas on education in his *Notes on the State of Virginia*, ed. by William Peden (Chapel Hill: University of North Carolina Press for the Institute of Early American History and Culture, 1955), 146–47, among others.

38. See Moncure Daniel Conway, *George Washington's Rules of Civility Traced to their Sources and Restored* (London: Chatto & Windus, 1890), esp. 11–36; John C. Fitzpatrick, *George Washington Himself: A Common-Sense Biography Written from His Manuscripts* (Indianapolis: Bobbs-Merrill, 1933), 19–31; and Douglas Southall Freeman, *George Washington: A Biography*, 7 vols. (New York: Charles Scribner's Sons, 1948–55), I: 125–34. Marye, formerly Marie, was a French Huguenot who arrived in Virginia by way of England.

39. Douglass Adair, "A Note on Certain of Hamilton's Pseudonyms," *WMQ* 3rd ser., 12 (April 1955):284; Reinhold, *Classica Americana*, 27; and Robert Middlekauff, "A Persistent Tradition: The Classical Curriculum in Eighteenth Century New England," *WMQ* 3rd ser., 18 (January 1961):55.

40. Although girls and young women received what we would call elementary and secondary education alongside their male counterparts, college, through the seventeenth and eighteenth centuries, was a male domain. Women, however, continued to receive additional education through home tutorials by itinerants and parents.

41. *Nevv England's First Fruits*, 13. See also Hawke, *Colonial History*, 233, and reprint in Massachusetts Historical Society *Collections* 1 (Boston: For the Society, 1792), 242–48.

42. *Nevv England's First Fruits*, 13. "Tully" was an Englished version of Marcus *Tullius* Cicero; today we normally use his cognomen, Cicero. Tully and Sallust generally were the first authors to whom beginning colonial Latinists were introduced. For additional discussion of the popularity of these two authors, see below, chapter 3, nn. 30 and 31.

43. Morison, *Harvard College*, 1:81.

44. Shores, *Origins*, for additional details.

45. "Proceedings of the Trustees, 11 November 1701," in Franklin Bowditch Dexter, ed., *Documentary History of Yale University: Under the Original Charter of the Collegiate School of Connecticut 1701–1745* (New Haven: Yale

University Press, 1916), 29–30. See also Ebenezer Baldwin, *Annals of Yale College, from Its Foundation, to the Year 1831*, 2nd ed. (New Haven: B. & W. Noyes, 1838); and Oviatt, *Beginnings of Yale*, 423.

46. Wright, *Cultural Life*, 131–132; Reinhold, *Classica Americana*, 27; and Middlekauff, "Persistent Tradition," 54.

47. *The New-York Gazette or Weekly Post-Boy*, 3 June 1754, quoted in Alden T.Vaughan, ed., *America before the Revolution, 1725–1775* (Englewood Cliffs, N.J.: Prentice-Hall, 1967), 91–93.

48. Quoted in *Annals of America*, 1:371. See also Courtlandt Canby, "A Note on the Influence of Oxford College Upon William and Mary College in the Eighteenth Century," *WMQ* 2nd ser., 21 (July 1941):243–47.

49. Arthur O. Norton, "Harvard Text-Books and Reference Books of the Seventeenth Century," *PCSM 28 Transactions 1930–1933* (Boston: By the Society, 1935), 362; and *New England's First Fruits*, 15.

50. For a look at what books students were reading, see Robert F. Seybolt, "Student Libraries at Harvard, 1763–1764," *PCSM 28 Transactions 1930–1933* (Boston: By the Society, 1935). Samuel Johnson's *Dictionary* and John Locke's *Essay on Human Understanding* were very popular, but so were the classics, with Seybolt listing 22 copies of Virgil's works, 17 of Cicero's, 14 Greek grammars, 12 Latin grammars, and 5 copies of Caesar's *Commentaries*, and a few of Sir Roger L'Estrange's popular *Seneca's Morals*, 450–57.

51. Quotation from Middlekauff, "Persistent Tradition," 54; Edmund S. Morgan, "Ezra Stiles: The Education of a Yale Man, 1742–1746," *HLQ* 17 (May 1954):259; Norton, "Harvard Text-Books," 362; and Morgan, *The Gentle Puritan: A Life of Ezra Stiles, 1727–1795* (New Haven: Yale University Press for the Institute of Early American History and Culture, 1962), 47.

52. Morgan, *Gentle Puritan*, 387–88.

53. *New England's First Fruits*, 18–20; Norton, "Harvard Text-Books," 364.

54. George Lyman Kittredge, "A Harvard Salutatory Oration of 1662," *PCSM 28 Transactions 1930–1933* (Boston: By the Society, 1935), 16–24.

55. Lyman H. Butterfield, ed., *Letters of Benjamin Rush*, 2 vols. (Princeton: Princeton University Press, 1951), 2:1067. See also Richard M. Gummere, *Seven Wise Men of Colonial America* (Cambridge: Harvard University Press, 1967), 65–66, 70. Rush and John Adams carried on a lengthy correspondence in their later years, much of it arguing over the validity of a classical education. In 1810, for instance, Rush argued that Adams's position favoring a classical education did not hold water. "Napoleon," Rush penned, "would have been just what he is had he never read a page of ancient history," Butterfield, *Rush Letters*, 2:1073. According to the Corsican's own writings (see chapter 4 below), Rush was wrong.

56. Frederic Hudson, *Journalism in the United States, from 1690 to 1872* (New York: Harper & Row, 1969), 124–25.

57. Donald Robert Come, "The Influence of Princeton on Higher Educa-

tion in the South Before 1825," *WMQ* 3rd ser., 2 (October 1945):361–62; Middlekauff, "Persistent Tradition," 55; James McLachlan, "Classical Names, American Identities: Some Notes on College Students and the Classical Traditions in the 1770s," in Eadie, *Classical Traditions*, 96–97.

58. Come, "Princeton," 382, 387, 366; Gummere, *American Colonial Mind*, 156–57. Freneau and Brackenridge collaborated on a "rhapsodic epic, 'The Rise Glory of America . . . ,' " for the 1771 commencement:

Where the Mississippi stream,
By forests shaded, now runs weeping on,
Nations shall grow, and states not less in fame
Than Greece and Rome of old! We too shall boast
Our Scipios, Solons, Catos, sages, chiefs.

59. Carl L. Becker, *The Declaration of Independence: A Study in the History of Political Ideas* (New York: Alfred A. Knopf, 1922; New York: Vintage Books, 1962), 51.

60. See Michael Kraus, "Literary Relations Between Europe and America in the Eighteenth Century," *WMQ* 3rd ser., 1 (July 1944):210–34. For additional sources, see Gephart, *Revolutionary America*, 2:999–1010.

61. Adair, "Hamilton's Pseudonyms," 288–89; also reprinted in Trevor Colbourn, ed., *Fame and the Founding Fathers: Essays by Douglass Adair* (New York: W. W. Norton, 1974).

62. Adair, "Hamilton's Pseudonyms," 288–89. This article must be read along with Thomas P. Govan, "Alexander Hamilton and Julius Caesar: A Note on the Use of Historical Evidence," *WMQ* 3rd ser., 32 (July 1975): 475–80.

63. I used Joseph Addison, *The Works of the Right Honourable Joseph Addison*, ed. by Henry G. Bohn, 6 vols., new ed. (London: George Bell and Sons, 1881), with *Cato. A Tragedy*, found on 1:165–227.

64. Act 4, sc. 4; Kenneth Silverman, *A Cultural History of the American Revolution* (New York: Thomas Y. Crowell, 1976), 76.

65. When *Cato* was first performed in 1713, both sides of the political spectrum claimed it as their own; Addison, astutely, maintained political neutrality.

66. See, among others, Margaret M. Forbes, "Addison's *Cato* and George Washington," *CJ* 55 (1959–60):210–12, who notes that in 1758 there was a production of the play at Belvoir, Virginia, with the role of Cato's daughter, Marcia, played by Mrs. Fairfax. See also Frederic M. Litto, "Addison's *Cato* in the Colonies," *WMQ* 3rd ser., 23 (July 1966):431–49; Robert H. Land, "The First Williamsburg Theater," *WMQ* 3rd ser., 5 (July 1948):359–74; and Paul L. Ford, *Washington and the Theatre* (New York: Dunlap Society, 1899).

67. Smith, *Delegates*, 2:62.

68. Adair, "Hamilton's Pseudonyms," 288–89. Adair appears to have paraphrased Carl Becker. See Colbourn, "Jefferson's Use of the Past," 59. See also

McLachlan, "Classical Names," 94; Colbourn, *Lamp of Experience*, vii; and Ellis, "Habits of Mind," 152–53.

Washington's personal library was no exception to Adair's postulation, and his books reflect a man of eclectic tastes. Washington was not an intellectual in the mold of Jefferson or John Adams (few were), but, as a curious and practical man, when faced with a new problem, he read deeply and broadly. An ardent experimenter, Washington stayed abreast of innovations in agriculture by reading the current literature and exchanging letters with leading agronomists. A romantic at heart, he owned volumes of *Don Quixote* and *Tom Jones*, and as an underrated student of history, he nevertheless perused popular histories by the Abbé de Vertot, Smollet, Stanyan, and a critical work on Cromwell. And, as a veteran, he was particularly interested in his books on Marshal Turenne, Gustavus Adolphus, Jeney on partisan war, Turpin de Crisse, and Marshal de Saxe. See Appleton P. C. Griffin, comp., *A Catalogue of the Washington Collection in the Boston Athenaeum* (Boston: Boston Athenaeum, 1897), esp. 482–562.

69. The best classical library in the colonies belonged to James Logan of Philadelphia. See Edwin Wolf, *The Library of James Logan of Philadelphia, 1674–1751* (Philadelphia: The Library Company of Philadelphia, 1974). For just a smattering of other book lists, see: Shores, *Origins*, esp. 238–68; "Library of Charles Dick," *WMQ* 1st ser., 18 (October 1909):112–113; "Library of Col. William Fleming," *WMQ* 1st ser., 6 (January 1898):158–64; "Libraries in Colonial Virginia," *WMQ* 1st ser., 3 (July 1894–April 1895):43–45, 132–34, 246–53 and 8 (July 1899–January 1900):18–22, 77–79, 145–50; Anne Floyd Upshur and Ralph T. Whitelaw, "Library of the Rev. Thomas Teackley," *WMQ* 2nd ser., 22 (July 1943):298–303; James Napier, "Some Book Sales in Dumfries, Virginia, 1794–1796," *WMQ* 3rd ser., 10 (July 1953):441–445; Samuel Eliot Morison, "Old School and College Books in the Prince Library," *More Books* (Bulletin of the Boston Public Library) 11 (March 1936):77–93; Reinhold, *Classica Americana*, 28–30, 41–49, esp. 41, nn. 37–41; and Reinhold, ed., *The Classick Pages: Classical Reading of Eighteenth-Century Americans* (University Park, Pa.: Pennsylvania State University Press for the American Philological Association, 1975).

70. W. Jackson Bate, *Samuel Johnson* (New York: Harcourt Brace Jovanovich, 1975), 517.

71. Charles H. Sherrill, *French Memories of Eighteenth-Century America* (New York: Charles Scribner's Sons, 1915), 232–33.

3. The Diffusion of Knowledge

1. Oddly enough, the loudest voices among republican zealots decrying classical education as useless were, like Benjamin Rush, from the revolutionary generation whose leadership, almost to a man, was classically trained. Appar-

ently, what was useless in the 1790s and 1800s had proved fairly useful in 1775–76 and 1787.

2. Quoted in Albert C. Gaudin, *The Educational Views of Charles Rollin* (New York: Thesis Publishing, 1939), 15.

3. Bate, *Samuel Johnson*, 25. The grammar school where Johnson studied (Lichfield), matriculated an earlier eighteenth-century wordsmith whose work, as already noted, was closely read in the colonies—Joseph Addison, ibid., 22n.

4. Becker, *Declaration of Independence*, 24–25. See also the earlier (6 July 1775) "Declaration of the Causes and Necessity of Taking Up Arms," in Charles C. Tansill, comp., *Documents Illustrative of the Formation of the Union of American States* (Washington, D.C.: Government Printing Office, 1927), 10–17.

5. Boyd, *Jefferson Papers*, 11:44; Reinhold, *Classica Americana*, 24.

6. This was an oft-used phrase of Washington's who, immediately after the war and in the latter days of his presidency, longed to retire to Mt. Vernon and his "vine and fig" or "fig and vine."

7. Reinhold, *Classick Pages*, 19, discusses some of these critics. See also his "Opponents of Classical Learning in America During the Revolutionary Period," *American Philosophical Society Proceedings* 112 (August 1968):221–34.

8. Quoted in Becker, *Declaration of Independence*, 43–44.

9. Quoted in Reinhold, *Classica Americana*, 40; Bate, *Samuel Johnson*, 195, 199.

10. Henry Fielding, *The History of Tom Jones, A Foundling*, 2 vols., ed. by Fredson Bowers (Middletown, Conn.: Wesleyan University Press, 1975), 2:620.

11. My thanks to Professor Forrest McDonald for this information.

12. John Dickinson, *Letters from a Farmer in Pennsylvania*, in Forrest McDonald, ed., *Empire and Nation* (Englewood Cliffs, N.J.: Prentice-Hall, 1962), quotations on 19, 22, 7, respectively, and see also 14, 33, 35, 38, 41–42, 45, 50, 58, 68, 73–74, 77, and 84, for classical references; Sam Adams to Arthur Lee, 4 March 1775, in Smith, *Delegates*, 1:321, who employs a Dickinson Latinism as a closing; Reinhold, *Classica Americana*, 22–26; Richard M. Gummere, "John Dickinson, the Classical Penman of the Revolution," *CJ* 52 (November 1956):81–83. See also Milton Ellis, "Richard Lee II, Elizabethan Humanist or Middle-Class Planter?," *WMQ* 2nd ser., 21 (January 1941):30; Peden, "Jefferson's Libraries," 265–66; Randall Stewart, "Puritan Literature and the Flowering of New England," *WMQ* 3rd ser., 3 (July 1946):321; S. H. Nulle, "Julian in America," *CJ* 61 (January 1966):166; and Stephen Botein, "Cicero as Role Model for Early American Lawyers: A Case Study in Classical 'Influence,' " *CJ* 73 (April–May 1978):314.

13. Quoted in William Frost, *Dryden and the Art of Translation* (Yale Studies in English, vol. 128) (New Haven: Yale University Press, 1955), 2. As Frost cogently notes, the quality of these translations varied a great deal.

14. May, *Enlightenment in America*, 36; Botein, "Cicero as Role Model," 315.

15. Colbourn, *Lamp of Experience*, 22.

16. Factors were commercial representatives who, for a percentage, handled a colonist's affairs in Great Britain.

17. Among works published in the colonies was Benjamin Franklin's edition of *Cato's Moral Distichs Englished in Couplets*, trans. by James Logan (Philadelphia: B. Franklin, 1935), noted in Leonard W. Larrabee et al., eds., *The Papers of Benjamin Franklin*, twenty-seven vols. to date (New Haven: Yale University Press, 1959–), 2:130–31. See also C. A. Herrick, "The Early New-Englanders: What Did They Read?," *The Library* 3rd ser., 9 (January 1918):2, 7; Samuel Eliot Morison, "The Library of George Alcock, Medical Student, 1676," *PCSM* 28 *Transactions 1930–1933* (Boston: By the Society, 1935):350–57, which contained many medical books but also Horace, Hesiod, Plutarch, Cicero, and Aristotle; Charles F. Robinson and Robin Robinson, "Three Early Massachusetts Libraries," ibid., 107, 115; and Howard Mumford Jones, "Desiderata in Colonial Literary History," *PCSM* 32 *Transactions 1933–1937* (Boston: By the Society, 1937), esp. 434, where he discusses the "extraordinary intellectual energy" of American colonists.

18. Sometimes also seen as Ludwig Wilhelm Brhuggemann and Ludwig Wilhelm Brueggemann.

19. Quoted in Reinhold, *Classick Pages*, 13. See also May, *Enlightenment in America*, 36; William Reitzel, "The Purchasing of English Books in Philadelphia, 1790–1800," *Modern Philology* 35 (November 1937):157–71; Howard Mumford Jones, "The Importation of French Literature in New York City, 1750–1800," *Studies in Philology* 28 (October 1931):235–51; and Jones, "The Importation of French Books in Philadelphia, 1750–1800," *Modern Philology* 32 (November 1934):157–77.

20. For Brüggemann, I used the copy in the Library of Congress, Rare Books Collection: *A View of the English Editions, Translations and Illustrations of the Ancient Greek and Latin Authors, with Remarks* (Stettin: John Samuel Leich, 1797), and *A Supplement to the View of the English Editions, Translations and Illustrations of the Ancient Greek and Latin Authors, with Remarks* (Stettin: John Samuel Leich, 1801). Both are available in reprint, ibid., 2 vols. (New York: Burt Franklin, 1971). See also the dated C. H. Conley, *The First English Translations of the Classics* (New Haven: Yale University Press, 1927); G. S. Gordon, ed., *English Literature and the Classics* (Oxford: Clarendon Press, 1912); and Henry Burrows Lathrop, *Translations from the Classics into English from Caxton to Chapman, 1477–1620* (Madison: University of Wisconsin Press, 1932; New York: Octagon Books, 1967), esp. his "Chronological List of Translations," 311–18. Brüggemann, adding works until the 1790s, is more complete.

21. Martha Walling Howard, *The Influence of Plutarch in the Major European Literature of the Eighteenth Century* (Chapel Hill: University of North Carolina Press, 1970), 195; Michael Grant, *The Ancient Historians* (New York: Charles Scribner's Sons, 1970), 406.

22. Garry Wills, *Cincinnatus: George Washington & The Enlightenment: Images of Power in Early America* (Garden City, N.Y.: Doubleday, 1984), 117, 126.

23. Grant, *Ancient Historians*, 317.

24. Carl L. Becker, *Everyman His Own Historian: Essays on History and Politics* (New York: F. S. Crofts, 1935), 49.

25. Howard, *Plutarch*, 7; McDonald, *Novus*, 67; Reinhold, *Classica Americana*, 151–52; May, *Enlightenment in America*, 36; and Colbourn, *Fame and the Founding Fathers*, esp. Adair's essay of the same title. As Harold T. Parker pointed out, Plutarch was also a great favorite of French revolutionaries, *Cult of Antiquity*, 17.

26. See also Howard, *Plutarch*, 15–32.

27. See Robert Adger Law, "The Text of 'Shakespeare's Plutarch,' " *HLQ* 6 (February 1943):197; Grant, *Ancient Historians*, 405.

28. Harold C. Syrett, ed., *The Papers of Alexander Hamilton*, 26 vols. (New York: Columbia University Press, 1961–79), 1:391–407.

29. Brüggemann, *A View*, 313–24, 481–532, 580–611, 690–97.

30. Eivion Owen, "Caesar in American Schools Prior to 1860," *CJ* 31 (January 1936):212–14.

31. Quoted in Reinhold, *Classick Pages*, xix.

32. Quoted in Hamerow, *Reflections*, 52. Although professional historians may argue this point, a modern parallel exists. For a great many Americans, knowledge of history comes not from academic histories but from the historical novels of James Michener and John Jakes.

33. McDonald, *Novus*, 67; Colbourn, *Lamp of Experience*, 22, and his invaluable "Appendix II," 199–232.

34. Gribbin, "Rollin's Histories," 611; Reinhold, *Classick Pages*, 157; Gummere, *Seven Wise Men*, 10; and Botein, "Cicero as Role Model," 315.

35. Lyman H. Butterfield, ed., *Adams Family Correspondence*, 4 vols. (Cambridge: Belknap Press of Harvard University Press, 1963), 1:142.

36. Butterfield, *Rush Letters*, 1:535.

37. I used Charles Rollin, *The Ancient History of the Egyptians, Carthaginians, Assyrians, Babylonians, Medes and Persians, Grecians, and Macedonians; including a History of the Arts and Sciences of the Ancients*, 2 vols. in 1 (New York: Harper & Brothers, 1841); Rollin, *The Roman History From the Foundations of Rome to the Battle of Actium: That is, To the End of the Commonwealth*, 15 vols. (London: John and Paul Knapton, 1750); and Vertot, *The History of the Revolutions That happened in the Government of the Roman Republic*, 2 vols., 5th ed., trans. by Ozell (London: D. Midwinter, 1740). There are dozens of English editions of Rollin; consult the *National Union Catalogue*.

38. Reinhold, *Classick Pages*, 158. Rollin's *Histories*, Vertot's History, and Montesquieu's *Considérations sur les causes de la grandeur des Romains et de leur décadence* (also popular in the colonies) were often assigned in prerevolutionary French colleges or awarded as prizes; Parker, *Cult of Antiquity*, 16n.

39. May, *Enlightenment in America*, 39; Howard, *Plutarch*, 7. For one measure of Rollin's popularity, see the important work of David Lundberg and Henry F. May, "The Enlightened Reader in America," *AQ* 28 (Summer 1976):262–93, esp. 278–79; and Jones, "French Books in Philadelphia," 163.

40. Quoted in Reinhold, *Classica Americana*, 56.

41. For the influence of Rollin on American military thinking, a good starting point would be David A. Tretler, "The Making of a Revolutionary General: Nathanael Greene, 1742–1779," Ph.D. dissertation, Rice University, 1986, esp. 94–105. For a people well versed in biblical miracles, particularly those of Exodus, the victory of the "10,000" Greeks over Darius's "100,000"-man army at Marathon was quite believable.

42. Quoted in Hamerow, *Reflections*, 213.

43. Commager, "Leadership," 654–55.

44. Parson Weems quoted in Wills, *Cincinnatus*, 35. See also Howard, *Plutarch*, 58–59, 33.

45. To modern users and abusers of history, Forrest McDonald issued a caveat. In dealing with the past, we must strive to "be cautious in bringing to bear concepts and information that were not available to the eighteenth-century subjects," adding that "it is readily demonstrable that eighteenth-century Americans were sometimes uninformed about the past, including their own past, but they acted on the basis of their own knowledge and understanding, not ours," *Novus*, xii.

46. Gribbin, "Rollin's Histories," 614.

47. See George C. Brauer, Jr., "Alexander in England: The Conqueror's Reputation in the Late Seventeenth and Eighteenth Centuries," *CJ* 76 (October–November 1980):36–37; and, for but one example, Bate, *Samuel Johnson*, 311.

48. Drawn from Morgan, *Puritan Political Ideas*, xxxv–xxxvi.

49. Interestingly enough, Steele was an ex-officer of the Coldstream Guards; many fellow officers disliked his literary efforts which they considered uncomplimentary toward the army. In turn, Steele thought little of his messmates' intellectual capabilities; in fact, to this day, the Guards are still known as "the woodenheads." See Lee McCardell, *Ill-Starred General: Braddock of the Coldstream Guards* (Pittsburgh: University of Pittsburgh Press, 1958), 22–23, 32, 36.

50. The essay form was "vastly more popular in America than in England," noted Colbourn, *Lamp of Experience*, 9, although Samuel Johnson, author of *The Ambler* and *The Idler* might have disagreed. See also Smart, "Private Libraries," 37, who describes the *Spectator* as being very popular in Virginia; Shipton, "Literary Leaven," who notes the same for New England; and May, *Enlightenment in America*, 36–37, 41.

51. Quoted in Louis C. Schaedler, "James Madison, Literary Craftsman," *WMQ* 3rd ser., 3 (October 1946):515.

52. *Common-Sense*, 11 June, 1737, quoted in Elizabeth Christine Cook, *Literary Influences in Colonial Newspapers* (New York: Columbia University Press, 1912), 63–64.

53. Kraus, "Literary Relations," 224; Cook, *Newspapers*, 4, 17; and see also Robert M. Weir, "The Role of the Newspaper Press in the Southern Colonies on the Eve of the Revolution: An Interpretation," in Bailyn and John B.

Hench, eds., *The Press & the American Revolution* (Worcester: American Antiquarian Society, 1980), 99–150.

54. For just one example see B[enjamin] West, *The New-England Almanack, or Lady's and Gentleman's Diary* (Providence: John Carter, 1774). The Addison-Steele (and others) personalized essay became the accepted and the *only* style in colonial and revolutionary America. Modern political columnists are lineal descendants of these two highly influential Britons.

55. Robert J. Allen, ed., *Addison and Steele: Selections from "The Tatler" and "The Spectator"* (New York: Holt, Rinehart & Winston, 1957; reprint 1966), x.

56. Bate, *Samuel Johnson*, 50.

57. I used R[oger] L'Estrange, *Seneca's Morals by way of Abstract*, 7th ed. (London: M. Bennet, 1699).

58. *Cato*, act 5, sc. 2.

59. Hugh F. Rankin, *The Theater in Colonial America* (Chapel Hill: University of North Carolina Press, 1960), 93, 115, 139, 193; and Oral Sumner Coad and Edwin Mims, Jr., *The American State* (New Haven: Yale University Press, 1929), 12–13, 16.

60. L'Estrange, *Seneca's Morals*, 37.

61. Samuel Eliot Morison, *The Young Man Washington* (Cambridge: Harvard University Press, 1932), 14–18.

62. C. Crispus Sallustius, *The War with Cataline*, trans. by J. C. Rolfe, rev. ed. (Loeb series) (Cambridge: Harvard University Press, 1931; reprint 1971), 112.

63. May, *Enlightenment in America*, 41; James Thomas Flexner, *George Washington: The Forge of Experience (1732–1775)* (Boston: Little, Brown, 1965), 240–43; Wills, *Cincinnatus*, 8, 134–37; H. C. Montgomery, "Washington the Stoic," *CJ* 31 (February 1936):371–73, and Conway, *Washington's Rules of Civility*. See also Barry Schwartz, *George Washington: The Making of an American Symbol* (New York: Free Press, 1987).

64. Lathrop, *Translations*, 18.

65. Samuel Croxhall, *Fables of Aesop; and Others*, 13th ed. (London: n.p., 1786); Reinhold, *Classica Americana*, 149).

66. Diary entry, January 1759, Lyman H. Butterfield, ed., *Diary and Autobiography of John Adams*, 4 vols. (Cambridge: Harvard University Press, 1961–62), 1:66, 74.

67. *De Officiis* 1.35.

68. *Cato's Letters* 4: nos. 121, 126, 133. See also ibid. no. 108, 24; 3: no. 102, 311, 313; ibid. no. 100, 296, 299, among many examples.

69. Larrabee et al., *Franklin Papers*, 1:8–45; 2:130–31.

70. Quoted by Socrates in Xenophon, *Memorabilia and Oeconomius*, trans. by E. C. Marchant (Loeb series) (New York: G. P. Putnam's Sons, 1923), 1. 2. 54.

71. Vertot, *History of the Revolutions*, 1:35–37, quoted in Reinhold, *Classick Pages*, 195.

72. Vertot, *History of the Revolutions*, 1:13–14.
73. Quoted in *Cato's Letters*, no. 18, 1:119.
74. Vertot, *History of the Revolutions*, 1:11–12.
75. *Cato's Letters*, no. 17, 1:114–115.
76. Reinhold, *Classick Pages*, 158.
77. Larrabee et al., *Franklin Papers*, 2:222.
78. See Cook, *Newspapers*, for examples. A survey of the almanac collection at the John Carter Brown Library reveals just how replete these handy booklets were with classical terminology and mythology. For just a few citations, see Richard Saunders, *Poor Richard Improved* (Philadelphia: B. Franklin and D. Hall, 1749); Benjamin West, *The New-England Almanack* (Providence: John Carter, 1773); and N[athaniel] Ames, *The Astronomical Diary* (Boston: John Draper, 1761). See also Milton Drake, comp., *Almanacs of the United States*, 2 vols. (New York: Scarecrow Press, 1962).
79. N.W., *An Almanack of Celestial Motions and Aspects for the (Dionysion) Year of the Christian Aera, 1707* (Boston: B. Green, 1707).
80. Flexner, *Forge of Experience*, 242.
81. As just one source of many, for New Hampshire slaves bearing classical names, see Richard M. Gummere, "Classical Precedents in the Writings of James Wilson," *PCSM* 32 *Transactions 1933–1937* (Boston: By the Society, 1937), 527.
82. Highet, *Classical Tradition*, 400; see also any good map of upstate New York.
83. Flexner, *Forge of Experience*, 242.
84. *Cato,* act 2, sc. 4. There is another passage (act 2, sc. 1) which might have influenced or inspired Henry. Sempronius cries:

> My voice is still for war.
> Gods! can a Roman senate long debate
> Which of the two to chose, slavery or death!

Charles L. Cohen's "The 'Liberty or Death' Speech: A Note on Religion and Revolutionary Rhetoric," *WMQ* 3rd ser., 38 (October 1981):702–17, discusses biblical, some classical, and most revolutionary rhetoric in Henry's dynamic speech, but he ignores the influence of either above-mentioned passages in *Cato*. See also McDonald, *Novus*, 10; Litto's excellent "Addison's *Cato* in the Colonies," 431–49; Land, "First Williamsburg Theater," esp. 372–73; David S. Lovejoy, "Henry Marchant and the Mistress of the World," *WMQ* 3rd ser., 12 (July 1955):387; Edward A. Wyatt IV, "Three Petersburg Theatres," ibid., 2nd ser., 21 (April 1941):83–84; John Loftis' enlightening "The London Theaters in Early Eighteenth-Century Politics," *HLQ* 18 (August 1955):369–93; and Forbes, "Addison's *Cato*," 210–12.
85. *Cato,* act IV, sc. 4. This particular passage had a strong influence on young revolutionary zealots such as Colonels Alexander Hamilton, John Laurens, Henry Lee, and Alexander Scammell, all of whom not only shared a

love of the classics but who were all very close to His Excellency, George Washington.

Less likely, but possibly, Hale, whose statue stands before the headquarters building of the Central Intelligence Agency, was also influenced by a passage from *Cato's Letters* in which a letter from Brutus (a great hero to republicans) to Cicero is quoted:

> What was the End of killing the Tyrant [Julius Caesar], but to be free from Tyranny?— A ridiculous Motive, and an empty Exploit, if our Slavery survives him?—Oh, who is it that makes Liberty his Care? Liberty which ought to be the Care of all Men, as 'tis the Benefit and Blessing of all! For myself, I cannot lose but with my Life, my Resolution to maintain in Freedom my Country, which I have set free. (no. 23, 1:170)

86. David L. Jacobson, ed., *The English Libertarian Heritage: From the Writings of John Trenchard and Thomas Gordon in The Independent Whig and Cato's Letters* (Indianapolis: Bobbs-Merrill, 1965), xxxvn, lvi–lvii. See also Bailyn, *Ideological Origins*, 44–45. Reading *Cato's Letters* gives one a solid foundation for understanding eighteenth-century American republican ideology. The authors quote from many classical and popular sources well-known to their colonial readers. For the purposes of this book, as will be seen in part III, the writings of the two authors (Trenchard and Gordon) were particularly important to the development of the revolutionary generation's attitudes toward the military in time of peace and war.

87. John Robert Moore, "Dr. Johnson and Roman History,"*HLQ* 12 (May 1949):311, 314.

88. Charles F. Mullet, "Ancient Historians and 'Enlightened' Reviewers," *The Review of Politics* 21 (July 1959): 550–51.

89. Arthur H. Buffington, "The Puritan view of War," *PCSM* 28 *Transactions 1930–1933* (Boston: By the Society, 1935), 68.

90. Rollin, *Ancient History*, 420–57.

91. Quoted in Marcus Cunliffe, *Soldiers & Civilians: The Martial Spirit in America 1775–1865* (Boston: Little, Brown, 1968), 66–67.

92. Ibid.

4. Learning about Warfare

1. Jones, *Strange New World*, 115.

2. Christopher Duffy, *The Military Experience in the Age of Reason* (London: Routledge & Kegan Paul, 1987; New York: Atheneum, 1988), 50.

3. The French created an artillery school at Douai in 1679, and the Royal Military Academy for Engineer and Artillery officer-cadets was founded in Woolwich, England, in 1741. See André Corvisier, *Armies and Societies in Europe, 1494–1789*, trans. by Abigail T. Siddall (Bloomington: Indiana University Press, 1979), 103–9; and John Childs, *Armies and Warfare in Europe, 1648–1789* (Manchester: Manchester University Press, 1982), 93–95.

4. For a list of these tracts, see Robin Higham, ed., *A Guide to the Sources*

of British Military History (Berkeley: University of California Press, 1971); Higham, ed., *A Guide to the Sources in United States Military History* (Hamden, Conn.: Archon Books, 1975); Higham and Don Mrozek, eds., ibid., *Supplement I* (Hamden, Conn.: Archon Books, 1981); ibid., *Supplement II* (Hamden, Conn.: Archon Books, 1986); and Houlding, *Fit for Service*, esp. 151–256, 426–34.

5. Quoted in S. L. A. Marshall, *Men Against Fire: The Problem of Battle Command in Future War* (New York: William Morrow, 1947), 116. Marshall's general themes retain some value, but they must be read alongside the critical comments of Roger D. Spiller, "S. L. A. Marshall and the Ratio of Fire," *RUSI* 133 (Winter 1988): 63–71; David H. Hackworth and Julie Sherman, *About Face: The Odyssey of an American Warrior* (New York: Simon and Schuster, 1989), 548–86, and Fredric Smolen, "The Secret of the Soldiers Who Didn't Shoot," *American Heritage* 40 (March 1989):37–45.

6. The term *Strategy* was not regularly employed in the eighteenth century, but, from the Greek word for general *(strategoi)*, its etymology is apparent: the primary concern of a general in war. See also Russell F. Weigley's seminal "American Strategy: A Call for a Critical Strategic History," in Don Higginbotham, ed., *Reconsiderations on the Revolutionary War* (Westport, Conn.: Greenwood Press, 1978), 32–53.

7. David G. Chandler, *The Campaigns of Napoleon: The Mind and Method of History's Greatest Soldier* (New York: Macmillan, 1966), 161, 4–11, 136–37, 133–201; Liddell Hart, *Ghost of Napoleon*, 38; Larry H. Addington, *The Patterns of War since the Eighteenth Century* (Bloomington: Indiana University Press, 1984), 17; Gerald Gilbert, *The Evolution of Tactics* (London: Hugh Rees, 1907), xiv; and for additional advice on reading history, see Edward Cooke, *The Character of Warre, or The Image of Martial Discipline* (London: Thomas Purfoot, 1626), esp. chapter 17.

8. Quoted in Gilbert, *Evolution of Tactics*, xiv. See also Jay Luvaas, ed. and trans., *Frederick the Great on the Art of War* (New York: Free Press, 1966), 343. This is Frederick's post–Seven Years' War revision of an earlier treatise. See "The Instructions of Frederick the Great for His Generals, 1747," trans. by Thomas R. Phillips, in Phillips, ed., *Roots of Strategy: A Collection of Military Classics* (Harrisburg, Pa.: Military Service Publishing, 1940; reprint ed., Harrisburg, Pa.: Stackpole Books, 1985). Frederick had fifty copies of these "Instructions" distributed among his key officers in 1747 on an oath of secrecy. Captured along with a general by the Austrians in 1760, they were quickly translated and published in several languages, including English (1762). These "Instructions" from 1747 were studied intensely by revolutionary Americans.

9. Carl von Clausewitz, *On War*, ed. and trans. by Michael E. Howard and Peter Paret (Princeton: Princeton University Press, 1976), 173–74. Reading this fine translation should be prefaced by the superlative introductory essays of Howard, Paret, and Bernard Brodie.

10. Quoted from Hegel's *Lectures on the Philosophy of History* in Hamerow, *Reflections on History*, 229.

11. Mao Tse-tung [Zedong], *Selected Military Writings of Mao Tse-tung* (Peking: Foreign Language Press, 1963), 76; John Morgan Dederer, *Making Bricks Without Straw: Nathanael Greene's Southern Campaigns and Mao Tse-tung's Mobile War*, Fore. by Russell F. Weigley (Manhattan, Kans.: Sunflower University Press, 1983), 15.

12. Quoted in Marshall, *Men against Fire*, 107.

13. Chandler, *Campaigns of Napoleon*, 135–37.

14. Quoted in Marshall, *Men against Fire*, 107.

15. Socrates quoted in Xenophon, *Memorabilia* 2. 1. 28.

16. Chevalier de la Valiere, *The Art of War* (Philadelphia: Robert Bell, 1776), 61, iv. This translation was a favorite of the American high command.

17. Liddell Hart, *Great Captains Unveiled* (Boston: Little, Brown, 1927; Freeport, N.Y.: Books for Libraries Press, 1967), 126. Italics in original.

18. Quoted in Duffy, *Military Experience*, 140.

19. Thomas Styward, *The Path waie to Martiall Discipline, divided into two Bookes, verie necesarie for young Souldiers, or for all such as loveth the proffesion of Armes* (London: T. East, 1581), 2.

20. Quoted in Xenophon, *Memorabilia* 3. 1. 6.

21. Frederick, "Instructions," 346.

22. Christopher Duffy, *Frederick the Great: A Military Life* (London: Routledge & Kegan Paul, 1985), 322; Frederick, "Instructions," 349, 348–51. See also Rollin, *Ancient History*, 122–23; de la Valiere, *Art of War*, 56–58; and the definition of "General" in George Smith, *An Universal Military Dictionary, Or a Copious Explanation of the Technical Terms &c. Used in the Equipment, Machinery, Movements, and Military operations of an Army* (London: J. Millan, 1779). Smith was the inspector of the Royal Military Academy at Woolwich.

23. De la Valiere, *Art of War*, 57.

24. Rollin, *Ancient History*, 123.

25. Xenophon, *Cyropaedia*, 2 vols., trans. by Walter Miller (Loeb series) (New York: Macmillan, 1914–24), 5.3.47. As Professor Donald Kagan enlightened me, Cyrus lived and died in the sixth century B.C.; Xenophon, who wrote as if at Cyrus's knee, lived 150 years later.

26. F. E. Adcock, *The Roman Art of War under the Republic* (Martin Classical Lecturers VIII) (Cambridge: Harvard University Press, 1940), 120; Adcock, *The Greek and Macedonian Art of War* (Berkeley: University of California Press, 1957), 85; Duffy, *Frederick*, 327; Frederick, "Instructions," 346; and see also Gunter E. Rothenberg, "Maurice of Nassau, Gustavus Adolphus, Raimondo Montecuccoli, and the Military Revolution' of the Seventeenth Century," in Peter Paret, ed., *Makers of Modern Strategy from Machiavelli to the Nuclear Age* (Princeton: Princeton University Press, 1986), 61–62; Morison, *Young Man Washington*, 23.

27. *King Henry V*, act. 3, sc. 6.

28. Roger [Boyle], Earl of Orrery, *A Treatise of the Art of War: Dedicated to the Kings Most Excellent Majesty* (London: Henry Herringman, 1677), 149.

29. Frederick, "Instructions," 344–47; Duffy, *Frederick*, 327; and Morison, *Young Man Washington*, 23.

30. Howard, *Plutarch*, 189; [Thomas] Webb, *A Military Treatise on the Appointments of the Army* (Philadelphia: W. Dunlap, 1759), 20.

31. Matthew Suttcliffe, *The Practice, Proceedings, and Lawes of armes, described out of the doings of most valiant and expert Captaines, and confirmed both by ancient, and moderne examples, and praecedents* (London: Christopher Barker, 1593), A5.

32. See Smith, *Military Dictionary*, v, of many.

33. G. F. R. Henderson, *The Science of War: A Collection of Essays and Lectures, 1891–1903*, ed. by Neill Malcolm (London: Longmans, Green, 1913), 101.

34. Ibid., 174.

35. Hans Delbrück, *History of the Art of War: Within the Framework of Political History*, trans. by Walter J. Renfroe, Jr., 4 vols. (Westport, Conn.: Greenwood Press, 1975–86), 1:96–97. Actually there were also Thebans at this famous battle, but they surrendered. As Delbrück remarked about the Thespians, "If the sacrifice of the Spartiates, who form a warrior class, is a deed of eternally memorable heroism, then the voluntary participation of the citizen militia of a small city seems to surpass human capabilities," ibid., 97n. For just one example of Thermopylae in the American press, see the *Virginia Gazette*, 30 December 1780, quoted in Frank Moore, ed., *Diary of the American Revolution from Newspapers and Original Documents*, 2 vols. in 1 (New York: Charles Scribner, 1860; New York: *The New York Times* & Arno Press, 1969), 886–87.

36. To John Banister, in John C. Fitzpatrick, ed., *The Writings of George Washington from the Original Manuscripts, 1745–1799*, 39 vols. (Washington, D.C.: Government Printing Office, 1931–44), 11:286. Hereinafter cited as *GW Writings*.

37. E. M. Lloyd, *A Review of the History of Infantry*, new ed. (Westport, Conn.: Greenwood Press, 1976), 33.

38. Frederick, "Instructions," 349–50.

39. Quoted in Gilbert, *Evolutions of Tactics*, xiv; Oliver Lyman Spaulding, *Pen and Sword in Greece and Rome* (Princeton: Princeton University Press, 1933), 4n; and Henderson, *Science of War*, 166, 170, among others. Jean-Charles de Folard's (1669–1752) *Histoire de Polybe*, 6 vols. (Paris: n.p., 1727–30), was less a pure translation than a platform for Folard to expound upon his ideas on the art of war. See Duffy, *Military Experience*, 53.

40. C. Crispi Sallustii, *Bellem Catilinarium, et Jurgurthinum, Ex optime atque accuratissima Gottlieb Cortii editione expressum, or, Sallust's History of Cataline's Conspiracy and the War with Jurgurtha, According to the excellent and accurate edition of Gottlieb Cortius*, trans. by John Mair, 3rd ed. (Edinburgh: David Willison, 1770), 2.

41. Caesar, *The Gallic War*, trans. by H. J. Edwards (Loeb series) (Cambridge: Harvard University Press, 1966), xii.

42. Quoted in Chandler, *Campaigns of Napoleon*, 137.

43. Quoted in Gilbert, *Evolution of Tactics*, 143.

44. Quoted from Frontinius in Edward N. Luttwak's superb, *The Grand Strategy of the Roman Empire: From the First Century A.D. to the Third* (Baltimore: John Hopkins University Press, 1976), 121.

45. Quoted in Marshall, *Men against Fire*, 114–15.

46. Luvaas, *Frederick the Great*, 47.

47. Thucydides, 3.82.

48. Arther Ferrill, *The Origins of War: From the Stone Age to Alexander the Great* (London: Thames and Hudson, 1985), 217; William H. McNeill, *The Pursuit of Power: Technology, Armed Force, and Society since A.D. 1000* (Chicago: University of Chicago Press, 1982), 146; Oliver Lyman Spaulding, Jr., Hoffman Nickerson, and John Womack Wright, *Warfare: A Study of Military Methods from the Earliest Times* (New York: Harcourt, Brace, 1925), 3–4, 5–7; Gwynne Dyer, *War* (New York: Crown, 1985), 72; and Geoffrey Parker, *The Military Revolution: Military Innovation and the Rise of the West, 1500–1800* (New York: Cambridge University Press, 1988), 2–7, among others.

49. Background drawn from the following: Theodore Ropp, *War in the Modern World*, new rev. ed. (New York: Collier Books, 1962), esp. 12; Michael Howard, *War in European History* (New York: Oxford University Press, 1976), 13–15, 55. Also helpful were Corvisier, *Armies and Societies;* John U. Nef, *War and Human Progress: An Essay on the Rise of Industrial Civilization* (Cambridge: Harvard University Press, 1950); Bernard Brodie and Fawn M. Brodie, *From Crossbow to H-Bomb: The Evolution of the Weapons and Tactics of Warfare*, rev. and enlged. ed. (Bloomington: Indiana University Press, 1973); Paul M. Kennedy, *The Rise and Fall of the Great Powers: Economic Change and Military Conflict From 1500 to 2000* (New York: Random House, 1987); and Robert L. O'Connell, *Of Arms and Men: A History of War, Weapons, and Aggression* (New York: Oxford University Press, 1989).

50. Felix Gilbert, "Machiavelli: The Renaissance of the Art of War," in Paret, ed., *Makers of Modern Strategy*, 21; Luttwak, *Grand Strategy;* S. E. Stout, "Training Soldiers for the Roman Legion," *CJ* 21 (April 1921): 425–27; and Charles R. Shrader, "The Influence of Vegetius' De re militari," *MA* 45 (December 1981):167–72. See M. J. D. Cockle, *A Bibliography of Military Books up to 1642* (London: Holland Press, 1900; reprint. 1957), 9–11; and Niccolo Machiavelli, *The Arte of Warre*, trans. by Peter Whithorne (London: n.p., 1560), which went through several editions. There remains something of a paradox inherent in Machiavelli's writing. On the one hand, he suggests realpolitik in *The Prince;* on the other, there was the patriotic, Vegetian-influenced Machiavelli of *The Art of War*. Certainly, much of the latter may be extrapolated for use by disciples of the former, but there remains a republican flavor in *The Art of War*—from classical influence, no doubt—that does not mesh easily with the realism of *The Prince*.

51. Jay Luvaas described Vegetius's *De Re Militari* as "one of the most

influential military treatises in the Western world from Roman times until the time of Frederick," *Frederick the Great*, 55 n. 12. I am grateful to Professor Michael Mallet for much needed clarification.

52. Among the copies of Vegetius's work I have examined are those in the Library of Congress, both in the Rare Book Room and in the Rosewald Collection: *De Re Militari* (Cologne: N[icolaus] G[oetz], [ca. 1475]; ibid., (Romae: Silber, 1487); *Fl. Vegetii Renati De re militari libri quatuor. Sexti Iulii Frontini De strategematis libri totidem. Aeliani De instruen dis aciebus unus* (Lutetiae: C. Wechelum, 1532), which combines the work of Vegetius, Frontinius, and Aelian; ibid., (Parisiis: C. Perier, 1553); ibid., (Antverpiae: Christophorum Plantinum, 1585); *The foure bookes of Flavius Vegetius Renatus, briefelye contayninge a plaine forme, and perfect knowledge of martiall police, feates of chiualrie, and whatsoeuer pertayneth to warre*, trans. by John Sadler (London: Thomas Marshe, 1572); *Military Instructions of Vegetius, in five books*, trans. by John Clarke (London: W. Griffin, 1767), for which Lt. Clarke received a promotion to captain; *Commentaires sur les institutions militaires de Végèce*, trans. by Turpin de Crissé (Paris: Nyon l'aîné, 1783), plus various editions in Spanish, German, Italian, and Swedish published before 1800. See also Dianne Bornstein, "Military Manuals in Fifteenth-Century England," *Mediaeval Studies* 37 (1972):469–77; Bornstein, "Military Strategy in Malory and Vegetius' *De re militari*," *Comparative Literature Studies* 9 (1972):123–29; Bornstein, "The Scottish Prose Version of Vegetius' *De re militari*," *Studies in Scottish Literature* 8 (1971):174–83; W. Goffert, "The Date and Purpose of Vegetius' *De re militari*," *Traditio* 33 (1977):65–100; Cockle, *Bibliography*, 1, 3–4, 14, 41, 155; Brüggemann, *A View*, 745–47; J. Wiseman, "L'Epitoma re militari de Végèce et sa fortune au Moyen Age," *Le Moyen Age* 85 (1979):13–29; Lathrop, *Translations*; Cooke, *The Character of Warre*; James Turner, *Pallas Armata: Military Essayes on the Ancient Grecian, Roman, and Modern Art of War* (London: M. W., 1683), esp. 87–94; and [Nicholas Boone], *Military Discipline: The Souldier, or Expert Artilleryman* (Boston: By Author, 1701), who considered Plutarch, Vegetius, Xenophon, Homer, and others "an old heap of stuff," (3).

53. Charles W. Jones, "Bede and Vegetius," *Classical Review* 46 (1932):248–49; Delbrück, *History of the Art of War*, 2:203; Spaulding et al., *Warfare*, 294; and Christine de Pisan, *Faits d'armes et de chevalerie* (Westminster: William Caxton, 1489).

54. Quoted in Delbrück, *History of the Art of War*, 2:203. For more on this controversial turn-of-the-century historian, see Arden Bucholz, *Hans Delbrück & The German Military Establishment: War Images in Conflict* (Iowa City: University of Iowa Press, 1985).

55. Napoleon quoted in Chandler, *Campaigns of Napoleon*, 137; Carnot quoted in Oliver L. Spaulding, Jr., "The Ancient Military Writers," *CJ* 28 (June 1933):657. That the essence of things never changes may be seen in the biting satire of Francis Grose, *Advice to the Officers of the British Army: With the Addition of some Hints to the Drummer and Private Soldier*, 7th ed. (London: G. Kearsley,

1783), 60. American servicemen of World War II were convinced that medics used thin, sharp needles when administering shots to officers, saving the big, dull needles for enlisted men. Grose sarcastically advises eighteenth-century medical personnel, "Keep two lancets [for bleeding]; a blunt one for the soldiers, and a sharp one of the officers: this will be making a proper distinction between them."

56. Alfred P. Dorjahn and Lester K. Born, "Vegetius and the Decay of the Roman Army," *CJ* 30 (December 1934), esp. 158. "The patriotic writer can see only the ruinous and ruined contemporary society about him; in contrast to this his attention is eagerly fixed upon the staunch soldiarity of the past history of his race."

57. Delbrück, *History of the Art of War*, 2:203.

58. Ropp, *War in the Modern World*, 32n.

59. Delbrück, *History of the Art of War*, 2:203.

60. See Dederer, *Making Bricks without Straw*, 15; Samuel B. Griffith, ed., *Sun Tzu: The Art of War* (New York: Oxford University Press, 1963; reprint. 1981); Tao Hanshang, *Sung Tzu's Art of War*, trans. by Yuan Shibing (New York: Stirling, 1987); and the first Western translation by Jesuit Joseph Amiot, *Art Militaire Des Chinois, ou recueil D'anciens Traites Sur la Guerre, composés avant l'ere chrétienne, Par Differents Generaux Chinois* (Paris: Didot L'aîne, 1772), esp. 45–159.

61. Spaulding et al., *Warfare*, 419.

62. Luvaas, *Frederick the Great*, 26.

63. My thanks to Professor Robin Higham on this point.

64. Vegetius, "The Military Institutions of the Romans," from the trans. by John Clarke, in Phillips, *Roots of Strategy*, 124, hereinafter cited as Vegetius, "Military Institutions." See also Lester K. Born, "Roman and Modern Military Science: Some Suggestions for Teaching," *CJ* 29 (October 1933):14; and Luttwak, *Grand Strategy*.

Vegetius's comments on preparedness are worth nothing in full: "He, therefore, who desires peace, should prepare for war. He who aspires to victory, should spare no pains to form his soldiers. And he who hopes for success, should fight on principle, not chance. No one dares to offend or insult a power of known superiority in actions." Or, as one seventeenth-century commander paraphrased it: "he that will injoy Peace with his Neighbors, must always be prepared for War," Charles V, *Political and Military Observations, Remarks and Maxims, of Charles V, Late Duke of Lorrain, General of the Emperor's Forces*, trans. by Rupert Beck (London: J. Jones & W. Hawes, 1699), 38–39.

65. See the sources in James Michael Hill, *Celtic Warfare, 1591–1763* (Edinburgh: John Donald, 1986), and Forrest McDonald, "Prologue," in McWhiney, *Cracker Culture*, xxi–xliii.

5. The European Inheritance

1. Howard, *War in European History*, 55; McNeill, *Pursuit of Power*, 117, 63; Addington, *Patterns of War*, 2; and Ropp, *War in the Modern World*, 19.

As will be seen, this conflict between realization of a need for external defense and a very real fear of internal oppression by these security forces runs as a thread through Western political-military thought and practice from classical times to the eighteenth century and beyond.

2. Howard, *War in European History*, 62; and see also McNeill, *Pursuit of Power*, 117, 63; Addington, *Patterns of War*, 2; and Ropp, *War in the Modern World*, 19. Kennedy, *Rise and Fall*, esp. his "Introduction" and first chapter, were helpful.

3. Luttwak, *Grand Strategy*, 135; Kennedy, *Rise and Fall*, xvi, 17.

4. Quoted in Parker, *Military Revolution*, 10.

5. Ibid., 10–12, among others.

6. Ibid., 14.

7. Ibid., 2. The fall of Constantinople stands out as a significant blip on the time-space continuum, yet, as Michael Mallet has suggested to me, the forces for change already existed in Europe with the Italians leading the way.

8. Philippe Contamine, *War in the Middle Ages*, trans. by Michael Jones (New York: Basil Blackwell, 1984), 139, and the fine bibliography, 309–60; McNeill, *Pursuit of Power*, 89–90.

9. Ropp, *War in the Modern World*, 27; Dyer, *War*, 72; H. W. Koch, *The Rise of Modern Warfare, 1618–1815* (Englewood Cliffs, N.J.: Prentice-Hall, 1981), 8–25; and the seminal article by Geoffrey Parker, "The 'Military Revolution,' 1560–1660—a Myth?," *JMH* 48 (June 1976), esp. 208–9, which he extends in *Military Revolution*. Insights gained from this article and book are valuable to students of war of any period. See also Emmanuel B. Leroy Ladurie, "Recent Historical 'Discoveries,' " *Daedalus* 106 (Fall 1977), esp. 146.

10. Howard, *War in European History*, 37. For example, during the Thirty Years' War the population of Germany fell from 21 million to 13 million— including those who fled—with civilians faring much worse than soldiers, Childs, *Armies and Warfare*, 9.

11. Kennedy, *Rise and Fall*, 71.

12. Quoted in Rothenberg, "Maurice, Gustavus, Montecuccoli," 35; Ropp, *War in the Modern World*, 27; Dyer, *War*, 72; and Howard, *War in European History*, 37.

13. Vegetius, "Military Institutions," 126.

14. Ibid., 75.

15. Ibid., 120.

16. Ibid., 172. See also Graham Webster, *The Roman Imperial Army of the First and Second Centuries A.D.*, 3rd ed. (London: A & C Black, 1985).

17. Howard, *War in European History*, 56; quotation from the introduction to John Bingham, trans., *The Tactiks of Aelian Or art of Embattling an army after*

ye Grecian manner (London: Laurence Lisle, 1616). This work features "The exercise military of ye English by ye order of that great Generall Maurice of Nassau Prince of Orange." See also Geoffrey Parker, ed., *The Thirty Years' War*, rev. ed. (London: Routledge & Kegan Paul, 1987), 205.

18. Howard, *War in European History*, 56; McNeill, *Pursuit of Power*, 117; Duffy, *Military Experience*, 15; Parker, *The Thirty Years' War*, 205–7; Adcock, *Roman Art of War*, 12, 15, 19, 83; Rothenberg, "Maurice, Gustavus, Montecuccoli," 41; Lloyd, *Review of the History of Infantry*, 99; and Jacob de Gheyn, *The Exercise of Armes for calivres, mvskettes, and pikes after the ordre of His Excellence Maurits, Prince of Orange* (The Hag[u]e: n.p., 1608), esp. its terrific woodcut prints.

19. Kennedy, *Rise and Fall*, 71.

20. On this point, A. C. Houlding's *Fit for Service* should be consulted.

21. Duffy, *Military Experience*, 6–7.

22. Delbrück, *History of the Art of War*, 4:177, 189, 252–54. See also Firth, *Cromwell's Army*, 276–310, and Childs, *Armies and Warfare*, 67. Biblical admonitions forbade the administration of more than thirty-nine lashes, and revolutionary Americans followed this directive. Washington repeatedly sought to raise the number of punishment strokes, and Congress eventually did, but only minimally.

23. Or, as Christopher Duffy, *Military Experience*, 101, writes, soldiers have always been "drawn irresistibly towards whatever will do themselves the most harm."

24. Quoted in R. R. Palmer, "Frederick the Great, Guibert, Bülow: From Dynastic to National War," in Paret, *Makers of Modern Strategy*, 91 and 93–94. See also Howard, *War in European History*, 56–57.

25. McNeill, *Pursuit of Power*, 130–31, 133, 138.

26. Ropp, *War in the Modern World*, 56.

27. Suttcliffe, *Practice, Proceedings, and Lawes of armes*, 21.

28. Quoted in Lloyd, *Review of the History of Infantry*, 102.

29. Firth, *Cromwell's Army*, 187. See also Nef, *War and Human Progress*, 65–88. Nef's work is exciting in its breadth and scope, it also should be read with a caveat. Writing in the immediate aftermath of World War II and filled with revulsion over the war just ended and fearful of nuclear conflict, Nef often imparts a mid–twentieth-century interpretation to the past.

30. Ibid., 25.

31. Quoted in Duffy, *Military Experience*, 98.

32. Quoted in Elbridge Colby, *Masters of Mobile Warfare* (Princeton: Princeton University Press, 1943), 92–93. See also Donald M. Frame, trans., *Voltaire: Candide, Zadig, and Selected Stories* (New York: New American Library, 1961), esp. 18–19.

33. In the Thirty Years' War, some 25,000 Scots alone fought for the Protestant side. Parker, *Thirty Years' War*, 194.

34. Kennedy, *Rise and Fall*, 67.

35. Rothenburg, "Maurice, Gustavus, Montecuccoli," 47–48; Ropp, *War in the Modern World*, 53; and Hew Strachan, *European Armies and the Conduct of War* (London: Allen & Unwin, 1983), 9.

36. Lloyd, *Review of the History of Infantry*, 177, 184; Strachan, *European Armies*, 15; Ropp, *War in the Modern World*, 57; and Duffy, *Frederick*, 296–300.

37. Quoted in Duffy, *Frederick*, 245.

38. On the phalanx and on Greek warfare in general, a good source is W. Kendrick Pritchett, *The Greek State at War*, 4 vols. (Berkeley: University of California Press, 1974–85), esp. vols. 1 and 2.

39. The Spanish *tercio* was modeled on the Roman legion, even to carrying a *gladius* (a short, stabbing sword); but the Spanish conformed to gunpowder realities by thinning their formations to protect their musketeers. Ironically, the original *gladius* was a Spanish sword borrowed by the Romans.

40. Delbrück, *History of the Art of War*, 3:553–90; Ropp, *War in the Modern World*, 22; Charles W. C. Oman, *The Art of War in the Middle Ages A.D. 378–1515*, rev. and ed. by John H. Beeler (Ithaca: Cornell University Press, 1953), 73–115; and Howard, *War in European History*, 15. Regarding the abundance of arms in colonial America, see chap. 6, n. 11.

41. Ropp, *War in the Modern World*, 29; Contamine, *War in the Middle Ages*, 147; Parker, *Military Revolution*, 18; and Gilbert, *Evolution of Tactics*, 6. It is from the phalanx where the modern term "rank and file" has its etymology.

42. Kennedy, *Rise and Fall*, 70–71.

43. The term "line of communication" is used here in its modern sense; in seventeenth- and eighteenth-century terminology, it meant the united trenchworks surrounding a besieged work. See Smith, *Military Dictionary*.

44. Parker, *Military Revolution*, 26.

45. Henry Guerlac, "Vauban: The Impact of Science on War," in Paret, *Makers of Modern Strategy*, 67, 65–66, 79; Childs, *Armies and Warfare*, 145–48.

46. Guerlac, "Vauban," noted that: "Antiquity was still the great teacher in all that concerned the broader aspects of military theory and the secrets of military genius. Vegetius and Frontinius were deemed indispensable" as was Caesar, 71–72. See also Christopher Duffy's invaluable *Siege Warfare: The Fortress in the Age of Vauban and Frederick the Great* (London: Routledge & Kegan Paul, 1984), esp. 6, 78, 107.

47. Quoted in Ropp, *War in the Modern World*, 43–44.

48. Louvois also borrowed from antiquity and introduced an inspector general to the French army in 1668. The first was a former drillmaster whose name almost immediately entered the public domain, typifying the discipline of the times—Lieutenant Colonel Martinet.

49. Duffy, *Siege Warfare*, 2:78, 6, 107; Guerlac, "Vauban," 65–67, 79; Koch, *Rise of Modern Warfare*, 69; *War in the Modern World*, 43–44; and Rothenberg, "Maurice, Gustavus, Montecuccoli," 51, who notes that after the fall of Magdeburg in 1631, twenty-five thousand citizens were slaughtered and the

town burned, an incident Schiller described as "a murderous scene for which history can find no words and the art of writing no pen," Nef, *War and Human Progress*, 138.

50. Much of what follows is drawn from the excellent work of: Childs, *Armies and Warfare*, esp. 2; Duffy, *Military Experience;* Parker, *Military Revolution;* and the superb study by Martin van Creveld, *Supplying War: Logistics from Wallenstein to Patton* (Cambridge: Cambridge University Press, 1977).

51. Nef, *War and Human Progress*, 250–70, for just one example, grossly misrepresents conditions to buttress his overall argument.

52. Dyer, *War*, 63.

53. Strachan, *European Armies*, 15.

54. Grady McWhiney and Perry Jamieson, *Attack and Die: Military Tactics and the Southern Heritage* (University, Ala.: University of Alabama Press, 1982), 19. To contrast these with Napoleon's "butcher's bills," see Chandler, *Campaigns of Napoleon*, 1118–21.

55. Parker, *Military Revolution*, 43, 39–40. Bonaparte's army corps rarely exceeded thirty-five thousand troops. Each corps thus drew supplies and forage from its own area, concentrating only when the time for battle grew close.

56. For example, see Donald W. Engels, *Alexander the Great and the Logistics of the Macedonian Army* (Berkeley: University of California, 1978; reprint. 1980).

57. Luvaas, *Frederick the Great*, 308.

58. Chandler, *Campaigns of Napoleon*, 164; Strachan, *European Armies*, 41; Delbrück, *History of the Art of War*, 4:412; and McNeill, *Pursuit of Power*, 147.

"Tooth-to-tail" means the number of men required to maintain combat troops in the field: the smaller and more efficient the "tail," the larger the "tooth." For example, Strachan, ibid., 10, depicted a typical eighteenth-century Prussian infantry regiment as having 2,200 combatants, 2,400 noncombatants, and 1,200 draft horses. Potatoes, however, only provided human forage along the march; if an army remained immobile too long, it starved.

59. Parker, *Military Revolution*, 65–66. See also Van Creveld, *Supplying War*, 9–26; Palmer, "Frederick, Guibert, Bülow," 94–95; McNeill, *Pursuit of Power*, 144, 159; Rothenberg, "Maurice, Gustavus, Montecuccoli," 54; Parker, "Military Revolution," 209–10; Nef, *War and Human Progress*, 323; H. C. B. Rogers, *The British Army of the Eighteenth Century* (New York: Hippocrene Books, 1977), 119–127; Kennedy, *Rise and Fall*, 65; and Colby, *Masters of Mobile Warfare*, 25–26.

60. In spite of industrialized mechanization, transporting bulky forage or trying to find it locally remained the bane of armies through World War II (the Wehrmacht, as historian Richard DiNardo reminded me, was never more than 50 percent mechanized). In the First World War, for instance, the British shipped 750,000 tons of POL (petroleum, oil, and lubricants) to the Western Front; they also shipped 5,500,000 tons of oats and hay. Ropp, *War in the Modern World*, 29n.

61. See "rations" in Smith, *Military Dictionary*, wherein the British army (circa 1779) substituted a daily allowance of one pound each of beef and biscuit, plus peas, butter, and rice per soldier.

62. Van Creveld, *Supplying War*, 25. Twenty pounds of daily feed per horse is not much. In 1779 in his dictionary under "forage," George Smith suggests that the daily allowance for a cavalry mount should be twenty pounds of hay, ten pounds of oats, and five pounds of straw, Smith, *Military Dictionary*.

63. Parker, *Military Revolution*, 76, and see graph on 186.

64. Luvaas, *Frederick the Great*, 16.

65. Van Creveld, *Supplying War*, 25.

66. Luvaas, *Frederick the Great*, 16.

67. Palmer, "Frederick, Guibert, Bülow," 95.

68. Vegetius, "Military Institutions," 143.

69. Quoted in Hackworth and Sherman, *About Face*, 560.

70. Vegetius, "Military Institutions," 128.

71. Quoted in Kennedy, *Rise and Fall*, 71.

72. Vegetius, "Military Institutions," 128.

73. Kennedy, *Rise and Fall*, 85.

74. What might be best described as an offensive-defense. That is, an active, nonpassive, nonstatic defense in which the counterattack, the counteroffensive was always in the forefront of the commander's mind. This concept had a great influence on Washington's strategic thinking by late 1776, and later, on Napoleon's.

75. Frederick, "Instructions," 321.

76. Thucydides 5.70.

77. Maurice de Saxe, "My Reveries Upon the Art of War," trans. by Thomas R. Phillips, in Phillips, *Roots of Strategy*, 202–5. See also Saxe, *Mes Reveres, Ouvrage posthume de Maurice Comte de Saxe*, trans. by Abbé Perau, 2 vols. (Amsterdam and Leipzig: Arkstee and Merkus, 1757). Saxe's work was influential on Frederick, and later, translated into English, upon American officers in the Revolution and even on Napoleon. Saxe drew heavily from Vegetius and to a lesser extent from Frontinius and other classical authors, including Polybius. Saxe also borrowed from Chevalier Folard's *Histoire sur Polybe* (1727–30).

78. Saxe, "My Reveries," 298. These words carry the same message as those of the much-lauded Sun Tzu (see n. 69 above).

79. Ibid. See also Smith, *Military Dictionary*, who begins his definition of the term "Battles": "*Battles* have ever been the last resource of good generals." The Swiss-born Baron Antoine Henri Jomini, Marshal Ney's chief-of-staff and later a Russian general, wrote voluminously on the art of war, advocating maneuver over battle, unlike Saxe who perceived maneuver as a means of gaining tactical and moral ascendency.

80. Frederick, "Instructions," 391. See also Liddell Hart, *Ghost of Napoleon*, 47; Liddell Hart, *Great Captains*, 39–75, 150–52, 155; and Donald Armstrong,

"The *Blitzkrieg* in Caesar's Campaigns," CJ 37 (December 1941), 141, 143. Battle "may be, as Carlyle says, the quintessence of years of labor compressed into an hour," quoted in Colby, *Masters of Mobile Warfare*, 6. Two great captains of the seventeenth century who spent two years campaigning against one another without coming to battle (Turenne and Montecuccoli) knew that battle was the focus of all war. "It is a paradox to hope for victory without fighting," wrote Montecuccoli. "The goal of the man who makes war is to fight in the open field to win a victory," quoted in Liddell Hart, *Great Captains*, 21. The influence of Saxe on Liddell Hart's "indirect approach" seems readily apparent. See Liddell Hart, *Strategy*, 2nd rev. ed. (London: Faber & Faber, 1954; reprint. 1967; New York: New American Library, 1974).

    81. McNeill, *Pursuit of Power*, 159–63; Liddell Hart, *Ghost of Napoleon*, 16–17; Liddell Hart, *Strategy*, 63–93; Howard, *War in European History*, 58–60; Rothenberg, "Maurice, Gustavus, Montecuccoli," 45–48; and Dyer, *War*, 61, among others.

    82. Houlding, *Fit for Service*, 280, who also notes that aiming would have done little good for the Brown Bess had no rear sight.

    83. Quoted in ibid., 279–80.

    84. Humphrey Bland, *A Treatise of Military Discipline; In which is Laid down and Explained The Duty of the Officer and Soldier Thro' the several Branches of the Service*, 4th ed. (London: Sam. Buckley, 1740), 145.

    85. A European contemporary (1779) also questioned the Prussian rate of fire. While acknowledging that it might be possible to achieve this rate on a relatively sedate firing range unencumbered by packs, on a battlefield, heavily loaded, tired, frightened, thirsty soldiers may only fire "as many as one or at the most two rounds in a minute" (quoted in Duffy, *Military Experience*, 210).

    86. Dyer, *War*, 62–63.

    87. Houlding, *Fit for Service*, 262–63.

    88. Ropp, *War in the Modern World*, 50n.

    89. Houlding, *Fit for Service*, 137–45; Duffy, *Military Experience*, 210–11, 248, 260, among others.

    90. Duffy, *Military Experience*, 252–53, 241–42, 211.

    91. Basil P. Hughes, *Firepower: Weapons Effectiveness on the Battlefield, 1630–1850* (New York: Charles Scribner's Sons, 1974), 26, 64. On the other hand, the stopping power of a musket was formidable: French musket balls weighed twenty-two to the pound and the British, fourteen to the pound (ibid., 11).

    92. Quoted in Strachan, *European Armies*, 24. This was the high tide of the bayonet. At Borodino, one of the bloodiest battles of the Napoleonic Wars, the French fired an average of only ten rounds per man (Ropp, *War in the Modern World*, 47). The subsequent nineteenth-century shift from smoothbore to mass-produced rifles should have sent all bayonets to museums, but doctrines, tradition, and training manuals, through World War II, insisted on its continued usefulness. See McWhiney and Jamieson, *Attack and Die*, 76–80, and S. L. A. Marshall, *The Soldier's Load and the Mobility of a Nation* (Washington,

D.C.: Combat Forces Press, 1950), 16, who writes that more Americans were killed in the Pacific theater of World War II by swords than by bayonets (see caveat regarding Marshall's work, chap. 5, n. 5).

93. Quoted in Duffy, *Military Experience*, 211–12.

94. Quoted in Luvaas, *Frederick the Great*, 143.

95. Phillips, ed., *Roots of Strategy*, 307. For every fifteen soldiers who marched with Frederick in 1756, only one remained by 1762, such were the casualties in this "limited" war (Duffy, *Military Experience*, 309).

96. Quoted in Luvaas, *Frederick the Great*, 146.

97. Adcock, *Roman Art of War*, 10.

98. See McWhiney and Jamieson, *Attack and Die*, esp. chap. 1, and Richard E. Beringer, Herman Hattaway, Archer Jones, and William N. Still, Jr., *Why the South Lost the Civil War* (Athens: University of Georgia Press, 1986), 48–49. That Europeans ignored the valuable and bloody lessons of the American Civil War may be seen in Jay Luvaas's excellent *The Military Legacy of the Civil War: The European Inheritance*, new ed. (Lawrence: University Press of Kansas, 1988), and Thomas Pakenham, *The Boer War* (New York: Random House, 1979), among others.

99. Bland, *Treatise of Military Discipline*, 133–34. See also D. B. Horn and Mary Ransome, eds., *English Historical Documents, 1714–1784* (New York: Oxford University Press, 1957), 615.

100. Robert S. Quimby, *The Background of Napoleonic Warfare: The Theory of Military Tactics in Eighteenth-Century France* (New York: Columbia University Press, 1957).

101. McNeill, *Pursuit of Power*, 163.

6. The American Experience

1. Any discussion of colonial militia presents scholars with a conundrum: because the militia reflected the evolving values and structures of each colony at differing times, almost any generalization about militia may be challenged to some degree. Bearing this caveat in mind, the reader should also recognize that the definitive work on *any* colony's militia—much less an overall synthesis—remains to be written. Even William L. Shea describes his admirable *The Virginia Militia in the Seventeenth-Century* (Baton Rouge: Louisiana State University Press, 1983), ix, as "a pioneering effort." For additional background on colonial military affairs, among others see Douglas Edward Leach's excellent *Arms for Empire: A Military History of the British Colonies in North America, 1607–1763* (New York: Macmillan, 1973); Leach, *Flintlock and Tomahawk: New England in King Philip's War* (New York: W. W. Norton, 1958; reprint. 1966); Leach's bibliographic essays in Higham, *Guide to the Sources*, Higham and Mrozek, ibid., *Supplement I* and *II;* Howard H. Peckham, *The Colonial Wars, 1689–1762* (Chicago: University of Chicago Press, 1964); Fred Anderson's superb study, *A People's Army: Massachusetts Soldiers and Society in the Seven Years'*

War (Chapel Hill: University of North Carolina Press for the Institute of Early American History and Culture, 1984); E. Wayne Carp, "Early American Military History: A Review of Recent Work," *VMHB* 94 (July 1986): 259–84; and Don Higginbotham's provocative and illuminating "The Early American Way of Wars: Reconnaissance and Appraisal," *WMQ* 3rd ser., 44 (April 1987):230–73.

2. Quoted in James Muldoon, "The Indian as Irishman," *EIHQ* 111 (October 1975):277.

3. For a smattering of the many works readily available to those thinking of immigrating to America from the late sixteenth century, see Louis B. Wright and Elaine W. Fowler, eds., *English Colonization of North America* (New York: St. Martin's Press, 1968), and any edition of Richard Hakluyt's *The Principal Navigations*, originally published in 1589 and 1598–1600.

4. See Louis Morton, "The Origins of American Military Policy," *MA* 22 (Summer 1958):75, and Douglas Edward Leach, "The Military System of Plymouth Colony," *NEQ* 24 (September 1951):343.

5. See Allan R. Millett and Peter Maslowski, *For the Common Defense: A Military History of the United States* (New York: Free Press, 1984), 2, and John E. Ferling, *A Wilderness of Miseries: War and Warriors in Early America* (Westport, Conn.: Greenwood Press, 1980), 10–11.

6. Quoted from 1624 in Leo Francis Stock, ed., *Proceedings and Debates of the British Parliament Respecting North America*, 5 vols. (Washington, D.C.: Carnegie Institution, 1924), 1:65.

7. Leach, "Military System," 343, 346; William Bradford, *Of Plymouth Plantation: The Pilgrims in America*, ed. by Harvey Wish (New York: Capricorn Books, 1962), 40–44, 65–66; Timothy H. Breen, "English Origins and New World Development: The Case of the Covenanted Militia in Seventeenth-Century Massachusetts," *Past & Present* 57 (November 1972):81–82; William L. Shea, "The First American Militia," *MA* 46 (February 1982):15; and Morton, "Origins of American Military Policy," 75. See also Daniel R. Campbell, " 'Amongst the many glorious workes of the late Kinge': The Successful Settlement of Virginia," *Southern Historian* 6 (1985):3–11.

8. Francis Grose, *Military Antiquities Respecting a History of the English Army from the Conquest to the Present Time*, 2 vols. (London: n.p., 1786–88), 1:9. The term "trainband" comes from "trained band" or in the spelling of the period, a "trayned band."

9. Morton, "Origins of American Military Policy," 76; Shea, "First American Militia," 18, among others.

10. See Lindsay Boynton, *The Elizabethan Militia, 1558–1638* (London: Routledge & Kegan Paul, 1967), esp. chaps. 7–8, and J. R. Western's excellent *The English Militia in the Eighteenth Century: The Story of a Political Issue, 1660–1802* (London: Routledge & Kegan Paul, 1965).

11. Morton, "Origins of American Military Policy," 76–77; Shea, "First American Militia," 18. That the eighteenth-century colonists were the "most

heavily armed peoples on earth" appears to conflict with the dire shortage of arms suffered by Americans throughout the Revolution. The term is relative; compared with other peoples Americans *were* the most heavily armed. But a hodgepodge of ancient and homemade muskets, fowling pieces, and shotguns, all of different calibers and quality, made for a logistical nightmare since an army requires uniformity of arms. Also, many men appeared in continental camps unarmed, having left the family musket at home, for defense and shooting for the table. During the war, weapons burst, were broken, or left on the battlefield by militia anxious to leave the war and return home.

12. Cunliffe, *Soldiers and Civilians*, 392.

13. Buffington, "Puritan View of War," 68.

14. See Peter Brock, *Pacificism in the United States: From the Colonial Era to the First World War* (Princeton: Princeton University Press, 1968), who over-emphasizes the impact pacificism had on American conceptions of war through the Revolution.

15. Cunliffe, *Soldiers and Civilians*, 25, among many others.

16. Quoted in Richard Slotkin, *Regeneration through Violence: The Mythology of the American Frontier, 1600–1860* (Middletown, Conn.: Wesleyan University Press, 1973), 163. For a few modern examples of the dangers of smoking in combat, see Hackworth and Sherman, *About Face*, 96, 248, 510.

17. Quoted in Andrew McFarland Davis, "John Harvard's Life in America, or Social and Political Life in New England in 1637–1638," *PCSM* 12 *Transactions 1908–1909* (Boston: By the Society, 1911), 39.

18. Quoted in Stanley Pargellis, ed., *Military Affairs in North America, 1748–1765: Selected Documents from the Cumberland Papers in Windsor Castle* (Hamden, Conn.: Archon Books, 1969), 237.

19. To Abigail Adams in Butterfield, *Adams Family Correspondence*, 2:336; Frederick called for wars to be "short and lively," Palmer, "Frederick, Guibert, Bülow," 102.

20. Parker, *Military Revolution*, 43–44.

21. Houdling, *Fit for Service*, 2.

22. Washington to president of Congress, 8 September 1776, *GW Writings*, 6:28.

23. Mao, *Writings*, 246; Dederer, *Making Bricks without Straw*, 14.

24. Washington to New York Legislature, 16 December 1776, *GW Writings*, 6:384.

25. A point reaffirmed by none other than George C. Marshall. See Neustadt and May, *Thinking in Time*, 249.

26. Leach, "Military System," 343.

27. See John W. Shy, *Toward Lexington: The Role of the British Army in the Coming of the American Revolution* (Princeton: Princeton University Press, 1965), 6, 17; Millett and Maslowski, *For the Common Defense*, 3; Morton, "Origins of American Military Policy," 79–80; and Millis, *Arms and Men*, 22–23, among others.

28. Quoted in H. Telfer Mook, "Training Day in New England," *NEHQ* 11 (December 1938):681, and see also 675–90; Shy, *Toward Lexington*, 6; and Ronald L. Boucher, "The Colonial Militia as a Social Institution: Salem, Massachusetts," *MA* 37 (December 1973):125–30.

29. Thomas Venn and John Lacy, *Military & Maritime Discipline in Three Books* (London: E. Tyler and R. Holt, 1672; London: Robert Boulton, 1683), 6.

30. Leach, "Military System," 343, 364; Morrison Sharp, "Leadership and Democracy in the Early New England System of Defense," *AHR* 50 (January 1945):252; Morton, "Origins of American Military Policy," 79–80; Millett and Maslowski, *For the Common Defense*, 3; and Millis, *Arms and Men*, 22–23.

31. Morton, "Origins of American Policy," 80; Strachan, *European Armies*, 29.

32. Quoted in Hart, *American History*, 1:237.

33. Quoted in Houlding, *Fit for Service*, 376n.

34. John K. Mahon, "Anglo-American Methods of Indian Warfare, 1676–1794," *MVHR* 45 (September 1958):254. See also Don Higginbotham, *George Washington and the American Military Tradition* (Mercer University Lamar Memorial Lectures 27) (Athens: University of Georgia Press, 1985), 9–10, 12; and Slotkin, *Regeneration through Violence*, esp. 3–4.

35. Duffy, *Military Experience*, 209.

36. Suttcliffe, *Practice, Proceedings, and Lawes of armes*, 63.

37. Barnabe Rich, *Dialogue between Mercury and an English Soldier* (1574), quoted in Firth, *Cromwell's Army*, 3n.

38. *Henry IV*, pt. 1, act 4, sc. 2.

39. A "scapegallows" is defined in Francis Grose's *A Classical Dictionary of the Vulgar Tongue* (London: S. Hooper, 1785), as someone "who deserves and has narrowly escaped the gallows." Fred Anderson's *A People's Army* has evoked well-deserved praise, not only for its content but for his approach. For this reader, his chapter one "Overview" spawned innumerable ideas which is, after all, the ideal of any history.

40. Israel Stoughton to John Winthrop, July 1637, quoted in Sharp, "Leadership and Democracy," 245.

41. Millett and Maslowski, *For the Common Defense*, 5, 8; Sharp, "Leadership and Democracy," 245; Morton, "Origins of American Military Policy," 80; Breen, "English Origins," 83; and Shy, *Toward Lexington*, 7, 15.

42. Depending upon time and place, however, nonwhite and non-English males often served in the militia. For example, while a 1652 Massachusetts law "enjoyned" "all Scotsmen, Negers, & Indians inhabiting with or servants to the English" from attending militia musters as they had been doing, (quoted in Breen, "English Origins," 86), in the Yamasee Wars in South Carolina (1715–28), Afro-Southern slaves were armed and fought well. Some communities accepted blacks into their militia, others did not.

43. Leach, "Military System," 364.

44. Shy, *Toward Lexington*, 6.

45. Ibid. See also Craven, *Southern Colonies*, 170–71, 276–77, 306; and Higginbotham, *George Washington*, 9–12, among others.

46. Leach, "Military Systems," 347.

47. See Stephen Saunders Webb, *The Governors-General: The English Army and the Definition of the Empire, 1569–1681* (Chapel Hill: University of North Carolina Press, 1979), 431–513. See also his "Army and Empire: English Garrison Government in Britain and America, 1569 to 1763," *WMQ* 3rd ser., 34 (1977):1–31. Military and ex-military men had served as governors-general of Ireland since the sixteenth century. Employing officers in this capacity became the norm in the eighteenth century; for instance, Charles, Lord Cornwallis, who surrendered to Washington at Yorktown, later became Viceroy of India and, following that assignment, finished his career in Ireland.

48. E. Milton Wheeler, "Development and Organization of the North Carolina Militia," *NCHR* 41 (Summer 1964):311, 315.

49. A point Professor Donald Snow has made to me on more than one occasion.

50. Pargellis, *Military Affairs*, 19.

51. Webb, *Governors-General*, and "Army and Empire," should be read along with Higginbotham's "Early American Way of War," 245–46, Richard R. Johnson's "The Imperial Webb: The Thesis of Garrison Government in Early America Considered," *WMQ* 3rd ser., 43 (July 1986):408–30, along with Webb's rebuttal, "The Data and Theory of Restoration Empire," ibid., 431–59.

A rebuttal of Webb's thesis—highly provocative, massively documented—is well beyond the scope of this work, nor is it, at this point, warranted. Webb advanced his preliminary thesis in *Governors-General* which he proposed as only the first of several volumes elaborating his views, something that has forestalled both criticism and praise. At this point I am neither convinced nor unconvinced by his arguments, but I do applaud his intellectual vigor and his determined efforts to answer his challengers. Whether Webb's thesis receives general acceptance, the historical profession as a whole should welcome attempts at broad, stimulating new arguments rather than immediately trying to disparage them. If it appears that I have given Webb short shrift, it stemmed from my own efforts to remain focused on my own topic.

52. Quoted in Breen, "English Origins," 88.

53. Sharp, "Leadership and Democracy," 253; Morton, "Origins of American Military Policy," 80; and Breen, "English Origins," 87–88. As *Cato* later observed: "Some Inequality there must be; the danger is that it be not too great: Where there is absolute Equality, all Reverence and Awe, two Checks indispensable to Society, would be lost; and where Inequality is too great, all Intercourse and Communication is lost" (*Cato's Letters*, no. 43, 2:71).

54. Quoted in Breen, "English Origins," 89.

55. Drawn in part from John W. Shy, "The American Military Experi-

ence: History and Learning," *JIH* 1 (February 1971):211; reprinted in his *A People Numerous and Armed: Reflections on the Military Struggle for American Independence* (New York: Oxford University Press, 1976), 225–58. Shy's work has inspired many of the ideas contained herein and curbed some of the excesses.

56. See Ferling, *Wilderness of Miseries, passim.*

57. The first of Cromwell's army's Articles of War dealt with blasphemy: "First, Let no man presume to Blaspheme the holy and blessed Trinity, . . . upon paine to have his Tongue bored with a red-hot Iron" (quoted in Firth, *Cromwell's Army*, 400). See also Sharp, "Leadership and Democracy," 246, and Samuel Sewall, *The Diary of Samuel Sewall*, ed. by Harvey Wish (New York: Capricorn Books, 1967), which is replete with colonial punishments.

58. Muldoon, "Indian as Irishman," 280.

59. See Alden T. Vaughan and Edward W. Clark, eds., *Puritans among the Indians: Accounts of Captivity and Redemption, 1676–1724* (Cambridge: Belknap Press of Harvard University Press, 1981), 9, 33–35, 140–43; Emma Lewis Coleman, ed., *New England Captives Carried to Canada between 1677 and 1760 During the French and Indian Wars*, 2 vols. (Portland, Maine: Southworth Press, 1925); and Wilcomb E. Washburn, *The Indian in America* (New York: Harper & Row, 1975), esp. 82–83, 111–25, 130.

60. Isa. 42. 13; Patrick D. Miller, Jr., "God the Warrior: A Problem in Biblical Interpretation and Apologetics," *Interpretation* 19 (January 1965): 39–46.

61. Shy, "American Military Experience," 211–13; Millett and Maslowski, *For the Common Defense*, 12; Mahon, "Anglo-American Methods," 264; Bradford, *Of Plymouth Plantation*, 182–83; and Ferling, *Wilderness of Miseries*, 21, 43–44.

62. John Josselyn, *An Account of Two Voyages to New-England*, 2nd ed. (London: B. Widdowes, 1675), in *CMHS* 3rd ser., 3 (1833):309.

63. See A. V. B. Norman and Don Pottinger, *English Weapons and Warfare, 449–1660* (New York: Thomas Y. Crowell, 1966; New York: Dorset Press, 1979). Even in the late seventeenth century, however, some Massachusetts Bay leaders continued to discount Native American martial skills. "Lieft [Lieutenant]" Lion Gardener removed an arrow from one of his men, "and presumed to sent [it] to the Bay, because they had said that the arrows of the Indians were of no force" (quoted in Gardener, "Lieft. Lion Gardener His Relation of the Pequot Warres, 1660," in *CMHS*, 3rd ser., 3 [1833]:144).

64. Gardener, "Lieft. Lion Gardener," 153.

65. Quoted in Shea, "First American Militia," 16. See also Bradford, *Of Plymouth Plantation*, 183–84.

66. Bradford, *Of Plymouth Plantation*, 40–41.

67. A poem for the month of December in Daniel Travis, *An Almanack* (Boston: E. Fleet, 1723).

68. Jack S. Radabaugh, "The Militia in Colonial Massachusetts," *MA* 18 (Spring 1954):2; Millett and Maslowski, *For the Common Defense*, 11–12; and

Gary B. Nash, *Red, White, and Black: The Peoples of Early America* (Englewood Cliffs, N.J.: Prentice-Hall, 1974), esp. chap. 4.

69. These concepts will be detailed in part III.

70. See Leonard Liggio's provocative and illuminating "English Origins of Early American Racism," *Radical History Review* 3 (1976):1–36. My thanks to Ellen Shapiro McDonald for bringing this article to my attention. See also Nicholas Canny, "The Ideology of English Colonization: From Ireland to America," *WMQ* 3rd ser., 30 (1973):575–98.

71. Howard Mumford Jones, "Origins of the Colonial Idea in England," *PAPS* 85 (1942):463–65. The modern slang expression "made their bones" might be more appropriate.

72. See for but one example, ibid., 450–52.

73. Howard Mumford Jones, *Ideas in America* (Cambridge: Harvard University Press, 1944), 52. See also Muldoon, "Indian as Irishman," 269, among others.

74. Quoted in David Beers Quinn, *The Elizabethans and the Irish* (Ithaca: Cornell University Press for the Folger Shakespeare Library, 1966), 23.

75. William Thomas, *The Pilgrim: A dialogue on the Life and Actions of King Henry the Eighth*, ed. by J. A. Froude (London: Parker, Son, and Bourn, 1861), 66.

76. Daniel Gookin, "Historical Collections of the Indians of New England," in *CMHS* 1st ser., 1 (1792):149.

77. Quinn, *Elizabethans and the Irish*, 26, 24; Barnabe Rich, *The Irish Hvbbvb or, The English Hve and Crie. Briefely pvrsving the Base conditions, and most notorious offences of this vile, vaine, and wicked age* (London: John Marriot, 1617), 4; Rich, *A New Description of Ireland: Wherein is described the disposition of the Irish whereunto they are inclined* (London: Thomas Adams, 1610), 25–26, who describes Irish butter making (Irish butter, "more loathsome than toothsome"): "It is holden among the Irish, to bee a presagement of some misfortune, to keepe their milking vessals cleanly, and that if they should either scald or wash them, some vnlucky misadventure would surely betide them."; and Rych [Rich], *A Trve and A Kind Excuse Written in Defense of that Booke, intiuled* A New Description of Irelande (London: Thomas Adams, 1612).

78. Quoted in Quinn, *Elizabethans and the Irish*, 24.

79. Muldoon, "Indian as Irishman," 270, 272, 269–70. See also Quinn, *Elizabethans and the Irish*, 155.

80. See, among others, G. A. Hayes-McCoy, "Gaelic Society in Ireland in the Sixteenth Century," *HS* 4 (1963):45–61. Employing indigenous forces to defeat native opponents (who knew the enemy better) has ancient precedents, and, in fact, some colonists saw the value in this. Lion Gardener offered to pay local Indians for each Pequot head they sent him; after receiving twelve heads, he fulfilled the "contract" ("Lieft Lion Gardener," 150). The original precursor of Daniel Boone and Davy Crockett, John Church, recognized that the best weapon against Amerindians were other natives, but such was the

colonial loathing of intercultural mixing and so strong was the Irish example, that magistrates followed the English model and sold captive Indians into slavery. Ironically, shipped to the West Indies (primarily Barbados) they toiled alongside thousands of Irish (and Scots) deported from their native lands. See Slotkin, *Regeneration through Violence*, 162–63.

81. Quoted in Jones, *Ideas in America*, 54.

82. Thomas Morton, *New English Canaan or New Canaan. Containing an Abstract of New England, Composed in Three Bookes* (Amsterdam: Jacob Frederick Stam, 1637), 24.

83. "Prohibition of Irish Manners and Customs," in Constantia Maxwell, ed., *Irish History from Contemporary Sources (1509–1610)* (London: George Allen & Unwin, 1923), 166–67, a most valuable source, hereinafter cited as Maxwell, *Irish History*.

84. Quoted in Jones, "Origins of the Colonial Idea," 45n.

85. Hill, *Celtic Warfare*, 17; Lord Mountjoy quoted in Hayes-McCoy, "Gaelic Society," 57.

86. Thomas Churchyard, *A generall rehearsall of warres, wherein is five hundred severall services of land and sea: as sieges, battailles, skirmiches, and encounters* (London: Edward White, 1579), 121. See also James Turner Johnson, *Ideology, Reason, and the Limitation of War: Religious and Secular Concepts, 1200–1740* (Princeton: Princeton University Press, 1975), 141–42.

87. Churchyard, *generall rehearsall*, 124; and Shy, "American Military Experience," 212.

88. Sir Nicholas Malbie, 4 October 1579, quoted in James Hogan and N. McNeill O'Farrell, eds., *The Walsingham Letter-Book or Register of Ireland, May 1578 to December 1579* (Dublin: Stationary Office for the Irish Manuscripts Commission, 1959), 202.

89. "Minute of the most gross error, long since committed and still continued, in the Wars of Ireland, and the way to redress the same, briefly declared," (1599), quoted in Maxwell, *Irish History*, 219.

90. T. Gainsford, *The Glory of England* (1618) quoted in Maxwell, *Irish History*, 219.

91. "Minute of the most gross error," in Maxwell, *Irish History*, 220. Even earlier, a correspondent of Henry VIII wrote in 1540 of the "great hardness and misery these Irishmen can endure, both of hunger, cold, thirst, and evil lodging, more than the inhabitants of any other land" (quoted in ibid., 229).

92. Quoted in Parker, *Military Revolution*, 119. Change the date to the 1960s and, instead of Irish or Indian, read Viet Cong, and one wonders if Santayana was not right after all. English officers in Ireland and colonial Americans would have understood the psychological damage the oft-repeated Vietnam War adage, "the night belongs to Charlie" had on American soldiers, though they would have substituted "bog" and "forest," respectively.

93. Sir John Dowdall, January 1599, quoted in Maxwell, *Irish History*, 213.

94. Ernest George Atkinson, ed., *Calendar of the State Papers Relating to*

Ireland, of the Reign of Elizabeth, 1600, March–October, Preserved in the Public Record Office (London: Mackie, 1903), 24.

95. Quoted in Hill, *Celtic Warfare*, 31. Not so oddly, the Romans employed a similar strategy against guerrillas.

96. Fynes Moryson quoted in Maxwell, *Irish History*, 198–200.

97. Josselyn, *Account of Two Voyuages*, 295.

98. William Saxey, Chief Justice of Munster to Sir Robert Cecil, 1598, quoted by Philip O'Sullivan Beare (1621), quoted in Maxwell, *Irish History*, 211–12.

99. Shy, "American Military Experience," 212; Hill, *Celtic Warfare*, 30–32. For instance, see Mountjoy's "Ordinances to be Observed during the Wars in Ireland, 1600," in Great Britain, *Calendar of the Carew Manuscripts*, ed. by J. S. Brewer and William Bullen, 6 vols. (London: Longmans Green, 1867–71), 3:367–68. See also G. A. Hayes-McCoy, *Irish Battles* (London: Longmans, Green, 1969); Cyril Falls, *Elizabeth's Irish Wars* (London: Methuen, 1950); J. F. Lydon, *The Lordship of Ireland in the Middle Ages* (Dublin: Gill and Macmillan, 1972); and Aidan Clarke, "Colonial Identity in Early Seventeenth-Century Ireland," HS 11 (1976):57–71.

100. Jones, *Ideas in America*, 54.

101. Mahon, "Anglo-American Methods," 254.

102. Shy, "American Military Experience," 214.

103. "John Talcott's Letter to Sir Edmund Andros, 5 December 1687," in *CMHS* 3rd. ser., 3 (1833):168.

104. Ibid.

105. Duffy, *Military Experience*, 15; Millis, *Arms and Men*, 16; Shy, "American Military Experience," 214; Millett and Maslowski, *For the Common Defense*, 11, 27, 34.

106. *Cato's Letters*, no. 17, 1:113.

107. Quoted in Alan Rogers, *Empire and Liberty: American Resistance to British Authority, 1755–1763* (Berkeley: University of California Press, 1974), 63.

108. *GW Writings*, 29:41–42.

109. Houlding, *Fit for Service*, 31, who comments that while the English hated the French, they "hated everyone else as well."

110. John Childs, *The Army of Charles II* (London: Routledge & Kegan Paul, 1876), 21.

111. In the Revolution, Loyalists and Germans invariably were assigned the worse duties or most dangerous posts. This policy may be said to have backfired at Trenton.

112. Quoted in Moore, *Diary of the American Revolution*, 215.

113. See Peter E. Russell's excellent "Redcoats in the Wilderness: British Officers and Irregular Warfare in Europe and America, 1740 to 1760," *WMQ* 3rd ser., 35 (October 1978):629–52.

114. Quoted in Slotkin, *Regeneration through Violence*, 232.

115. The term is from Houlding, *Fit for Service*, 2–3. The "Howes" and "Wolfes" are used as types for neither the elder brother of General William and Admiral Richard Howe nor the victor of the Plains of Abraham survived the war.

116. Archibald Kennedy, *Serious Advice to the Inhabitants of the Northern Colonies on the Present Situation of Affairs* (New York, 1755), quoted in Rogers, *Empire and Liberty*, 49. In 1775, British troops assaulting Breed's Hill that hot June day carried eighty-pound packs in the first wave. Unfortunately, after the war this commonsensical piece of wisdom was lost, for on June 1944, Americans landed on Easy Red Beach in Normandy carrying an identical load (plus wearing impregnated clothing over regular uniforms and toting gas masks; when emptied of its original load, the latter, according to my late father, were superb for protecting cigars). See Marshall, *Soldier's Load*, 25, 28.

117. Roger, *Liberty and Empire*, 49.

118. Ibid.

119. I am grateful to Professor Pete Maslowski for making me clarify this point. Specialists in European history continue to consider the American Revolutionary War as an aberration with literally no impact on the art of war, a lead American historians have generally followed. For example, see Peter Paret, "Colonial Experience and European Reform at the End of the Eighteenth Century," *BIHR* 37 (May 1964):47–59; Piers Mackesy, "What the British Army Learned," in Ronald Hoffman and Peter J. Albert, eds., *Arms and Independence: The Military Character of the American Revolution* (Charlottesville: University Press of Virginia for the United States Capitol Historical Society, 1984), 191–215; and Theodore Ropp, "The General Military Significance of the American Revolution," ibid., 216–30, among others. The lessons of the Revolutionary War were generally ignored by most Europeans (as was the case with *all* American wars; see Jay Luvaas's superb *Military Legacy of the Civil War*). Indirectly, however, the American war and revolution provided both future militarists and revolutionaries with significant examples, validation, and, above all, inspiration. No matter how minimal their American service, certainly August von Gneisenau and John Moore learned a great deal in their first war—the American Revolution. See Roger Parkinson, *Moore of Corunna* (London: Hart Davis, Macgibbon, 1976).

120. Higginbotham, *George Washington*, esp. chap. 1; Fitzpatrick, *George Washington Himself*, chaps. 9–14, among others. See also Dederer, "Origins of Robert E. Lee's Bold Generalship."

121. Alan Rogers makes a telling point: the low opinions that *both* Americans *and* British formed of each other's martial abilities were not quickly forgotten (*Empire and Liberty*, 72).

122. For ideas related to this subject (and for much more), I acknowledge my debt to Douglas Edward Leach's *Roots of Conflict: British Armed Forces and Colonial Americans, 1677–1763* (Chapel Hill: University of North Carolina Press, 1986).

123. Anderson, *A People's Army*, 25.

124. At Louisbourg, an aide told Wolfe that his newly formed Light Infantry "reminded some of the troops Xenophon organized to fight off the Carducci. Wolfe replied: 'It was there [in the Anabasis] that I got the idea. But those who have not read history think it novel with me' " (quoted in Colby, *Masters of Mobile Warfare*, 4).

125. Lieutenant-Colonel Caroline Bird (1750) quoted in Houlding, *Fit for Service*, 168.

126. See Ira D. Gruber's excellent "Classical Influences on British Strategy in the War for American Independence," in Eadie, *Classical Traditions*, 182–84, 189. My thanks to Dr. Norman Fiering, Director, John Carter Brown Library, for bringing this work to my attention.

127. See John Henry Stanley, "Preliminary Investigation of Military Manuals of American imprint Prior to 1800," M.A. thesis, Brown University, 1964, who chronologically lists military-related laws, drill manuals, and the few works published in America on the art of war, 63–97. See also Francis S. Drake, *Life and Correspondence of Henry Knox, Major-General in the Revolutionary Army* (Boston: Samual G. Drake, 1873), which includes: *A Catalogue of Books, Imported and to be Sold by Henry Knox, at London Book-Store* (Boston: n.p., 1772).

III. *The Intellectual Origins of American Conceptions of War*

1. For but one example, see Amphitryon's remonstrance to Lycus's comments about Hercules in Euripides's *Madness of Hercules* (188–204). Amphitryon extolls the martial virtues of the bow, "the crown of wise inventions," and offers advice, sound to any military situation. If a spearman breaks his weapon, Amphitryon says, he is SOL (soldier out of luck, to use the polite phrase), but:

> . . . he whose hand is cunning with the bow,—
> Yet still hath store wherewith to avert the death.
> Afar he stands, yet beats the foeman back,
> And wound with shafts unseen, watch as they will;
> Yet never bares his body to the foe,
> But is safe-warded; and in battle this
> Is wisest policy, still to harm all foes
> That beyond range shrink not, oneself unhurt.

2. *Cato's Letters*, no. 106, 4:7, in an essay entitled, "Of Plantations and Colonies," ibid., 3–12.

7. *War in the Colonial Mind: Sources*

1. Cotton Mather, *The Present State of New-England* (Boston: Samuel Green, 1690; New York: Haskell House, 1972), 43.

2. Quoted in Roland H. Bainton, *Christian Attitudes toward War and Peace: A Historical Survey and Critical Re-evaluation* (London: Hodder and Stoughton, 1960; reprint. 1961), 115.

3. Quoted in ibid., 24.

4. Eccles. 3.1, 8.

5. Quoted in William Chase Greene, "Ancient Attitudes toward War and Peace," *CJ* 39 (June 1944):526.

6. Vegetius, "Military Institutions," 124.

7. Thucydides, 1. 954. See also Greene, "Ancient Attitudes," 525.

8. Thucydides, 1. 144.

9. Quoted in Xenophon, *Memorabilia* 3. 5. 8.

10. Euripides, *Madness of Hercules*, 126–29.

11. Quoted in Greene, "Ancient Attitudes," 516.

12. Commager, "Leadership," 655.

13. Quoted in Duffy, *Frederick*, 243.

14. Quoted in the *Ohio State Journal*, 12 August 1880, in Lloyd Lewis, *Sherman: Fighting Prophet* (New York: Harcourt, Brace, 1982), 636. See also B. H. Liddell Hart, *Sherman: Soldier, Realist, American* (New York: Dodd, Mead, 1929), 310; and Ferrill, *Origins of War*, 9.

15. Pindar, Fragment 110. The cautionary words of veterans, then and now, usually remain unheard.

16. Quoted in Greene, "Ancient Attitudes," 525.

17. Quoted by Alexander Hamilton in Syrett, *Hamilton Papers*, 1:401.

18. See James C. Ballagh, ed., *Letters of Richard Henry Lee*, 2 vols. (New York: Macmillan, 1911–14), 1:198, for just one example.

19. John Stuart Mill quoted in Grant, *Ancient Historians*, 27.

20. See Delbrück, *History of the Art of War*, 1:69–70.

21. Something akin to a universal peace came to the Greek city-states only after their conquest by Alexander.

22. Pritchett, *Greek State*, 2:4–33, for trials of Greek generals, and 34–35, for civilian control and supervisors. Like the eighteenth-century French, generals also served as admirals.

23. Ferrill, *Origins of War*, 142.

24. Plato, *The Republic* 5. 16.

25. Quoted in Gummere, "Dickinson," 83.

26. Plato, *The Republic* 5, 15–16.

27. Ibid. See also Childs, *Armies and Warfare*, 22.

28. *The Republic* 2. 14.

29. Adcock, *Roman Art of War*, 83.

30. Childs, *Armies and Warfare*, 2, among others.

31. Quoted in Reinhold, *Classick Pages*, 103.

32. Sallustius, *War with Cataline*, 7.

33. Cicero, *De Officiis* 1, 24.

34. Brian Caven, *Punic Wars* (New York: St. Martin's Press, 1980), 260.

35. Rollin, *Ancient History*, 2:426, and see also 425–27. Plato also extolled

the virtues of military instruction for the young. See Barnabe Rich, *Vox Militis: Foreshewing What Perils Are Procvred Where the people of this, or any other Kingdome liue without regard of Marshall discipline* (London: B. A., 1625), 4.

36. Cicero, *De Officiis* 1. 33.

37. Ibid. 1. 34.

38. Stout, "Training Soldiers," 425–46; Suttcliffe, *Practice, Proceedings, and Lawes of armes*, 64, who quotes from Livy on the subject.

39. Although there is an enormous amount of literature on all of these aspects—military, ideological, and otherwise—see Rollin, *Ancient History*, 1:426, or any other eighteenth-century popular history, for these were the primary sources for colonial views.

40. From Juvenal's *Satires*, quoted in Louis Smith, *American Democracy and Military Power: A Study of Civil Control of the Military Power in the United States* (Chicago: University of Chicago Press, 1951; reprint. 1956), 2.

41. Vertot, *History of Revolutions*, 1:3.

42. Ibid., 2.

43. Quoted in L'Estrange, *Seneca's Morals*, 94.

44. Vertot, *History of Revolutions*, 1:13–14.

45. Adcock, *Roman Art of War*, 85.

46. Rollin, *Ancient History*, quoted in Reinhold, *Classick Pages*, 160.

47. Also translated as "military power must be subordinate to civil authority." This is also the motto of the state of Wyoming.

48. Vertot, *History of Revolutions*, 1:37, quoted in Reinhold, *Classick Pages*, 195.

49. Sallustii, *Bellum Catilinarium*, 14. See also St. Augustine of Hippo quoted in Rich, *Vox Militis*, 10.

50. Sallust quoted in Reinhold, ed., *Classick Pages*, 103.

51. Quoted in *Cato's Letters*, no. 26, 1:199.

52. Vertot, *History of Revolutions*, 1:13–14.

53. Sallust quoted in Reinhold, *Classick Pages*, 105.

54. *Cato's Letters*, no. 26, 1:198.

55. Ibid., no. 27, 1:203.

56. Shy, *Toward Lexington*, 6.

57. Kenneth J. Pratt, "Roman Anti-Militarism," *CJ* 51 (October 1955):21.

58. Delbrück, *History of the Art of War*, 2:509–10.

59. William Hooper to James Iredell, 26 April 1774, in Don Higginbotham, ed., *The Papers of James Iredell*, 2 vols. (Raleigh, N.C.: Department of Cultural Resources, Division of Archives and History, 1976), 1:232.

60. Pratt, "Roman Anti-Militarism," 23–24; William Hardy Alexander, "War in the *Aeneid*," *CJ* 40 (February 1945): 261–73; and George E. Duckworth, "Virgil and War in the *Aeneid*," *CJ* 41 (December 1945):104–7, which builds on Alexander's work.

61. Frank Hewitt Cowles, "Virgil's Hatred of War," *CJ* 29 (February 1934):361, 359.

62. Quoted in Duckworth, "Virgil and War," 105.

63. Quoted in Greene, "Ancient Attitudes," 532.

64. Bainton, *Christian Attitudes*, 41.

65. Cicero, *De Re Publica* 1. 4. 8.

66. Ibid., 6. 10.

67. Ibid., 20. 33. "Eas artis, quae efficant ut usui civitati simus; id enim esse praeclarissimum sapientaie munus maximumque virtutis vel documentum vel officium puto."

68. Ibid., 7. 27. Or as Plato wrote in *The Republic* (1. 347), "good men will not consent to hold office for the sake of either money or of honour."

69. Also known as Cato the Elder. He was the great-grandfather of the Stoic philosopher and statesman, Cato the Younger, (95–46 B.C.), the hero of Addison's play.

70. Quoted in Cicero, *De Officiis* 1. 11.

71. Virgil's *Georgics*, in fact, was a denunciation of the civil wars which occurred in the aftermath of Caesar's assassination.

72. Cicero, *De Officiis* 1. 12.

73. Ibid., 23.

74. Ibid., 11.

75. Ibid., 11, 13.

76. Ibid., 12, 23.

77. John D. Tooke, *The Just War in Aquinas and Grotius* (London: S.P.C.K., 1965), xii. Following the decline of papal power and the advent of absolutism, just war and related theoretical concepts were perceived in secular terms. That is, controlling war between nations was seen as the first step in adjudicating international differences.

78. The literature on just war theory and all its related aspects is vast. I used a variety of primary and secondary sources, but by no means made a complete survey. Bainton's *Christian Attitudes* and Johnson's *Ideology, Reason* present somewhat differing perspectives (Johnson is critical of some of Bainton's arguments), but both are good surveys with excellent bibliographies. See also Michael Walzer, *Just and Unjust Wars: A Moral Argument with Historical Illustrations* (New York: Basic Books, 1978), esp. chaps. 1–3; M. H. Keen, *The Laws of War in the Late Middle Ages* (London: Routledge and Keegan Paul, 1965); Frederic Russell, *Just War in the Middle Ages* (New York: Cambridge University Press, 1975); James Muldoon's well-crafted *Popes, Lawyers, and Infidels: The Church and the Non-Christian World, 1250–1550* (Philadelphia: University of Pennsylvania Press; 1979) and Brian Bond, "The 'Just War' in Historical Perspective," *History Today* (February 1966):111–19.

79. See W. S. M. Knight, *The Life and Works of Hugo Grotius* (Grotius Society Publications No. 4) (London: Sweet & Maxwell, 1925); Hugo de Groot [Grotius], *The Rights of War and Peace, Including the Law of Nature and of Nations*, trans. by A. C. Campbell (New York: M. Walter Dunne, 1901); Emmerich de Vattel, *The Law of Nations, Or, Principles of the Law of Nature, Applied to the Conduct and Affairs of Nations and Sovereigns*, rev. ed. (Philadelphia: P. N. Nicklin and T. Johnson, 1820); and McDonald, *Novus*.

80. This all-to-brief summarization does great injustice to an important and rich area of study, but, for the purposes here, it cannot be helped.

81. Tooke, *Just War*, 11; Bainton, *Christian Attitudes*, 96. To the young Augustine, "war was chronic in the City of Man," but temporary temporal conflict resolution had little effect on eternal peace. Quoted in Michael Walzer, "Exodus 32 and the Theory of Holy War: The History of a Citation," *HTR* 61 (January 1968):5.

82. Johnson, *Ideology, Reason*, 34, 39.

83. Tooke, *Just War*, 21–22.

84. Quoted in Johnson, *Ideology, Reason*, 90, and see also 91–92.

85. Yale University Press, *The Complete Works of St. Thomas More: The Yale Edition of the Complete Works of St. Thomas More*, 15 vols. to date (New Haven: Yale University Press, 1963–   ), vol. 4: *Utopia*, ed. by Edward Surtz and J. H. Hexter, book 2 *(Military Affairs of the Utopians)*, 199. Hereinafter cited as *More*.

86. Quoted in Nef, *War and Human Progress*, 136, 165.

87. *More*, 207–9.

88. My thanks to Professor Michael Mallet for clarifying this point.

89. McNeill, *Pursuit of Power*, 76; Gilbert, "Machiavelli," 26.

90. *More*, 201.

91. Ibid., 201, 217, 203, 205.

92. Ibid., 203–5. For an excellent history of political assassination, see Franklin L. Ford, *Political Murder: Tyrannicide to Terrorism* (Cambridge: Harvard University Press, 1985).

93. Quoted in Bainton, *Christian Attitudes*, 104. Rules of war and proscriptions against unnecessary violence can only be adhered to if there is discipline and if the governing polity concurs. For instance, the well-disciplined Swiss pikemen were expressly forbidden to take prisoners, and any taken had to be executed. See Delbrück, *History of the Art of War*, 2:653.

94. *More*, 203–5.

95. Ibid., 135; McNeill, *Pursuit of Power*, 68.

96. Sir John Davies (1612) quoted in Muldoon, "Indian as Irishman," 276n.

97. Bainton, *Christian Attitudes*, 104.

98. Nef, *War and Human Progress*, 42, 200. Some, like Donne, saw gunpowder weapons as so destructive as to make war unfightable.

99. Walzer, "Exodus 32," 8.

100. Nef, *War and Human Progress*, 115.

101. See Michael Walzer, *The Revolution of the Saints* (Cambridge: Harvard University Press, 1965), esp. 270.

102. Walzer, "Exodus 32," 5.

103. Delbrück, *History of the Art of War*, 3:218.

104. "Whether Soldiers, Too, Can Be Saved (1527)," in Martin Luther, *Luther's Works*, ed. by Jaroslaw Pelikan and Helmut T. Lehman, gen. eds., 55 vols. (St. Louis: Concordia Publishing House and Philadelphia: Fortress Press, 1955–86), 46:96. Hereinafter cited as *Luther*.

105. Ibid., 118.

106. Ibid., 122.

107. Ibid., 120–21. See also Num. 14.40–45, 21.21–30, Deut. 2.26–37.

108. Ibid., 112, 111.

109. Ibid., 47:13–15, 19–20, 30.

110. Ibid., 46:121. Or, as Childs, *Armies and Warfare*, 23, quotes him: When war was inevitable, then "go to it with might and main, show that you are men of mettle. War is not waged by thinking about it," Luther wrote, "It is serious business that dulls the teeth of even the proudest, fiercest and most defiant fire-eater, leaving him scarcely able to bite into fresh butter."

111. Luther, *Works*, 46:96.

112. See John H. Geerken, "Machiavelli Studies Since 1969," *JHI* 37 (April–June 1976): 352.

113. Quoted in Alfredo Bonadeo, "Montaigne on War," *JHI* 46 (September 1985): 424.

114. Jacob Zeitlin, ed. and trans. *The Essays of Michel de Montaigne*, 3 vols. (New York: Alfred A. Knopf, 1934), 3:242, 244.

115. Quoted in Richard H. Cox, *Locke on War and Peace* (Oxford: Clarendon Press, 1960), 175, and see also 172–73.

116. *Luther*, 46:118.

117. Ibid., 121.

118. Cox, *Locke on War*, 173.

119. From the *2nd Treatise*, quoted in Clough, *Intellectual Origins*, 151.

120. See McDonald and McDonald, *Requiem*, 39–58, and Larry Bowman, *Captive American Prisoners during the American Revolution* (Athens: Ohio University Press, 1976), among others. British prisoners held by the Americans fared better, but not by much.

121. Duffy, *Frederick*, 295. Eighteenth-century European armies often tore down whole villages not from vindictiveness but to use the rubble for field fortifications. See Childs, *Armies and Warfare*, 155.

122. For a fine overview of the biblical way of war or rules of war, see Deut. 20.10–20.

123. Gummere, *American Colonial Mind*, 3–4, 97; Ellis, "Habits of Mind," 158–59.

124. Isa. 32.22; and *An Abstract Of the Lavves of Nevv England*, 18, in Peter Force, comp., *Tracts and Other Papers, Relating Principally to the Origins, Settlement, and Progress of the Colonies in North America, From the Discovery of the Country to the Year 1776*, 4 vols. (Washington, D.C.: Peter Force, 1836–47; reprint ed., New York: Peter Smith, 1947), 2.

125. Ps. 115.16, a verse often cited by colonials for claiming territory not directly occupied by the Indians. See Washburn, *Indian in America*, 83. Another favorite verse justifying land takeovers was Ps. 72.8–9: "He shall have dominion also from sea to sea, and from the river unto the ends of the earth. They that dwell in the wilderness shall bow before him; and his enemies shall lick the dust."

126. Daniel Gookin (1674), "Historical Collections," 141.

127. Abbot, *Mr. Abbot's Sermon*, 3, 1.

128. Morton, *New English Canaan*, 23. See also Force, comp., *Tracts and Other Papers*, 2:18. The native North American population, having no natural immunity, had already been devastated from prior contact with Europeans. The first European explorers and fishermen took gold, silver, potatoes, corn, chilies, and cod back to the Old World, but left diseases which cut an awful swath through the Indians.

129. Gookin, "Historical Collections," 148; Josselyn, "Account of Two Voyages," 294.

130. See Amos Adams, *A Discourse Before and at the Desire of the Ancient and Honourable Artillery-Company, at Boston, June 4, 1759; Being the Anniversary of their Election of Officers* (Boston: Z. Fowle and S. Draper, 1759), 13, among many others.

131. Rich, *The Fruites of Long Experience* (London, 1604), quoted in Sharp, "Leadership and Democracy," 246.

132. Adams, *Discourse Before*, 15; Buffington, "Puritan View of War," 73; Morgan, *Puritan Political Ideas*, xxiv; and Vaughan and Clark, *Puritans among Indians*, 1–4, among many others.

133. Leo F. Solt, *Saints in Arms: Puritanism and Democracy in Cromwell's Army* (Stanford: Stanford University Press, 1959), 26. To cite even the major works consulted or on this topic would create a vast bibliography. For interested readers, go to any library card catalog and refer to "Miller, Perry" as an excellent starting point.

134. Quoted in Sharp, "Leadership and Democracy," 247. If one substitutes "virtue" for "faith," then it is almost as if Sallust was writing. See also Richard Slotkin and James K. Folsom, eds., *So Dreadfull A Judgment: Puritan Responses to King Philip's War, 1676–1677* (Middletown, Conn.: Wesleyan University Press, 1978).

135. Mather, *Present State of New-England*, 28.

136. Quoted in Vaughan and Clark, *Puritans among Indians*, 31.

137. Rev. John Williams quoted in Vaughan and Clark, *Puritans among Indians*, 1; Deut. 2.9, Josh. 7.10–11, among others.

138. Increase Mather, *A Discourse Concerning the Grace of Courage, wherein the Nature, Beneficialness, and Necessity of that Vertue for all Christians, is described* (Boston: B. Green, 1710), 16–17, among others, discusses the significance of the Armada.

139. Colman, *Sermon Preached*, 25.

140. Deut. 20.10–11.

141. See A. Malamat, "The War of Gideon and Midian: A Military Approach," *PEQ* (January–April 1953):61–65.

142. Deut. 20.16–17.

143. Ebenezer Gay, *Zechariah's Version of Christ's Martial Glory open'd and apply'd in a Sermon Preach'd at the Desire of the Honourable Artillery Company, in Boston, June 3, 1728* (Boston: For J. Eliot, J. Phillips, and B. Long, 1728), 9,

24; Zech. 1.8; and for commonly used New Testament verses justifying war and the military profession, see Luke 3.13, 7.10, Acts 10, and Mark 12.17.

144. Exod. 15.3, quoted in Edmund Calamy, comp., *Cromwell's Soldier's Bible: Being a Reprint, in Facsimile, of "The Souldier's Pocket Bible," Compiled by Edmund Calamy, and Issued for the Use of the Commonwealth Army in 1643,* intro. by Garnet Wolseley (London: Elliot Stock, 1895), 15. Hereinafter cited as *Calamy.* For just a few works focusing on the biblical way of war, see Yigael Yadin, *The Art of Warfare in Biblical Lands: In Light of Archaeological Study,* trans. by M. Pearlman, 2 vols. (New York: McGraw-Hill, 1963); Yadin, "Some Aspects of the Strategy of Ahab and David (I K[ings] 20; II Sam. 11)," *Biblica* 36(1955): 332–51; Marion J. Benedict Rollins, *The God of the Old Testament in Relation to War* (New York: Teachers College, Columbia University, 1927); Malamat, "War of Gideon," 61–65; Peter C. Craigie, *The Problem of War in the Old Testament* (Grand Rapids, Mich.: William B. Eerdmans, 1978); Craigie, " 'Yaweh is a Man of Wars,' " *SJT* 22(1969): 183–88; A. Gelston, "The Wars of Israel," *SJT* (September 1964): 325–31; Waldemar Janzen, "War in the Old Testament," *MQR* 46(April 1972): 155–66; and Miller, "God the Warrior," 39–46.

145. Judg. 8.6; Yadin, *Art of Warfare,* 2:260.

146. Gardener, "Lieft. Lion Gardener," 150.

147. Craigie, *Problem of War,* 53.

148. George Fox and several other Quakers presented Charles II with a petition in 1660 that condemned "all wars and strife and fightings with outward weapons, for any end or purpose whatever." Quoted in George Clark, *War and Society in the Seventeenth Century* (Cambridge: Harvard University Press, 1958), 14. See also Buffington, "Puritan View of War," 71.

149. Quoted from *Leviathan* in Daniel R. Beaver, "Cultural Change, Technological Development and the Conduct of War in the Seventeenth Century," in Russell F. Weigley, ed., *New Dimensions in Military History: An Anthology* (San Rafael, Calif.: Presidio Press, 1975), 76. Hobbes was read in the colonies, but he was not a favorite.

150. Williams to Winthrop, 1645, in Massachusetts Historical Society, *The Winthrop Papers 1498–1649,* 5 vols. (Boston: Plimpton Press, 1929–47), 5:32.

151. Quoted in Buffington, "Puritan View of War," 72.

152. Mather, *Discourse Concerning the Grace of Courage,* 39–40, and see also Judg. 11.27, Gen. 14.13, 16, and 1 Sam. 11.1. See also Daniel Shute, *A Sermon Preached to the Ancient and Honorable Artillery Company in Boston, New-England, June 1, 1767* (Boston: Edes and Gill, 1767), 21, 27; Simeon Howard, *A Sermon Preached to the Ancient and Honorable Artillery-Company, in Boston, New-England, June 7, 1773* (Boston: John Boyles, 1773), 20, among others.

153. Walzer, "Exodus 32," 11.

154. Craigie, *Problem of War,* 22.

155. Quoted in William Kyle Smith, *Calvin's Ethics of War* (Annapolis, Md.: Westminister Foundation of Annapolis, 1972), 14, 16; Walzer, "Exodus

32," 12; and Alice M. Baldwin, *The New England Clergy and the American Revolution* (Durham, N.C.: Duke University Press, 1928), 36.

156. Josh. 7; 1 Sam. 15; Miller, "God the Warrior," 40; and Gelston, "Wars of Israel," 327.

157. Craigie, *Problem of War*, 35; Miller, "God the Warrior," 41.

158. Samuel Willard, *A Compleat Body of Divinity in Two Hundred and Fifty Expository Lectures on the Assembly's Shorter Catechism* (Boston: B. Green and S. Kneeland, 1726), 658, 660, 667.

159. *Calamy*, 3.

160. Gay, *Zechariah's Vision*, 32.

161. Abbot, *Mr. Abbot's Sermon*, 12.

162. Samuel Davies, *The Curse of Cowardice, A Sermon Preached to the Militia of Hanover County, in Virginia, at a General Muster, May 8, 1758.* (London: n.p., 1758; reprint. Boston: Z. Fowle and S. Draper, 1759), 4.

163. Gay, *Zechariah's Vision*, 31; Ps. 144.1.

164. 2 Chron. 32.78 quoted in *Calamy*, 3.

165. Quoted in Johnson, *Ideology, Reason*, 122. See also William Gouge, *The Whole-Armor of God or the Spiritvall Fvrnitvre which God hath provvided to keepe safe every Christian Sovldier from the assaults of Satan* (London: Iohn Beale, 1616), 18, who notes that *"A Christians Course of life is a warfare"*; and Gouge, *Gods Three Arovves: Plague, Famine, Svvord, In three Treatises* (London: George Miller, 1631), 414, 425, wherein he quotes Vegetius's famous dictum twice.

166. Gardener, "Lieft. Lion Gardener," 149–50; *Nevv England's First Fruits*, 21; and Mather quoted in Slotkin, *Regeneration through Violence*, 162.

167. Sharp, "Democracy and Leadership," 248.

168. Solt, *Saints in Arms*, 8–13; *Calamy*, throughout.

169. See Frank Moore, ed., *The Patriot Preachers of the American Revolution, with Biographical Sketches, 1766–1783* (New York: L. A. Osborne, 1860).

170. Baldwin, *New England Clergy*, 126; Craigie, *Problem of War*, 28; Jer. 48.10.

171. See Harry S. Stout, "Religion, Communications, and Ideological Origins of the American Revolution," *WMQ* 3rd ser., 34 (October 1977):519–41; O. Peabody Natick, *Artillery Election Sermon, 1732* (Boston: n.p., 1732), a strong advocate of militia training and preparing for war so that this "might happily prevent much Bloodshed, and perhaps prevent there ever being another War" (30); and any of the other sermons quoted herein or listed in the bibliography.

172. Adams, *Discourse Before*, 21.

173. Quoted in Stewart, "Puritan Literature," 331.

174. Colman, *Sermon Preached*, 26.

8. The English Legacy

1. Samuel Johnson, "The Bravery of the English Common Soldiers," (1760?), in Johnson, *Political Writings*, ed. by Donald J. Greene (New Haven: Yale University Press, 1977), 281.

2. Within their cultural milieu and native environment, the Scots and Irish, along with Amerindians and other warrior-hunter-herder tribesmen, were fierce warriors and fighters, but they lacked the discipline and regimentation required among soldiers. Taken out of their natural environs, trained, disciplined, and "come to understand themselves, the wont hath not a better Souldier" ([M.S.], *A Discovrse concerning the Rebellion in Ireland* [London: Richard Lownes, 1642], 22).

3. Quoted in Harry Rothwell, ed., *English Historical Documents 1189–1327* (New York: Oxford University Press, 1975), 321. See also Carl Stephenson and Frederick George Marcham eds., *Sources of English Constitutional History: A Selection of Documents from A.D. 600 to the Present* (New York: Harper & Brothers, 1937), 123.

4. *More*, 217.

5. Some three thousand shipwrecked Spaniards from the Armada did make it ashore in Ireland, but most were immediately put to the sword. See Parker, *Military Revolution*, 32. Had the Spanish managed a beachhead, in all likelihood they would have captured London, for the English forces assembling to meet them were poorly organized and unequal to the task.

6. Johnson, *Ideology, Reason*, 84. The impact of the Armada's failure on subsequent events in America is often ignored. For some one hundred years (1560–1660) the English fought holy wars—first against Catholic Spain in the Channel and helping the Dutch, then in the Civil War—and their victories proved to them that God truly was on their side. Also, this affirmed the role and superiority of militia over regular, professional armies in the English mind, though not in fact. Thus the combined mythos of holy war and militia weighed heavily on colonial conceptions of war.

7. Barnabe Rich, *A Pathway to Military Practice*, quoted in Firth, *Cromwell's Army*, 3; Rich, *Vox Militis*, 53, in which he pretty much repeats himself.

8. Suttcliffe, *Practice, Proceedings, and Lawes of armes*, 62.

9. Quoted in Firth, *Cromwell's Army*, 2.

10. Kennedy, *Rise and Fall*, 62. Charles I, against the wishes of Parliament, sent forces to assist French Huguenots near La Rochelle in 1627, but this turned into another fiasco. Among the British in the Dutch service were some excellent units. See Robert Monro, *Monro His Expedition with the Worthy Scots Regiment (Called Mac-Keyes Regiment) levied in August 1616* (London: William Jones, 1637), the first English regimental history.

11. From "The Lamentation of a Bad Market, or the Disbanded Soldier," quoted in Firth, *Cromwell's Army*, 272. See also another ballad, "The Maunding Soldier, or the Fruit of War is Beggary," quoted in ibid.

12. Thomas Churchyard, *A Pleasant Discourse of Court and Wars* (1596) quoted in Alexander Boswell, ed., *Fonde's Caducae* (London: Achinleck Press, 1816), 26.

13. Grose, *Classical Dictionary;* Breen, "English Origins," 79; Henry J. Webb, *Elizabethan Military Service: The Books and the Practice* (Wisconsin: University of Wisconsin Press, 1965), 174; and Childs, *Armies and Warfare,* 174.

14. Childs, *Armies and Warfare,* 102.

15. Geoffrey Gates, *The Defense of the Militarie Profession* (1579), quoted in Webb, *Elizabethan Military Science,* 72.

16. [Boyle], *Treatise of the Art of War,* 15.

17. Rich, *Vox Militis,* 2. With the wording slightly altered, this same quotation may be found in Rich, *Allarme to England, foreshewing what perilles are procured, where the people live without regarde of Martiall lawe* (London: Christopher Barker, 1578), 1.

18. Quoted in Webb, *Elizabethan Military Science,* 43.

19. Rich, *Vox Militis,* v.

20. [Boyle], *Treatise of the Art of War,* 5. See also Hill, *Celtic Warfare,* 47.

21. Quoted in Firth, *Cromwell's Army,* 5.

22. John of Gaunt, *King Richard II,* act 2, sc. 1.

23. Quoted in Firth, *Cromwell's Army,* 6. Also in Nef, *War and Human Progress,* 21.

24. Quoted in Lois G. Schwoerer, *"No Standing Armies!": The Antiarmy Ideology in Seventeenth-Century England* (Baltimore: Johns Hopkins University Press, 1974), 10.

25. Rich, *Irish Hvbbvb,* 8.

26. Rich, *Vox Militis,* 38.

27. Quoted in Schwoerer, *"No Standing Armies!",* 11.

28. Sir John Falstaff, *King Henry IV,* pt. 1, act 4, sc. 2.

29. Millis, *Arms and Men,* 18–19.

30. *More,* 496.

31. Fenne, *Fennes Fruites* (London, 1590), quoted in Paul A. Jorgensen, *Shakespeare's Military World* (Berkeley: University of California Press, 1956), 192. In 1744, Benjamin Franklin printed a version of this work which was apparently widely known:

> War begets Poverty,
> Poverty peace;
> Peace makes Riches flow,
> (Fate ne'er doth cease).
> Riches produce Pride,
> Pride is War's Ground;
> War begets Poverty, &c.
> The World goes round.

Found in R. Saunders, *A Pocket Almanac for the Year 1744* (Philadelphia: B. Franklin, 1744), in Larabee et al., *Franklin Papers,* 2:401. See also Clark, *War and Society*, 141, who produces a version supposedly written by a German who emigrated to Pennsylvania long after Fenne's work was published.

32. Stuart's *War and American Thought* offers different perspectives on certain concepts contained herein, but his book spurred many of my inquiries, and I readily acknowledge my debt.

33. A great many sources were consulted for this and the following paragraphs. Among them, see: Lawrence Delbert Cress, "Radical Whiggery on the Role of the Military," *JHI* 40 (January–March 1979): 43–60, esp. 44–46, which along with his superb *Citizens in Arms: The Army and the Militia in American Society to the War of 1812* (Chapel Hill: University of North Carolina Press, 1982), was invaluable; McDonald, *Novus;* Zera S. Fink, *The Classical Republicans: An Essay in the Recovery of a Pattern of Thought in Seventeenth Century England* (Northwestern University Studies in the Humanities No. 9) (Evanston: Northwestern University Press, 1945); Andrew Browning, ed., *English Historical Documents 1660–1714* (New York: Oxford University Press, 1953); and some background drawn from George L. Haskins, *The Growth of English Representative Government* (Philadelphia: University of Pennsylvania Press, 1948; New York: A. S. Barnes, 1960); and Norman F. Cantor, ed., *William Stubbs on the English Constitution* (New York: Thomas Y. Crowell, 1966).

34. The essays collected in J. G. A. Pocock, ed., *Three British Revolutions: 1641, 1688, 1776* (Princeton: Princeton University Press, 1980), are generally illuminating and provocative for this period. In particular, see Lawrence Stone, "The Results of the English Revolutions of the Seventeenth Century," 23–108, and Pocock's introductory essay, 3–20. These essays not only reveal the wealth of scholarship in these areas but the difficulty that this author had in remaining narrowly focused on his topic.

35. See *Cato's Letters*, no. 40, 2:55.

36. To detail the conflict between king and Parliament during the early colonial period is beyond the scope of this work. The Parliamentary Petition of Rights (1628), and the wars in Scotland and Ireland of the late 1630s and early 1640s all strained relations between Crown and Parliament.

37. [Andrew Fletcher], *A Discourse of Government with relation to Militia's* (Edinburgh: n.p., 1698), 24.

38. Quoted in Firth, *Cromwell's Army*, 13. Many military works address the Civil War and Cromwell's army, but Firth is the place to start as it is really an excellent piece of history, well written, superbly researched, and thought provoking.

39. Ibid., 17.

40. Ibid., 17–30.

41. Lewy, *Religion and Revolution*, 130.

42. Quoted in Solt, *Saints in Arms*, 14.

43. Edward Peyton, *A Divine Catastrophe of the Kingly Family of the House of Stuarts: or, A Short History of the Rise, Reign, and Ruine Thereof* (London: Giles Calvert, 1652), 6, 80.

44. Edward Waterhouse, *A Discourse and Defence of Arms and Armory, Shewing the Nature and Rises of Arms and Honour in England, from the Camp, the Court, the City: under the two later of which, are contained Universities and Courts of Inn* (London: Samuel Mearne, 1660), 47.

45. Parker, *Military Revolution*, 33.

46. Solt, *Saints in Arms*, 17; A. S. P. Woodhouse, ed., *Puritanism and Liberty: Being the Army Debates (1647–9) from the Clarke Manuscripts with Supplementary Documents*, 2nd ed. (Chicago: University of Chicago Press, 1951), 20–21. See also Ian Gentles, "The Arrears of Pay of the Parliamentary Army at the End of the First Civil War," *BIHR* 48 (May 1975): 52–63. In the colonies, fulfillment of a contract was a serious legal and moral obligation. Colonists recognized early on that if one reneged on a contract, one would forever be untrustworthy. A breach of contract was as much a sin as a breach of the covenant with God.

47. Peyton, *Divine Catastrophe*, 104.

48. Woodhouse, *Puritanism*, 21; Firth, *Cromwell's Army*, 348.

49. Quoted in Firth, *Cromwell's Army*, 351.

50. Peyton, *Divine Catastrophe*, 103.

51. This lesson was on the minds of American republicans some 130 years later when an American army (particularly its officers) at Newburgh, New York, with its pay in arrears and postwar emoluments threatened by congressional and state inaction, sought redress. Only the singular character of Washington, the personal loyalty he engendered, and a dramatic speech by him, drawn from Addison's *Cato*, forestalled a potential subversion of the Revolution, leaving the virtuous American tradition and doctrine of civilian control of the military unsullied.

52. *Cato's Letters*, no. 25, 1:194.

53. Quoted in Firth, *Cromwell's Army*, 375.

54. Quoted in ibid., 377.

55. Ibid., 379, 380.

56. See the *Disbanding Act, 1660*, in Browning, *English Historical Documents*, 802–3.

57. Caroline Robbins, "The 'excellent' use of Colonies. A Note on Walter Moyle's Justification of Roman Colonies, *ca.* 1699," *WMQ* 3rd ser., 23 (October 1966): 623. As much as the authors of *Cato's Letters* despised Cromwell, they nonetheless held him in higher regard than either Alexander or Caesar (no. 49, 2:117). On the other hand, in words that were surely noticed by colonial readers, they wrote that Cromwell "headed an Army which pretended to fight for Liberty; and by that Army became a bloody Tyrant: As I once saw a Hawk very generously rescue a Turtle Dove from the Persecution of the Crows, and then eat him up himself" (ibid., no. 95, 3:246). In the colonies, Cromwell was loathed for his dictatorial policies, but since he was also a Puritan and staunch defender of the Protestant faith, he was not excoriated in colonial pamphlets as much as one would expect.

58. *Cato's Letters*, no. 60, 2:234.

59. McNeill, *Pursuit of Power*, 139.

60. *Cato's Letters*, no. 63, 2:265–66.

61. Cress, *Citizens in Arms*, 18.

62. For more on the army's police role, see Houlding, *Fit for Service*, and Tony Hayter, *The Army and the Crowd in Mid-Georgian England* (Totowa, N.J.: Rowman and Littlefield, 1978).

63. Rogers, *British Army*, 38; Childs, *Armies and Warfare*, 185.

64. Schwoerer, *"No Standing Armies!"*, 21; Gentles, "Arrears of Pay," 59.

65. Childs, *Armies and Warfare*, 175. See John Todd White, "Standing Armies in Time of War: Republican Theory and Military Practice During the American Revolution," Ph.D. dissertation, George Washington University, 1978, 45–46, among others on quartering problems in colonial America.

66. Hayter, *Army and the Crowd*, 21. Soldier-baiting was another English antimilitary tradition carried to America; the most famous incident was, of course, the "Boston Massacre."

67. Very much the colonial belief. See Shy, *Toward Lexington*, vii, among others.

68. Neatly summarized by Stone, "Results," 63.

69. See Browning, *English Historical Documents*, 122–28, 812–13.

70. *Cato's Letters*, no. 20, 1:131.

71. The collected or primary works of these writers have all been published and are available at most major libraries or through interlibrary loan. Interpretive secondary works abound, but as Forrest McDonald advised me long ago, start with the originals and make up your own mind.

72. Natick, *Artillery Sermon*, 39.

73. Davies, *Curse of Cowardice*, 24.

74. Shy, *Toward Lexington*, vii.

75. General Orders, 25 July 1777, *GW Writings*, 8:456.

76. "Power is like Fire," *Cato* wrote, "it warms, scorches, or destroys, according as it is watched, provoked, or increased. It is dangerous as useful" (*Cato's Letters*, no. 25, 1:192).

77. Schwoerer, *"No Standing Armies!"*, 155. See also her "The Literature of the Standing Army Controversy, 1697–1699," *HLQ* 28 (May 1965), 187–212. Unable to criticize William directly, *Cato* later ascribed the problem to "Court Parasites" (*Cato's Letters*, no. 13, 1:85) or "Creatures and Tools of Power" (ibid., no. 93, 3:235).

78. For just a sampling of arguments both pro and con, see—among the radical Whigs—[Fletcher], *Discourse of Government;* [John Trenchard], *An Argument, Showing, that a Standing Army Is Inconsistent with a Free Government, and absolutely destructive to the Constitution of the English Monarchy* (London: n.p., 1697); [Trenchard], *A Short History of Standing Armies in England* (London: n.p., 1698); these may be found in Richard H. Kohn, ed., *Anglo-American Antimilitary Tracts 1697–1830* (New York: Arno Press, 1979); and for an opposing

view, the moderate Whig position, as it were, see [Daniel Defoe], *A Brief Reply to the History of Standing Armies in England. With some Account of the Authors* (London: n.p., 1698). The controversy continued on well into the eighteenth century. See *Cato's Letters*, throughout; [Charles Jenkinson, earl of Liverpool], *A Discourse on the Establishment of a National and Constitutional Force in England* (London: R. Griffiths, 1757); William Bollan, *Continued Corruption, Standing Armies, and Popular Discontents considered; And the Establishment of the English Colonies in America* (London: J. Almon, 1768), esp. 4–20 which borrows heavily from *Cato's Letters*; *No Standing Army in the British Colonies or an Address to the Inhabitants of the Colony of New-York. Against Unlawful Standing Armies* (New York: John Holt, 1775); and [Buchan, David Stewart Erskine, *11th earl of*], *Letters on the Impolicy of a Standing Army, in Time of Peace, and On the Unconstitutional and illegal Measure of Barracks* (London: D. J. Easton, 1793). A recent study approaching this argument from a strictly legalistic perspective, thereby ignoring many social, political, and military aspects, is John Phillip Reid, *In Defiance of the Law: The Standing-Army Controversy, The Two Constitutions, and the Coming of the American Revolution* (Chapel Hill: University of North Carolina Press, 1981). For a light-hearted parody of all these anonymous tracts and pamphlet wars, see Fart-in-Hand-O Puff-Indorst [Jonathan Swift], *The Benefit of Farting Farther Explain'd, Vindicated, Maintain'd, Against Those Blunderbusses Who will not allow it to be concordant to the Cannon Law*, 2nd ed. (London: A. Moore, 172?).

79. [Fletcher], *Discourse of Government*, 26.

80. *Cato's Letters*, no. 99, 3:285.

81. William and Mary (of Orange) had brought several companies of their Dutch household guards with them upon assuming the Crown.

82. In fact, as Larry Cress cogently notes in his excellent *Citizens in Arms*, the moderate Whig position was never fully detailed until Adam Smith's *An Inquiry into the Nature and Causes of the Wealth of Nations* was published in 1776. Read as a socioeconomic-military proscription instead of as purely an economic work, *The Wealth of Nations* takes on new meaning for the eighteenth century and modern times.

83. Cress, *Citizens in Arms*, 25.

84. Houlding, *Fit for Service*, 8.

85. [Defoe], *Brief Reply*, 2–3.

86. Schwoerer, *"No Standing Armies!"*, 160, 185–86; Cress, *Citizens in Arms*, 28–32.

87. [Defoe], *Brief Reply*, 14.

88. Schwoerer, *"No Standing Armies!"*, 184.

89. See especially John W. Wilkes, "British Politics Preceding the American Revolution," *HLQ* 29 (August 1957): 301–19; Cress, *Citizens in Arms*, 21.

90. As a matter of fact, even this standing army was regularly put to route by undisciplined Scottish clansmen armed with traditional weapons. See Parker, *Military Revolution*, 35; Hill, *Celtic Warfare*, throughout. As to why this

happened, the most recent and best work on the eighteenth-century British army is Houlding, *Fit for Service.*

91. So much could be crammed in a merchant vessel that it was far less costly to send supplies by ship to the West Indies than to send wagons of victuals to an inland post. On the other hand, this points out how cheap life was at this time. Yellow fever and malaria proved deadlier foes than most battlefield opponents. For instance, the 38th Foot, numbering 700 men, was sent to the West Indies in 1738. In 1745 the regiment returned to England with only 492 enlisted—and this was after an additional *960* recruits had been sent out to the West Indies (Houlding, *Fit for Service,* 15–16, among others).

92. Tony Hayter's *Army and the Crowd* discusses this in great detail. Before the eighteenth century, crowd control consisted of a magistrate or lone soldier reading the Riot Act (if twelve or more persons continued in the area following the reading, they became felons). After this time, however, rioting became more regular and severe. In the Gordon Riots of 1780, London authorities lost control, and it required thousands of troops to put things in order. Houlding points out that between 1740 and 1775 alone there were 159 major riots in England (*Fit for Service,* 60).

Regular soldiers have traditionally loathed crowd control. For one thing, they are neither trained nor equipped for it; it is not their primary mission. If they react as soldiers, they are fearsome brutes; if they try to reason with their fellow citizens, they are liable to injury. Moreover, employing regular troops in a civilian riot situation, unless as a simple show of force, promotes poor disciplinary practices and resentment among the troops.

93. Quoted in Holding, *Fit for Service,* 60.

94. Ibid., 60–61, 74.

95. [Fletcher], *Discourse of Government,* 39.

96. [Jenkinson], *Discourse on the Establishment,* 58.

97. *Cato's Letters* "probably had more impact in America than any other single Opposition effort," to quote Larry Cress, *Citizens in Arms,* 21.

98. Tacitus quoted in *Cato's Letters,* no. 76, 3:84.

99. Trenchard and Gordon translated Cicero's "Eundem Magistratum, ni interfuerint decem Anni, ne quis capito" as "That no Man should bear the same Magistracy when he had borne before but after an Interval of ten Years" (*Cato's Letters,* no. 115, 4:84); Ibid., 86; and see also no. 24, 1:179.

100. Ibid., no. 40, 2:55. See also no. 55, 2:165.

101. Ibid., no. 72, 3:54, in an essay entitled: "In absolute Monarchies the Monarch seldom rules, but his Creatures instead of him.—That sort of Government [is] a Gradation of Tyrants." "All this further proves," added *Cato,* "that Men and Societies have no possible human Security but certain and express laws" (ibid., 45).

102. Ibid., no. 63, 2:262.

103. Ibid., no. 25, 1:193. See also [Jenkinson], *Discourse on the Establishment,* 49, wherein the future Lord Liverpool borrows many of his ideas from *Cato.*

104. *Cato's Letters*, no. 65, 2:285, in an essay entitled: *"Military Virtue produced and supported by Civil Liberty."*

105. Ibid., no. 95, 3:252. In reading through the four volumes of *Cato's Letters*, I detected a change of tone in Trenchard's contributions, something of a—and I hesitate to use the word—paranoia seemed to creep into his writing. His prose remains extremely clear and powerful, but a certain shrillness appears, not evident in his earlier work. Toward the end of *Cato*, Trenchard apparently was quite ill. Perhaps his shrillness is a reflection of a man desperately seeking to make one more point before Time, the tyrant that no person can overcome, claimed him.

106. Ibid., no. 95, 3:254, 255. Samuel Johnson makes a similar point in his "Remarks on the Militia Bill" (1756), in his *Political Writings*, 183.

107. *Cato's Letters*, no. 94, 3:236.

108. As the eighteenth century progressed, the British army was composed less of "scapegallows" and more of men dislocated and put out of work by economic and agrarian changes. Sylvia R. Frey's excellent *The British Soldier in America: A Social History of Military Life in the Revolutionary Period* (Austin: University of Texas Press, 1981) should be consulted along with her fine essay in John Ferling, ed., *The World Turned Upside Down: The American Victory in the War of Independence* (Westport, Conn.: Greenwood Press, 1988), 165–83. On the other hand, the all-important popular perception of British soldiers (and, indeed, soldiers in general) in England and America was little altered—they were still, to use the Iron Duke's words, the "scum of the earth."

109. See Felix Gilbert, "The English Background of American Isolationism in the Eighteenth Century," *WMQ* 3rd ser., 1 (April 1944): 138–60, who discusses the influence of British writers (particularly Lords Bolingbroke and Chesterfield and the very influential James Burgh) on nascent American foreign policy. The roots of this extend further back than Gilbert explored, but this remains as an important article.

110. *Cato's Letters*, no. 11, 1:66.

111. Ibid., no. 55, 2:169. Also, "Against any Man using unlawful Force, every Man has a Right to use Force" (167). As W. Jackson Bate has shown, Samuel Johnson's reputation as an arch-Tory cannot be accepted at face value. He cites an argument Johnson had with historian Sir Adam Fergusson: "Why all this childish jealousy of the power of the crown?" Johnson asked rhetorically, ". . . in no government can power be abused long. Mankind will not bear it. If a sovereign oppresses his people to a great degree, they will rise and cut off his head" (Bate, *Johnson*, 197).

112. *Cato's Letters*, no. 74, 3:73, an essay which also contains the following: "Conquest, or Fighting for Territory, is, for the most part, the most shameless Thing in the World. Government is either designed for the People's Good, or else I know not what Business it has in the World" (74).

113. See essays nos. 93–95.

114. The essay, "The terrible Consequences of a War to England, and the

Reasons against engaging in one," ibid., no. 85, 3:166–74, discusses this fully.

115. Ibid., 168.

116. Ibid., no. 93, 3:233.

Afterword

1. Martin and Lender, *A Respectable Army*, 20 and xi–xii.

2. As one German professional officer noted in 1781, "since we made no effort to smother the rebellion at the beginning, when it could have been done at small cost, the rebels couldn't help become soldiers. Moreover, their trade is increasing every day." Carl Von Baurmeister, *Revolution in America: Confidential Letters and Journals 1776–1784 of Adjutant General Major Baurmeister of the Hessian Forces*, trans. by Bernhard A. Ulendorf (New Brunswick, N.J.: Rutgers University Press, 1957; Westport, Conn., Greenwood Press, 1973), 426.

3. Cress, *Citizens in Arms*, 51.

4. Tansill, *Documents Illustrative of the Formation*, 14, 10–17.

5. Charles Royster, *A Revolutionary People at War: The Continental Army and American Character, 1775–1783* (Chapel Hill: University of North Carolina Press for the Institute of Early American History and Culture, 1979; New York: W. W. Norton, 1981), throughout. See also E. Wayne Carp, *To Starve the Army at Pleasure: Continental Army Administration and American Political Culture, 1775–1783* (Chapel Hill: University of North Carolina Press, 1984).

6. Quoted in Martin and Lender, *A Respectable Army*, 33.

7. Ibid., 18–20.

8. Washington's army outside Boston had to be completely rebuilt in the winter of 1775–76 in the face of the enemy. The next winter, Washington's famous attack on Trenton was dictated in large part because his army's enlistments were due to expire on the first of January. Only by calling upon the personal loyalty of his men was Washington able to expand this small tactical but immense psychological victory by defeating a British force at Princeton before retiring unpursued to try and survive until that spring's levies reached him.

As a general, Washington has never received his due. Always compared with the great eighteenth-century commanders such as Napoleon, Frederick the Great, and others, he invariably falls short. But which of these Great Captains had to conduct a war under the conditions that Washington did, worrying more about keeping a few men in the field than building an army and having to obey civilian masters who both feared and loathed the army he led on their behalf? Even after his men became soldiers, the failure of the states to meet their quotas of recruits and supplies left him concerned more with food and fodder than operational maneuver.

9. Regarding detachments, Washington's main army furnished units for numerous commands and expeditions. The bulk of Horatio Gates's Continental Line that proved so decisive at Saratoga were regiments detached by

Washington. The absence of these troops—because of the Saratoga campaign and because Gates delayed in returning them—at Brandywine Creek and Germantown very likely was the difference between defeat and victory.

A casual reading of Washington's letters reflects his intense dislike of the militia system even late in the war. In his Circular Letter to the States of 18 October 1780, he wrote about "carrying on a War with Militia." "The Idea is chimerical, and that we have so long persisted in it is a reflection on the judgment of a Nation so enlightened as we are, as well as strong proof of the empire of prejudice [against armies] over reason" (*GW Writings*, 20:209).

10. Cress, *Citizens in Arms*, 60.

11. See in particular the excellent study by John Todd White, "Standing Armies in Time of War," 112–15.

12. Butterfield, *Rush Letters*, 1:157.

13. In "Correspondence of Ezra Stiles, President of Yale College, and James Madison, President of William and Mary College, 1780," *WMQ* 2nd ser., 7 (October 1927): 293.

14. *GW Writings*, 20:459.

15. To John Banister, 21 April 1778, *GW Writings*, 11:285–86, for just one of many citations.

16. Ibid., 291.

17. Cress, *Citizens in Arms*, 57.

18. At the heart of any successful military insurgency is disciplined subordination, whether the movement's armed forces remain guerrilla in nature or escalate through various stages into a regular army capable of waging high intensity warfare. Disciplined troops—guerrillas or otherwise—commanded by leaders unswervingly dedicated to a clearly defined objective but flexible in their operational strategy and tactical execution can be defeated only by equally well-trained, well-led, and well-motivated opponents, no matter what technological advantages the latter might have.

19. Martin and Lender, *A Respectable Army*, 20.

20. Cress, *Citizens in Arms*, 51.

21. Ibid., 53.

22. Quoted in Saul K. Padover, ed., *The Complete Madison: His Basic Writings* (New York: Harper & Brothers, 1953), quotations on 341, 340, 263.

23. For an excellent overview of this, see James Kirby Martin, "The Continental Army," in Ferling, *World Turned Upside Down*, 19–34. In spite of much carping, militia did do valuable service during the war. As John Shy cogently noted, "the war was a political education conducted by military means, and no one learned more than the apathetic majority as they scurried to restore some measure of order in their lives." "The American Revolution Considered as a Social Movement," in Stephen Kurtz and James H. Hutson, eds., *Essays on the American Revolution* (Chapel Hill, N.C.: University of North Carolina Press, 1973), 147. Unknowingly, militia proved to be a primary "educator." In small towns and villages, for most Americans, militia units

were the Revolution, representatives of Congress and windows to a distant world. In the field, they occasionally performed well. Not only did militiamen flesh out the lean Continental ranks in battle but their very unreliability that drove Washington, Greene, and others mad also ensured that a British commander never could be too sure of his opponents' strength. Particularly in the South, formed into what were for the most part undisciplined guerrilla bands, militia played an important role in disrupting British pacification measures and communications, gathering intelligence, and keeping the Revolution alive. See Dederer, *Making Bricks without Straw*, 46, and the sources cited therein.

   24. Cress, *Citizens in Arms*, 57.

   25. Seen in the writings of several Continental officers, this line more than likely comes from *Henry V*, act 4, sc. 3:

> We few, we happy we band of brothers;
> For he to-day that sheds his blood with me
> Shall be my brother; be he ne'er so vile,
> This day shall gentle his condition;
> And gentlemen in England now a-bed
> Shall think themselves accurs'd they were not here,
> And hold their manhoods cheap while any speaks
> That fought with us upon Saint Crispin's day.

Bibliography

Primary

Abbot, Hull. *Mr. Abbot's Sermon Preach'd to the Artillery-Company in Boston, June 2, 1735.* Boston: S. Kneeland and T. Green, 1735.

Abbot, W. W.; Twohig, Dorothy; Chase, Philander D.; and Runge, Beverly H., eds. *The Papers of George Washington: Presidential Series.* 3 vols. Charlottesville: University Press of Virginia, 1983– .

———. *The Papers of George Washington: Revolutionary War Series.* 2 vols. to date. Charlottesville: University Press of Virginia, 1985– .

Adams, Amos. *A Discourse Before and at the Desire of the Ancient and Honourable Artillery-Company, at Boston, June 4, 1759: Being the Anniversary of their Election of Officers.* Boston: Z. Fowle and S. Draper, 1759.

Adams, Charles Francis, ed. *The Works of John Adams, Second President of the United States, with a Life of the Author.* 10 vols. Boston: Little, Brown, 1850–56.

Addison, Joseph. *The Works of the Right Honourable Joseph Addison.* Ed. by Henry G. Bohn. 6 vols., new ed. London: George Bell and Sons, 1881.

Allen, Robert J., ed. *Addison and Steele: Selections from "The Tatler" and "The Spectator."* New York: Holt, Rinehart, & Winston, 1957. Reprint 1966.

Ames, N[athaniel]. *The Astronomical Diary.* Boston: John Draper, 1761.

Amiot, Joseph. *Art Militaire Des Chinois, ou recueil D'anciens Traites Sur la Guerre. composés avant l'ere chrétienne, Par Differents Generaux Chinois.* Paris: Didot L'aîne, 1772.

The Annals of America. 24 vols. Chicago: Encyclopedia Britannica, 1968.

Arrian. *The Campaigns of Alexander.* Trans. by Aubrey de Sélincourt. Rev. by J. R. Hamilton. New York: Dorset Press, 1971. Reprint 1986.

Atkinson, Ernest George, ed. *Calendar of the State Papers Relating to Ireland, of the Reign of Elizabeth, 1600, March–October, Preserved in the Public Record Office.* London: Mackie, 1903.

Bailyn, Bernard, ed. *Pamphlets of the American Revolution*. 1 vol. to date. Cambridge: Harvard University Press, 1965–.

Ballagh, James C., ed. *The Letters of Richard Henry Lee*. 2 vols. New York: Macmillan, 1911–14.

Baurmeister, Carl von. *Revolution in America: Confidential Letters and Journals 1776–1784 of Adjutant General Major Baurmeister of the Hessian Forces*. Trans. by Bernhard A. Ulendorf. New Brunswick, N.J.: Rutgers University Press, 1957. Reprint. Westport, Conn.: Greenwood Press, 1973.

Bingham, John, trans. *The Tactiks of Aelian Or art of Embattling an army after ye Grecian manner*. London: Laurence Lisle, 1616.

Birch, J[ohn] F[rancis]. *Memoir on the National Defense*. London: J. Stockdale, 1808.

Bland, Humphrey. *A Treatise of Military Discipline; In which is Laid down and Explained The Duty of the Officer and Soldier, Thro' the several Branches of the Service*. 4th ed. London: Sam. Buckley, 1740.

Bollan, William. *Continued Corruption, Standing Armies, and Popular Discontents considered; And the Establishment of the English Colonies in America*. London: J. Almon, 1768.

[Boone, Nicholas]. *Military Discipline: The Souldier, or Expert Artilleryman*. Boston: By the Author, 1701.

Boswell, Alexander, ed. *Fonde's Caducae*. London: Achinleck Press, 1816.

Boswell, James. *The Life of Samuel Johnson*. Garden City, N.Y.: Doubleday, 1946.

Boyd, Julian P., ed. *The Papers of Thomas Jefferson*. 22 vols. to date. Princeton: Princeton University Press, 1950– .

[Boyle], Roger, earl of Orrery. *A Treatise of the Art of War: Dedicated to the Kings Most Excellent Majesty*. London: Henry Herringman, 1677.

Bradford, William. *Of Plymouth Plantation: The Pilgrims in America*. Ed. by Harvey Wish. New York: Capricorn Books, 1962.

Browning, Andrew, ed. *English Historical Documents 1660–1714*. New York: Oxford University Press, 1953.

Brüggemann, Lewis William, comp. *A Supplement to the View of the English Editions, Translations and Illustrations of the Ancient Greek and Latin Authors, with Remarks*. Stettin: John Samuel Leich, 1801. Reprint. New York: Burt Franklin, 1971.

———. *A View of the English Editions, Translations and Illustrations of the Ancient Greek and Latin Authors, with Remarks*. Stettin: John Samuel Leich, 1797. Reprint. New York: Burt Franklin, 1971.

[Buchan, David Stewart Erskine, 11th earl of]. *Letters on the Impolicy of a Standing Army, in Time of Peace. and On the Unconstitutional and illegal Measure of Barrachs*. London: D. J. Easton, 1793.

Butterfield, Lyman H., ed. *Adams Family Correspondence*. 4 vols. Cambridge: Belknap Press of Harvard University Press, 1963.

———. *Diary and Autobiography of John Adams*. 4 vols. Cambridge: Harvard University Press, 1961–62.

————. *Letters of Benjamin Rush*. 2 vols. Princeton: Princeton University Press, 1951.

Caesar, Gaius Julius. *The Civil Wars*. Trans. by A. G. Peskett. Loeb Classical Library. New York: Macmillan, 1914.

————. *The Conquest of Gaul*. Trans. by S. A. Handford. Rev. by Jane F. Gardner. Penguin Classics. New York: Penguin Books, 1982.

————. *The Gallic War*. Trans. by H. J. Edwards. Loeb Classical Library. Cambridge: Harvard University Press, 1966.

Calamy, Edmund, comp. *Cromwell's Soldier's Bible: Being a Reprint, in Facsimile, of "The Souldier's Pocket Bible," Compiled by Edmund Calamy, and Issued for the Use of the Commonwealth Army in 1643*. Intro. by Garnet Wolseley. London: Elliot Stock, 1895.

Charles V. *Political and Military Observations, Remarks and Maxims, of Charles V. Late Duke of Lorrain, General of the Emperor's Forces*. Trans. by Rupert Beck. London: J. Jones and W. Hawes, 1699.

Churchyard, Thomas. *A generall rehearsall of warres, wherein is five hundred severall services of land and sea: as sieges, battailles, skirmiches, and encounters*. London: Edward White, 1579.

Cicero. *De Officiis*. Trans. by Walter Miller. Loeb Classical Library. New York: Macmillan, 1913.

————. *De Re Publica, De Legibus*. Trans. by Clinton Walker Keyes. Loeb Classical Library. New York: G. P. Putnam's Sons, 1928.

Clausewitz, Carl von. *On War*. Ed. and trans. by Michael Howard and Peter Paret. Princeton: Princeton University Press, 1976.

Clough, Wilson Ober, ed. *Intellectual Origins of American National Thought: Pages from the Books Our Founding Fathers Read*. 2nd rev. ed. New York: Corinth Books, 1961.

Cockle, M. J. D., comp. *A Bibliography of Military Books up to 1642*. London: Holland Press, 1900. Reprint. 1957.

Coleman, Emma Lewis, ed. *New England Captives Carried to Canada between 1677 and 1760 during the French and Indian Wars*. 2 vols. Portland, Maine: Southworth Press, 1925.

Colman, Benjamin. *A Sermon Preached to the Honourable and Ancient Artillery Company in Boston, June 5, 1738*. Boston: J. Draper, 1738.

Colonial Society of Massachusetts. *Transactions* 12 *1908–1909*. Boston: By the Society, 1911.

————. *Transactions* 28 *1930–1933*. Boston: By the Society, 1935.

————. *Transactions* 32 *1933–1937*. Boston: By the Society, 1937.

Conway, Moncure Daniel. *George Washington's Rules of Civility Traced to their Sources and Restored*. London: Chatto & Windus, 1890.

Cooke, Edward. *The Character of Warre, or The Image of Martiall Discipline*. London: Thomas Purfoot, 1626.

"Correspondence of Ezra Stiles, President of Yale College, and James Madison, President of William and Mary College, 1780." *William and Mary Quarterly* 2nd Ser., 7 (October 1927): 292–96.

Croxhall, Samuel. *Fables of Aesop and Others.* 13th ed. London: n.p., 1786.

Davies, Samuel. *The Curse of Cowardice, A Sermon Preached to the Militia of Hanover County, in Virginia, at a General Muster, May 8, 1758.* London: n.p., 1758. Reprint. Boston: Z. Fowle and S. Draper, 1759.

[Defoe, Daniel]. *A Brief Reply to the History of Standing Armies in England. With some Account of the Authors.* London: n.p., 1698.

Dexter, Franklin Bowditch, ed. *Documentary History of Yale University: Under the Original Charter of the Collegiate School of Connecticut 1701–1745.* New Haven: Yale University Press, 1916.

Ewald, Johann. *Diary of the American War: A Hessian Journal.* Trans. by Joseph P. Tustin. New Haven: Yale University Press, 1979.

Feuquieres, Antoine de Pas. *Memoirs Historical and Military: Containing a distinct View of all the Considerable States of Europe.* 2 vols. London: T. Woodward, 1736. Reprint. Westport, Conn.: Greenwood Press, 1968.

Fielding, Henry. *The History of Tom Jones, A Foundling.* Ed. by Fredson Bowers. 2 vols. Middletown, Conn.: Wesleyan University Press, 1975.

Fitzpatrick, John C., ed. *The Writings of George Washington from the Original Manuscripts, 1745–1799.* 39 vols. Washington, D.C.: Government Printing Office, 1931–44.

[Fletcher, Andrew]. *A Discourse of Government With relation to Militia's.* Edinburgh: n.p., 1698.

Folard, Jean-Charles de. *Histoire de Polybe.* 6 vols. Paris: n.p., 1727–30.

Force, Peter, comp. *Tracts and Other Papers, Relating Principally to the Origins, Settlement, and Progress of the Colonies in North America, From the Discovery of the Country to the Year 1776.* 4 vols. Washington, D.C.: Peter Force, 1836–47. Reprint. New York: Peter Smith, 1947.

Frame, Donald M., trans., *Voltaire: Candide, Zadig and Selected Stories.* New York: New America Library, 1961.

Gay, Ebenezer. *Zechariah's Vision of Christ's Martial Glory open'd and apply'd in a Sermon Preach'd at the Desire of the Honourable Artillery Company, in Boston, June 3, 1728.* Boston: For J. Eliot, J. Phillips, and B. Long, 1728.

Gheyn, Jacob de. *The Exercise of Armes for calivres, mvskettes, and pikes after the ordre of His Excellence Maurits, Prince of Orange.* The Hag[u]e: n.p., 1608.

Gouge, William. *Gods Three Arovves: Plague, Famine, Svvord. In three Treatises.* London: George Miller, 1631.

———. *The Whole-Armor of God or the Spiritvall Fvrnitvre which God hath provided to keepe safe euery Christian Sovldier from the assaults of Satan.* London: Iohn Beale, 1616.

Great Britain. *Calendar of the Carew Manuscripts.* Ed. by J. S. Brewer and William Bullen. 6 vols. London: Longmans, Green, 1867–71.

Griffin, Appleton P. C., comp. *A Catalogue of the Washington Collection in the Boston Athenaeum.* Boston: Boston Athenaeum, 1897.

Griffith, Samuel B., ed. *Sun Tzu: The Art of War.* New York: Oxford University Press, 1963. Reprint. 1981.

Groot, Hugo de [Grotius]. *De jure belli ac pacis.* London: T. Warren, 1654.

———. *De jure belli ac pacis.* Trans. by W. Evats. London: M. W., 1682.

———. *De jure belli ac pacis.* Ed. by J. Morrice. London: D. Brown, 1715. Reprint. 1738.

———. *The Rights of War and Peace, Including the Law of Nature and of Nations.* Trans. by A. C. Campbell. New York: M. Walter Dunne, 1901.

Grose, Francis. *Advice to the Officers of the British Army: With the Addition of some Hints to the Drummer and Private Soldier.* 7th ed. London: G. Kearsley, 1783.

———. *A Classical Dictionary of the Vulgar Tongue.* London: S. Hooper, 1785.

Hart, Albert Bushnell, ed. *American History told by Contemporaries.* 10 vols. New York: Macmillan 1897.

Hawke, David, ed. *U.S. Colonial History: Readings and Documents.* Indianapolis: Bobbs-Merrill, 1966.

Herodotus. *The Histories.* Trans. by Aubrey de Sélincourt. Rev. by A. R. Burn. Penguin Classics. New York: Penguin Books, 1972. Reprint. 1984.

———. *The Persian Wars.* Trans. by George Rawlinson. New York: Modern Library, 1942.

———. *Works.* 4 vols. Trans. by A. D. Yodley, Loeb Classical Library. New York: G. P. Putnam's Sons, 1920–24.

Higginbotham, Don, ed. *The Papers of James Iredell.* 2 vols. Raleigh, N.C.: Department of Cultural Resources, Division of Archives and History, 1976.

Hogan, James, and O'Farrell, N. McNeill, eds. *The Walsingham Letter-Book or Register of Ireland, May 1578 to December 1579.* Dublin: Stationary Office for the Irish Manuscripts Commission, 1959.

Homer. *The Iliad.* 2 vols. Trans. by A. T. Murray. Loeb Classical Library. New York: G. P. Putnam's Sons, 1924–25.

Horn, D. B., and Ransome, Mary, eds. *English Historical Documents, 1714–1783.* New York: Oxford University Press, 1957.

Howard, Simeon. *A Sermon Preached to the Ancient and Honorable Artillery-Company, in Boston, New-England, June 7, 1773.* Boston: John Boyles, 1773.

Jacobson, David L., ed. *The English Libertarian Heritage: From the Writings of John Trenchard and Thomas Gordon in "The Independent Whig" and "Cato's Letters."* Indianapolis: Bobbs-Merrill, 1965.

Jefferson, Thomas. *Notes on the State of Virginia.* Ed. by William Peden. Chapel Hill: University of North Carolina Press for the Institute of Early American History and Culture, 1955.

[Jenkinson, Charles, earl of Liverpool]. *A Discourse on the Establishment of a National and Constitutional Force in England.* London: R. Griffiths, 1757.

Johnson, Samuel. *A Dictionary of the English Language: in which the Words are deduced from their Originals, and Illustrated in their Different Significations.* 2 vols. London: W. Strahan, 1755.

———. *Political Writings.* Ed. by Donald J. Greene. New Haven: Yale University Press, 1977.

Kohn, Richard H., ed. *Anglo-American Antimilitary Tracts 1697–1830.* New York: Arno Press, 1979.

Larabee, Leonard W.; Bell, Whitfield J., Jr.; Boatfield, Helen C.; and Fineman, H. Helene, eds. *The Papers of Benjamin Franklin.* 27 vols. to date. New Haven: Yale University Press, 1959– .

L'Estrange, R[oger]. *Seneca's Morals by way of Abstract.* 7th ed. London: M. Bennet, 1699.

"Libraries in Colonial Virginia." *William and Mary Quarterly* 1st ser., 3 (July 1894–April 1895): 43–45, 132–34, 246–53; 8 (July 1899–January 1900): 18–22, 77–79, 145–50.

"Library of Charles Dick." *William and Mary Quarterly* 1st ser., 18 (October 1909):118–19.

"Library of Col. William Fleming." *William and Mary Quarterly* 1st ser., 6 (January 1898): 158–64.

Luther, Martin. *Luther's Works.* Ed. by Jaroslaw Pelikan and Helmut T. Lehman, gen. eds. 55 vols. St. Louis: Concordia Publishing House and Philadelphia: Fortress Press, 1955–86.

Luvaas, Jay, ed. and trans. *Frederick the Great on the Art of War.* New York: Free Press, 1966.

McDonald, Forrest, ed. *Empire and Nation.* Englewood Cliffs, N.J.: Prentice-Hall, 1962.

Machiavelli, Niccolo. *The Arte of Warre.* Trans. by Peter Whithorne. London: n.p., 1560.

Makintosh, R[obert]. *Comments on the Growing Breach between the American Colonies and England.* London: n.p., 1770.

Mao Tse-tung. *The Selected Military Writings of Mao Tse-tung.* Peking: Foreign Language Press, 1963.

———. *Six Essays on Military Affairs.* Peking: Foreign Language Press, 1972.

Massachusetts Historical Society. *Collections* 1st ser. 1. Boston: For the Society, 1792.

———. *Collections.* 3rd ser. 3. Boston: For the Society, 1833.

———. *The Winthrop Papers 1498–1649.* 5 vols. Boston: Plimpton Press, 1929–47.

Mather, Increase. *A Discourse Concerning the Grace of Courage, wherein the Nature, Beneficialness, and Necessity of that Vertue for all Christians, is described.* Boston: B. Green, 1710.

Maxwell, Constantia, ed. *Irish History from Contemporary Sources (1509–1610).* London: George Allen & Unwin, 1923.

Monro, Robert. *Monro His Expedition with the Worthy Scots Regiment (Called MacKeyes Regiment) levied in August 1616.* London: William Jones, 1637.

Montesquieu, Baron de. *The Spirit of the Laws.* Trans. by Thomas Nugent. 2 vols. in 1. New York: Hafner, 1949. Reprint. 1966.

Moore, Frank, ed. *Diary of the American Revolution from Newspapers and Original Documents.* 2 vols. in 1. New York: Charles Scribner, 1860; New York: *The New York Times* & Arno Press, 1969.

————. *The Patriot Preachers of the American Revolution, with Biographical Sketches, 1766–1783.* New York: L. A. Osborne, 1860.

Morgan, Edmund S., ed. *Puritan Political Ideas 1558–1794.* Indianapolis: Bobbs-Merrill, 1965.

Morison, Samuel Eliot. "Old School and College Books in the Prince Library." *More Books* (Bulletin of the Boston Public Library) 11 (March 1936): 77–93.

Morton, Thomas. *New English Canaan or New Canaan. Containing an Abstract of New England. Composed in Three Bookes.* Amsterdam: Jacob Frederick Stam, 1637.

[M.S.]. *A Discovrse concerning the Rebellion in Ireland.* London: Richard Lownes, 1642.

Napier, James. "Some Book Sales in Dumfries, Virginia, 1794–1796." *William and Mary Quarterly* 3rd ser., 10 (July 1953): 441–45.

Natick, O. Peabody. *Artillery Election Sermon, 1732.* Boston: n.p., 1732.

Nevv England's First Fruits: In Respect, First of the Conversion of some, Conviction of divers, Preparation of sundry of the Indians. 2. Of the progresse of Learning, in the Colledge at Cambridge in Massachusetts Bay. London: R. O. and G. D., 1643.

Nicolli, Allardyce, ed. *[George] Chapman's Homer: The Illiad, The Odyssey and the Lesser Homerica.* 2 vols., 2nd ed. Bollingen Series 41. Princeton: Princeton University Press, 1967.

No Standing Army in the British Colonies or an Address to the Inhabitants of the Colony of New-York, Against Unlawful Standing Armies. New York: John Holt, 1775.

Padover, Saul K., ed. *The Complete Madison: His Basic Writings.* New York: Harper & Brothers, 1953.

Pargellis, Stanley, ed. *Military Affairs in North America, 1748–1765: Selected Documents from the Cumberland Papers in Windsor Castle.* Hamden, Conn.: Archon Books, 1969.

Peckham, Howard H., ed. *The Toll of Independence: Engagements & Battle Casualties of the American Revolution.* Chicago: University of Chicago Press, 1974.

Peyton, Edward. *A Divine Catastrophe of the Kingly Family of the House of Stuarts: or, A Short History of the Rise, Reign, and Ruine Thereof.* London: Giles Calvert, 1652.

Phillips, Thomas R., ed. *Roots of Strategy: A Collection of Military Classics.* Harrisburg: Military Service Publishing, 1940. Reprint. Harrisburg: Stackpole Books, 1985.

Pindar. *The Odes of Pindar.* Trans. by John Sandys. Loeb Classical Library. Cambridge: Harvard University Press, 1915. Reprint. 1961.

Pisan, Christine de. *Faits d'armes et de chevalerie.* Westminster: William Caxton, 1489.

Plato. *The Republic.* 2 vols. Trans. by Paul Shorey. Loeb Classical Library. Cambridge: Harvard University Press, 1963.

Plutarch. *Plutarch's Lives.* 11 vols. Trans. by Bernadotte Perrin. Loeb Classical Library. New York: G. P. Putnam's Sons, 1914–26.

Polybius. *The Histories.* 6 vols. Trans. by W. R. Paton. Loeb Classical Library. New York: G. P. Putnam's Sons, 1922–27.

Publications of the Colonial Society of Massachusetts. *See* Colonial Society of Massachusetts.

Reinhold, Meyer, ed. *The Classick Pages: Classical Reading of Eighteenth-Century Americans.* University Park, Pa.: Pennsylvania State University Press for the American Philogical Association, 1975.

Rich, Barnabe. *Allarme to England, foreshewing what perilles are procured, where the people live without regarde of Martiall lawe.* London: Christopher Barker, 1578.

———. *The Irish Hvbbvb or, The English Hve and Crie. Briefely pvrsving the Base conditions, and most notorious offences of this vile, vaine, and wicked age.* London: John Marriot, 1617.

———. *A New Description of Ireland: Wherein is described the disposition of the Irish whereunto they are inclined.* London: Thomas Adams, 1610.

———. [Rych]. *A Trve and A Kind Excuse Written in Defense of that Booke,* intiuled A New Description of Irelande. London: Thomas Adams, 1612.

———. *Vox Militis: Foreshewing What Perils Are Procvred where the people of this, or any other Kingdome liue without regard of Marshall discipline.* London: B. A., 1625.

Rollin, Charles. *The Ancient History of the Egyptians, Carthaginians, Assyrians, Bablylonians, Medes and Persians, Grecians, and Macedonians: including a History of the Arts and Sciences of the Ancients.* 2 vols. in 1. New York: Harper & Brothers, 1841.

———. *The Roman History From the Foundations of Rome to the Battle of Actium: That is, To the End of the Commonwealth.* 15 vols. London: John and Paul Knapton, 1750.

Rothwell, Harry, ed. *English Historical Documents 1189–1327.* New York: Oxford University Press, 1975.

Sallustii, C. Crispus. *Bellum Castilinarium, et Jurgurthinum, Ex optime atque accuratissima Gottlieb Cortii editione expressum, or Sallust's History of Catline's Conspiracy and the War with Jurgurtha, According to the excellent and accurate edition of Gottlieb Cortius.* Trans. by John Mair. 3rd ed. Edinburgh: David Willison, 1770.

Sallustius, C. Crispus. *The War with Cataline.* Trans. by J. C. Rolfe. Rev. ed. Loeb Classical Library. Cambridge: Harvard University Press, 1931. Reprint. 1971.

Saunders, Richard. *Poor Richard Improved.* Philadelphia: B. Franklin and D. Hall, 1749.

Saxe, Maurice de. *Mes Reveres. Ouvrage posthume de Maurice Comte de Saxe.* Trans. by Abbé Perau. 2 vols. Amsterdam and Leipzig: Arkstee and Merkus, 1757.

Sewall, Samuel. *The Diary of Samuel Sewall.* Ed. by Harvey Wish. New York: Capricorn Books, 1967.

Shakespeare, William. *The Complete Works of William Shakespeare Comprising His Plays and Poems.* Intro. by B. Hodek. London: Spring Books, 1958. Reprint. 1967.

Shurtleff, Nathaniel B., ed. *Records of the Governor and Company of the Massachusetts Bay in New England.* 5 vols. Boston: W. White, 1853–4.

Shute, Daniel. *A Sermon Preached to the Ancient and Honorable Artillery Company in Boston, New-England, June 1, 1767.* Boston: Edes and Gill, 1767.

Slotkin, Richard, and Folsom, James K., eds. *So Dreadfull a Judgment: Puritan Responses to King Philip's War, 1676–1677.* Middletown, Conn.: Wesleyan University Press, 1978.

Smith, George. *An Universal Military Dictionary, Or a Copious Explanation of the Technical Terms &c. Used in the Equipment, Machinery, Movements, and Military operations of an Army.* London: J. Millan, 1779.

Smith, Paul H.; Gawalt, Gerard W.; Plakas, Rosemary Fry; and Sheridan, Eugene R., eds. *Letters of Delegates to Congress 1774–1789.* 15 vols. to date. Washington, D.C.: Library of Congress, 1976– .

Stephenson, Carl, and Marcham, Frederick George, eds. *Sources of English Constitutional History: A Selection of Documents from A.D. 600 to the Present.* New York: Harper & Brothers, 1937.

Stock, Leo Francis, ed. *Proceedings and Debates of the British Parliaments Respecting North America.* 5 vols. Washington, D.C.: Carnegie Institution, 1924.

Styward, Thomas. *The Path waie to Martiall Discipline, divided into two Bookes, verie necessarie for young Souldiers, or all such as loveth the proffesion of Armes.* London: T. East, 1581.

Suttcliffe, Matthew. *The Practice, Proceedings, and Lawes of armes, described out of the doings of most valiant and expert Captaines, and confirmed both by ancient, and moderne examples, and praecedents.* London: Christopher Barker, 1593.

[Swift, Jonathan] Puff-Indorst, Fart-in-Hand-O. *The Benefit of Farting Farther Explain'd, Vindicated, Maintain'd, Against Those Blunderbusses Who will not allow it to be concordant to the Cannon Law.* 2nd ed. London: A. Moore, 172?.

Syrett, Harold C., ed. *The Papers of Alexander Hamilton.* 26 vols. New York: Columbia University Press, 1961–79.

Tacitus. *The Annals of Imperial Rome.* Trans. and intro. by Michael Grant. Rev. ed. New York: Dorset Books, 1961. Reprint. 1980.

———. *The Histories.* Trans. by Kenneth Wellesley. Penguin Classics. New York: Penguin Books, 1964; 1984.

Tansill, Charles A. *Documents Illustrative of the Formation of the American States.* Washington, D.C.: Government Printing Office, 1927.

Tao Hanzhang. *Sun Tzu's Art of War.* Trans. by Yuan Shibing. New York: Stirling, 1987.

Taylor, Robert J.; Kline, Mary-Jo; and Lint, Greg L., eds. *Papers of John Adams.* 6 vols. to date. Cambridge: Belknap Press of Harvard University Press, 1977– .

Thomas, William. *The Pilgrim: A Dialogue on the Life and Actions of King Henry the Eighth*. Ed. by J. A. Froude. London: Parker, Son, and Bourn, 1861.

Thucydides. *History of the Peloponnesian War*. 4 vols. Trans. by Charles Forster Smith. Loeb Classical Library. Cambridge: G. P. Putnam's Sons, 1919–23.

———. *History of the Peloponnesian War*. Trans. by Rex Warner. Intro. by M. I. Finley. Penguin Classic. New York: Penguin Books, 1954. Reprint. 1985.

Travis, Daniel. *An Almanack*. Boston: E. Fleet, 1723.

[Trenchard, John]. *An Argument, Showing, that a Standing Army Is Inconsistent with a Free Government, and absolutely destructive to the Constitution of the English Monarchy*. London: n.p., 1697.

———. *A Short History of Standing Armies in England*. London: n.p., 1698.

Trenchard, John, and Gordon, Thomas. *Cato's Letters: or, Essays on Liberty, Civil and Religious, and Other Important Subjects*. 4 vols., 6th ed. corrected. London: J. Walthoe, 1755; 4 vols in 2, New York: Da Capo Press, 1971.

Turner, James. *Pallas Armata: Military Essayes on the Ancient Grecian, Roman, and Modern Art of War*. London: M. W., 1683.

Upshur, Anne Floyd, and Whitelaw, Ralph T. "Library of the Rev. Thomas Teackley." *William and Mary Quarterly* 2nd ser., 22 (July 1943): 298–308.

Valiere, Chevalier de la. *The Art of War*. Philadelphia: Robert Bell, 1776.

Vattel, Emmerich de. *The Law of Nations, Or, Principles of the Law of Nature, Applied to the Conduct and Affairs of Nations and Sovereigns*. Rev. ed. Philadelphia: P. N. Nicklin and J. Johnson, 1829.

Vaughan, Alden T., ed. *America Before the Revolution, 1725–1775*. Englewood Cliffs, N.J.: Prentice-Hall, 1967.

Vaughan, Alden T., and Clark, Edward W., eds. *Puritans among the Indians: Accounts of Captivity and Redemption, 1676–1724*. Cambridge: Belknap Press of Harvard University Press, 1981.

[Vegetius], Flavius Vegetius Renatus. *Commentaires sur les institutions militaires de Végèce*. Trans. by Turpin de Crissé. Paris: Nyon l'aine, 1783.

———. *De Re Militari*. Cologne: N[icolaus] G[oetz], [ca. 1475].

———. *Fl. Vegetii Renati De re militari libri quatuor. Sexti Iulii Frontini De strategematis libri totidem. Aeliani De instruen dis aciebus unus*. Lutetiae: C. Wechelum, 1532.

———. *Fl. Vegetii Renati De re militari libri quatuor. Sexti Iulii Frontini De strategematis libri totidem. Aeliani De instruen dis aciebus unus*. Parisiis: C. Perier, 1553.

———. *Fl. Vegetii Renati De re militari libri quatuor. Sexti Iulii Frontini De strategematis libri totidem. Aeliani De instruen dis aciebus unus*. Antverpiae: Christophorum Plantinum, 1585.

———. *The foure bookes of Flavius Vegetius Renatus, briefelye contayninge a plaine forme, and perfect knowledge of martiall policye, feates of chiualrie, and whatsoeuer pertayneth to warre*. Trans. by John Sadler. London: Thomas Marshe, 1572.

———. *Military Instructions of Vegetius, in five books*. Trans. by John Clarke. London: W. Griffin, 1767.

Venn, Thomas, and Lacy, John. *Military and Maritime Discipline in Three Books.* London: E. Tyler and R. Holt, 1672; London: Robert Boulton, 1683.

Vertot, Abbé de. *The History of the Revolutions That happened in the Government of the Roman Republic.* 2 vols. 5th ed. Trans. by Ozell. London: D. Midwinter, 1740.

Virgil. *Aeneid.* 2 vols. Trans. by H. Rushton Fairclough. Rev. ed. Loeb Classical Library. Cambridge: Harvard University Press, 1946.

W., N. *An Almanack of Celestial Motions and Aspects for the (Dionysion) Year of the Christian Aera, 1707.* Boston: B. Green, 1707.

Warner, Rex, trans. *Fall of the Roman Republic: Six Lives by Plutarch.* Intro. by Robin Seager. Penguin Classics. New York: Penguin Books, 1958. Reprint. 1986.

Waterhouse, Edward. *A Discourse and Defence of Arms and Armory, Shewing the Nature and Rises of Arms and Honour in England, from the Camp, the Court, the City: under the two later of which, are contained Universities and Courts of Inn.* London: Samuel Mearne, 1660.

Webb, [Thomas]. *A Military Treatise on the Appointments of the Army.* Philadelphia: W. Dunlap, 1759.

West, Benjamin. *The New-England Almanack.* Providence: John Carter, 1773.

West, B[enjamin]. *The New-England Almanack, or Lady's and Gentleman's Diary.* Providence: John Carter, 1774.

Willard, Samuel. *A Compleat Body of Divinity in Two Hundred and Fifty Expository Lectures on the Assembly's Shorter Catechism.* Boston: B. Green and S. Kneeland, 1726.

Wolf, Edwin. *The Library of James Logan of Philadelphia, 1674–1751.* Philadelphia: The Library Company of Philadelphia, 1974.

Wolfe, James. *General Wolfe's Instructions to Young Officers: Also His Orders for a Battalion and an Army.* London: J. Millan, 1768.

Woodhouse, A. S. P., ed. *Puritanism and Liberty: Being the Army Debates (1647–49) from the Clarke Manuscripts with Supplementary Documents.* 2nd ed. Chicago: University of Chicago Press, 1951.

Wright, Louis B., and Fowler, Elaine W., eds. *English Colonization of North America.* New York: St. Martin's Press, 1968.

Xenophon. *Cyropaedia.* 2 vols. Trans. by Walter Miller. Loeb Classical Library. New York: Macmillan, 1914–24.

———. *Memorabilia and Oeconomicus.* Trans. by E. C. Marchant. Loeb Classical Library. New York: G. P. Putnam's Sons, 1923.

Yale University. *The Complete Works of St. Thomas More: The Yale Edition of the Complete Works of St. Thomas More.* 15 vols. to date. New Haven: Yale University Press, 1963– .

Zeitlin, Jacob, ed. and trans. *The Essays of Michel de Montaigne.* 3 vols. New York: Alfred A. Knopf, 1934.

Secondary

REFERENCE WORKS

Blanco, Richard L., comp. *The War of the American Revolution: A Selected Annotated Bibliography of Published Sources.* New York: Garland, 1984.

Drake, Milton, comp. *Alamanacs of the United States.* 2 vols. New York: Scarecrow Press, 1962.

Dupuy, R. Ernest, and Dupuy, Trevor N., eds. *The Encyclopedia of Military History from 3500 B.C. to the Present.* 2nd rev. ed. New York: Harper & Row, 1986.

Gephart, Ronald M., comp. *Revolutionary America 1763–1789: A Bibliography.* 2 vols. Washington, D.C.: Library of Congress, 1984.

Higham, Robin, ed. *A Guide to the Sources in British Military History.* Berkeley: University of California Press, 1971.

———. *A Guide to the Sources in United States Military History.* Hamden, Conn.: Archon Books, 1975.

Higham, Robin, and Mrozek, Donald J., eds. *A Guide to the Sources in United States Military History: Supplement I.* Hamden, Conn.: Archon Books, 1981.

———. *A Guide to the Sources in United States Military History: Supplement II.* Hamden, Conn.: Archon Books, 1986.

BOOKS

Adcock, F. E. *The Greek and Macedonian Art of War.* Berkeley: University of California Press, 1957.

———. *The Roman Art of War under the Republic.* Martin Classical Lectures VIII. Cambridge: Harvard University Press, 1940.

Addington, Larry H. *The Patterns of War since the Eighteenth Century.* Bloomington: Indiana University Press, 1984.

Adelman, Jonathan R. *Revolution, Armies, and War: A Political History.* Boulder, Colo.: Lynne Rienner, 1985.

Anderson, Fred. *A People's Army: Massachusetts Soldiers and Society in the Seven Years' War.* Chapel Hill: University of North Carolina Press for the Institute of Early American History and Culture, 1984.

Bailyn, Bernard. *The Ideological Origins of the American Revolution.* Cambridge: Belknap Press of Harvard University Press, 1967.

Bailyn, Bernard, and Hench, John B., eds. *The Press and the American Revolution.* Worcester, Mass.: American Antiquarian Society, 1980.

Bainton, Roland H. *Christian Attitudes toward War and Peace: A Historical Survey and Critical Re-evaluation.* London: Hodder and Stoughton, 1960. Reprint. 1961.

Baldwin, Alice M. *The New England Clergy and the American Revolution.* Durham, N.C.: Duke University Press, 1928.

Baldwin, Ebenezer. *Annals of Yale College, from Its Foundation, to the Year 1831.* 2nd. ed. New Haven: B. & W. Noyes, 1838.

Bate, W. Jackson. *Samuel Johnson.* New York: Harcourt Brace Jovanovich, 1975.

Becker, Carl L. *The Declaration of Independence: A Study in the History of Political Ideas.* New York: Alfred A. Knopf, 1922. Reprint. New York: Vintage Books, 1962.

————. *Everyman His Own Historian: Essays on History and Politics.* New York: F. S. Crofts, 1935.

Beeler, John. *Warfare in Feudal Europe 730–1200.* Ithaca: Cornell University Press, 1971. Reprint. 1984.

Behrens, C. B. A. *Society, Government and the Enlightenment: The Experiences of Eighteenth-Century France and Prussia.* London: Thames and Hudson, 1985.

Berringer, Richard E.; Hattaway, Herman; Jones, Archer; and Still, William N., Jr. *Why the South Lost the Civil War.* Athens: University of Georgia Press, 1986.

Boorstin, Daniel J. *The Americans: The Colonial Experience.* New York: Random House, 1958.

Bowman, Larry. *Captive American Prisoners during the American Revolution.* Athens: Ohio University Press, 1976.

Boynton, Lindsay. *The Elizabethan Militia, 1558–1638.* London: Routledge & Kegan Paul, 1967.

Bridenbaugh, Carl. *Mitre and Sceptre: Transatlantic Faiths, Ideas, Personalities, and Politics, 1689–1775.* New York: Oxford University Press, 1962.

Brock, Peter. *Pacifism in the United States: From the Colonial Era to the First World War.* Princeton: Princeton University Press, 1968.

Brodie, Bernard, and Brodie, Fawn M. *From Crossbow to H-Bomb: The Evolution of the Weapons and Tactics of Warfare.* Rev. and enlged. ed. Bloomington: Indiana University Press, 1973.

Bronowski, J., and Mazlish, Bruce. *The Western Intellectual Tradition.* New York: Harper & Brothers, 1960.

Bucholz, Arden. *Hans Delbrück and the German Military Establishment: War Images in Conflict.* Iowa City: University of Iowa Press, 1985.

Burnett, Edmund Cody. *The Continental Congress.* New York: Macmillan, 1941.

Cantor, Norman F., ed. *William Stubbs on the English Constitution.* New York: Thomas Y. Crowell, 1966.

Carp, E. Wayne. *To Starve the Army at Pleasure: Continental Army Administration and American Political Culture, 1775–1783.* Chapel Hill: University of North Carolina Press, 1984.

Caven, Brian. *The Punic Wars.* New York: St. Martin's Press, 1980.

Chandler, David G. *The Campaigns of Napoleon: The Mind and Method of History's Greatest Soldier.* New York: Macmillan, 1966.

Childs, John. *Armies and Warfare in Europe, 1648–1789.* Manchester: Manchester University Press, 1982.

Childs, John. *The Army of Charles II*. London: Routledge & Kegan Paul, 1976.

Cipolla, Carlo M. *Guns, Sails, and Empires: Technological Innovation and the Early Phases of European Expansion, 1400–1700*. New ed. Manhattan, Kans.: Sunflower University Press, 1985.

Clark, George. *War and Society in the Seventeenth Century*. Cambridge: Cambridge University Press, 1958.

Coad, Oral Sumner, and Mims, Edwin, Jr. *The American State*. New Haven: Yale University Press, 1929.

Colbourn, H. Trevor. *The Lamp of Experience: Whig History and the Intellectual Origins of the American Revolution*. Chapel Hill: University of North Carolina Press for the Institute of Early American History and Culture, 1965.

———, ed. *Fame and the Founding Fathers: Essays by Douglass Adair*. New York: W. W. Norton, 1974.

Colby, Elbridge. *Masters of Mobile Warfare*. Princeton: Princeton University Press, 1943.

Conley, C. H. *The First English Translations of the Classics*. New Haven: Yale University Press, 1927.

Contamine, Philippe. *War in the Middle Ages*. Trans. by Michael Jones. New York: Basil Blackwell, 1984.

Cook, Elizabeth Christine. *Literary Influences in Colonial Newspapers*. New York: Columbia University Press, 1912.

Corvisier, André. *Armies and Societies in Europe, 1494–1789*. Trans. by Abigail T. Siddall. Bloomington: Indiana University Press, 1979.

Cox, Richard H. *Locke on War and Peace*. Oxford: Clarendon Press, 1960.

Craigie, Peter C. *The Problem of War in the Old Testament*. Grand Rapids, Mich.: William B. Eerdmans, 1978.

Craven, Wesley Frank. *The Southern Colonies in the Seventeenth Century, 1607–1689*. Baton Rouge: Louisiana State University Press, 1949. Reprint. 1970.

Cress, Lawrence Delbert. *Citizens in Arms: The Army and the Militia in American Society to the War of 1812*. Chapel Hill: University of North Carolina Press, 1982.

Cunliffe, Marcus. *Soldiers and Civilians: The Martial Spirit in America 1775–1865*. Boston: Little, Brown, 1968.

Davidson, Philip. *Propaganda and the American Revolution, 1763–1783*. Chapel Hill: University of North Carolina Press, 1941.

Dederer, John Morgan. *Making Bricks without Straw: Nathanael Greene's Southern Campaigns and Mao Tse-tung's Mobile War*. Fore. by Russell F. Weigley. Manhattan, Kans.: Sunflower University Press, 1983.

Delbrück, Hans. *History of the Art of War: Within the Framework of Political History*. Trans. by Walter J. Renfroe, Jr. 4 vols. Westport, Conn.: Greenwood Press, 1975–86.

Drake, Francis S. *Life and Correspondence of Henry Knox, Major-General in the Revolutionary Army*. Boston: Samuel G. Drake, 1873.

Duffy, Christopher. *Frederick the Great: A Military Life*. London: Routledge & Kegan Paul, 1985.

————. *The Military Experience in the Age of Reason*. London: Routledge & Kegan Paul, 1987. Reprint. New York: Atheneum, 1988.

————. *Seige Warfare: The Fortress in the Age of Vauban and Frederick the Great*. 2 vols. London: Routledge & Kegan Paul, 1984.

Dyer, Gwynne. *War*. New York: Crown, 1985.

Eadie, John, ed. *Classical Traditions in Early America*. Ann Arbor, Mich.: Center for Coordination of Ancient and Modern Studies, 1976.

Earle, Edward Mead, ed. *Makers of Modern Strategy: Military Thought from Machiavelli to Hitler*. Princeton: Princeton University Press, 1943.

Echeverria, Durand. *Mirage in the West: A History of the French Image of American Society to 1815*. Princeton: Princeton University Press, 1957.

Engels, Donald W. *Alexander the Great and the Logistics of the Macedonian Army*. Berkeley: University of California Press, 1978. Reprint. 1980.

Ewald, Alexander Charles. *The Life and Times of the Hon. Algernon Sydney, 1622–1683*. 2 vols. London: Tinsley Brothers, 1873.

Falls, Cyril. *Elizabeth's Irish Wars*. London: Methuen, 1950.

Ferling, John E. *A Wilderness of Miseries: War and Warriors in Early America*. Westport, Conn.: Greenwood Press, 1980.

————, ed. *The World Turned Upside Down: The American Victory in the War of Independence*. Westport, Conn.: Greenwood Press, 1988.

Ferrill, Arther. *The Origins of War: From the Stone Age to Alexander the Great*. London: Thames and Hudson, 1985.

Fink, Zera S. *The Classical Republicans: An Essay in the Recovery of a Pattern of Thought in Seventeenth Century England*. Northwestern University Studies in the Humanities No. 9. Evanston: Northwestern University Press, 1945.

Firth, C. H. *Cromwell's Army: A History of the English Soldier During the Civil Wars, the Commonwealth and the Protectorate*. 3rd ed. London: Methuen, 1921. Reprint. 1961.

————. *Essays Historical and Literary*. Oxford: Clarendon Press, 1938.

Fitzpatrick, John C. *George Washington Himself: A Common-Sense Biography Written from His Manuscripts*. Indianapolis: Bobbs-Merrill, 1933.

Flexner, James Thomas. *George Washington: The Forge of Experience (1732–1775)*. Boston: Little, Brown, 1965.

Ford, Franklin L. *Political Murder: From Tyrannicide to Terrorism*. Cambridge: Harvard University Press, 1985.

Ford, Paul L. *Washington and the Theatre*. New York: Dunlap Society, 1899.

Fortescue, John W. *A History of the British Army*. 13 vols. London: Macmillan, 1910–30.

Freeman, Douglas Southall. *George Washington: A Biography*. 7 vols. New York: Charles Scribner's Sons, 1948–55.

————. *R. E. Lee: A Biography*. Pulitzer Prize ed. 4 vols. New York: Charles Scribner's Sons, 1936.

Frey, Sylvia R. *The British Soldier in America: A Social History of Military Life in the Revolutionary Period*. Austin: University of Texas Press, 1981.

Frost, William. *Dryden and the Art of Transition*. Yale Studies in English, Vol. 128. New Haven: Yale University Press, 1955.

Gaudin, Albert C. *The Educational Views of Charles Rollin*. New York: Thesis Publishing, 1939.

Gilbert, Gerald. *The Evolution of Tactics*. London: Hugh Rees, 1907.

Goodman, Paul, ed. *Essays in American Colonial History*. New York: Holt, Rinehart & Winston, 1967.

Gordon, G. S., ed. *English Literature and the Classics*. Oxford: Clarendon Press, 1912.

Grant, Michael. *The Ancient Historians*. New York: Charles Scribner's Sons, 1970.

Gummere, Richard M. *The American Colonial Mind and the Classical Tradition: Essays in Comparative Culture*. Cambridge: Harvard University Press, 1963.

———. *Seven Wise Men of Colonial America*. Cambridge: Harvard University Press, 1967.

Guy, Alan J. *Oeconomy and Discipline: Officership and Administration in the British Army 1714–63*. Manchester: Manchester University Press, 1985.

Hackworth, David H., and Sherman, Julie. *About Face: The Odyssey of an American Warrior*. New York: Simon & Schuster, 1989.

Hamerow, Theodore S. *Reflections on History and Historians*. Madison: University of Wisconsin Press, 1987.

Haskins, George L. *The Growth of English Representative Government*. Philadelphia: University of Pennsylvania Press, 1948. Reprint. New York: A. S. Barnes, 1960.

Hayes-McCoy, G. A. *Irish Battles*. London: Longmans, Green, 1969.

Hayter, Tony. *The Army and the Crowd in Mid-Georgian England*. Totowa, N.J.: Rowman and Littlefield, 1978.

Henderson, G. F. R. *The Science of War: A Collection of Essays and Lectures, 1891–1903*. Ed. by Neill Malcolm. London: Longmans, Green, 1913.

Herr, Richard, and Parker, Harold T., eds. *Ideas in History: Essays Presented to Louis Gottschalk by His Former Students*. Durham, N.C.: Duke University Press, 1965.

Higginbotham, Don. *George Washington and the American Military Tradition*. Mercer University Lamar Memorial Lectures No. 27. Athens: University of Georgia Press, 1985.

———. ed. *Reconsiderations on the Revolutionary War*. Westport, Conn.: Greenwood Press, 1978.

Highet, Gilbert. *The Classical Tradition: Greek and Roman Influences on Western Literature*. New York: Oxford University Press, 1957.

Hill, James Michael. *Celtic Warfare, 1595–1763*. Edinburgh: John Donald, 1986.

Hindle, Brooke. *The Pursuit of Science in Revolutionary America, 1735–1789*. Chapel Hill: University of North Carolina Press for the Institute of Early American History and Culture, 1956.

Hoffman, Ronald, and Albert, Peter J., eds. *Arms and Independence: The Military Character of the American Revolution*. Charlottesville: University Press of Virginia for the United States Capitol Historical Society, 1984.

Houlding, J. A. *Fit for Service: The Training of the British Army, 1715–1795*. Oxford: Clarendon Press, 1981

Howard, Martha Walling. *The Influence of Plutarch in the Major European Literature of the Eighteenth Century*. Chapel Hill: University of North Carolina Press, 1970.

Howard Michael. *War in European History*. New York: Oxford University Press, 1976.

Hudson, Frederic. *Journalism in the United States, from 1690 to 1872*. New York: Harper & Row, 1969.

Hughes, Basil P. *Firepower: Weapons Effectiveness on the Battlefield, 1630–1850*. New York: Charles Scribner's Sons, 1974.

Johnson, James Turner. *Ideology, Reason, and the Limitation of War: Religious and Secular Concepts, 1200–1740*. Princeton: Princeton University Press, 1975.

Jones, Howard Mumford. *Ideas in America*. Cambridge: Harvard University Press, 1944.

———. *O Strange New World—American Culture: The Formative Years*. New York: Viking Press, 1964.

Jorgensen, Paul A. *Shakespeare's Military World*. Berkeley: University of California Press, 1956.

Kammen, Michael. *People of Paradox: An Inquiry Concerning the Origins of American Civilization*. New York: Alfred A. Knopf, 1972; New York: Vintage Books, 1973.

Keen, M. H. *The Laws of War in the Late Middle Ages*. London: Routledge and Kegan Paul, 1965.

Kennedy, Paul M. *The Rise and Fall of the Great Powers: Economic Change and Military Conflict from 1500 to 2000*. New York: Random House, 1987.

Knight, W. S. M. *The Life and Works of Hugo Grotius*. Grotius Society Publications No. 4. London: Sweet & Maxwell, 1925.

Koch, H. W. *The Rise of Modern Warfare, 1618–1815*. Englewood Cliffs, N.J.: Prentice-Hall, 1981.

Korshin, Paul J., ed. *The American Revolution and Eighteenth Century Culture: Essays from the 1976 Bicentennial Conference of the American Society for Eighteenth-Century Studies*. New York: AMS Press, 1976.

Kraus, Michael. *The North Atlantic Civilization*. Princeton: Van Nostrand, 1957.

Kurtz, Stephen, and Hutson, James H., eds. *Essays on the American Revolution*. Chapel Hill: University of North Carolina Press, 1973.

Lathrop, Henry Burrows. *Translations from the Classics into English from Caxton to Chapman, 1477–1620*. Madison: University of Wisconsin Press, 1932. Reprint. New York: Octagon Books, 1967.

Leach, Douglas Edward. *Arms for Empire: A Military History of the British Colonies in North America, 1607–1763*. New York: Macmillan, 1973.

———. *Flintlock and Tomahawk: New England in King Philip's War*. New York: W. W. Norton, 1958. Reprint. 1966.

———. *Roots of Conflict: British Armed Forces and Colonial Americans, 1677–1763*. Chapel Hill: University of North Carolina Press, 1986.

Lewis, Lloyd. *Sherman: Fighting Prophet*. New York: Harcourt, Brace, 1932.

Lewy, Guenther. *Religion and Revolution*. New York: Oxford University Press, 1974.

Liddell Hart, B. H. *The Ghost of Napoleon*. London: Faber & Faber, 1933.

———. *Great Captains Unveiled*. Boston: Little, Brown, 1927; Freeport, N.Y.: Books for Libraries Press, 1967.

———. *Sherman: Soldier, Realist, American*. New York: Dodd, Mead, 1929.

———. *Strategy*. 2nd rev. ed. London: Faber & Faber, 1954. Reprint. 1967; New York: New American Library, 1974.

Lind, Millard C. *Yaweh Is a Warrior: The Theology of Warfare in Ancient Israel*. Scottsdale, Pa.: Herald Press, 1980.

Lloyd, E. M. *A Review of the History of Infantry*. New ed. Westport, Conn.: Greenwood Press, 1976.

Luttwak, Edward N. *The Grand Strategy of the Roman Empire: From the First Century A.D. to the Third*. Baltimore: Johns Hopkins University Press, 1976.

Luvaas, Jay. *The Military Legacy of the Civil War: The European Inheritance*. New ed. Lawrence: University Press of Kansas, 1988.

Lydon, J. F. *The Lordship of Ireland in the Middle Ages*. Dublin: Gill and Macmillan, 1972.

McCardell, Lee. *Ill-Starred General: Braddock of the Coldstream Guards*. Pittsburgh: University of Pittsburgh Press, 1958.

McDonald, Forrest. *E Pluribus Unum: The Formation of the American Republic, 1776–1790*. Boston: Houghton Mifflin, 1965; Indianapolis: Liberty Press, 1979.

———. *Novus Ordo Seclorum: The Intellectual Origins of the Constitution*. Lawrence: University Press of Kansas, 1985.

McDonald Forrest, and McDonald, Ellen Shapiro. *Requiem: Variations on Eighteenth-Century Themes*. Lawrence: University Press of Kansas, 1988.

McNeill, William H. *The Pursuit of Power: Technology, Armed Force, and Society since A.D. 1000*. Chicago: University of Chicago Press, 1982.

McWhiney, Grady. *Cracker Culture: Celtic Ways in the Old South*. Tuscaloosa: University of Alabama Press, 1988.

McWhiney, Grady, and Jamieson, Perry. *Attack and Die: Military Tactics and the Southern Heritage*. University, Ala.: University of Alabama Press, 1982.

Maier, Pauline. *The Old Revolutionaries: Political Lives in the Age of Samuel Adams*. New York: Alfred A. Knopf, 1980.

Marshall, S. L. A. *Men against Fire: The Problem of Battle Command in Future War*. New York: William Morrow, 1947.

————. *The Soldier's Load and the Mobility of a Nation.* Washington, D.C.: Combat Forces Press, 1950.

Martin, James Kirby, and Lender, Mark Edward. *A Respectable Army: The Military Origins of the Republic, 1763–1789.* Arlington Heights, Ill.: Harlan Davidson, 1982.

May, Henry F. *The Enlightenment in America.* New York: Oxford University Press, 1976.

Miller, Perry, ed. *The American Puritans: Their Prose and Poetry.* Garden City, N.Y.: Doubleday, 1956.

————. *The New England Mind: From Colony to Province.* New ed. Boston: Beacon Press, 1961.

Millett, Allan R., and Maslowski, Peter. *For the Common Defense: A Military History of the United States.* New York: Free Press, 1984.

Millis, Walter. *Arms and Men: A Study of American Military History.* New York: G. P. Putnam's Sons, 1956; New Brunswick, N.J.: Rutgers University Press, 1981.

Morgan, Edmund S. *American Slavery American Freedom: The Ordeal of Colonial Virginia.* New York: W. W. Norton, 1975.

————. *The Gentle Puritan: A Life of Ezra Stiles, 1727–1795.* New Haven: Yale University Press for the Institute of Early American History and Culture, 1962.

Morgan, Edmund S., and Morgan, Helen M. *The Stamp Act Crisis: Prologue to Revolution.* New, rev. ed. New York: Collier Books, 1963.

Morison, Samuel Eliot. *The Founding of Harvard College.* Cambridge: Harvard University Press, 1935.

————. *Harvard College in the Seventeenth Century.* 2 vols. Cambridge: Harvard University Press, 1936.

————. *The Intellectual Life of Colonial New England.* Ithaca: Cornell University Press, 1936; New York: New York University Press, 1956.

————. *The Young Man Washington.* Cambridge: Harvard University Press, 1932.

Muldoon, James. *Popes, Lawyers, and Infidels: The Church and the Non–Christian World, 1250–1550.* Philadelphia: University of Pennsylvania Press, 1979.

Nash, Gary B. *Red, White, and Black: The Peoples of Early America.* Englewood Cliffs, N.J.: Prentice-Hall, 1974.

Nef, John U. *War and Human Progress: An Essay on the Rise of Industrial Civilization.* Cambridge: Harvard University Press, 1950.

Neustadt, Richard E., and May, Ernest R. *Thinking in Time: The Uses of History for Decision-Makers.* New York: Free Press, 1986.

Norman, A. V. B., and Pottinger, Don. *English Weapons and Warfare, 449–1660.* New York: Thomas Y. Crowell, 1966; New York: Dorset Press, 1979.

O'Connell, Robert L. *Of Arms and Men: A History of War, Weapons, and Aggression.* New York: Oxford University Press, 1989.

Oman, Charles W. C. *The Art of War in the Middle Ages A.D. 378–1515.* Rev. and ed. by John H. Beeler. Ithaca: Cornell University Press, 1953.

Oviatt, Edwin. *The Beginnings of Yale (1701–1726).* New Haven: Yale University Press, 1916.

Pakenham, Thomas. *The Boer War.* New York: Random House, 1979.

Paret, Peter, ed. *Makers of Modern Strategy from Machiavelli to the Nuclear Age.* Princeton: Princeton University Press, 1986.

Parker, Geoffrey. *The Military Revolution: Military Innovation and the Rise of the West, 1500–1800.* New York: Cambridge University Press, 1988.

————, ed. *The Thirty Years' War.* Rev. ed. London: Routledge & Kegan Paul, 1987.

Parker, Harold T. *The Cult of Antiquity and the French Revolutionaries: A Study in the Development of the Revolutionary Spirit.* Chicago: University of Chicago Press, 1934.

Parkinson, Roger. *Moore of Corunna.* London: Hart Davis, Macgibbon, 1976.

Peckham, Howard H. *The Colonial Wars, 1689–1762.* Chicago: University of Chicago Press, 1964.

Pocock, J. G. A., ed. *Three British Revolutions: 1641, 1688, 1776.* Princeton: Princeton University Press, 1980.

Pritchett, W. Kendrick. *The Greek State at War.* 4 vols. Berkeley: University of California Press, 1974–85.

Quimby, Robert S. *The Background of Napoleonic Warfare: The Theory of Military Tactics in Eighteenth-Century France.* New York: Columbia University Press, 1957.

Quinn, David Beers. *The Elizabethans and the Irish.* Ithaca: Cornell University Press for the Folger Shakespeare Library, 1966.

Rabb, Theodore K., ed. *The Thirty Years' War.* 2nd ed. Lanham, Md.: University Press of America, 1981.

Rankin, Hugh F. *The Theater in Colonial America.* Chapel Hill: University of North Carolina Press, 1960.

Reid, John Phillip. *In Defiance of the Law: The Standing-Army Controversy, The Two Constitutions, and the Coming of the American Revolution.* Chapel Hill: University of North Carolina Press, 1981.

Reinhold, Meyer. *Classica Americana: The Greek and Roman Heritage in the United States.* Detroit: Wayne State University Press, 1984.

Robbins, Caroline. *Absolute Library: A Selection from the Articles and Papers of Caroline Robbins.* Ed. by Barbara Taft. Hamden, Conn.: Archon Books for the Conference on British Studies and Wittenberg University, 1982.

————. *The Eighteenth-Century Commonwealthmen: Studies in the Transmission, Development and Circumstance of English Liberal Thought from the Restoration of Charles II until the War with the Thirteen Colonies.* Cambridge: Harvard University Press, 1959.

Rogers, Alan. *Empire and Liberty: American Resistance to British Authority, 1755–1763.* Berkeley: University of California Press, 1974.

Rogers, H. C. B. *The British Army of the Eighteenth Century*. New York: Hippocrene Books, 1977.

Rollins, Marion J. Benedict. *The God of the Old Testament in Relation to War*. New York: Teachers College, Columbia University, 1927.

Ropp, Theodore. *War in the Modern World*. New, rev. ed. New York: Collier Books, 1962.

Royster, Charles. *Light-Horse Harry Lee and the Legacy of the American Revolution*. New York: Alfred A. Knopf, 1981.

————. *A Revolutionary People at War: The Continental Army and American Character, 1775–1783*. Chapel Hill: University of North Carolina Press for the Institute of Early American History and Culture, 1979. Reprint. New York: W. W. Norton, 1981.

Russell, Frederic. *Just War in the Middle Ages*. New York: Cambridge University Press, 1975.

Schwartz, Barry. *George Washington: The Making of an American Symbol*. New York: Free Press, 1987.

Schwoerer, Lois G. *"No Standing Armies!": The Antiarmy Ideology in Seventeenth-Century England*. Baltimore: Johns Hopkins University Press, 1974.

Scouller, R. E. *The Armies of Queen Anne*. Oxford: Clarendon Press, 1966.

Shea, William L. *The Virginia Militia in the Seventeenth-Century*. Baton Rouge: Louisiana State University Press, 1983.

Sherrill, Charles H. *French Memories of Eighteenth-Century America*. New York: Charles Scribner's Sons, 1915.

Shores, Louis. *Origins of the American College Library*. Nashville: George Peabody College for Teachers, 1934.

Shy, John W. *A People Numerous and Armed: Reflections on the Military Struggle for American Independence*. New York: Oxford University Press, 1976.

————. *Toward Lexington: The Role of the British Army in the Coming of the American Revolution*. Princeton: Princeton University Press, 1965.

Silverman, Kenneth. *A Cultural History of the American Revolution*. New York: Thomas Y. Crowell, 1976.

Slotkin, Richard. *Regeneration through Violence: The Mythology of the American Frontier, 1600–1860*. Middletown, Conn.: Wesleyan University Press, 1973.

Smith, Louis. *American Democracy and Military Power: A Study of Civil Control of the Military Power in the United States*. Chicago: University of Chicago Press, 1951. Reprint. 1956.

Smith, William Kyle. *Calvin's Ethics of War*. Annapolis, Md.: Westminister Foundation of Annapolis, 1972.

Solt, Leo F. *Saints in Arms: Puritanism and Democracy in Cromwell's Army*. Stanford: Stanford University Press, 1959.

Souleman, Elizabeth V. *The Vision of World Peace in Seventeenth and Eighteenth-Century France*. New York: G. P. Putnam's Sons, 1941.

Spaulding, Oliver Lyman, Jr. *Pen and Sword in Greece and Rome*. Princeton: Princeton University Press, 1933.

Spaulding, Oliver Lyman, Jr.; Nickerson, Hoffman; and Wright, John Womack. *Warfare: A Study of Military Methods from the Earliest Times*. New
York: Harcourt, Brace, 1925.

Strachan, Hew. *European Armies and the Conduct of War*. London: Allen &
Unwin, 1983.

Stuart, Reginald C. *War and American Thought: From the Revolution to the Monroe
Doctrine*. Kent: Kent State University Press, 1982.

Tooke, John D. *The Just War in Aguinas and Grotius*. London: S.P.C.K., 1965.

Vagts, Alfred. *A History of Militarism: Romance and Realities of a Profession*. New
York: W. W. Norton, 1937.

Van Creveld, Martin. *Supplying War: Logistics from Wallenstein to Patton*. Cambridge: Harvard University Press, 1977.

————. *Technology and War: From 2000 B.C. to the Present*. New York: Free
Press, 1989.

Van Tassel, David D., and McAhren, Robert W., eds. *European Origins of
American Thought*. Chicago: Rand McNally, 1969.

Vaughan, Alden T. *New England Frontier: Puritans and Indians, 1620–1675*.
Rev. ed. New York: W. W. Norton, 1975.

Walton, Clifford. *History of the British Standing Army, A.D. 1660–1700*. London: Harrison and Sons, 1894.

Walzer, Michael. *Exodus and Revolution*. New York: Basic Books, 1985.

————. *Just and Unjust Wars: A Moral Argument with Historical Illustrations*.
New York: Basic Books, 1978.

————. *The Revolution of the Saints*. Cambridge: Harvard University Press,
1965.

Washburn, Wilcomb E. *The Indian in America*. New York: Harper & Row,
1975.

Webb, Henry J. *Elizabethan Military Science: The Books and the Practice*. Wisconsin: University of Wisconsin Press, 1965.

Webb, Stephen Saunders. *The Governors-General: The English Army and the
Definition of the Empire, 1569–1681*. Chapel Hill: University of North Carolina Press, 1979.

Webster, Graham. *The Roman Imperial Army of the First and Second Centuries
A.D.* 3rd ed. London: A & C Black, 1985.

Weigley, Russell F., ed. *New Dimensions in Military History: An Anthology*. San
Rafael, Calif.: Presidio Press, 1975.

Western, J. R. *The English Militia in the Eighteenth Century: The Story of a
Political Issue, 1660–1802*. London: Routledge & Kegan Paul, 1965.

Wills, Garry. *Cincinnatus: George Washington and The Enlightenment: Images of
Power in Early America*. Garden City, N.Y.: Doubleday, 1984.

Wood, Gordon. *The Creation of the American Republic, 1776–1787*. Chapel Hill:
University of North Carolina Press for the Institute of Early American
History and Culture, 1969. Reprint. New York: W. W. Norton, 1972.

Wright, Louis B. *The Cultural Life of the American Colonies, 1607–1763*. New
York: Harper & Row, 1957.

Yadin, Yigael. *The Art of Warfare in Biblical Lands: In Light of Archaeological Study*. Trans. by M. Pearlman. 2 vols. New York: McGraw-Hill, 1963.

ARTICLES

Adair, Douglass. "A Note on Certain of Hamilton's Pseudonyms." *William and Mary Quarterly* 3rd ser., 12 (April 1955): 282–97.

Alexander, William Hardy. "War in the *Aeneid*." *Classical Journal* 40 (February 1945): 261–73.

Armstrong, Donald. "The *Blitzkrieg* in Caesar's Campaigns." *Classical Journal* 37 (December 1941): 138–43.

Beall, Otto T., Jr. "Aristotle's Master Piece in America: A Landmark in the Folklore of Medicine." *William and Mary Quarterly* 3rd ser., 20 (April 1963): 207–22.

Best, Edward R., Jr. "The Literate Roman Soldier." *Classical Journal* 62 (December 1966): 122–27.

Bloom, Edward A., and Bloom, Lilian D. "Addison on Moral Habits of the Mind." *Journal of the History of Ideas* 21 (July–September): 409–27.

Bonadeo, Alfredo. "Montaigne on War." *Journal of the History of Ideas* 46 (September 1985): 417–26.

Bond, Brian. "The 'Just War' in Historical Perspective." *History Today* (February 1966): 111–19.

Born, Lester K. "Roman and Modern Military Science: Some Suggestions for Teaching." *Classical Journal* 29 (October 1933): 13–22.

Bornstein, Dianne. "Military Manuals in Fifteenth-Century England." *Mediaeval Studies* 37 (1972): 469–77.

———. "Military Strategy in Malory and Vegetius' *De re militari*." *Comparative Literature Studies* 9 (1972): 123–29.

———. "The Scottish Prose Version of Vegetius' *De re militari*." *Studies in Scottish Literature* 8 (1971): 174–83.

Botein, Stephen. "Cicero as Role Model for Early American Lawyers: A Case Study in Classical 'Influence.' " *Classical Journal* 73 (April–May 1978): 313–21.

Boucher, Ronald L. "The Colonial Militia as a Social Institution: Salem, Massachusetts." *Military Affairs* 37 (December 1973): 125–30.

Brauer, George C., Jr. "Alexander in England: The Conqueror's Reputation in the Late Seventeenth and Eighteenth Centuries." *Classical Journal* 76 (October–November 1980): 34–47.

Breen, Timothy H. "English Origins and New World Developments: The Case of the Covenanted Militia in Seventeenth-Century Massachusetts." *Past & Present* 57 (November 1972): 74–96.

Campbell, Daniel R. " 'Amongst the many glorious workes of the late Kinge': The Successful Settlement of Virginia." *Southern Historian* 6 (1985): 3–11.

Canby, Courtlandt. "A Note on the Influence of Oxford College upon William and Mary College in the Eighteenth Century." *William and Mary Quarterly* 2nd ser., 21 (July 1941): 243–47.

Canny, Nicholas. "The Ideology of English Colonization: From Ireland to America." *William and Mary Quarterly* 3rd ser., 30 (1973): 575–98.

Carp, E. Wayne. "Early American Military History: A Review of Recent Work." *Virginia Magazine of History and Biography* 94 (July 1986): 259–84.

Carter, Alice. "Analyses of Public Indebtedness in Eighteenth-Century England." *Bulletin of the Institute of Historical Research* 24 (November 1951): 173–81.

Clarke, Aidan. "Colonial Identity in Early Seventeenth-Century Ireland." *Historical Studies* 11 (1976): 57–71.

Cohen, Bernard I. "The Eighteenth-Century Origins of the Concept of Scientific Revolution." *Journal of the History of Ideas* 37 (April–June 1976): 257–88.

Cohen, Charles. "The 'Liberty or Death' Speech: A Note on Religion and Revolutionary Rhetoric." *William and Mary Quarterly* 3rd ser., 38 (October 1981): 702–17.

Colbourn, H. Trevor. "Thomas Jefferson's Use of the Past." *William and Mary Quarterly* 3rd ser., 15 (January 1958): 56–70.

Come, Donald Robert. "The Influence of Princeton on Higher Education in the South Before 1825." *William and Mary Quarterly* 3rd ser., 2 (October 1945): 359–96.

Commager, Henry Steele. "Leadership in Eighteenth Century America and Today." *Daedalus* 90 (Fall 1961): 652–74.

Cowles, Frank Hewitt. "Virgil's Hatred of War." *Classical Journal* 29 (February 1934): 357–74.

Craigie, Peter C. " 'Yaweh Is a Man of War.' " *Scottish Journal of Theology* 22 (1969): 183–88.

Cress, Lawrence Delbert. "Radical Whiggery on the Role of the Military." *Journal of the History of Ideas* 40 (January–March 1979): 43–60.

Dederer, John Morgan. "Making Bricks without Straw: Nathanael Greene's Southern Campaigns and Mao Tse-tung's Mobile War." *Military Affairs* 48 (October 1983): 115–21.

———. "The Origins of Robert E. Lee's Bold Generalship: A Reinterpretation." *Military Affairs* 49 (July 1985): 117–23.

Dorjahn, Alfred P., and Born, Lester K. "Vegetius and the Decay of the Roman Army." *Classical Journal* 30 (December 1934): 148–58.

Douglas, Elisha P. "German Intellectuals and the American Revolution." *William and Mary Quarterly* 3rd ser., 17 (April 1960): 200–218.

Duckworth, George E. "Virgil and War in the *Aeneid.*" *Classical Journal* 41 (December 1945): 104–7.

"Education in Colonial Virginia." *William and Mary Quarterly* 1st ser., 6 (January 1898): 171–87.

Ellis, Joseph. "Habits of Mind and an American Enlightenment." *American Quarterly* 28 (Summer 1976): 150–64.

Ellis, K. L. "British Communications and Diplomacy in the Eighteenth Century." *Bulletin of the Institute of Historical Research* 31 (May 1958): 159–67.

Ellis, Milton. "Richard Lee II, Elizabethan Humanist or Middle-Class Planter?" *William and Mary Quarterly* 2nd ser., 21 (January 1941): 29–32.

Fann, Willerd R. "On the Infantryman's Age in Eighteenth Century Prussia." *Military Affairs* 41 (December 1977): 165–70.

Firth, C. H. "The Undeserved Neglect of Earlier English Historians by Their Successors." *Bulletin of the Institute of Historical Research* 5 (November 1927): 65–69.

Forbes, Margaret M. "Addison's *Cato* and George Washington." *Classical Journal* 55 (1959–60): 210–12.

Geerken, John H. "Machiavelli Studies since 1969." *Journal of the History of Ideas* 37 (April–June 1976): 351–68.

Gelston, A. "The Wars of Israel." *Scottish Journal of Theology* 17 (September 1964): 325–31.

Gentles, Ian. "The Arrears of Pay of the Parliamentary Army at the End of the First Civil War." *Bulletin of the Institute of Historical Research* 48 (May 1975): 52–63.

Gilbert, Felix. "The English Background of American Isolationism in the Eighteenth Century." *William and Mary Quarterly* 3rd ser., 1 (April 1944): 138–60.

Goffert, W. "The Date and Purpose of Vegetius' *De re militari*." *Traditio* 33 (1977): 65–100.

Govan, Thomas P. "Alexander Hamilton and Julius Caesar: A Note on the Use of Historical Evidence." *William and Mary Quarterly* 3rd ser., 32 (July 1975): 475–80.

Graham, Gerald S. "Considerations on the War of American Independence." *Bulletin of the Institute of Historical Research* 22 (May 1949): 22–34.

Greene, William Chase. "Ancient Attitudes toward War and Peace." *Classical Journal* 39 (June 1944): 513–32.

Gribbin, William. "Rollin's Histories and American Republicanism." *William and Mary Quarterly* 3rd ser., 29 (October 1972): 611–22.

Gummere, Richard M. "John Dickinson, the Classical Penman of the Revolution." *Classical Journal* 52 (November 1956): 81–88.

———. "Some Classical Side Lights on Colonial Education." *Classical Journal* 55 (1959–60): 223–32.

Hatton, R. M. "John Robinson and the Account of Sueden." *Bulletin of the Institute of Historical Research* 28 (November 1955): 128–59.

Hayes-McCoy, G. A. "Gaelic Society in Ireland in the Sixteenth Century." *Historical Studies* 4 (1963): 45–61.

Herrick, C. A. "The Early New-Englanders: What Did they Read?" *The Library* 3rd ser., 9 (January 1918): 1–17.

Higginbotham, Don. "The Early American Way of War: Reconnaissance and Appraisal." *William and Mary Quarterly* 3rd ser., 44 (April 1987): 230–73.

Howard, Leon. "The Influence of Milton on Colonial American Poetry." *Huntington Library Bulletin* 9 (April 1936): 63–89.

Janzen, Waldemar. "War in the Old Testament." *Mennonite Quarterly Review* 46 (April 1972): 155–66.

Johnson, Richard R. "The Imperial Webb: The Thesis of Garrison Government in Early American Considered." *William and Mary Quarterly* 3rd ser., 43 (July 1986): 408–30.

Jones, Charles W. "Bede and Vegetius." *Classical Review* 46 (1932): 248–49.

Jones, Howard Mumford. "The Importation of French Books in Philadelphia, 1750–1800." *Modern Philology* 32 (November 1934): 157–77.

———. "The Importation of French Literature in New York City, 1750–1800." *Studies in Philology* 28 (October 1931): 235–51.

———. "Origins of the Colonial Idea in England." *Proceedings of the American Philosophical Society* 85 (1942): 448–65.

Jorgensen, Paul A. "Military Rank in Shakespeare." *Huntington Library Quarterly* 14 (November 1950): 17–41.

Kraus, Michael. "Literary Relations between Europe and America in the Eighteenth Century." *William and Mary Quarterly* 3rd ser., 1 (July 1944): 210–34.

Ladurie, Emmanuel B. Leroy. "Recent Historical 'Discoveries.' " *Daedalus* 106 (Fall 1977): 141–55.

Land, Robert H. "The First Williamsburg Theater." *William and Mary Quarterly* 3rd ser., 5 (July 1948): 359–74.

Landrum, Grace Warren. "The First Colonial Grammar in English." *William and Mary Quarterly* 2nd ser., 19 (July 1939): 272–85.

Lane, Jack C. "America's Military Past: The Need for New Approaches." *Military Affairs* 41 (October 1977): 109–13.

Law, Robert Adger. "The Text of 'Shakespeare's Plutarch.' " *Huntington Library Quarterly* 6 (February 1943): 197–203.

Leach, Douglas Edward. "The Military System of Plymouth Colony." *New England Quarterly* 24 (September 1951): 342–64.

Liggio, Leonard. "English Origins of Early American Racism." *Radical History Review* 3 (1976): 1–36.

Litto, Frederic M. "Addison's *Cato* in the Colonies." *William and Mary Quarterly* 3rd ser., 23 (July 1966): 431–49.

Loftis, John. "The London Theaters in Early Eighteenth-Century Politics." *Huntington Library Quarterly* 18 (August 1955): 369–93.

Lokken, Roy N. "The Concept of Democracy in Colonial Political Thought." *William and Mary Quarterly* 3rd ser., 16 (October 1959): 568–80.

Lovejoy, David S. "Henry Marchant and the Mistress of the World." *William and Mary Quarterly* 3rd ser., 12 (July 1955): 375–98.

Lundberg, David, and May, Henry F. "The Enlightened Reader in America." *American Quarterly* 28 (Summer 1976): 262–93.

Mahon, John K. "Anglo-American Methods of Indian Warfare, 1676–1794." *Mississippi Valley Historical Review* 45 (September 1958): 254–75.

Malamat, A. "The War of Gideon and Midian: A Military Approach." *Palestine Exploration Quarterly* (January–April 1953): 61–65.

Meyer, D. H. "The Uniqueness of the American Enlightenment." *American Quarterly* 28 (Summer 1976): 165–86.

Middlekauff, Robert. "A Persistent Tradition: The Classical Curriculum in Eighteenth Century New England." *William and Mary Quarterly* 3rd ser., 18 (January 1961): 54–67.

Miller, Patrick D., Jr. "God the Warrior: A Problem in Biblical Interpretation and Apologetics." *Interpretation* 19 (January 1965): 39–46.

Montgomery, H. C. "Washington the Stoic." *Classical Journal* 31 (February 1936): 371–73.

Mook, H. Telfer. "Training Day in New England." *New England Historical Quarterly* 11 (December 1938): 675–97.

Moore, John Robert. "Dr. Johnson and Roman History." *Huntington Library Quarterly* 12 (May 1949): 311–14.

Morgan, Edmund S. "Ezra Stiles: The Education of a Yale Man, 1742–1746." *Huntington Library Quarterly* 17 (May 1954): 251–68.

Morton, Louis. "The Origins of American Military Policy." *Military Affairs* 22 (Summer 1958): 75–82.

Muldoon, James. "The Indian as Irishman." *Essex Institute Historical Quarterly* 111 (October 1975): 267–89.

Mullet, Charles F. "Ancient Historians and 'Enlightened' Reviewers." *The Review of Politics* 21 (July 1959): 550–65.

———. "Classical Influences on the American Revolution." *Classical Journal* 35 (November 1939): 92–104.

———. "Roman Precedents and British Colonial Policy in 1770." *Huntington Library Quarterly* 7 (November 1943): 97–104.

Nulle, S. H. "Julian in America." *Classical Journal* 61 (January 1966): 165–77.

Owen, Eivion. "Caesar in American Schools Prior to 1860." *Classical Journal* 31 (January 1936): 212–14.

Paret, Peter. "Colonial Experience and European Military Reform at the End of the Eighteenth Century." *Bulletin of the Institute of Historical Research* 37 (May 1964): 47–59.

———. "Education, Politics, and War in the Life of Clausewitz." *Journal of the History of Ideas* 29 (July–September 1968): 394–408.

Parker, Geoffrey. "The 'Military Revolution,' 1560–1660—a Myth?" *Journal of Modern History* 48 (June 1976): 195–214.

Peden, William. "Some Notes Concerning Thomas Jefferson's Libraries." *William and Mary Quarterly* 3rd ser., 1 (July 1944): 265–72.

Pratt, Kenneth J. "Roman Anti-Militarism." *Classical Journal* 51 (October 1955): 21–25.

Radabaugh, Jack S. "The Militia of Colonial Massachusetts." *Military Affairs* 18 (Spring 1954): 1–18.

Radin, Max. "The Promotion of Centurions in Caesar's Army." *Classical Journal* 10 (April 1915): 300–311.

Reinhold, Meyer. "Opponents of Classical Learning in America during the Revolutionary Period." *American Philosophical Society Proceedings* 112 (August 1968): 221–34.

Reitzel, William. "The Purchasing of English Books in Philadelphia, 1750–1800." *Modern Philology* 35 (November 1937): 157–71.

Robbins, Caroline. "The 'excellent' use of Colonies. A Note on Walter Moyle's Justification of Roman Colonies, *ca.* 1699." *William and Mary Quarterly* 3rd ser., 23 (October 1966): 630–26.

Russell, Peter E. "Redcoats in the Wilderness: British Officers and Irregular Warfare in Europe and America, 1740 to 1760." *William and Mary Quarterly* 3rd ser., 35 (October 1978): 629–52.

Schaedler, Louis C. "James Madison, Literary Craftsman." *William and Mary Quarterly* 3rd ser., 3 (October 1946): 515–33.

Schwoerer, Lois G. "The Literature of the Standing Army Controversy, 1697–1699." *Huntington Library Quarterly* 28 (May 1965): 187–212.

Sharp, Morrison. "Leadership and Democracy in the Early New England System of Defense." *American Historical Review* 50 (January 1945): 244–60.

Shea, William L. "The First American Militia." *Military Affairs* 46 (February 1982): 15–18.

Shipton, Clifford K. "Literary Leaven in Provincial New England." *New England Quarterly* 9 (June 1936): 203–17.

Shrader, Charles R. "The Influence of Vegetius' De re militari." *Military Affairs* 45 (December 1981): 167–72.

Shy, John W. "The American Military Experience: History and Learning." *Journal of Interdisciplinary History* 1 (February 1971): 205–28.

Smart, George K. "Private Libraries in Colonial Virginia." *American Literature* 10 (March 1938): 24–52.

Smoler, Fredric. "The Secret of the Soldier's Who Didn't Shoot." *American Heritage* 40 (March 1989): 37–45.

Spaulding, Oliver L., Jr. "The Ancient Military Writers." *Classical Journal* 28 (June 1933): 657–69.

Spiller, Roger J. "S.L.A. Marshall and the Ratio of Fire." *Journal of the Royal United Service Institute* 133 (Winter 1988): 63–71.

Stewart, Randall. "Puritan Literature and the Flowering of New England." *William and Mary Quarterly* 3rd ser., 3 (July 1946): 319–42.

Stout, Harry S. "Religion, Communications, and Ideological Origins of the American Revolution." *William and Mary Quarterly* 3rd ser., 34 (October 1977): 519–41.

Stout, S. E. "Training Soldiers for the Roman Legion." *Classical Journal* 21 (April 1921): 423–13.

Stuart, Reginald C. " 'Engines of Tyranny': Recent Historiography on Standing Armies during the Era of the American Revolution." *Canadian Journal of History* 19 (1984): 183–99.

Todd, Frederick P. "Our National Guard." *Military Affairs* 5 (1941): 73–86, 153–70.

Walzer, Michael. "Exodus 32 and the Theory of Holy War: The History of a Citation." *Harvard Theological Review* 61 (January 1968): 1–14.

Webb, Stephen Saunders. "Army and Empire: English Garrison Government in Britain and America, 1569 to 1763." *William and Mary Quarterly* 3rd ser., 34 (January 1977): 1–31.

———. "The Data and Theory of Restoration Empire." *William and Mary Quarterly* 3rd ser., 43 (July 1986): 431–49.

Wheeler, E. Milton. "Development and Organization of the North Carolina Militia." *North Carolina Historical Review* 41 (Summer 1964): 307–23.

Wilkes, John W. "British Politics Preceding the American Revolution." *Huntington Library Quarterly* 20 (August 1957): 301–19.

Wisemen, J. "L'*Epitoma re militari* de Végèce et sa fortune au Moyen Age." *Le Moyen Age* 85 (1979): 13–29.

Wood, Gordon S. "Conspiracy and the Paranoid Style: Causality and Deceit in the Eighteenth Century." *William and Mary Quarterly* 3rd ser., 39 (July 1982): 401–41.

Wright, Louis B. "The 'Gentleman's Library' in Early Virginia: The Literary Interests of the First Carters." *Huntington Library Quarterly* 1 (October 1937): 3–61.

———. "Intellectual History and the Colonial South." *William and Mary Quarterly* 3rd ser., 16 (April 1959): 214–27.

———. "Literature in the Colonial South." *Huntington Library Quarterly* 10 (May 1947): 297–315.

Wyatt, Edward A., IV. "Three Petersburg Theatres." *William and Mary Quarterly* 2nd ser., 21 (April 1941): 83–110.

Yadin, Yigael. "Some Aspects of the Strategy of Ahab and David (I K[ings] 20; II Sam. 11)." *Biblica* 36 (1955): 332–51.

UNPUBLISHED SOURCES

Hall, Graeme J. L. "The Guerrilla as Midwife: The End of the Union (Ireland) and the Mandate (Palestine)." Ph.D. dissertation, The University of Alabama, 1988.

Stanley, John Henry. "Preliminary Investigation of Military Manuals of American Imprint Prior to 1800." M.A. thesis, Brown University, 1964.

Templin, Thomas E. "Henry 'Light-Horse Harry' Lee: A Biography." Ph.D. dissertation, University of Kentucky, 1975.

Tretler, David A. "The Making of a Revolutionary General: Nathanael Greene: 1742–1779." Ph.D. dissertation, Rice University, 1986.

White, John Todd. "Standing Armies in the Time of War: Republican Theory and Military Practice during the American Revolution." Ph.D. dissertation, George Washington University, 1978.

Index

Abercrombie, Gen. James, 138
Achilles, 63
Adair, Douglass, quoted, 41, 42
Adams, Abigail, 42; quoted, 51
Adams, John, 48, 51, 119, 211, 229 n 58; classical influence, 57, 227 n 50; quoted, 16, 34–35, 42, 118
Adams, Samuel, 59, 182
Adaptation, 6–7, 18–19, 142. *See also* Americans; Whig, Whigs
Adcock, F. E., 109
Addison, Joseph, 21, 41, 49, 57, 61; essay form, 54–55; popularity, 54–55; quoted, 42, 56, 60; schooling, 230 n 3
Adolphus, Gustavus, 74, 78, 91, 92, 99, 100, 106, 191
Aegean Sea, 155
Aeneid, 38; epic of war, 161–62. *See also* Virgil
Aesop, 43, 57
African-Americans, 18, 19, 200; classical names, 59; in militia, 252 n 42
Africanus, Scipio (Publius Cornelius Scipio), 30, 53, 76, 228 n 58; quoted, 78
Afro-Americans. *See* African-Americans
Afro-Southerners. *See* African-Americans
Age of Reason, 31, 92; effect on war, 126; formality, 67
Agrippa, Marcus Vipsanius, 186
Alexander the Great, 41, 69, 71, 74, 76, 78, 85, 101, 102; unpopularity, 53

Ambler, The, 233 n 50. *See also* Johnson, Dr. Samuel
Ambrose, Saint, 165
America, idea of, 27–28
Americans: colonists, 25; balance in life, 150; bonds, 9, 16–17, 23–24, 45, 60, 206, 207; disunity, 2, 15–16, 60; fear of corruption, 54, 58; fear of forest and Native Americans, 128, 256 n 92; Irish influence, 129–36, 175; Old Testament Christians, 17, 127, 176; paradoxical nature, 17–19, 116, 127, 205, 215; relations with natives, 174–75; uniqueness, 113, 147. *See also* Conceptions of war; History; Native Americans; Reading
American warfare, 126–29; brutality, 127–29, 135–43, 148; change in attitude, 139–43; collecting heads/scalps, 176, 255 n 80; combined operations, 138–39; employing natives, 255–56 n 80; English model, 136–43; Irish model, 129–36, 175–76. *See also* British army
Amerindians. *See* Native Americans
Anabaptists, 117
Anabasis, 259 n 121. *See also* Xenophon
Ancient History. *See* History
Anderson, Fred, quoted, 141
Andros, Sir Edmund, 136
Angles, 183

309